JOE HILL

JOE HILL

by Gibbs M. Smith

Published by the
University of Utah Press
Salt Lake City, Utah

iv

FOR MY PARENTS AND C.

Acknowledgments

Several individuals generously aided in the preparation of this work. I benefited from conversations or correspondence with Professor Wallace Stegner, Mr. Barrie Stavis, Professor Vernon Jensen, Mr. Patrick Renshaw, Mr. Pete Seeger, Professor Melvyn Dubofsky, Mr. William Chance, Mr. Louis Moreau, Mr. Bruce Phillips, Mr. Kjell Persson, Mr. John Takman, Professor William H. Friedland, Mrs. Olive W. Burt, and Mrs. Ester Dahl, among others.

Librarians and archivists in both the United States and Sweden have been helpful and gracious. I especially wish to express my gratitude to the staffs of the following institutions with which I worked: the Wayne State University Labor History Archives, the Labadie Collection of the University of Michigan Library, the State Historical Society of Wisconsin, the University of Utah Libraries, the Utah State Historical Society, the University of California (Santa Barbara) Library, the Hoover Institution on War, Revolution, and Peace at Stanford University, the Library of Congress, the National Archives, the Manuscript Division of The New York Public Library, the Regional Oral History Office of the Bancroft Library at the University of California (Berkeley), and the Archives of the Royal Ministry for Foreign Affairs and Arbetarrörelsens Arkiv in Sweden.

The use of the I.W.W.'s resources extended by General Secretary-Treasurer Carl Keller was an invaluable asset.

To the several individuals who read the manuscript, I offer special thanks. Professor Philip C. Sturges, Professor James L. Clayton, and Professor Alfred A. Cave, all of the University of Utah, encouraged and made helpful criticisms at an early stage. Mr. Fred Thompson of the Industrial Workers of the World and Professor Philip Taft of Brown University by their informed criticisms each made a valuable contribution.

Mrs. Jean Bickmore White, Mrs. Iola Smith, the staff of the University of Utah Press, Dr. G. Gibbs Smith, and Miss ShruDeLi Smith provided assistance at crucial stages in the preparation of the book.

I am grateful for the contributions of Mrs. Joyce L. Kornbluh and Professor Archie Green which appear in this book, as well as for their advice and friendship.

I especially appreciate the assistance given by my wife Catherine. But for her enduring patience and help, the completion of this work would not have been possible.

Finally, I wish to thank Ammon Hennacy, who introduced me to Joe Hill.

Gibbs M. Smith
Santa Barbara

Grateful acknowledgment is made to the following for permission to reprint passages from the works indicated: Barrie Stavis for *The Man Who Never Died*, copyright © 1951 (under the title *Joe Hill*), 1954, 1959, by Barrie Stavis. Charles Scribner's Sons for *The Timber Beast* by Archie Binns, copyright © 1944; and for *From Here to Eternity* by James Jones, copyright © 1951. Doubleday & Company, Inc., for *Big Jim Turner* by James Stevens, copyright © 1945, 1948 by James Stevens. Harcourt, Brace & World, Inc., for *The People, Yes* by Carl Sandburg, copyright © 1936 by Harcourt, Brace & Co. Houghton Mifflin Company for *The Ninth Wave* by Eugene Burdick, copyright © 1956; and for *Nineteen Nineteen* by John Dos Passos, copyright © 1930 by John Dos Passos, 1946 by John Dos Passos and Houghton Mifflin Co. *Industrial and Labor Relations Review* for "The Legend of Joe Hill," by Vernon H. Jensen (April 1951). International Publishers for *The Case of Joe Hill* by Philip S. Foner, copyright © 1965 by International Publishers; and for "Joe Hill Listens to the Praying" by Kenneth Patchen from *Proletarian Literature in the United States: An Anthology*, Granville Hicks et al., eds., copyright © 1935. MCA Music for "I Dreamed I Saw Joe Hill Last Night," lyrics by Alfred Hayes, music by Earl Robinson, copyright © 1938 by MCA Music, a division of MCA Inc.; copyright renewed 1965 and assigned to MCA Music. All rights reserved. Oak Publications for *The Letters of Joe Hill* by Philip S. Foner, copyright © 1965 by Oak Publications, a division of Embassy Music Corporation. Wallace Stegner for *The Preacher and the Slave*, copyright © 1950 by Wallace Stegner.

Sources of Illustrations: Arbetarrörelsens Arkiv, Stockholm: 45, 46, 49; Archie Green, Urbana, Ill.: 8, 29, 32, 37; C. E. McCann, San Pedro, Calif.: 57; George Ballis and Farm Workers Press, Delano, Calif.: 208; *International Socialist Review*: 145, 184, 189, 190; Olive Burt, Salt Lake City: 64, 77, 176; *Salt Lake Herald-Republican*: 68, 69, 76, 78, 89, 112, 182; *Salt Lake Tribune*: 118; Mrs. Scotty Jenkins, Eureka, Calif.: 90; *Solidarity*: 173, 180; *Sunset* Magazine: 139; Utah State Historical Society Archives: 133, 136; Wayne State University Labor History Archives, Detroit: 176, 185, 187.

Table
of
Contents

The Industrial Workers of the World

Intro-duction by Joyce Kornbluh

Although more than half a century separates Joe Hill's life from the civil rights and New Left movements of today, some of the current songs of protest are directly related to the past efforts of the Industrial Workers of the World, the "One Big Union" to which Hill dedicated himself. Indeed, the I.W.W. singing, songwriting, sitdowns, and free speech fights have provided some of the philosophy and models for the New Left. "We're all leaders," said an unknown I.W.W. in Everett, Washington, in 1917 when the sheriff asked, "Who the hell's your leader anyhow?"—an anecdote used by C. Wright Mills to introduce his 1948 book *The New Men of Power* and a sentiment vocalized by some of the young radicals today. As social historian Howard Zinn points out in comparing the I.W.W. with the New Left: "The parallels are striking . . . the plunging into areas of maximum danger; the impatience with compromises and gradualist solutions; the deep suspicion of politics . . . the emphasis on direct, militant, mass action . . . the migrant, shabby existence of the organizer . . . the songs and humor; the dream of a new brotherhood."

If Joe Hill were to return to earth he probably still would be writing songs about "Pie in the Sky." For despite the Square Deals, the New Freedoms, the New Deals, the New Frontier, and the Great Society, the goal of rendering people secure from the dread of war and the fear of want in a democratic society has not been realized. It was this spirit of the future that animated Joe Hill and other rebels in the I.W.W. and was capsulated in Joe Hill's famous sentence, still used in radical rhetoric today: "Don't mourn: organize."

The I.W.W. emerged as a result of two forces: the frustration of eastern radicals who wished to influence the American Federation of Labor and the Knights of Labor toward their socialist ideas, and the militant philosophy of the Western Federation of Miners. The class-war character of many industrial struggles west of the Mississippi had led to previous attempts to organize workers into industrial unions. Leaders of the Western Federation of Miners, their unions shaken by crushing strikes in Colorado and Idaho, formed first the Western Labor Union, then the American Labor Union to strengthen their organization and broaden their base of support (the W.F.M. had broken away from the A.F.L. in 1897).

Late in 1904, W.F.M. leaders initiated a meeting in Chicago of six radical spokesmen to consider plans for a new national, revolutionary union. They invited thirty prominent socialists and labor radicals to a secret conference in the same city in January 1905. The January Conference drafted the Industrial Union Manifesto, an analysis of industrial and social relations from the revolutionary viewpoint which spelled out labor's grievances, criticized existing craft unions for creating a skilled labor aristocracy, and suggested ". . . one big industrial union . . . founded on the class struggle." Printed in great quantities, the Manifesto was sent around the country. All workers who agreed with its principles were invited to attend a convention in Chicago, beginning on June 27, 1905, to found a new, revolutionary, working-class organization.

At the founding convention were nearly 200 delegates from thirty-four organizations—socialists, anarchists, radical miners—all advocates of industrial unionism. They were united in their opposition to the craft union philosophy and conservative practices of the American Federation of Labor and by their desire to replace the capitalist system with a cooperative commonwealth of workers. Individual A.F.L. unions, composed mainly of skilled workers, had refused to organize the unskilled in the rapidly expanding industries, and as a federation the A.F.L. had repudiated the Knights of Labor policy of organizing all workers, skilled and unskilled alike.

Machinery and advancing technology were progressively eliminating the need for skilled craftsmen, even in the early years of the twentieth century. The closing of the frontier had diminished opportunities for workers to stake claims in the West. Waves of immigrants, many attracted to this country by the promises of company propaganda and the recruitment of company agents, found that their skills and vocational backgrounds were frequently not utilized in the American factory system. Giant corporations were growing in power; and, in what has been termed "The Progressive Era," a new consensus of businessmen, liberals, and government officials was attempting to regulate benignly through governmental process the growing combinations of interstate capital. As Howard Zinn has written, "In retrospect, the I.W.W. appears to have been a desperate attempt to disrupt this structure before its rivets turned cold."

The I.W.W. delegates viewed the American economy in Marxian terms. They believed that the class struggle was inherent in the very nature of a capitalist system and, since all value was produced by labor, that employers were parasites who exploited workers in their control over industry and society. Government, existing laws and institutions were all the creation of the capitalists and were used by them to further their rule. The I.W.W. held that since the employers had united into great combinations of capital to maintain their supremacy it was necessary to organize all workers, skilled and unskilled, into industrial unions in order to wage effective war on the integrated power of modern industry. Presiding at the Chicago meetings was "Big Bill" Haywood, an organizer for the Western Federation of Miners, who opened the sessions. "Fellow Workers: This is the Continental Congress of the Working Class. We are here to confederate the workers of this country into a working-class movement in possession of the economic powers, the means of life, in control of the machinery of production and distribution without regard to capitalist masters."

In One Big Union the strength of all organized workers
would converge to a common center.

In summary, the I.W.W. held that (1) employers and workers have diametrically conflicting interests; (2) the wage system must be replaced by an industrial society controlled by workers themselves; (3) labor unions must be organized on industrial rather than craft lines; (4) labor's goals must be secured by industrial rather than political action; and (5) a new moral code emphasizing the rights of human life and happiness must replace the capitalist system's emphasis on the rights of property. Most of these ideas were clearly expressed in the Preamble to the I.W.W. constitution, written during those days in June 1905, with its ringing words that over the next decades were to be translated into many languages.

> The working class and the employing class have nothing in common. There can be no peace so long as hunger and want are found among millions of working people, and the few, who make up the employing class, have all the good things of life.
>
> Between these two classes a struggle must go on until the workers of the world organize as a class, take possession of the earth and the machinery of production, and abolish the wage system.
>
> We find that the centering of the management of industries into fewer and fewer

hands makes the trade unions unable to cope with the ever growing power of the employing class. The trade unions foster a state of affairs which allows one set of workers to be pitted against another set of workers in the same industry, thereby helping defeat one another in wage wars. Moreover, the trade unions aid the employing class to mislead the workers into the belief that the working class have interests in common with their employers.

These conditions can be changed and the interest of the working class upheld only by an organization formed in such a way that all its members in any one industry, or in all industries if necessary, cease work whenever a strike or lockout is on in any department thereof, thus making an injury to one an injury to all.

Instead of the conservative motto, "A fair day's wage for a fair day's work," we must inscribe on our banner the revolutionary watchword, "Abolition of the wage system."

It is the historic mission of the working class to do away with capitalism. The army of production must be organized, not only for the every-day struggle with capitalists, but also to carry on production when capitalism shall have been overthrown. By organizing industrially we are forming the structure of the new society within the shell of the old. (As amended in 1908)

Any wage earner could be a member of the new organization, regardless of occupation, race, creed, or sex. It made no difference to the I.W.W. if he were black or white, American or foreign born. An immigrant with a paid-up union card in his own country was eligible for immediate membership. Initiation fees and dues were made very low. Labor-management contracts were viewed as an interference with labor's only weapon—the strike. Contracts were also rejected because they kept workers from declaring strikes when the employer might be most vulnerable. The "social general strike" was recommended as the most effective weapon with which to overthrow the capitalist system, and Labor Day was set on May first, a date of significance for European and American radicals. Militarism was condemned and membership could be denied to anyone who joined the state militia or police.

"Big Bill" Haywood who chaired the sessions at the founding convention was to become one of the most colorful and forceful labor leaders in American history. From the start of the meetings, Haywood vocalized the interest in organizing forgotten, unskilled workers, those without votes and without unions. "I do not care a snap of my fingers whether or not the skilled workers join the industrial movement at this time," he shouted at one point in the proceedings. "We are going down into the gutter to get at the mass of workers and bring them up to a decent plane of living."

The industrial unionism which the I.W.W. delegates propounded was a unique American contribution to revolutionary labor theory and practice. Not only would industrial unions parallel the concentration of American industry, they would become the basis for the socialist society of the future—"By organizing industrially we are forming the structure of the new society within the shell of the old." An article in the I.W.W. newspaper *Solidarity* was to state at a later time, "The I.W.W. is organizing for pork chops in the present and for a new social system." I.W.W. songwriter Ralph Chaplin made this philosophy immortal in a stanza from the labor hymn "Solidarity Forever," which he wrote in 1915—the "Marching Song of Industrial Freedom."

In our hands is placed a power greater than their hoarded gold;
Greater than the might of armies magnified a thousand fold,
We can bring to birth a new world from the ashes of the old,
For the Union makes us strong.

For much of the founding convention, debate focused on the role of political action versus direct action for the new industrial movement. Many of the
delegates were against "political action at the capitalist ballot box," since politics had no meaning for a large portion of the working class—women, migrants,
aliens, southern blacks—who were unable to vote. Fundamentally, many of the
"direct actionists" questioned the value of reforms gained through the state,
since the capitalist government, they held, was a "committee to look after the
interests of the employers." In a class war in which "all peace as long as the
wage system lasts is but an armed truce," sheer economic power alone would
decide economic and social questions between conflicting forces.

In addition to their antagonism toward all types of politicians, many of
the delegates to the I.W.W. founding convention feared that the newly formed
organization would be dominated by the Socialist Labor Party and by the Socialist Party. And indeed, the value of political action was given its most forceful defense by Daniel DeLeon, the leader of the Socialist Labor Party, who
argued at the I.W.W. Chicago meetings that it was the "civilized means of making progress." "Every class struggle is a political struggle," held DeLeon, who
stated, however, that it was necessary ". . . to gather behind that ballot, behind
that united political movement, the Might which alone is able when necessary,
to take and hold." The political clause in the I.W.W. Preamble was sustained by
a sizable majority at the 1905 convention, yet the controversy over direct versus political action was to lead to major cleavages in the I.W.W. and come to a
focus three years later at the 1908 convention.

Within a year after the founding convention, a split occurred in the I.W.W.
which involved issues of moderate or revolutionary tactics. The Western Federation of Miners seceded, leaving the I.W.W. with only about half its initial
60,000 members. DeLeon, Vincent St. John, and Haywood—the more revolutionary leaders—were left in control of the organization but internal controversy continued, stimulated by the issue of political action. At the 1908
convention, Daniel DeLeon, who opposed the antipolitical position, was ex-
pelled from the meetings on a technicality. With his followers from the I.W.W.,
DeLeon set up a rival organization with headquarters in Detroit. Never more
than a propaganda group for the Socialist Labor Party, the DeLeon faction
changed its name in 1915 to the Workers' International Industrial Union and
was formally dissolved in 1925.

With DeLeon's ouster, the delegates to the 1908 convention deleted from
the Preamble all references to political activity. Many of the delegates were
westerners imbued with the frontier tradition of direct action. A group of
twenty, dubbed the "Overalls Brigade," had made their way to the Chicago
meetings by traveling in freight cars and camping in hobo jungles. These prag-

matic westerners helped in the next few years to shape the long-range policies of the I.W.W. The antipolitical philosophy of the I.W.W. leadership was reinforced by syndicalist theory, but a syndicalism, in contrast to the European model, which advocated industrial rather than craft unions and a more integrated economic organization of society with highly centralized working class control.

For the next decade, the I.W.W. became a militant expression of class war in the U.S., directing or taking part in at least 150 strikes. The I.W.W. used the strike as a vehicle of agitation and a tactic to strengthen working class solidarity. Strikes were part of the guerilla warfare against the employer as well as a means to eventually overthrow the capitalist system. In the words of one I.W.W. writer: "Strikes are mere incidents in the class war; they are tests of strength, periodic drills in the course of which the workers train themselves for concerted action. This training is most necessary to prepare the masses for the final 'catastrophe,' the general strike which will complete the expropriation of the employers."

The general strike was viewed in the broadest sense as the peaceful taking over of the means of production once the workers had been organized and capitalism had proved its inefficiency. It would be brought about, said Haywood and other I.W.W. organizers, by the "folded arms" of the workers. "When we strike now, we strike with our hands in our pockets," Haywood told a reporter in 1913. "We have a new kind of violence, the havoc we raise with money by laying down our tools." This philosophy was voiced eloquently by I.W.W. strike leader Joseph Ettor, addressing Lawrence, Massachusetts, textile workers in 1912. He said:

> If the workers of the world want to win, all they have to do is recognize their own solidarity. They have nothing to do but fold their arms and the world will stop. The workers are more powerful with their hands in their pockets than all the property of the capitalists. As long as the workers keep their hands in their pockets, the capitalists cannot put theirs there. With passive resistance, with the workers absolutely refusing to move, lying absolutely silent, they are more powerful than all the weapons and instruments that the other side have for attack.

Until the time of the general strike, however, the workers must be inspired with a sense of militancy and class solidarity. Although I.W.W. activists were excellent in setting up strike committees, encouraging rank and file participation and welding diverse nationality groups into a cohesive force, I.W.W. organizers rarely remained after a strike to build a strong union organization. Once a strike was won, no contracts would be recognized. Only temporary "truces" could be effected on the battlefield of capital and labor. The philosophy of the general strike was expressed in one of the colorful I.W.W. songs:

> Why do you make agreements that divide you when you fight,
> And let the bosses bluff you with the contract's "sacred right?"
> Why stay at work when other crafts are battling with the foe;
> You must all stick together, don't you know?

Tie 'em up! Tie 'em up! That's the way to win;
Don't notify the bosses 'til hostilities begin;
Don't furnish chance for gunmen, scabs and all their like;
What you need is One Big Union and the One Big Strike!

I.W.W. members "tied up" their bosses by assorted forms of harassment on the job, often called "sabotage" or "conscientious withdrawal of efficiency"—harassment which proved to be the most controversial concept affecting the organization.

The tactics of direct action evolved from the nature of working conditions of I.W.W. members who frequently had to resort to short, decisive actions in place of costly, long-term strikes. Although it might be impossible to maintain picket lines across thousands of miles of prairie wheat fields, it was possible to leave signs warning: "$3.00 a day—shocks right side up. $2.00 a day—shocks upside down." Strikes on the job were means of gaining practical concessions quickly, as well as part of the long-term battle to weaken the capitalist system.

I.W.W. sabotage aimed to ". . . hit the employer in his vital spot, his heart and soul, in other words, his pocketbook." It encompassed actions which might disable machinery, slacken production, spoil a product, or reduce a company's profits by telling the truth about its merchandise. Sabotage was defined as another form of coercion, part of the internal industrial process, rather than physical violence. However, bold rhetoric continued to dramatize industrial evils in the I.W.W. literature and propaganda and the wooden shoe and black cat symbols for sabotage appeared widely in I.W.W. song, prose, and illustration between 1913 and 1917. Stickers and circulars showed a hunched black cat baring its claws, and the words "sab cat," "kitten," "fix the job," were used to suggest or threaten striking on the job, direct action, and workers' power.

Although it would be difficult at this time to document whether or not I.W.W. members practiced lawlessness and violence, many investigators over the years have concluded that such reports were exaggerated and that there is no evidence that I.W.W. members engaged in destructive sabotage as has been charged. Indeed, despite the emphasis on direct action, the I.W.W. avoided violence and destruction. However, bold free speech fights and inflammatory propaganda brought the impact of the organization to the doorstep of many communities across the country, and its revolutionary theories and militant strikes resulted in legal and illegal attempts to suppress the organization. Its success in organizing rebellions of immigrant factory workers, the expansion of its membership in the mines, lumber forests, and midwest harvest fields led to savage opposition in the press, persecution by federal and state government agencies, and violence against many members of the organization from illegal vigilante groups.

From 1905 to 1914, economic conditions in the United States aggravated labor discontent. Rising prices, stationary wages, a series of depressions, and widespread unemployment provided a backdrop for I.W.W. activities. After the financial panic of 1908, unemployment in all trades was close to 36 percent.

Stickers were issued promoting solidarity and workers' power.

Millions of unemployed drifted in search of work from one town to another, most making their way on freight cars, and finding temporary jobs harvesting crops, sawing lumber, cutting ice, building roads, laying railroad ties. In 1908, although a minimum of $800 a year was necessary to support a family, half the adult fathers earned under $600 and a quarter earned under $400 a year.

The most important strikes which the I.W.W. directed or took part in include the Goldfield, Nevada, miners' strike of 1906-1907; the Lawrence, Massachusetts, textile workers' strike of 1912; a lumber workers' strike in the same year in Louisiana and Arkansas; the Paterson, New Jersey, silk workers' strike of 1913; and the iron workers' strike on the Masabi Range in Minnesota in 1916. The I.W.W.'s most important units were made up of workers in lumbering, construction, agriculture, dock work, and marine transport, but it was also successful for periods of time in eastern textile towns, in Colorado's coal mines, and in the oil fields of Oklahoma. Although the organization never had more than about 100,000 members at the peak of its activities, it shook the nation with an impact disproportionate to its size.

Three stars on the I.W.W. banner, printed on all items of propaganda, were labeled "Education," "Organization," "Emancipation." Education was carried on through propaganda leagues, industrial education clubs, hundreds of thousands of leaflets, Sunday educational meetings, and widespread circulation of its newspapers, *Solidarity* and *The Industrial Worker*, both started in 1909. By the end of 1912, foreign-language branches of the I.W.W. were publishing newspapers in French, Italian, Spanish, Portuguese, Yiddish, Russian, Polish, Slavic, Lithuanian, Hungarian, Swedish, and Japanese. Most I.W.W. union halls included libraries of I.W.W. literature and books by Marx, Darwin, Spencer, Voltaire, Jack London, Thomas Paine, government publications, and a wide range of material on economics and social sciences. Unemployed I.W.W. members frequently spent much time in public libraries reading philosophy, economics, and science. Jailed during free speech fights or organizing campaigns and strikes, members would set up their own circulating prison libraries, publish a handwritten I.W.W. prison newspaper, and occasionally stage prison "entertainments," which might include book reviews, debates, lectures, and educational skits.

Some of the best educational material published by the I.W.W. was included in the "Little Red Song Book." As one I.W.W. organizer wrote in 1912, "There are 38 songs in the I.W.W. songbook and out of that number 24 are educational and I can truthfully say that every one of them is almost a lecture in itself." The songbook was started by the Spokane branch of the I.W.W. about 1909 and was given the provocative subtitle, "Songs To Fan the Flames of Discontent." There have been over thirty editions of the songbook from 1909 to the present time, which have included more than 180 songs. Folklorist John Greenway has called the I.W.W. songbook ". . . the first great collection of labor songs ever assembled for utilitarian purposes . . . ." Over the years, the contents of the "Little Red Song Book" dramatized the class-conscious philosophy of the I.W.W. and reflected in many of the items the spirit, humor, and experiences of migratory and seasonal workers. Although the I.W.W.'s most talented and prolific songwriter was Joe Hill, other contributors included Richard Brazier, Ralph Chaplin, Covington Hall, and Laura Payne Emerson. I.W.W. songs were sung on picket lines, in hobo jungles, at mass meetings, during free speech demonstrations—wherever members gathered to agitate for a new world built "from the ashes of the old."

The I.W.W. pioneered in the use of free speech fights—not to defend a constitutional principle or to attract publicity, but to recruit members in the "slave market" sections of cities where unemployed workers gathered between jobs. From 1907 to 1917, the Wobblies conducted some 30 such struggles to establish the right to speak on street corners to workers about job conditions. Each followed a similar pattern. Organizers would issue a call through handbills and press for "foot loose rebels" to come to a certain town where a campaign would be under way. In answer, hundreds of members and sympathizers would arrive by boxcar, attempt to mount soapboxes, and be thrown into jails. Soon the crowded prisons, clogged municipal court machinery, and high costs of supporting extra police and extra prisoners would lead the town fathers to rescind the municipal ordinance against street organizing and to release jailed radicals.

The boldness and intransigence of the I.W.W. rebels exasperated town officials, aroused wrath and frequent violence among respectable town burghers, and frequently turned the free speech campaigns into bitter, bloody fights. As the *San Diego Tribune* editorialized about the I.W.W. radicals during a 1912 free speech campaign in that city, "Hanging is none too good for them. They would be much better dead for they are absolutely useless in the human economy. They are the waste material of creation and should be drained off into the sewer of oblivion, there to rot in cold obstruction like any other excrement."

The *Tribune* also called for the shooting or hanging of all I.W.W. members in the jails, which, it claimed, ". . . would end the trouble in an hour." Vigilante committees, frequently in collusion with police and local officials, would seize I.W.W. prisoners on their release from jail, load them into cars, drive to the edge of town, beat and club them, and warn them not to return. In some cases the victims were tarred and feathered, others were stripped naked and left to make their way to shelter, and still others were pistol whipped and shot. In 1912, in response to demands from several California organizations to investigate vigilante brutality against I.W.W. free speech campaigners, California governor Hiram Johnson appointed a fact-finding commission. The investigation report emphasized the passive resistance of the I.W.W. campaigners and the lack of violence or drunkenness among I.W.W. members; it also scored the police for "needless brutality" and substantiated the reports of beatings by ". . . so called vigilantes . . . part of whom were police officers, part constables, and part private citizens." None of the vigilantes, however, was ever apprehended or tried.

Early in January 1912, the focus of I.W.W. activities moved east to a dramatic, ten-week strike of 25,000 textile workers in Lawrence, Massachusetts. This became the most widely publicized I.W.W. conflict, acquainting the nation with the plight of poorly-paid, foreign-born factory workers, dramatizing the problems of child labor in the mills and disseminating the organization's philosophy of radical unionism. Lawrence was a new kind of strike—the first time such large numbers of unorganized foreign-born workers were following the leadership of the I.W.W. "They are always marching and singing," wrote reporter Mary Heaton Vorse. "The tired, gray crowds ebbing and flowing perpetually into the mills had waked and opened their mouths to sing." And in the *American Magazine* of April 1912, Ray Stannard Baker observed:

> It is not short of amazing, the power of a great idea to weld men together . . . . There was in it a peculiar, intense vital spirit, a religious spirit if you will, that I have never felt before in any strike . . . . At first, everyone predicted that it would be impossible to hold these divergent people together, but aside from the skilled men, some of whom belong to craft unions, comparatively few went back to the mills.

In the I.W.W. local in Lawrence, membership swelled to 10,000 in the year following the strike, but dropped to 400 by 1914 as I.W.W. leaders scattered to other areas of industrial conflict, leaving behind a loosely-knit organization. In addition, the employers initiated an espionage system in the mills to counter any further radical influence. A fifty-percent speedup of the textile machines after 1912 led to widespread unemployment and offset the wage increases that had been gained by the strike settlement.

But the immediate effect of the Lawrence strike was to hearten textile workers in other eastern cities and to prepare for the next large I.W.W. strike in the silk mills of Paterson, New Jersey, within the year. The strike also made a profound impression on the public and the rest of the labor movement by dramatizing the plight of foreign-born workers in crowded industrial areas and communicating the spirit of their rebellion. Following the Lawrence strike, literary critic Kenneth McGowan wrote in *Forum Magazine*:

> Whatever its future, the I.W.W. has accomplished one tremendously big thing, a thing that sweeps away all twaddle over red flags and violence and sabotage, and that is the individual awakening of "illiterates" and "scum" to an original, personal conception of society and the realization of the dignity and rights of their part in it. They have learned more than class consciousness; they have learned consciousness of self.

Preceding and during World War I, the I.W.W. took an antimilitarist stand, opposed the entrance of the United States into the war, and continued to lead strikes in contrast to the no-strike pledge of the A.F.L. Since the 1905 founding of the I.W.W., the organization had opposed war not only on the basis of antimilitarism, but on the grounds of antinationalism and anticapitalism as well. "In a broad sense," said I.W.W. soapboxer J. P. Thompson, "there is no such thing as a foreigner. We are all native-born members of this planet and for members of it to be divided into groups or units and taught that each nation is better than others leads to clashes and world war. We ought to have in the place of national patriotism, the idea that one people is better than another, a broader concept—that of international solidarity."

As early as 1914, the I.W.W. declared itself officially opposed to World War I in a convention resolution which stated: "We as members of the industrial army will refuse to fight for any purpose except the realization of industrial freedom." I.W.W. writers and speakers lambasted the European conflict as an object lesson in capitalist folly in which workers were being sent into slaughter to line the pockets of the owners of industry. I.W.W. leaders maintained that I.W.W. strikes of this period were not attempts to sabotage the war effort but industrial disputes to improve conditions for workers in agriculture, lumbering, and mining. A President's Mediation Commission investigating the I.W.W.-led strikes in Arizona supported this view. Although the strikes were denounced by many companies as pro-German and seditious, the Commission reported that ". . . they appeared to be nothing more than the normal results of the increased cost of living [and] the speeding up processes to which the mine management had been tempted by the abnormally high market price of copper."

However, frightened at the prospects of labor shortages at a time when there was a heightened demand for their products, employers vented their fury on dissenters, who, they claimed, were threatening national security and the capitalist system. In Tulsa, Oklahoma, the *Daily World* editorialized: "The first step in the whipping of Germany is to strangle the I.W.W.'s. Kill them, just as you would kill any other kind of snake. Don't scotch 'em; kill 'em dead. It's no time to waste money on trials and continuances and things like that. All that is necessary is the evidence and a firing squad." The charges that Wobblies were German agents or that their strikes were supported by the Kaiser's gold were

11

widespread but never verified by the slightest evidence. In fact, newspaper reporter Robert Breure, who interviewed Northwest lumber operators about the I.W.W., wrote that one employer told him: "In war—and a strike is war—anything is fair . . . . Of course, we have taken advantage of the general prejudice against them as an unpatriotic organization to beat their strike." Although the organization remained antimilitary after the United States entered the war, it neither officially opposed the draft nor staged any antiwar strikes.

Little effort went into protecting I.W.W. members from community hysteria. Army troops and community vigilante groups raided I.W.W. halls and members' homes across the country, dispersed outdoor gatherings, disrupted meetings, and jailed members. Across the country in 1917, 184 I.W.W. members were arrested by federal agents and charged with interfering with the war effort, encouraging resistance to the Selective Service Act, conspiring to cause insubordination and disloyalty in the armed forces and injuring citizens selling munitions to the government. Approximately 100 I.W.W. defendants, including Bill Haywood, were convicted and received severe sentences, twenty years' imprisonment in the case of the better-known leaders.

The post-war years were marked by further prosecutions of the I.W.W. under criminal syndicalism statutes of many states. In addition, considerable community hostility toward radicalism in all forms led to continued harassment of the organization. On Armistice Day, 1919, for example, a group of American Legion men in Centralia, Washington, attacked the I.W.W. hall during a much publicized community parade. In the fracas, four Legionnaires were killed and numerous I.W.W. members were rounded up and arrested. One young I.W.W., Wesley Everest, a war veteran still wearing his uniform, was dragged from the Centralia jail at night and lynched from a railroad trestle. Seven other I.W.W. prisoners were sentenced to jail for from twenty-five to forty years, and although seven of the jurymen repudiated their verdict after the trial and widespread national support mounted for the Centralia prisoners' release, most remained in jail until 1933.

Legal defense and amnesty campaigns sapped the strength of the organization for a number of years. In addition, controversy racked the membership over what terms the jailed members should accept for amnesty. Internal discord also focused around relations with the American Communist Party, organized in 1919. At first, the I.W.W. was sympathetic to the Bolshevik Revolution, and in 1920 Moscow wooed the I.W.W. to join the Communist International, praising the ". . . long and heroic service of the I.W.W. in the class war." Some I.W.W. leaders and activists, such as Bill Haywood, Elizabeth Gurley Flynn, George Hardy, and Charles Ashleigh, were attracted to Soviet communism. Indeed, Haywood skipped bail and fled to the Soviet Union, where he died in 1928. The majority of I.W.W. members, however, became increasingly critical of the Soviet system. As I.W.W. historian Fred Thompson writes:

> The repression of the Kronstad revolt in Russia, the role of the Communists during the seizure of industries by Italian workers in September 1920, and their division of the Italian labor movement . . . all such events made the I.W.W. realize that no matter how

"left" the Communists might be, they were still politicians, primarily concerned with getting and holding the power to rule.

The I.W.W. held to the belief in the gradual acquisition of control of industry by economic action on the job, in contrast to the Communist position which accepted industrial unionism but insisted that it is necessary to overthrow the capitalist state and organize a dictatorship of the proletariat in order to build a new society.

Following World War I, the I.W.W. became a victim of changing American industrial technology, changes which it had intellectually anticipated since its inception in 1905 and against which it continued to rebel. The expanding use of farm machinery threw thousands of migrant agricultural workers out of jobs. The "auto tramp" replaced the "bindle stiff" as whole families traveled by jalopy from one harvest to another, and "homeguards" instead of single transient workers were hired by the logging industry. In addition to the losses suffered through ruthless employer suppression during the "Open Shop" campaigns of the 1920's, the organization was confronted with fundamental changes in the work force and underwent further losses in membership. Many of its activists, jailed under state criminal syndicalism laws, were not released from prison until the middle or late 1920's. Despite these problems, however, the I.W.W. carried on its organizing activities for the next several decades, contributing its philosophy of industrial unionism and laying the groundwork for the mass organization of unskilled and foreign-born workers in the C.I.O. and many A.F.L. unions of the thirties and forties.

During the Depression, the I.W.W. joined with organizations of unemployed workers to set up Unemployed Unions to provide housing and food for the jobless. Throughout 1932 and 1933, I.W.W. organization and agitation in Detroit added impetus to the growing unrest of auto workers suffering from layoffs, wage cuts, and tensions of speed-up in the auto plants. Soapboxing, leafleting, a weekly radio program, and weekend socials in the Detroit I.W.W. hall provided the growth of a skeleton organization in some of the large auto plants which helped spur quickie strikes in the Briggs, Hudson, and Murray body plants. Some of the I.W.W. organizers moved on to Cleveland where, during the next few years, they organized members in several foundries and metal shops. Shops organized in 1934, such as the American Stove Company, were still in the I.W.W. in 1950, the longest record of collective bargaining in the I.W.W.'s history.

During World War II, spurts of I.W.W. activity carried on in western mining camps and along the waterfronts led *Business Week* to comment in January 1945: "The I.W.W. shows signs of life. In the metal shops of Cleveland, on the waterfront of San Diego, New Orleans, and New York, the dead past is stirring and men are carrying red cards." However, despite its opposition to the Communist Party which was reaffirmed in a 1946 convention resolution ("We look upon the Communist Party and its fledglings as a major menace to the working class . . . . The interests of world peace can best be served by labor movements

13

that clearly represent the interests of labor and not the interests of any political state"), the union was placed on Attorney General Tom Clark's list of subversive organizations. Soon afterward, the U.S. Treasury Department ruled that it was subject to a corporate income tax, and another blow came when the Wobbly leaders refused, on principle, to sign the noncommunist affidavit required by the 1947 Taft-Hartley Act and, in the process, lost the Cleveland local.

The I.W.W. persists to the present day, its headquarters still on Halsted Street in Chicago and its newspaper as lively and provocative as former I.W.W. publications. Recently it donated its archives to Wayne State University's Labor Archives in Detroit at a meeting commemorating the fiftieth anniversary of Joe Hill's death. Periodic, although sparsely attended, I.W.W. meetings are still held in a number of cities; small locals exist in several areas, and in recent years there has been a resurgent interest in I.W.W. philosophy and organization especially among young radicals on college campuses.

I.W.W. strike techniques—the sitdowns in Schenectady and Detroit, the chain picketing in Lawrence, the car caravans in Colorado—once considered revolutionary, became the practices of later A.F.L. and C.I.O. unions. The I.W.W. left its mark in the civil liberties field as well, when the free speech fights, and the trials and persecutions by vigilante groups aroused liberals across the country to the need for defense organizations to protect the rights of dissenters. I.W.W. fights for better conditions in the bunkhouses and on farms focused attention on the problems of migratory agricultural labor, and the agitation in the jails against notorious prison abuses eventually helped to bring about more humane prison conditions.

The influence and legend of the I.W.W. endures. Recent scholarly interest in the organization has led to articles in the press and periodicals, including a recent review, "Here Come the Wobblies," in the June 1967 issue of *American Heritage*. Recent books on the I.W.W. have included Patrick Renshaw's *The Wobblies* (Doubleday and Co., 1967); Philip S. Foner's *The Industrial Workers of the World, 1905-1917* (International Publishers, 1965); William Preston, Jr.'s *Aliens and Dissenters* (Harvard University Press, 1963); and Joyce Kornbluh's anthology *Rebel Voices* (The University of Michigan Press, 1964). Several articles on the organization by labor historian Philip Taft and by I.W.W. songwriter Richard Brazier have appeared in recent issues of *Labor History*. Labor folklorist Archie Green's monograph on the John Neuhaus Collection of I.W.W. song material (Institute of Labor and Industrial Relations, University of Illinois), and material on the I.W.W. in John Greenway's *American Folksongs of Protest* (University of Pennsylvania Press, 1953) focus on the contributions that I.W.W. songs have made to labor history and folklore.

To these is now added Gibbs Smith's thorough, scholarly volume on Joe Hill's life and influence, the most complete factual account to date, and a book which ably fills the existing gaps in information about Joe Hill's personal life and the circumstances surrounding his experiences in Utah.

Joe Hill's songs

Joe Hill, arriving in New York City
after emigrating from Sweden in 1902, worked in factories and mines, and on farms and waterfronts as he traveled from the east coast to San Pedro, California, where he joined the Industrial Workers of the World. In 1913, journeying east again—probably via freight train—Hill stopped to work in the mines of Utah. While in that state he was arrested, tried, and convicted of murdering a Salt Lake City grocer. Joe Hill's execution by a Utah firing squad in November of 1915 was preceded by appeals for clemency from thousands of sympathizers and such notables as Samuel Gompers, president of the American Federation of Labor; W. A. F. Ekengren, Swedish Minister to the United States; and President Woodrow Wilson.

Since then, the Joe Hill story has become legend. Nourished by the I.W.W. and other labor organizations, as well as by many writers of prose, verse, and lyric, Hill's legend has made him, like Paul Bunyan or Johnny Appleseed, a folk hero. His story has been told not only in America, but in his native Sweden, several western European countries, Russia, East Germany, and Australia. Today, the migrant Wobbly, shrouded in myth, can justly be called "the man who never died."

What was there about Hill that enabled him to survive in some sense his own death? There was, of course, the drama of his arrest and trial, and the climax of that morning in November 1915 when he was taken into the prison yard in Utah and shot through the heart by a five-man firing squad for his alleged crime. Memorable though this was, other men have been executed and have then been forgotten as quickly as their names were dropped from the headlines.

What, then, made the memory of Joe Hill live on in legend? To a large extent it was the legacy of his songs. Without them Hill would probably have been just another forgotten migrant worker, a denizen of the hobo jungles, a rider of the rails, a sleeper in haystacks, a man who worked too hard for too little.

At his best, Joe Hill, parodist and songsmith, was translator and scribe for the migrant workers and hobos of America, turning into lyrical expression their everyday experience of disillusionment, hardship, bitterness, and injustice. His lyrics, for the most part, are tough, hard-bitten, and scornful of what seemed to him the futility of trying to improve the worker's lot within the existing framework of American society. His few best songs of protest and parody won him a modest fame during his life and assured him a kind of immortality after his death. These, however, were not his only songs. There were a few romantic lyrics, filled with the clichés of sentimentality and unrecognizable as coming from the same hand. Hill wrote the music for his lyrics in only a few instances, usually setting his words to popular tunes of the time (1900-1915) or to familiar gospel and revival hymns.

Hill's better songs remain a part of our culture. It is true that many people, unaware of their original purpose "to fan the flames of discontent," know them simply because they are incorporated in popular songbooks, or because of the drama of his death, but others, in America and elsewhere, find his songs highly relevant today.

Fred Thompson, former editor of the *Industrial Worker* and I.W.W. historian, writes: "To many of us today nothing seems more relevant to this atomic age than Joe Hill's lines 'working men of all countries unite, side by side we for freedom will fight.' And our hopes still run to what can be done 'if workers take a notion' and realize that 'there is power in a band of working men.' "[1]

The I.W.W. was using songs to inspire militancy and solidarity in its ranks and to help enlist new members prior to the time Joe Hill joined the organization, probably in 1910. The date of the first I.W.W. parody is not certain, but the technique of using songs in organizational activities was perfected in Spokane, Washington, around 1908 by J. H. Walsh, a national organizer for the I.W.W., who moved to Spokane from Alaska, late in 1907.[2]

Commenting on the depressed economic conditions in the Pacific Northwest in 1907 and early 1908, Walsh explained the casual origin of Wobbly parodies: "There are so many hundred idle men in this country that many around headquarters [I.W.W. headquarters in Spokane] have little to do but to study the question, compose poetry and word up songs to old tunes. . . . Among the I.W.W. membership there are a few good singers as well as jawsmiths."[3]

Walsh's use of songs in organizing arose out of the I.W.W.'s opposition to employment practices in Spokane, the job-buying center for thousands of migratory workers who labored in the agricultural, mining, and lumber industries of the surrounding area. The I.W.W. was in Spokane to organize the ". . . thousands of wandering men who were exploited not only on the job, but who, whenever they came to town, were the prey of those who specialized in ways of deceit to rook workers of their wages."[4]

Probably the most ruthless among those who preyed on the migratory workers were the "employment sharks" or job merchants. After traveling great distances to the location of jobs purchased from the "sharks," workers would often discover the jobs did not even exist. In cooperation with employers, the sharks also sold real jobs which were terminated after a few days of work and sold again to other victims, with the shark and the employer dividing the worker's fee.[5]

In late 1908, as economic conditions began to improve and jobs were more readily available, the "employment agencies" became active. In retalia-

16

tion, the I.W.W. in Spokane warned incoming workers of the treachery of the sharks. Wobblies held outdoor public meetings to explain the practices of the agencies, called for their control by legislation, and urged that the workers refuse to buy jobs from fee-charging sharks. I.W.W. soapboxers, haranguing crowds of migrants in Spokane's tenderloin district, found themselves competing against the Salvation Army band with sufficient frequency to rouse the suspicion that the employment agencies had persuaded the band to time its performances to interfere with Wobbly meetings.[6]

It was Walsh who hit upon the idea of using I.W.W. parodies, some based

The One Big Union fought back at the exploiting class.

on Salvation Army tunes, to compete for the attention of crowds, and he organized a red-uniformed I.W.W. band to accompany the Wobbly singers.[7] Cards bearing improvised lyrics to familiar tunes were printed and sold to the audience. These Wobbly innovations began a noisy contest for followers between the I.W.W. and the Salvation Army.

The struggle against employment sharks evolved into the Spokane Free Speech Fight of 1909, which resulted in a Wobbly victory. During the Free Speech Fight, I.W.W. soapboxers were jailed en masse for violating a non-street-speaking ordinance passed by the city at the urging of the employment agencies.[8] The struggle ended with the revocation of the licenses of nineteen notorious sharks and the eventual passage of legislation regulating employment agencies in the area. The I.W.W. was also granted the right to organize through street meetings in Spokane.[9]

During and after the conflict with the employment sharks, the I.W.W. increased its use of songs to aid in enlistment work. A local Wobbly wrote: "Here in Spokane for the last two or three months at our agitational meetings, we have had a few songs by some of the fellow workers. It is really surprising how soon a crowd will form in the street to hear a song in the interest of the working class, familiar as they are with the maudlin sentimental music of the various religionists."[10]

Following this success in Spokane, Walsh further proved the popularity of

Wobbly songs during a cross-country trip to the I.W.W. national convention in Chicago in the autumn of 1908. Walsh and twenty fellow workers, later dubbed the "Overalls Brigade" because they wore denim overalls and red neckerchiefs, crossed the country from Portland, Oregon, to Chicago on freight trains. Wherever the "brigade" members stopped to camp in hobo jungles, they held organizational meetings and sold song cards while admonishing listeners to join the I.W.W. Walsh reported that in almost every town the songs "sold like hot cakes." When they reached Chicago, the "Overalls Brigade" had collected 200 dollars selling song cards for five cents apiece.[11]

About the time of the 1908 convention, a songbook committee, composed of two members from each of the Spokane I.W.W. locals, was formed. Richard Brazier, a member of the committee, reports that the compilation of the songbook was the work of the committee alone, making it truly a creation of the "rank and file itself."[12] The first edition, published in January 1909, was composed largely of songs submitted to the committee by local members. [13] The official title of the songbook was *Songs of the Workers* but it became much more widely known as the "Little Red Song Book." On August 19, 1909, the *Industrial Worker* carried an advertisement for the first edition.

With the publication of the songbook and the increased use of songs in organizational work, a debate developed within the I.W.W. over the extent to which songs should be used in the effort to enlist members.* One faction, convinced that the workers should be educated to the class struggle and its social

---

* The following viewpoints represent the argument of the faction which accepted the use of songs. Fred Isler in "Defense of the Song Method" (*Solidarity*, 20 January 1912, p. 4), answering an article by Wobbly F. W. Horn, who belittled the growing acceptance of songs in I.W.W. organizational work, argued:

> Songs of the revolutionary type have a part to play in the labor movement of the world, and in every country where workers are organized along revolutionary lines, songs reflecting the various phases of the movement are sung at public meetings. In France where the industrial unionists are numerically stronger than elsewhere, the "Internationale" has in many localities displaced the National Anthem. . . .

> Fellow worker Horn exaggerates a good deal when he states that the exponents of the song method go on the street to tell a few funny stories and sing a rag-time song. For the benefit of fellow workers who think as Horn does, I will inform them that one of the worst things a speaker has to contend with while on the soapbox is to gather a crowd, and I can assure them that it is not exactly pleasant for a speaker to have to talk for ten or twenty minutes to the curbstone or to a lonely telephone post before a crowd will gather. . . .

As the Wobblies increased their use of songs, articles began to appear in I.W.W. publications justifying their use by explaining that songs were traditional tools of social protest. One such article (*Solidarity*, 13 February 1915, p. 4) quoted from *The Development of the English Novel* by Wilbur L. Cross in attempting to place the I.W.W. song in folk tradition. The novel, according to Mr. Cross, developed out of the common folk's ". . . stories of their own lives, feelings and ways of looking at things." Their viewpoint held up to ". . . cynical ridicule the intrigues and frailties of the clergy; and gave a coarse realistic touch to the Arthurian fable." The writer in *Solidarity* commented:

> These words in large measure justify the existence of the I.W.W. songs. Many find these songs satirical, irreverent, coarse, and crude, though amusing. But they forget

and economic consequences through the written and spoken word, thought songs irrelevant to the work of education. Others, Joe Hill among them, felt the use of songs an important part of the educational effort.

> A pamphlet, no matter how good, is never read more than once, but a song is learned by heart and repeated over and over; and I maintain that if a person can put a few cold, common sense facts into a song, and dress them up in a cloak of humor to take the dryness off of them, he will succeed in reaching a great number of workers who are too unintelligent or too indifferent to read a pamphlet or an editorial on economic science.[14]

The debate was won by those favoring songs, and as the tunes gained popularity with the workers nearly all Wobblies became proud of them, viewing their music as one of the basic features distinguishing their organization from the A.F.L.[15] which had shown little inclination to produce its own body of traditional lore, song, and aphorism. Today, the I.W.W.'s place in the labor movement in America is preserved to a large extent by the spirit, vocabulary, and songs which the Wobblies willed to the more conservative majority of American workers.

19

Among the writers who produced the many parodies and the few original Wobbly songs were Richard Brazier, Ralph Chaplin, Laura Payne Emerson, Pat Brennan, Covington Hall, Charles Ashleigh, and T-Bone Slim. But, as Richard Brazier reportedly said, "The minute he [Joe Hill] appeared with his first, and then his second song, we all knew he was the great one."[16]

Joe Hill probably wrote his early I.W.W. songs in Malgren's Hall—used by the San Pedro I.W.W. local—and in the Sailors' Rest Mission in San Pedro. It was in these places that he was seen playing the piano, banjo, guitar, and violin. He also wrote songs while traveling and while in jail in Utah, but the Wobbly hall in San Pedro probably served as the most natural place for him to create. His San Pedro acquaintance Alexander MacKay has described him at work on his songs there.

> Joe was a real closed mouth guy, but he did loosen up in fine shape when he had a song on the griddle. I remember how he enjoyed giving his verses a workout on any of

---

that capitalist romance is just as unreal as the Arthurian one; and that it, too, needs to be exposed and laughed out of existence by another and more modern adaptation of a noble art. Cynical ridicule of pretentious and pious frauds, together with a virile presentation of actual conditions among the workers, told in their own way, is as necessary now as was the similar preceding effort of which Professor Cross writes so well. . . . Like the middle class which preceded it, the working class in order to perfect its revolution must first express itself. The I.W.W. songs are a means to this desirable end.

Elizabeth Balch ("Songs of Labor," *Survey*, 31, no. 14 [3 January 1914]: 412), a sympathetic observer of the I.W.W.'s use of song, spoke of the compatibility of I.W.W. songs with protest songs of the past. She noted that the I.W.W. had appropriated the "Marseillaise" and the "Internationale," which arose from social protests of past centuries, and identified the I.W.W. lyrics as part of a long history of protest songs. According to Miss Balch: "The I.W.W. has been quick to grasp the song as a band to hold varied nationalities together. It has become part of the new tactics, and like mass picketing, appeals to the imagination and gives those who take part a sense of solidarity and consecration."

us Wobs that were hanging around. One could say with considerable justice that the songs were communal production, because Joe always got tips and suggestions from whatever Wobs were in the neighborhood. I believe most of Joe's songs were composed on the Pedro waterfront.[17]

It is likely that Hill composed many songs prior to the appearance of his work in the "Little Red Song Book." Reportedly, he made up teasing verses about his brothers and sisters while a youth in Sweden, and it is likely that he entertained himself by "wording up" parodies after coming to America.

The first Joe Hill song to be published in the I.W.W. songbook was "The Preacher and the Slave," which appeared in the third edition in 1911.* A parody of the Salvation Army hymn "In the Sweet Bye and Bye," the song is an attack on the street corner mission and Salvation Army preachers who were prevalent on skid road in Hill's time. He satirizes the preachers who told "working stiffs" to accept their lot in life so they could qualify for "pie in the sky when they die."

> Long haired preachers come out every night,
> Try to tell you what's wrong and what's right;
> But when asked how 'bout something to eat
> They will answer with voices so sweet:
>
>> You will eat, bye and bye,
>> In that glorious land above the sky;
>> Work and pray, live on hay,
>> You'll get pie in the sky when you die.
>
> And the starvation army they play,
> And they sing and they clap and they pray.
> Till they get all your coin on the drum,
> Then they tell you when you are on the bum:
>
> If you fight hard for children and wife—
> Try to get something good in this life—
> You're a sinner and bad man, they tell,
> When you die you will sure go to hell.
>
> Workingmen of all countries unite,
> Side by side we for freedom will fight:
> When the world and its wealth we have gained
> To the grafters we'll sing this refrain:
>
>> You will eat, bye and bye.
>> When you've learned how to cook and to fry;
>> Chop some wood, 'twill do you good,
>> And you'll eat in the sweet bye and bye.[18]

---

* To explain the significance of Hill's songs to the I.W.W., as well as to present more clearly the meaning of individual songs, the background of songs for which there is available information will be presented. A complete listing of Hill's I.W.W. songs is presented in Appendix A. The songs appear in the text as they are found in the most recent edition of the "Little Red Song Book," with minor corrections made by Carl Keller, General Secretary-Treasurer of the I.W.W. The original spelling and punctuation (a fair amount of which has been preserved in the songbook) can also be seen in Appendix A.

Originally, Joe Hill included another verse, subsequently deleted from the I.W.W. songbook's version.

> Holy Rollers and jumpers come out;
> And they holler they jump and they shout;
> "Give your money to Jesus," they say,
> "He will cure all diseases today."[19]

The song ". . . was a clear breach with timidity, moralism, and the whole manner and content of the standard American culture,"[20] and abundant evidence attests to its popularity.[21] The rapid and widespread acceptance of this particular song, as well as other Hill parodies, derives in part from the familiar religious melodies to which their words were set. Most hobos learned religious hymns in the missions where they occasionally applied for food and shelter, and they could readily substitute Hill's new words for the old.[22] Thus, entering hobo tradition, they were carried by the folkstream throughout the land and reappeared in contemporary language and literature.[23]

Although, "The Preacher and the Slave"* remains Hill's best-known song, it is closely rivaled by several others, most notably, "Casey Jones—The Union Scab," a parody of the old railroad ballad.

Some confusion about the circumstances surrounding the writing of "Casey Jones—The Union Scab" has resulted from a widely accepted statement that the song was written at the Sailors' Rest Mission piano in San Pedro, adopted by Southern Pacific Railroad strikers for use in their 1911 strike, and then heard by a member of the San Pedro I.W.W. local who subsequently invited Hill to join the organization.[24] Contrary to this account, it is virtually certain that Hill was already a member of the I.W.W. when he wrote the song and that it was written in response to a strike involving 35,000 shopmen on the Illinois Central and the Harriman-owned lines, which included the Southern Pacific.[25]

The Harriman and Illinois Central Railroad System shopmen's strike (September 1911 through 1915) began when the nine craft unions organizing

---

* "The Preacher and the Slave" was not immediately credited to Joe Hill in the I.W.W. songbook. In the July 1911 and July 1912 editions, it was credited to F. B. Brechler, but beginning with the March 1913 (fifth) edition, and continuing to the present day, the song is credited to Hill. It is not known why the song was originally credited to Brechler. Joyce Kornbluh (*Rebel Voices: An I.W.W. Anthology* [Ann Arbor: University of Michigan Press, 1964], p. 179), speculates that Brechler may have been a pseudonym used by Hill.

There was a song by Frank Brechler, "Workers Shall the Master Rule Us," in the 1911 edition, which indicates that Brechler was probably a real person, not a pseudonym for Hill. However, there are no other songs in the several editions of the songbook credited to Brechler, and persons who have studied I.W.W. songwriting have no information concerning him except his name appearing in the 1911 songbook.

Possibly Joe Hill sent the song to the compilers of the songbook and it was credited to another by mistake, but it seems odd that the error, if it was an error, was not corrected until 1913. By the time the song was listed as Joe Hill's, he was a well-known Wobbly songwriter and probably corrected the mixup himself. It seems unlikely that the song would have been credited to Hill two years after its first appearance without concrete evidence that he was the author.

shopmen throughout the Harriman system met in the summer of 1911 and united in a "system federation." On July 1, 1911, all nine unions presented the same sixteen demands to the Harriman system companies. The strikers' basic demand was recognition of the union system federation as the collective bargaining agent for all nine craft unions.[26] Because the uniting of these craft unions into a federation seemed an important initial step toward the goal of organizing all workers in a given industry into one big union, the I.W.W. supported and worked for the strike and the federation.[27]

Railroad management rejected all sixteen union demands and refused to bargain except with one union at a time. They would not recognize the federation. The unions extended the deadline for company acceptance of their demands to September 30, apparently in the hope of avoiding a strike. In the interim, the railroad companies countered by laying off many union shopmen and recruiting non-union men to fill the vacancies. High fences were built around company property, bunks were installed in railroad cars for the non-union workers, arc lamps were installed around company yards, and guards were hired to protect workers and property.[28]

On September 30, 1911, the entire crew of 300 shopmen walked off the job in San Pedro, and 1,400 struck in Los Angeles. Similar walkouts occurred in other cities. Trains were kept moving, however. The non-union workers hired by the companies managed to keep the trains in a state of semi-repair,[29] * but they were kept moving primarily because the train-operating railroad union men—engineers, firemen, and brakemen—refused to strike with the shopmen, a situation leading to the eventual defeat of the strikers. The San Francisco local of the I.W.W. issued a sticker emphasizing the point:

RAILROAD MEN
NO SCAB SO DESPICABLE
AS A UNION SCAB
TIE UP THE ROAD
USE I.W.W. TACTICS
SOLIDARITY WINS[30]

---

* The striking union men issued bulletins warning of the danger involved in using trains maintained by non-union workers. During the strike, several boilers on steam engines exploded due to improper maintenance. A bulletin edited by Carl Person and printed in Clinton, Illinois (*Strike Bulletin*, 2, no. 10 [10 March 1914]: 4), editorialized on such an explosion.

> Engine 4037 exploded on the Southern Pacific Railroad. Miscellaneous repairs had been made on it by the strikebreakers (scabs) who are employed by this company—an aggregation of moral germs who know no more about a locomotive and its requirements than the cave dwellers knew about the higher principles of mathematics. And, because the Southern Pacific locomotives are being worked on by such men, they are in such a condition that explosions are frequent. . . .

The engine had been in for repairs. A number of staybolts had been applied, and the engine turned out of the shops without any of these staybolts being riveted. The crew riding in the engine was killed by the explosion.

It was the "Union Scab" Hill satirized in his "Casey Jones," referring to no particular individual but to all the union men who moved the trains during the strike.[31] The union scab who had to work because his craft union contract demanded it thereby helped defeat strikers from other craft unions—precisely the condition the I.W.W. hoped to change by uniting all workers into one big union.

"Casey Jones—The Union Scab," a satire on craft separatism, appeared as follows in the bulletin issued to the striking shopmen:

23

The Workers on the S. P. line to strike sent out a call;
But Casey Jones, the engineer, he wouldn't strike at all;
His boiler it was leaking, and its drivers on the bum,
And his engine and its bearings, they were all out of plumb.

    Casey Jones kept his junk pile running;
    Casey Jones was working double time;
    Casey Jones got a wooden medal,
      For being good and faithful on the S. P. line.

The workers said to Casey: "Won't you help us win this strike?"
But Casey said: "Let me alone, you'd better take a hike."
Then Casey's wheezy engine ran right off the worn-out track,
And Casey hit the river with an awful crack.

    Casey Jones hit the river bottom;
    Casey Jones broke his blooming spine,
    Casey Jones was an Angeleno,
      He took a trip to heaven on the S. P. line.

When Casey Jones got up to heaven to the Pearly Gate,
He said: "I'm Casey Jones, the guy that pulled the S. P. freight."
"You're just the man," said Peter, "our musicians went on strike;
You can get a job a-scabbing any time you like."

    Casey Jones got a job in heaven;
    Casey Jones was doing mighty fine;
    Casey Jones went scabbing on the angels,
      Just like he did to workers on the S. P. line.

The angels got together, and they said it wasn't fair,
For Casey Jones to go around a-scabbing everywhere.
The Angel Union No. 23, they sure were there,
And they promptly fired Casey down the Golden Stair.

    Casey Jones went to Hell a-flying.
    "Casey Jones," the Devil said, "Oh fine;
    Casey Jones, get busy shoveling sulphur—
      That's what you get for scabbing on the S. P. line."[32]

Among labor unions "Hill's version of 'Casey Jones' has become more popular than the original railroad ballad. It is one of the few songs that no labor-song anthologist would dare leave out."[33]

Songs became a distinguishing element of I.W.W.-supported strikes. Strike songs infused heterogeneous groups of workers with a sense of unity and solidarity. They were great morale builders and, as such, important organizing tools. I.W.W. strikes provided the inspiration for several of Hill's better known songs. "Where the Fraser River Flows," sung to the tune of "Where the River Shannon Flows," was written to aid construction workers laying track for the Canadian Northern Railroad Company in British Columbia who were striking because of low pay, unsanitary living conditions, bad food, and hazardous working conditions.[34]

Several months before the strike began the I.W.W. had established Local 327 in British Columbia and had sent men to organize the construction workers. By February 1912 the membership of the local had grown to 8,000. On March 27 the strike began; within a few days construction work along four hundred miles of track had stopped, and picket lines had been established in Vancouver, Seattle, Tacoma, Minneapolis, and San Francisco to keep job-hunting migrants from taking jobs in the strike area.[35] The following letter was received at *Solidarity* on May 3, 1912, from Lytton, British Columbia:

> The contractors' game was to force us to take station work, this is subcontracts, but they offered us the work at such ridiculously low prices we agreed among ourselves not to take any piece work from the contractors except at prices which we agreed upon. That would enable us to pay a decent wage in case we needed hired help. [Laborers would agree with the contractors to do a certain amount of station work for a specified sum of money.]
>
> We protested against the low prices offered by the contractors, and held off until late in the fall, but with financial ruin staring us in the face and winter coming on, we were forced to accept the conditions imposed upon us by these contractors, in the meantime strengthening our organization for the struggle which we knew must inevitably come and which took the form of a general strike or walkout, on March 27.
>
> The discontent was general all over the line, and the walkout started in Nelson & Benson's Camp 4, near Lytton. Within a few days the work was completely tied up, and is yet, notwithstanding all reports to the contrary, and until the workers demands for a minimum wage of $3 and a 9-hour day, and $5.25 a week for board are agreed to the fight will go on. . . .
>
> The strikers have conducted themselves peacefully, and have maintained good order in their ranks, but this cannot be said of the contractors and their paid hirelings and the police.[36]

Louis Moreau, a Wobbly "camp delegate" who helped organize the construction workers and who was on the committee that cared for the strikers during the walkout, remembers that Joe Hill, whom he had never met before, appeared in the strikers' camp in Yale, British Columbia,[37] about ten days after the walkout occurred. Several of the other Wobblies apparently knew Hill, who was very popular with everybody ". . . as he wrote several songs for the strikers who were fond of singing them." Moreau remembers seeing Joe Hill often in the office of the Yale strike secretary writing songs. "Where the Fraser River Flows" was written during the first few days Hill was in the camp.[38]

Judging from an article in the *Industrial Worker* in Spokane on May 9, 1912, the song gained rapid popularity. "The strikers on the Canadian Northern are singing songs as they carry on the strike. The songs are said to be the work of fellow worker J. Hill."[39] The *Industrial Worker* printed the song:

Fellow Workers, pay attention to what I'm going to mention,
For it is the clear contention of the workers of the world
That we should all be ready, true-hearted, brave and steady,
To rally 'round the standard when the Red Flag is unfurled.

    Where the Fraser River flows, each fellow worker knows,
    They have bullied and oppressed us, but still our Union grows.
    And we're going to find a way, boys, for shorter hours and better pay, boys!
    And we're going to win the day, boys; where the River Fraser flows.

For these gunny-sack contractors have all been dirty actors,
And they're not our benefactors, each fellow worker knows.
So we've got to stick together in fine or dirty weather,
And we will show no white feather, where the Fraser River flows.

Now the boss the law is stretching, bulls and pimps he's fetching,
And they are a fine collection, as Jesus only knows.
But why their mothers reared them, and why the devil spared them,
Are questions we can't answer, where the Fraser River flows.[40]

Alluding to other songs Hill wrote while in British Columbia, the *Industrial Worker*, after printing "Where the Fraser River Flows," regretted that lack of space prevented their publication. Louis Moreau recalls fragments of verse of three other songs and only the title of a fourth. The songs have not been published in the I.W.W. songbook or elsewhere, and Moreau is the only known source of information concerning them.

Moreau recalls the title "Mucker's Lament" or "Mucker's Dream" but nothing about the song. To the tune of "Wearing of the Green," Hill wrote "Martin Welch and Stuart," a parody on the names of the main contractors laying Canadian Northern track:

Martin Welch is mad as hell and don't know what to do,
And all his gunnysack contractors are feeling mighty blue;
For we have tied their railroad line and scabs refuse to come,
And we will keep on striking till we put them on the bum.
Till we put them on the bum, till we put them on the bum.
And we will keep on striking till we put them on the bum.

"The Wobblies drove those contractors nuts," Moreau recalls. "One day Martin came by our camp at Yale annex and started to talk to a bunch of Swedes that were sitting alongside of the road. When the groaning brigade, our singing sextet, started to sing the song Joe had made for him, Martin tore his hair and swore he'd get us."

Another song, "Skookum Ryan, the Walking Boss," was very popular and consisted of five or six stanzas of which Moreau remembers one:

Skookum Ryan the Walking Boss
Came tearing down the line,
Says he, "You dirty loafers take your coats off
Or go and get your time."

The remaining song Moreau remembers is "We Won't Build No More Railroads for Overalls and Snuff" and is, like "Martin Welch and Stuart," sung to the tune of "Wearing of the Green."

> We have got to stick together boys
> And fight with all our might.
> It's a case of no surrender;
> We have got to win this fight.
> From these gunnysack contractors,
> We will take no more bluff;
> And we won't build no more railroads
> For our overalls and snuff.
> For our overalls and snuff, for our overalls and snuff,
> We won't build no more railroads
> For our overalls and snuff.[41]

The I.W.W. strikers maintained order and policed themselves, penalizing anyone who drank liquor or perpetrated violence. The provincial police, unable to arrest strikers for criminal actions, began arresting them for "unlawful assemblage" and vagrancy.[42] Police raided the headquarters at Yale in late May and early June, giving Wobblies the choice of going back to work or to jail. Moreau, who was arrested and sentenced to six months in jail, recalls that "One thing puzzled us, we had not seen Joe Hill either during or after the raid and he was not among the ones [strikers] that had been sent to Westminster [a jail] as the Vancouver local later found out."[43] This seems consistent with Hill's characteristic ability to move in and out of the center of I.W.W. activity without losing his personal freedom—preserving an element of mystery.

Eventually, as the jails filled, the police relaxed their policy of arresting strikers. The strike ended in the fall of 1912 ". . . with some minor improvements for the workers."[44]

Another Joe Hill song, which evolved around the I.W.W.-led strike against the Lawrence, Massachusetts, textile mills in 1912, was "John Golden and the Lawrence Strike." This song, along with "Casey Jones—The Union Scab," and "Where the Fraser River Flows," appeared in the 1912 edition of the I.W.W. songbook, and it satirized the activities of John Golden, an American Federation of Labor official who attempted to gain control of the strike.

A majority of the unskilled laborers in the textile mills of Lawrence were recently arrived immigrants who received wages barely sufficient to sustain life. About half of Lawrence's 85,000 population over the age of fourteen had jobs in the mills, and health and living conditions were so deplorable that a local physician maintained that thirty-six out of every one hundred men and women working in the mills died before the age of twenty-five.[45]

The strike was precipitated by a law passed by the Massachusetts legislature reducing the work-week from fifty-six to fifty-four hours for women and children, beginning January 1, 1912. Workers struck spontaneously when the mill owners reduced wages to coincide with the reduced work-week.[46] The I.W.W., which had been increasing its strength among the mill workers since 1907, sent Joseph Ettor to lead the strikers. Arturo Giovannitti, representing

26

the Italian socialist newspaper *Il Proletario*, arrived from New York to take charge of strike relief and to work with Ettor. After a riot in which a woman striker was killed, Ettor and Giovannitti were jailed on charges of inciting violence and being accessories to murder. Shortly thereafter, William D. ("Big Bill") Haywood, secretary of the I.W.W., Elizabeth Gurley Flynn, and several other organizers arrived to fill the void.[47]

Prior to the walkout, no labor organization had succeeded in unifying the varied nationalities working in the Lawrence mills into a single unit. However, as indicated by a United States Senate investigation, the Lawrence strike developed into an organized struggle of 20,000 to 25,000 workers united in demanding an increase in wages and improved working conditions. The strike provided the mass of Lawrence workers their first opportunity to redress grievances. "The Lawrence strike was a social revolution."[48]

In addition to fighting the mill owners and many of Lawrence's leading citizens who had formed an anti-strike committee, the striking workers found themselves in a pitched battle with another union, the United Textile Workers of America, an affiliate of the American Federation of Labor. John Golden, president of the United Textile Workers, journeyed to Lawrence seeking to influence the Central Labor Union (the Lawrence branch of the United Textile Workers), to gain control of the dispute and to keep its members—skilled laborers—from joining the walkout. Golden was quoted in *Solidarity* as having said, "We must prevent the so-called labor strike leaders, the physical forcists, from getting control of the situation."[49] The I.W.W. charged that the mill owners, in particular William Wood, president of the American Woolen Company, wanted Golden to gain control of the strike, because they, in turn, could control him.

Lincoln Steffens, who visited Lawrence during the conflict, reported in *Solidarity* that workers hooted whenever John Golden was mentioned. "They understood that 'John Golden' was a signal to laugh and yell. And he and his name, you understand, were used to symbolize the A.F. of L. 'aristocratic labor' and a suspicious intimacy with capital."[50] Joe Hill's song, sung to the tune of "A Little Talk with Jesus," reflects the I.W.W.'s contempt for Golden and for American Woolen's William Wood.

In Lawrence, when the starving masses struck for more to eat,
And wooden headed Wood he tried the strikers to defeat,
To Sammy Gompers wrote and asked him what he thought,
And this is just the answer that the mailman brought:

A little talk with Golden makes it right, all right;
He'll settle any strike, if there is coin in sight;
Just take him out to dine and ev'rything is fine,
A little talk with Golden makes it right, all right.

The preachers, cops and money kings were working hand in hand,
The boys in blue, with stars and stripes were sent by Uncle Sam;
Still things were looking blue, 'cause every striker knew
That weaving cloth with bayonets is hard to do.

John Golden had with Mr. Wood a private interview,
He told him how to bust up the "I double double U."
He came out in a while and wore the Golden smile,
He said: "I've got all labor leaders skinned a mile."

John Golden pulled a bogus strike with all his "pinks* and stools."
He thought the rest would follow like a bunch of crazy fools.
But to his great surprise the "foreigners" were wise,
In one big solid union they were organized.

That's one time Golden did not make it right, all right;
In spite of all his schemes the strikers won the fight.
When all the workers stand united hand in hand,
The world with all its wealth will be at their command.[51]

As a result of Golden's dealings with the mill owners, the skilled workers who had walked out were offered a five percent pay increase and subsequently voted to return to work, deserting the mass of unskilled workers. Nevertheless, the unskilled continued the strike, demanding among other things a fifteen percent pay increase, double pay for overtime, and no discrimination against strikers. In mid-March, the mill owners, fearing that government intervention and investigation would jeopardize the high tariff on woolens, finally agreed to bargain. Offers of pay increases from five to twenty-two percent, time-and-a-quarter for overtime, and no discrimination against strikers led to the end of the strike on March 24, 1912.[52]

The remaining songs can be divided into several categories. Many portray the desirability of I.W.W. membership and predict dire consequences for those refusing to organize. There are songs which strike at the dishonest practices of employment sharks and songs which urge "on the job" sabotage. The problems of jobless migrants, unable to work because of infirmity or the unavailability of jobs, became fuel for lyrics, as did the antiwar position of the I.W.W.—a philosophy Hill wholeheartedly endorsed. Basic to the popular success of the songs were Hill's awareness of the plight of the worker and his brash, sardonic judgments against capitalists of every genre.

A strong current running through Hill's songs and writings is his belief in the power of a united working class. For the Salt Lake City branch of the Swedish-American organization Verdandi—headed by his friend Oscar W. Larson—Joe Hill wrote both the words and music to "Workers of the World Awaken."

Workers of the world, awaken!
Break your chains, demand your rights.
All the wealth you make is taken
By exploiting parasites.
Shall you kneel in deep submission
From your cradles to your graves?
Is the height of your ambition
To be good and willing slaves?

---

* Pinks are detectives from the Pinkerton Agency.

Joe Hill's call for working class solidarity
appeared on this sheet music, reprinted after his death.

Workers of the world, awaken!
Rise in all your splendid might;
Take the wealth that you are making,
It belongs to you by right.
No one will for bread be crying,
We'll have freedom, love and health,
When the grand red flag is flying
In the Workers' Commonwealth.[53]

This call to organize for a better life was echoed in "Everybody's Joining It" (the One Big Union), "What We Want" (a workers' paradise on earth), and was set to the martial rhythm of an old gospel hymn in "There Is Power in a Union."

While Hill was in jail in Salt Lake City, he received a letter from Sam Murray in San Francisco requesting a song about the souplines created by the depressed economic conditions existing simultaneously with the 1915 Panama-Pacific International Exposition. Murray suggested that Hill use the music of the song "It's a Long, Long Way to Tipperary." Hill replied:

30

> No, I have not heard that song about "Tipperary" but if you send it as you said you would I might try to dope something out about that Frisco Fair. I am not familiar with the actual conditions of Frisco at present; and when I make a song I always try to picture things as they really are. Of course a little pepper and salt is allowed in order to bring out the facts more clearly.
>
> If you send me that sheet music and give me some of the peculiarities and ridiculous points about the conditions in general on or about the fair ground, I'll try to do the best I can. Yours for the OBU.
>
> Joe Hill[54]

The result was "It's a Long Way Down to the Soupline."

> Bill Brown was just a working man like others of his kind.
> He lost his job and tramped the streets when work was hard to find.
> The landlord put him on the stem, the bankers kept his dough,
> And Bill heard everybody sing, no matter where he'd go:
>
> > It's a long way down to the soupline, it's a long way to go.
> > It's a long way down to the soupline, and the soup is thin I know.
> > Good bye, good old pork chops, farewell beefsteak rare;
> > It's a long way down to the soupline, but my soup is there.
>
> So Bill and sixteen million men responded to the call
> To force the hours of labor down and thus make jobs for all.
> They picketed the industries and won the four-hour day
> And organized a General Strike so men don't have to say:
>
> > It's a long way down to the soupline, it's a long way to go.
> > It's a long way down to the soupline, and the soup is thin I know.
> > Good bye, good old pork chops, farewell beefsteak rare;
> > It's a long way down to the soupline, but my soup is there.
>
> The workers own the factories now, where jobs were once destroyed
> By big machines that filled the world with hungry unemployed.
> They all own homes, they're living well, they're happy, free and strong,
> But millionaires wear overalls and sing this little song:
>
> > It's a long way down to the soupline, it's a long way to go.
> > It's a long way down to the soupline, and the soup is thin I know.
> > Good bye, good old pork chops, farewell beefsteak rare;
> > It's a long way down to the soupline, but my soup is there.[55]

Two months later, Hill wrote Murray again.

> I see you made a big thing out of the Tipperary song. [Murray had inserted in his letter, "We secured nearly fifty dollars by selling it for five cents for the Joe Hill de-

fense."] In fact, a whole lot more than I ever expected, I don't suppose that it would sell very well outside of Frisco, though by the way I got a letter from Swasey in N. Y. and he told me that "Casey Jones" made quite a hit in London and "Casey Jones," he was an Angeleno you know, and I never expected that he would leave Los Angeles at all.[56]

The "soupline" song did spread beyond "Frisco," however, when, with Hill's permission, it was adapted by Charles Ashleigh to fit conditions then existing in New York City. In a letter to Sam Murray dated March 22, 1915, Hill commented on its popularity.

> Yes, that Tipperary song is spreading like the smallpox they say. Sec. 69 [secretary of Local 69] tells me that there is a steady stream of silver from 'Frisco on account of it. The unemployed all over the country have adopted it as a marching song in their parades, and in New York City they changed it to some extent, so as to fit the brand of soup dished out in N. Y.[57]

Several songs and some of his writings show Hill's awareness that women, too, could aid in the "class struggle." On November 29, 1914, he wrote to the editor of *Solidarity*:

> The female workers are sadly neglected in the United States, especially on the West coast, and consequently we have created a kind of one-legged, freakish animal of a union, and our dances and blowouts are kind of stale and unnatural on account of being too much of a "buck" affair; they are too lacking the life and inspiration which the woman alone can produce.[58]

Soon afterward, Hill began corresponding with Elizabeth Gurley Flynn, a prominent I.W.W. organizer. A warm friendship developed through numerous letters and a visit she paid Hill in his jail cell. After having exchanged several letters with Miss Flynn, Hill wrote to his friend Sam Murray, ". . . have been busy working on a song named 'The Rebel Girl' (Words and Music), which I hope will help line up the women workers in the OBU."[59] Nine months later, as he faced execution, he wrote to her,

> You have been an inspiration and when I composed The Rebel Girl you was right there and helped me all the time. As you furnished the idea I will now that I am gone give you all the credit for that song, and be sure to locate a few more Rebel Girls like yourself, because they are needed and needed badly.[60]

"The Rebel Girl" clearly shows Hill's idea of the importance of women to the rebel cause, and while it was inspired by Miss Flynn, it was dedicated to all the women in the I.W.W.

> There are women of many descriptions
> In this queer world, as everyone knows,
> Some are living in beautiful mansions,
> And are wearing the finest of clothes.
> There are blue-blooded queens and princesses,
> Who have charms made of diamond and pearl;
> But the only and thoroughbred lady
> Is the Rebel Girl.

32

**Hill hoped "The Rebel Girl" would attract
more women to the ranks of the I.W.W.**

That's the Rebel Girl, that's the Rebel Girl!
To the working class she's a precious pearl.
She brings courage, pride and joy
To the fighting Rebel Boy;
We've had girls before, but we need some more
In the Industrial Workers of the World,
For it's great to fight for freedom
With a Rebel Girl.[61]

The advantages I.W.W. membership offered women workers are depicted
in two of Hill's songs, "The Girl Question" and "The White Slave." In "The Girl

Question," a young working girl who joins the I.W.W. to fight for better conditions is saved from a life of ruin. Another girl, without the organization to rely on, becomes "The White Slave." Cold and hungry, she succumbs to the temptations of an old "procuress."

> Come with me now, my girly, don't sleep out in the cold,
> Your face and tresses curly will bring you fame and gold,
> Automobiles to ride in, diamonds and silk to wear,
> You'll be a star bright, down in the red light,
> You'll make your fortune there.

All she finds in her new occupation, however, is ruin and disappointment. Hill concludes by pointing the finger of blame, not at the fallen girl, but at the unjust economic environment and the boss who forced her into temptation.[62]

33

Because of his belief that the panacea for all economic ills of the working class was the I.W.W., Joe Hill was particularly scornful of the worker who resisted organization. "Scissor Bill" became a mocking name for the man who ". . . says he never organized and never will."

> Scissor Bill, he wouldn't join the union,
> Scissor Bill, he says, "Not me, by heck!"
> Scissor Bill gets his reward in Heaven,
> Oh! sure. He'll get it, but he'll get it in the neck.[63]

"Mr. Block," was another "common worker" who insisted on believing he could improve his economic and social status by rejecting the teachings of the I.W.W. and keeping faith with the existing institutions and patterns for succeeding in American life. The song was almost certainly inspired by the cartoon strip "Mr. Block," written by Ernest Riebe and appearing in the *Industrial Worker*. Hill sarcastically notes that Block thinks ". . . he may be President some day." After trusting an employment "shark" who rooks him of "fare and fee," he joins the "great A. F. of L." in protest but receives from Sam Gompers only "our sympathy." He then votes for ". . . a Socialist for Mayor," but after the socialists are voted in, "a great big Socialistic Bull" raps him on the "block," and he realizes he has been wrong again. When ". . . the money kings in Cuba" blow up the gunboat *Maine*, patriotic Mr. Block gets angry and blames it on Spain. He goes off to battle, loses a leg, and is reduced to "peddling shoestrings," but still shouts, "Remember Maine, Hurrah! To Hell with Spain!" Reacting to Mr. Block's faith and optimism, Hill advises,

> Oh, Mr. Block, you were born by mistake,
> > You take the cake,
> > You make me ache.
> Tie a rock on your block and then jump in the lake,
> Kindly do that for Liberty's sake.[64]

Evidence of the popularity of "Mr. Block" and other Joe Hill songs within the I.W.W. appeared in an *Industrial Worker* article, dated April 17, 1913, relat-

Scornful "stickerettes" berated workers who
kept faith with capitalism and refused to organize.

ing the adventures of fifty Wobs as they traveled from San Francisco to Denver to participate in a free speech fight.

> Fifty miles from Salt Lake City we were sabotaged by an engineer on the Western Pacific. He reported his engine was in bad shape, the train crew was ordered to Salt Lake City with two cars only, leaving us detached in the dismal desert. We had no blankets, very little to eat and drink but amidst it all "Mr. Block" and "The White Slave" and other songs of Joe Hill's were rendered.[65]

Again, in the hop fields of California in 1913, three thousand laborers, gathered in the work camp on the Durst Brothers' Ranch, reportedly sang "Mr.

Block" at the height of their protest against unsanitary working conditions and low pay. Although it was estimated that only thirty of the three thousand workers protesting were active Wobblies, all of the workers had been unified into a single protest group and were singing Hill's song when ". . . the sheriff's posse came up in its automobiles."[66] In Salt Lake City in 1913, "Mr. Block" was sung to attract an audience for an I.W.W. street speaker.[67]

In addition to the lyrics dealing with union membership or the lack of it, Hill wrote several songs warning of the hazards of the migrant's particular way of life. Seeking to ridicule the corrupt practices of employment sharks, he turned his attention to those schemers who bilked the worker of his wages. In "Nearer My Job to Thee," a hobo, having bought a job from an employment agency, travels to the job site and finds, "Nothing but sand, by gee, job went up a tree."[68]

Another practice of the employment shark was exposed in "Coffee An'," in which a worker pays for a job, works a week, then is fired. When he tries to collect his pay, the clerk deducts ". . . road, school and poll tax and hospital fee," and declares that the worker owes the company fifty cents for his week's work.[69]

Hill also created a song reminding the worker that a little "sabotage" was sometimes necessary to help an employer realize the logic of his demands. "Conscientious withdrawal of efficiency" was not a mandate for violence, but rather for a sprinkling of sand in the workings of a machine, mysteriously broken bands around bundles of shingles, or, perhaps, as Hill illustrated in "Ta-ra-ra Boom De Ay," a slight slip at the right time. A Wob who was forced to work ". . . sixteen hours with hands and feet" threshing wheat, "accidentally" let his pitchfork slip into the cogwheels of the threshing machine with some very predictable results.

> Ta-ra-ra boom de ay! It made a noise that way,
> And wheels and bolts and hay went flying ev'ry way.
> That stingy rube said, "Well! A thousand gone to Hell."
> But I did sleep that night, I needed it all right.

Other incidents followed until the "rube" (boss) "cut the hours and raised the pay, gave ham and eggs for every day." Then the "accidents" ceased.[70]

Mindful, too, of the man who could not find work because of disability, age, or the scarcity of jobs, Hill wrote "Down in the Old Dark Mill" and "The Old Toiler's Message." These sentimentalized verses pictured drifting human derelicts, unable to work and reduced to keeping themselves alive by whatever means they could devise. Even for the able-bodied, jobs were often scarce and the futility and disillusionment Hill tried to convey in "The Tramp" were probably the common experience of many. A jobless wanderer is told time and time again as he searches for work:

> Tramp, tramp, tramp, keep on a-tramping,
> Nothing doing here for you;
> If I catch you 'round again, you will wear the ball and chain,
> Keep on tramping, that's the best thing you can do.

35

His crowning disappointment comes when he finally dies and is rejected, first by St. Peter, then by the Devil, both of whom repeat the same old admonition, "Keep on tramping, that's the best thing you can do."[71]

In "The Tramp," as well as several other songs, Hill takes the worker to heaven, to his "pie in the sky," and shows that conditions there are not much improved. Implicit in these songs is the message that the better life, if it is to come at all, must come now. Again, in "We Will Sing One Song," he emphasizes that membership in the I.W.W. can promote a better life. Set to the tune of "My Old Kentucky Home," the song lists the numerous woes of the worker: the meek and humble slave ". . . whose master reaps the profits of his toil"; the greedy master class who "live by robbing the ever-toiling mass"; the politician sly who talks of "changing the laws" while "living from the sweat of your brows"; the fallen girl whose "keepers" wine and dine on the profits of her immoral traffic; the "preacher fat and sleek" who tells of "homes in the sky"; the "poor and ragged tramp" who wanders aimlessly along the track because he's too old to work; the "children in the mills . . . made to work the pace that kills." The chorus and last verse provide Hill's solution.

> Organize! O, toilers, come organize your might;
> Then we'll sing one song of the Workers Commonwealth
> Full of beauty, full of love and health.

> Then we'll sing one song of the One Big Union Grand,
> The hope of the toiler and slave,
> It's coming fast; it is sweeping sea and land,
> To the terror of the grafter and the knave.[72]

In three songs, Hill echoed the I.W.W. policy which condemned war. His own ideas concerning war were reflected in a letter to Sam Murray. "Well war certainly shows up the capitalist system in the right light. Millions of men are employed at making ships and others are hired to sink them. Scientific management, eh, wot?"[73] The only kind of war Hill condoned is described in the song "Should I Ever Be a Soldier":

> Should I ever be a soldier, 'neath the Red Flag I would fight;
> Should the gun I ever shoulder, it's to crush the tyrant's might.
> Join the army of the toilers, men and women fall in line,
> Wage slaves of the world, arouse! Do your duty for the cause,
>   for Land and Liberty.[74]

"Stung Right" chronicles the lament of a worker enticed into joining "uncle Sammy's fleet" by promises of a trip around the world. According to Hill, the Navy, rather than improving his situation, worsens it by offering only hard work and bad food.[75] Also prominent in this category is the antiwar song, "Don't Take My Papa Away from Me," the last song Hill wrote. On November 18, 1915—one day before he was executed—he wrote Elizabeth Gurley Flynn: "Composed new song last week with music dedicated to the 'Dove of Peace.' "[76] The song sentimentally depicts the orphaning of a little girl as her father goes off to war and is killed ". . . mid the cannons' roar."[77]

**This song dramatized the Wobblies' view
of war as a destructive instrument of the capitalist class.**

The primary vehicle through which Hill's songs were disseminated and in which they have been preserved is the "Little Red Song Book." By 1913, the songbook, only four years old, was being printed in lots of fifty thousand.[78] During his lifetime, Hill's songs were also published in other I.W.W.-related songbooks. The Los Angeles local, for example, published a songbook selling for ten cents and containing at least thirteen of his songs. William Chance, a San Pedro Wobbly and friend of Hill remembers that Hill printed some songbooks on his own and sold them in San Pedro.[79] *Solidarity* reported in 1912 that San Pedro Local 245 was ". . . getting a songbook out."[80] Some of Hill's songs might have been included in that book, but there is no evidence confirming its existence.*

Hill's sentimental love songs never appeared in the "Little Red Song Book." These songs when analyzed today appear markedly inferior to his I.W.W. lyrics and give us a glimpse into an aspect of his personality about which little is known. Undeniably, it is an aspect of his personality contradictory to that admired by the I.W.W. Although several of Hill's I.W.W. songs exhibit a touch of sentimentality, none matches the three which follow. Two of them, "Come and Take a Joy-ride in My Aeroplane" and "Oh, Please Let Me Dance this Waltz with You," were found by police in his room in the house where he was arrested in Salt Lake City in 1914. The *Salt Lake Tribune* printed the songs.

COME AND TAKE A JOY-RIDE IN MY AEROPLANE

If you will be my sweetheart, I'll take you for a ride
Among the silv'ry clouds up in the sky.
Then, far away from sorrows like eagles we will glide,
And no one will be there but you and I.
Say, darling, if you'll be my little honey dove,
We'll fly above and coo and love.
I'll take you from this dusty earth to where the air
Is pure and crystal clear—and there
I'll give my promise to be true,
While gliding 'mong the silv'ry clouds with you.

Come and take a joy-ride in my aeroplane tonight,
Way beyond the clouds, where all the stars are shining bright.
There I'd like to look into your loving eyes of blue,
And if I should fall, then I know I'd fall in love with you.

---

* Regarding the other songbooks, the author has seen a copy of the Los Angeles songbook, reproductions from which can be found in Appendix A. The copy had pages missing that might have contained other Hill songs. The book can be dated to early 1913 by internal evidence; it is not known whether other editions were produced. None of the songs is unique; all appeared also in the "Little Red Song Book." Except for the "Internationale" by Eugene Pottier, all the songs are by Hill. A distinguishing feature of the book is a drawing by Joe Hill, dated 1912, which depicts the ship *Capitalism*, flying the flag of the merchants and manufacturers, sinking after hitting an iceberg labeled "I.W.W." The drawing is apparently based on the sinking of the *Titanic* which occurred in April 1912.

An unusual aspect of the book is the music on page 20 (with no words included) which was probably composed by Hill. No music was ever printed in the "Little Red Song Book." Also, in the Los Angeles songbook "The Preacher and the Slave" is called "The Preacher and the Bare Facts." The words are the same, however.

William Chance knew Hill in San Pedro in 1911, and it was then that he remembers Hill selling songbooks of his own work. This would indicate that Joe Hill printed his own songbook before many of his songs were published by the I.W.W.; "The Preacher and the Slave," Hill's first song to be included in the "Little Red Song Book," appeared in 1911.

If you will be my sweetheart, I'll take you to the stars,
The man in the moon will meet you face to face.
We'll take a trip to Venus, to Jupiter and to Mars,
And with the comets we will run a race.
We'll go to the milky way, where all the milk is sold
In cups of gold, so I was told.
Our little honeymooning trip shall be a scream,
A sweet and lovely dream.
Come, put your little head close to my heart,
And promise that we'll never, never part.[81]

OH, PLEASE LET ME DANCE THIS WALTZ WITH YOU   39

When I hear that melody, with its rhythmic harmony,
Then I feel just like I'd be in a dream entrancing,
And I'd like to float through space, softly glide from place to place,
With the fascinating grace of a fairy dancing.

    Oh, please let me dance this waltz with you,
    And look in your dreamy eyes of blue.
    Sweet imagination, smooth, gliding sensation,
    Oh, love, I would die just for dancing this waltz with you.

Listen to that mellow strain, come and let us waltz again.
Please don't let me ask in vain; I just feel like flying,
Put your head close to my heart, And we'll never, never part.
Come, my darling, let us start, from joy I'm nearly dying.[82]

The third thoroughly sentimental song, "My Dreamland Girl," was found in the Joe Hill file of the Archives of the Royal Ministry of Foreign Affairs in Stockholm, Sweden. It was printed on a small card, indicating that it had probably been for sale at one time.

MY DREAMLAND GIRL

Would you like to get acquainted with my Dreamland Girl divine?
Never was a picture painted fairer than this girl of mine.
Sweet and graceful like a pansy, bright and charming like a pearl,
She's the idol of my fancy, she's my own—my Dreamland Girl.

    Charming Fairy Queen of my dreams,
    Ever before me your face brightly beams:
    Night and day I'm dreaming of you,
    Some day my sweet dreams perhaps will come true.

She is coy and captivating, Venus-like in grace and pose,
With an air more fascinating than the fragrance of the Rose.
Like the stars her eyes are shining 'neath a wealth of golden hair,
And my heart is ever pining for my Dreamland Girl so fair.[83]

The existence of these works led to speculation that Hill wrote some non-I.W.W. songs professionally. The *Los Angeles Times*, for example, claimed that he wrote "... sentimental songs which were sold to eastern publishers."[84]

However, Richard Brazier, Hill's colleague in I.W.W. songwriting, doubts that the speculation is true.[85]

The most notable characteristic of Hill's work as a whole is the wide range of quality between his best and his worst songs. Hill, commenting on his own works to a newspaper reporter after his arrest in Utah, said:

> There are some defects in the harmony of my compositions but that is because of my lack of technical training. I am a man of little education and my modest accomplishments are due to a natural taste and some native talent in that direction. I have written lots of verses and songs and have composed the music for some of them. Most of the poems are of a revolutionary character and have been adopted by the revolutionary forces, such as the I.W.W. and the socialist organizations, as songs for use in revolutionary meetings.[86]

Most observers who have critically examined Hill's songs recognize that some are of lasting quality. Folklorist John Greenway, although critical of Hill's reputation as a martyr and of most of his work, states that two songs have permanent value, "Casey Jones—The Union Scab," and "The Preacher and the Slave." These, he feels, have ". . . attained the status of genuine folksongs." Of "The Preacher and the Slave," Greenway says, it ". . . is a classic, and nearly good enough to expiate all of Joe Hill's sins as a man and as a composer."[87] Author Wallace Stegner, too, feels that "The Preacher and the Slave" and "Casey Jones" are no longer I.W.W. songs or even labor songs, but have become folk songs.[88]

Nels Anderson, in his work on the American hobo, noted that Joe Hill holds the place of honor as a songwriter among the members of the I.W.W.,[89] while historian Henry F. May has stated that ". . . the harsh, tough, skeptical songs of Joe Hill convey most clearly the nature of the I.W.W.'s appeal to well brought-up intellectuals of radical sympathies."[90]

In his collection of American folk songs, Carl Sandburg said, "Hill was the I.W.W.'s star song writer and is the only outstanding producer of lyrics widely sung in the militant cohorts of the labor movement of America. Jails and jungles from the Lawrence, Massachusetts, woolen mills to the Wheatland, California, hop fields have heard the rhymes and melodies started by Joe Hill."[91] Sandburg's statement of praise should be qualified to include I.W.W. songwriter Ralph Chaplin, whose "Solidarity Forever" some feel to be the best labor song produced in America.[92]

George Milburn, writing during the 1930's on the culture of the hobo, noted that ". . . the most ingenious of the hobo parodists was an I.W.W. named Hillstrom. He signed himself Joe Hill."* Millburn commented that Hill's songs

---

* Joe Hill was at various periods in his life known by at least three different names. He was christened Joel Hägglund. After emigrating to America, he changed his name to Joe Hill, the name he used to sign his songs, and the name by which he was most widely known. After his arrest in Salt Lake City, he called himself Joseph Hillstrom. At least one report states that he also used the name of Nilsson while in America.

have become so popular that their original radical purpose has been forgotten; today they are heard at "... high school 'hobo day' masquerades and the luncheon club of Mr. Babbitt quite as often as they are at Wob meetings."[93]

A few of Joe Hill's I.W.W. songs, then, have survived the particular occasions of their creation and have become something they were not originally. In order to understand just what they were when Joe Hill wrote them, and to recapture the full impact they had on the Wobblies of that time, they must be considered in light of the conditions within which they were originally accepted and nourished. The world of the Wobblies was a world unto itself, with its own standards, developing its "... own body of traditional lore—song, tale, custom, aphorism—and within the enclave of the dominant society they abhorred, they used this folklore to transmit their own cultural values."[94] Alan Calmer, writing on the Wobbly in American literature noted that the aesthetic standard of the I.W.W. "... resulted in exaggerated praise of mere doggerel and jingle and tendentious compositions of the most blatant character—entirely because they expounded the point of view of the militant labor movement." Calmer contended that the I.W.W., lacking an understanding of past culture, equated aesthetics with ethics and, as a result, glorified any writings that dealt sympathetically with the worker. Viewed with this in mind, the success of Hill's songs among the working class can readily be understood, for Joc Hill's great virtue as a writer and the reason some of his songs were propelled into the folk heritage was that he was "... a genuine worker poet, who wrote always as a worker rather than as a writer."[95]

Calmer's premise is supported by I.W.W. praise of Hill's songs. A report from the British branch, appearing in *Solidarity*, called his work "... songs of sarcasm and truth, songs which brought the masters, their property and everything in connection with them into contempt by the workers."[96] Elizabeth Gurley Flynn said, "Joe Hill writes songs that sing, that lilt and laugh and sparkle, that kindle the fires of revolt in the most crushed spirit and quicken the desires for fuller life in the most humble slave."[97]

Ralph Chaplin, I.W.W. editor, artist, and organizer—and a songwriter in his own right—maintained that Joe Hill "... probably came about as close to being the laureate of labor as any poet the working class movement has yet produced." He described Hill's songs as being "As coarse as home-spun and as fine as silk; full of lilting laughter and keen-edged satire; full of fine rage and finer tenderness; simple, forceful and sublime songs; songs of and for the worker written in the only language he can understand and set to the music of Joe Hill's own heart."[98]

But perhaps a letter to President Woodrow Wilson, from an articulate man who claimed at the time he wrote to be working as a laborer on a state highway in California, best sums up the impact of Joe Hill's songs upon the audience for which they were written.

> I write you to save Joe Hillstrom from execution in Salt Lake, Utah for the reason that Hillstrom is the first and only true composer of working class songs and poetry. Hillstrom is the Bobby Burns of today, and if Joe is put to death, the working class will

41

lose a genius, who can if he lives, alleviate a lot of mental anguish among my kind. Joe understands our troubles, because he has had to sleep in barns and haystacks, and those who have never had to live such life can never understand the troubles we have in the jungles. . . . Men in your position of society do not understand, but Joe Hillstrom does, for he proves it in the songs he writes. I do not know Joe personally but have seen and distributed many of his writings, and think he is the greatest educator for true and sensible society. Hoping Mr. President that you do not let them put Joe Hillstrom to death, I remain yours for a true and sensible society.

Bernard Kyler[99]

From
greenhorn
Swede
to rebel
true-blue

2 Because of the efforts of various re-

searchers in recent years it is possible to piece together an account of Joe Hill's early life. Unfortunately, however, there remain periods prior to his arrest in Utah in January 1914 about which little is certain. Much of the difficulty in documenting his life stems from his unusual reluctance to talk about himself. One Wobbly, who claims to have lived with Hill in San Pedro, wrote in 1947: "I believe I knew Joe as well as anyone now alive, and that's not anything very much. As a matter of fact, Joe was a most reticent cuss. To drag anything biographical out of Joe was a man size job; the guy just wasn't a fluent talker."[1]

Another San Pedro acquaintance, William Chance, one of the few individuals alive today who actually knew Joe Hill, reports that he spent hours fishing with him off the wharf in San Pedro, but that their conversations were never personal and, instead, centered around the I.W.W.[2]

Writing from the Utah State Prison in 1915, Hill answered a request from a friend that he furnish some biographical information.

> Biography you say? No. Let's not spoil good writing paper with such nonsense— only the here and now is of concern to me. I am "a citizen of the world" and I was born on a planet called the earth. The exact spot where first I saw the light of day is of such slight importance that it deserves no comment—I haven't much to say about myself. Will only say that I have done what little I could to bring the flag of freedom closer to its goal.[3]

In addition to the problem of Hill's taciturnity, the nature of the legend that sprang up after his death makes it difficult to separate the facts from a preponderance of convenient explanations.

The first accurate information on Hill's birth and childhood became available after the publication of three articles about him in the May 1, 1949, issue of the Swedish magazine *Folket i Bild*. The writers received letters in response to their articles suggesting that the person variously known as Joe Hill and Joseph Hillstrom had been born Joel Hägglund in Gävle, Sweden. One of the most revealing of these letters, from Mrs. Ester Dahl, claimed that the man, Joe Hill, was almost certainly her brother, Joel Hägglund. In another letter there was speculation that the writer may have been a childhood friend of Hill in Gävle.[4]

With these meager clues as a starting point, Ture Nerman, since that time the author of a book on Joe Hill in Swedish, began an investigation. In the

Gävle parish office he discovered the records of the Hägglunds. These records matched Mrs. Dahl's account of her family, and the information was further verified by Nerman's correspondence with residents of Gävle who remembered the family.[5] With the residence in Gävle of the Hägglund family and Joel established, Nerman learned from Mrs. Dahl that a few weeks after Hill's execution in Salt Lake City, Utah, his aunt and uncle, who were living in Gävle, received official papers* from the United States verifying his conviction and execution.[6]

Joel Hägglund's mother and father, Margareta Katarina Hägglund and Olof Hägglund, had nine children, six of whom lived to maturity. The six surviving children were Ruben, Efraim, Paul, Joel, Judit, and Ester.[7] Joel Emmanuel (notwithstanding the fact that he later claimed it was of too slight importance to deserve comment) was born on October 7, 1879, in the family home at 28 Nedra Bergsgatan, Gävle, Sweden.[8] He began his sojourn "on a planet called the earth" in a family that his father could barely support with his meager salary as conductor on the Gävle-Dala Railroad.[9]

Devoutly religious,[10] the Hägglunds were members of the Waldenströmmare sect, an orthodox Lutheran group.[11] As a boy Hill was reportedly a diligent member of the Bethlehem Church Sunday School and attended Salvation Army meetings. For whatever significance it may have, it is known that on his examination, taken prior to confirmation in the church, he received a grade of C, the lowest given.[12]

In contrast to Hill's later activities, politics apparently was never mentioned in the Hägglund home. Mrs. Dahl recalls that, "We were taught to be obedient to God and the King and to submit to all authority."[13]

Although his later political ideals apparently did not evolve from his childhood environment, music, another passion of the adult Joe Hill, played an important role in the family's life. Both parents enjoyed music and often led their children in family singing.[14] The father built a four-octave organ which the entire family learned to play and which Joel used to accompany the family's singing.[15] Joel also learned to play the piano, the accordion, the guitar,[16] and his favorite instrument, the violin, which he once said he enjoyed even more than he did eating.[17]

During Ture Nerman's interviews with Gävle residents who remembered

---

* Utah officials had apparently learned of Hill's origins in Gävle from a Swedish woman in Salt Lake City, Athana Saccoss. Mrs. Saccoss had testified at Hill's trial that she knew him from childhood days in Gävle and had met him again in Salt Lake City just a few days prior to his arrest. It is almost certain that Mrs. Saccoss was the author of an anonymous letter written in December 1915 to the Swedish newspaper *Arbetarbladet* which stated that Joe Hill was actually Joel Hägglund from Gävle. *Arbetarbladet* carried an article based on the letter saying that the anonymous writer had known Hill in Gävle and had testified at his trial in Utah. The information on Hill's activities in Utah contained in the article corresponds with the testimony given by Mrs. Saccoss at the trial. For complete *Arbetarbladet* article translated from Swedish see Appendix B.

According to Mrs. Dahl, Utah officials addressed an inquiry about the Hägglund fam-

**Mrs. Hägglund and her children—
Joel (Joe Hill) stands at left and the baby is Ester Dahl.**

ily to the pastor in Gävle, who consulted the family records and replied that August and Ulrica Wennman were the family's only relatives living in Gävle in 1915 (Letter from Ester Dahl to the author, 20 November 1965, original in author's possession). Consequently, the official papers were sent to them. It was from the Wennmans that Ester Dahl learned of her brother's execution. In 1927, after her husband died, Ulrica Wennman destroyed the documents. She reportedly believed Hill to be guilty of the murder for which he was executed, and did not want to leave behind any evidence that she was related to a criminal. See Ture Nerman, *Arbetarsangaren Joe Hill: Mördare Eller Martyr?* (Stockholm, Sweden: Federativs Forlag, 1951), p. 29.

him as a boy, Joel was described as having a talent for music and being more withdrawn and serious minded than his brothers.[18] As a youth, just as later, he "... kept what he had inside himself," using his music as the principal outlet for his feelings. He composed songs about members of his family,[19] attended concerts at the hall of the workers' association in Gävle, and in his teens played a piano in a local cafe.[20]

In 1887, when Joel was eight years old, his father was injured while working on the railroad and died during an operation performed to stop internal bleeding.[21] After Olof Hägglund's death, the family, which had at best barely subsisted, now often went cold and hungry.[22] The children were forced to help support the family, and Joel first worked in a rope factory, then as a fireman on a steam-powered crane for the same company where his brother Paul worked as a machinist.[23]

Left: Joe Hill's father, Olof Hägglund.   Right: Joe Hill as a youth in Sweden.

Several years after his father's death, Joel was stricken with skin and joint tuberculosis.[24] He went by himself to Stockholm to receive X-ray treatment for the disease. When the treatments failed to cure the ailment, he was admitted to the Serafimer Hospital in Stockholm for a series of operations. Two of these, on his neck and nose, left him with an extremely thin nose and scars on his neck and face—distinguishing marks which were to play an important role in his later years. Between his intermittent stays in the hospital, from April 15 to October 3, 1900, he sustained himself by working at odd jobs in Stockholm.[25]

Back in Gävle after the operations, Joel turned once again to his music, attaching the bow of the violin to a bandage on his wrist and playing for hours.[26]

In January 1902, Mrs. Hägglund, ill since 1900 with a back ailment and having undergone nine operations within a period of a year and a half, died; with her death the family dissolved. Since the children were old enough to support themselves, they decided to sell the family home and venture out, each on his own.[27] Ruben, Efraim, Judit, and Ester moved to various cities in Sweden. Joel and Paul, believing that America was a land where one had only to "scrape gold off the ground," decided to emigrate in the fall of 1902.[28] With their share of the money received from the sale of the family home (6500 crowns or $1300, divided among the six children), they purchased passage to New York City on the Cunard Line's *Saxonia*.[29] While en route, Paul wrote a card—dated October 1902 and postmarked New York City—to Efraim in Göteborg. "Julle [Joel] and I will appear on a most magnificent concert on board this barge—a violin duet and piano, what do you think of that?"[30] Arriving in America with little money but hopes high, they had the advantage of a knowledge of English, written and spoken, for they had received training in the language at the Y.M.C.A. in Sweden and had studied an English dictionary.[31]

Much of the available information concerning Hill's arrival in America is contradictory. His own account, reportedly given to his attorney on the day before his execution, differs from Mrs. Dahl's. Hill remarked that he had come to America in 1902 to join his brother, Charlstrom, who was working as a railroad engineer in this country.[32] There seems no reason for Hill to have invented a fictitious brother except to obscure the facts and thus protect his family name.

Another version of his arrival in America comes from Ralph Chaplin, the I.W.W. editor, songwriter, and artist, whose account, until the early 1950's, was the only source of information in the United States about Hill's early life— outside of the sketchy facts known by the Utah authorities. In 1923 Chaplin published some "facts" about Hill's life that he had learned from John Holland, an inebriated Swede, in a Cleveland, Ohio, saloon in 1915.[33] Holland, who claimed to be Joe Hill's cousin, said Hill was born in Gävle in 1882 (three years later than the established date), and worked in Sweden as a sailor and later as a fireman on the National Railroad. Holland reportedly told Chaplin that he and Hill emigrated from Sweden to America together in 1902.[34] Two factors make all information from Chaplin's interview with Holland questionable: first, Holland was inebriated, and was talking about things which had happened a number of years earlier; second, Chaplin presumably did not write the article until eight years after the interview. Mrs. Dahl has speculated that John Holland was actually her brother Paul, since Chaplin's description of John Holland as a tall, blond Swede with deeply tanned skin, matched what she remembered of Paul's appearance.

Still another account, in the Swedish newspaper *Arbetarbladet*, states that Hill emigrated in 1902 with ". . . a few other people from Gävle."[35]

Although the various accounts of Hill's arrival in America differ, it ap-

47

pears almost certain that he came to America with his brother Paul in 1902. The card sent from the *Saxonia* and Ture Nerman's report of the parish record in Gävle of Joel and Paul's emigration in 1902 would seem to substantiate that conclusion.[36]

Between his arrival in America in 1902 and the fall of 1913 when he traveled to Utah, a few facts* concerning his activities and whereabouts can be presented. These are outlined below and developed more fully later in the chapter.

1905: Ester and Judit Hägglund received and saved Christmas cards from Joel postmarked Cleveland, Ohio.

1906: Joel Hägglund wrote a letter to his hometown newspaper in Gävle describing his experiences in the San Francisco earthquake.

1910:** On August 27 the I.W.W. publication *Industrial Worker* carried a letter signed by Joe Hill which was written in Portland, Oregon.

1911: Although Hill denied it, evidence indicates that he was in Mexico during the year. During a part of this year, Hill also reportedly shared a shack on the beach in Hilo, Hawaii, with Wobbly Harry "Mac" McClintock.

1911-13: William Chance and Alexander MacKay, together with John Holland and Tom Mooney, and Edward, John, and Frank Eselius—the brothers with whom Hill later stayed in Salt Lake City—mentioned knowing Hill in San Pedro during this time.

1912: John Makins, superintendent of the Sailors' Rest Mission in San Pedro, reported that Hill first visited his mission around this time. Also during this year, Wobbly Louis Moreau reported that Joe Hill was in British Columbia where he wrote several songs for I.W.W. members on strike against construction companies building the Canadian Northern Railroad.

Aside from the few available facts outlined above which serve to pinpoint Hill's whereabouts in the years 1905-1913, there is some additional information which may or may not be true. An attempt will be made in the following account to present all available information concerning Hill from the time of his arrival in the United States until his arrest in Utah in January 1914.

According to most accounts, Joel, after his arrival in New York City in 1902, remained in that city for a year working at various odd jobs, one of which was as a porter in a Bowery saloon. From New York, he moved on to Chicago where he worked for a time in a machine shop. He was fired from his job and

---

* A fact has been considered established if it has been learned from the person who experienced the event or from a document verifying the event, and if its accuracy is not challenged by other reliable information.

** Considered as "almost established" is the theory that Hill joined the I.W.W. some time in 1910.

blacklisted for attempting to organize the workers.* Changing his name from
Joel Hägglund to Joe Hill, presumably to escape the stigma of the blacklist, he
left Chicago after being there for about two months.[37]

A pattern of restlessness emerges from the facts about Hill's life in the
United States before his arrest in 1914. He traveled widely, apparently visiting
such far-removed locations as Philadelphia, the Dakotas, Spokane,[38] Portland,
and San Francisco. In 1905, he sent Christmas cards to his sisters from Cleveland, Ohio.[39]

**Joe Hill sent Christmas cards to Ester
and Judit postmarked Cleveland.**

In a letter dated April 24, 1906, and published on May 16, 1906, Hill
described the San Francisco Earthquake for his hometown newspaper, *Gefle
Dägblad*.

THE CATASTROPHE IN SAN FRANCISCO—
A RESIDENT OF GAVLE TELLS THE STORY

From a former resident of Gävle, Joel Hägglund, who was present at the terrible
catastrophe in San Francisco, we received a letter dated the twenty-fourth which gives
you some idea of what they had to go through there. He writes among other things:

I woke up on the morning of Wednesday, April 18, at 5:13 by being thrown out of
bed. I stood up by grabbing the door handle which I got hold of by accident, and after
opening the door, I managed to reach the stairway after much scuffling. How I managed to get down the stairs I can't really tell, but I went fast. I had come halfway down

---

* Ture Nerman's report of Hill's organizing activities so soon after coming to America
is not supported by other sources.

the third and last flight and began to hope I would make it, when suddenly the stairway fell in and I fell straight through the floor down into the basement.

I thought that my last moment had come, so I tried to recite one of the old hymns I had learned in Sunday School in Gävle. Then I closed my eyes and waited for my fate.

But then the shakings became weaker and weaker and finally they were completely still. I was pinned between some boards, but managed after some effort to get loose. I moved my arms and legs and found them still working. With the exception of some bruises on my right side and arm, I was completely unhurt. I heard voices and shouts and crept up until I saw a hole large enough for a man to crawl through. In a moment I was out in the street only to meet a sight still worse than was in the basement.

A large six story house on the other side of the street was flat as a pancake on the ground, and men, women and children were running around in complete disorder. Some had some clothing on, some had not more on than a newborn child, and to tell the truth, I wouldn't have taken a walk on main street in the suit I was wearing.

I got hold of a pair of trousers which fit me about as well as a pair of Swedish soldier's pants, and I went up to an opening where I had a good view of the city. It was a terrible sight to see the large houses, some in ruins, some similar to the leaning tower of Pisa. The ground was full of cracks, some nearly three feet wide, and here and there a dark smoke pillar came out of the ruins, which was the first indication of the terrible fire that later hit San Francisco. It didn't take long before red flames were seen in several places and as all the water pipes had broken and not a drop of water could be had, these spread with terrible speed and the city was changed within a few hours into one single lake of fire.

I saw many moving and heart rending scenes. Half-naked women carrying small children were driven from their homes. Some refused to leave their old homes, and were seized and bound to keep them from going back into the flames. So-called "martial" law was proclaimed immediately—that means momentary death for the least criminal act or disobedience. Two soldiers came and gave me an axe and put a large steel hat on me, and before I knew what it was all about, I was employed as a fireman in the San Francisco Fire Department. I worked for thirty-six hours without food or drink before I was released. My work consisted of helping old people from the fire, carrying out sick from the hospitals, saving valuables, etc. The officer who released me first wrote down my name, then he looked into my pockets for loot. If he had found any, I would have received an extra buttonhole in the vest for all my work and would probably have never written this letter.

Many tried to make money on this calamity and charge senselessly for food. A grocer who sold crackers, small cookies valued about 1/5 of a cent apiece, for ten cents apiece and eggs for two dollars a dozen made money by the barrels. But then the police were told. They came and gave away all he had to the people outside. Then they brought him out into the street, bound him to a pole and placed a sign over his head with the following inscription: "The man who sold crackers for ten cents apiece. Spit on him." All those who passed spit on him, and I couldn't resist the temptation to go forward and aim at his very long nose. It is hardly necessary here to say that he was a Jew.

My companion, Oscar Westergren, a well known person from Gävle, I have not seen since the day before the earthquake. I know not whether he is dead or alive, but I am hoping for the best. He may have received some kind of "forced labor."

The fire is not out everywhere and the formerly rich San Francisco is now only a smoking ruin. About a hundred frame houses are all that is left of the "Proud Queen on the Shores of the Pacific Ocean."[40]

In 1915—following Hill's execution in Utah—an anonymous person known only as "Mexico" reported that, in 1909, Joe Hill was instrumental in helping workers in a factory carry on sabotage against their employer. The purpose of the activity was to prevent the company from continuing production of internal combustion engines during a strike. Judging from the article, Hill was not employed in the factory but had helped organize the workers in retaliation against company strikebreakers.

JOE HILL, A SUCCESSFUL SABOTAGE

Joe Hill, who didn't know him? He the honest fighter in whom there was no guile. I am reminded of an episode in the year 1909. We, or more correctly I, worked in a fairly large shop where we made motors. There were about 300 employees from many different areas, but many were Swedes. Several were married and lived on the ground of the company. There was no association to take care of our interest.

It was fairly decent as long as the old foreman was there. But then he went the way of all flesh, and another one came in his place, a German-born devil. He was young, and foolish, which was still worse. The Taylor system was started at once, of course. He was friendly to start with, but when he couldn't press any more work from us, our salary was lowered 20% without our knowing anything about it.

We had taken a lot from him before, but this was too much. Finally we gathered together and protested, with the result that we were all driven out. What to do? Everything was chaos, and to top it all, the company got many strike breakers through Farlay, the great strike breaker chieftain.

Then it was suggested between us that we should choose some from among us who would organize sabotage against the company. We should get at least some revenge. But we got much revenge, instead, thanks to Joe Hill. He had heard about our fight; he organized us; he brought order out of chaos, accustomed as he was to such situations. He enjoyed sabotage. Eight were picked, among them the undersigned. We were employed by the company again, but not at the same jobs as before. Before we started, Hill gave us the well thought out counsel not to carry anything in our pockets that could betray us, and it was good advice.

My closest companion was a man from Ireland by the name of Downey. He ran the large lathe. It stopped in the afternoon as still as a mountain. Then you should have seen the German's face when he found that the bearings were torn by sand as if they had been chopped with a chisel and hammer. And they were so busy with all the orders.

Both the machines that I was supposed to test were to go to Japan. Control engineers were at the shop so there was no way of doing a poor job. I filled the machines in all weak spots with as much sand as I had time for. It really hurt me to see all those beautiful drilled camshafts ruined. But tell me, dear readers, what great values do you think are wasted in the great unjustified world fight? Our fight is justified.

A consequence of my work, as you can understand, was that everything that was damaged had to be made over to meet the required standards. That cost money. The bosses were running around like wild chickens. The German was full of wrath. Add to this the fact that all those people were not able to work, then you will understand the situation. The general confusion made it easier for us eight to fulfill our purpose, which was to cause as much havoc as we had time to, and to look out for spies of which there were plenty. But everything went fine thanks to Hill's ability to organize us.

I was arrested the following day as was Downey, and we were questioned. In America it is called the third degree and those who have been through that know what it means: no food, no sleep in forty-eight hours while they try to get one to confess. When one of the torturers quits, another one starts. Also, there were under the table dealings by the company to try to get the police to torture us and send us to the work house for a few years. It didn't succeed. We were freed two days later because of lack of evidence.

But Hillstrom had not been idle. He got together means to help those that needed it most and when two weeks had passed, the company was willing to talk. Everything was decided fairly well to the advantage of the workers. However, Downey and I were not rehired. Hillstrom offered to fight for us, but I for my part, was happy to leave the place, as was Downey. When the discussions were finished, there were many who in

51

their hearts thanked Hill who came as a saving angel and brought order and organization to our discussions.

I met him two years later in another city. We talked about this episode. Well, he said, "That is not the first time that I have been in such a situation, and I am sure it won't be the last either."

Now he is murdered. Now probably there will be no last time when the one that could not be bent, when the righteous fighter in his own person, leads the fight against oppression. The enemy has murdered him but the acts of his life are still alive. Peace over him.*

Mexico[41]

All information capable of substantiation indicates that Hill joined the I.W.W. in San Pedro in 1910, the same year the local was formed. Commenting on his arrival in that city, Hill said: "I went to Los Angeles and then to San Pedro, where I became associated with members of the I.W.W. who were employed at the wharfs. I took an active interest in the San Pedro local of the I.W.W. and for several years I served as secretary of the local."[42]

This statement of Hill's is borne out by Alexander MacKay, who worked with him on the San Pedro waterfront, and by William Chance, who met Hill in San Pedro in 1911.[43] Tom Mooney and the Eselius brothers claimed to have known Hill in San Pedro, but didn't mention his I.W.W. activity, during the years 1911 to 1913.[44]

In his report of the circumstances surrounding the creation of "Casey Jones—The Union Scab," Ralph Chaplin concluded that Hill was invited to join the I.W.W. following a Southern Pacific Railroad strike in the summer of 1911.[45] However, there is no other evidence to support Chaplin's assertion that Hill joined in 1911. Adding to the probability that Hill was a member in 1910 is a letter he wrote from Portland, Oregon, to the *Industrial Worker*.

Another Victim of the Uniformed Thugs   On the Road, August 11th, 1910

While strolling through the yards at Pendleton, Ore., I saw a fellow sitting on a tie pile. He had his left hand all bandaged up and hanging useless by his side, and the expression on his face was the most hopeless I ever saw. Seeing that he was one of my class I went up and asked him how it happened, and he told me a tale that made the blood boil in my veins. Like many others, he floated into Roseville Junction, Cal., a town noted for murders and bloodshed. He had a few cents and did not have to beg, but the bull of that worthy town did not like the way he parted his hair, I guess, so they told him to make himself scarce around there. After a bit a train pulled out and he tried to obey the orders, but that upholder of law and justice saw him and habitually took a shot at him. His intentions were, of course, the very best, but being a poor shot he only succeeded in crushing the man's hand. The poor fellow might starve to death though, so that blood-thirsty hyena may not get so badly disappointed after all. Not

---

* This article raises several questions for which there are no available answers. How, for instance, did Hill know about the strike and gain the leadership of the strikers? Was Hill a member of the I.W.W. or some other labor organization at this time? From all indications he did not join the I.W.W. until a year later in 1910. Had Hill been in such situations before as he allegedly claimed? Since the author of the article failed to mention his own name, the factory name, or the city in which the episode occurred, it is difficult to substantiate the account or to prove it wrong.

being satisfied with disabling the man for life, he struck him several blows on the head and face with a "sapper" (rubber hose with chunks of lead in the end.) Then he threw him in the "tank" without any medical aid whatever, although the hand was bleeding badly. The next morning about 5 o'clock he got a couple of kicks for breakfast and told that if he dared to show his face around there again it would be the grave yard for him. He told me he could not sleep much because the hand was aching all the time and he wished he could get it cut off, because it was no good anyway. Now, fellow workers, how long are those hired murderers, whose chief delight it is to see human blood flowing in streams, going to slaughter and maim our class. There is only one way to stop it—only one remedy—to unite on the industrial field. Yours,

JOE HILL,
Portland Local, No. 92[46]

Despite Hill's statement to the contrary, it seems certain that he was among the group of Wobblies who in 1911 rallied to the cause inspired by Ricardo Flores Magón and Enrique Flores Magón, brothers who plotted from Los Angeles to overthrow the government of Mexico. With its large Mexican population and its proximity to Mexico, Los Angeles became the seat of the Mexican Liberal Party dedicated to the overthrow of dictator Porfirio Diaz.[47] When Diaz was ousted by Francisco Madero in 1910, the Magón brothers and other radicals formed a junta and planned to take advantage of the chaotic political situation in Mexico to seize Baja California and accomplish the "emancipation" and "industrial freedom" of the working class in Mexico.[48]

With an initial enrollment of eighteen, the "army" of the rebels swelled to several hundred, composed largely of wandering hobos eager for adventure. Joe Hill was reportedly in charge of enlisting I.W.W. members from Los Angeles into the rebel ranks.[49] The choice of Hill would have been logical, for he was well known in radical circles in that region and probably knew the Magón brothers.[50]

In January 1911, the rebels took Mexicali by force of arms. Later that spring, a small force of approximately forty rebels took the town of Tecate about thirty miles from Tijuana and prepared to engage the Mexican army. A letter appearing in the *Industrial Worker*, appealing for help for the men fighting in Mexico, reported on conditions there: "So far, only a few of the I.W.W. boys have been killed and the revolution has been only supported by the Mexicans and American members of the Liberal Junta, and the members of the I.W.W. locals down here in California, and right now about half of the 250 insurrectos here in Tia Juana are members of the I.W.W."[51]

Another letter to *Solidarity* describes the conditions in Tijuana.

A Visit to Mexico

Yesterday I visited Tiajuana, Mex., the town recently captured and now held by the rebels. It is a border town and only a short distance from San Diego. Immediately after the battle tourists and others from that city, mostly YMCA boys, poured into the town and looted the stores and private houses, taking everything of value they could carry away. Of course the capitalist press at first had scary headlines about the awful insurrectos and how they looted even private homes etc.

As soon as the last federal soldier had disappeared across the line and the dead and wounded had received attention, the rebels began to reconstruct things in the old town of Tiajuana. The first thing they did was to open the jail and let all the prisoners go free. Only the walls of the old bastille stand to remind the passerby of the awful days of the past.

The bull ring is in ashes. The custom house and all other public buildings have been taken possession of and appropriated to the use of the army.

The wonder of the visitors and the United States soldiers on the border is that in that little town today, although an army is encamped there, no jail or guardhouse is needed.

Most of the rebels are Americans. Many of them I had seen on other fields of battle, the economic field, and as I shook hands with them, while cartridge belts and guns made up a conspicuous part of their apparel, I knew it was the same old battle, only in a different form than of old. . . .[52]

The rebel ranks were torn by dissension. Few things seemed to go well, and the campaign ended with the defeat of a hundred men at Tijuana on June 22, 1911, when, outnumbered by well supplied Mexican troops, the rebels retreated to the United States.[53]

Shortly before his execution in 1915, Hill in a statement to his attorney disclaimed any involvement in the affair: "I was acting as secretary [of the San Pedro local] when a mob was reported to have attempted to loot Tijuana from the American side. I have been credited with having been a lieutenant of that mob, but this is absolutely untrue. I was then at San Pedro and there heard of the affair."[54]

This statement contradicts reports from Hill's fellow workers—as well as indications from Hill himself—that he participated in the abortive invasion.[55] Perhaps the strongest evidence of Hill's involvement comes from Wobbly Sam Murray, a friend and correspondent of Hill's, who, in published statements and in letters to friends, claimed to have been with Hill in Mexico.[56] In a letter to Murray from prison, Hill alludes to a degree of familiarity with the situation in Mexico: "The other day we [the Joe Hill Defense Fund] got ten bucks from a company of soldiers stationed on the Mexican line. How is that old top? Maybe they are remembering some of the cigars in glass bottles they smoked at the expense of the 'Tierra e Liberated' bunch [one of the names by which the rebel army was known]."[57]

The *Los Angeles Times*, in a 1915 article summarizing Hill's career in San Pedro, made this reference to his activities in Mexico:

When he first arrived Hill worked steadily and lived quietly. . . . Then he fell in with the I.W.W. colony that were making their headquarters here. Having accepted the doctrine of the organization he became bitter toward society. Soon he quit working and went to Mexico with a roving band of I.W.W. raiders. He returned after a few months and was never steadily employed afterwards.[58]

In a satirical article, "The People," Hill indicates a personal involvement with conditions during the invasion.

When the Red Flag was flying in Lower California there were not any of "the people" in the ranks of the rebels. Common working stiffs and cow-punchers were in the majority, with a little sprinkling of "outlaws," whatever that is.

"The people" used to come down there on Sunday in their stinkwagons to take a look at "The wild men with their Red Flag" for two-bits a look. But if the Mexican or the Indian regiment happened to be a little overjoyed from drinking "mescal" and took a notion to have a bit of sociable target practice, or to try to make buttonholes for one another without taking their clothes off, then "the people" would almost break their legs to get to their stinkwagons and make a bee-line for the "Land of the Graft and the Home of the Slave."

Well, it is about time that every rebel wakes up to the fact that "the people" and the workingclass have nothing in common. Let us sing after this "The Workers' flag is deepest red" and to hell with "the people."[59]

In an apparent attempt to incite rebels to use force where necessary in taking Baja California, Hill wrote: "Workers may find out that the only 'machine' worth while is the one which the capitalists use on us when we ask for more bread for ourselves and our families. The one that works with a trigger. All aboard for Mexico!"[60]

During the winter of the same year, 1911, Hill is also reported to have been in the Hawaiian Islands. "Mac" McClintock, a Wobbly, claimed that he, Joe Hill, and Pat Kelly shared a shack on the beach at Hilo, Hawaii. They were employed ". . . as longshoremen—loading raw sugar in the holds of the American-Hawaiian Sugar boats."[61] McClintock stated that they stayed there two or three months, and each time the mail boat came, Hill received several letters, forwarded by a Scandinavian seamen's mission in San Pedro, which he burned after reading.[62] McClintock's story coincides with a statement in John Holland's account to Ralph Chaplin that when Hill's "viking spirit" could stand it no longer, he would sign on ships sailing between Los Angeles and Honolulu. [63]

In keeping with the mysteriousness of Hill's life, there is contradictory information from various sources as to the possibility that Hill participated in Wobbly free speech fights in Spokane (1909) and Fresno (1911). One Wobbly, Ted Fraser, reportedly claimed in a speech at a meeting in London, England, that he first met Hill in Los Angeles, and that he later fought alongside him in free speech fights in Spokane and Fresno.[64] On the other hand Richard Brazier, a Wobbly who was unquestionably in the Spokane fight, strongly doubts that either Fraser or Hill was there.[65] Hill's involvement in the Fresno free speech fight is equally doubtful.

Another account of an attempt to participate in a free speech fight comes from William Chance, who maintains that Hill was on his way to the San Diego fight of 1912 when he was captured by vigilantes in Oceanside, California, and beaten so severely that he could not continue.[66]

Those Wobs who reached San Diego were met by violent opposition. Vigilantes met trains on the only line into town, ordered the Wobs off, beat them, made them run the gauntlet—two lines of men with clubs or sticks—and forced them back onto trains headed north.[67] Those who made it into town were arrested en masse and the jails were soon filled. Some, not so fortunate, were captured and beaten. Ben Reitman, a free speech sympathizer—but not a Wobbly—was abducted and beaten while in San Diego with the anarchist Emma

Goldman.[68] Free speech sympathizers among the San Diego citizenry received the same brutal treatment.[69]

As described in Chapter 1, Hill, during a strike against construction contractors on the Canadian Northern Railroad in 1912, put in an appearance at the strikers' camp near Yale, British Columbia, where he wrote one of his most popular songs, "Where the Fraser River Flows."[70]

From Canada, Hill apparently returned to San Pedro in time for the I.W.W.-inspired dockworkers' strike which took place during July of 1912. The San Pedro press reported that the Wobblies organized the Italian dockworkers and called a strike against the Banning Company on Crescent Wharf.[71] Two hundred Italians walked off the job on July 21, 1912.[72] Their principal demands were an increase in pay from thirty to forty cents an hour and a nine-hour working day. The strike was conceived and planned at the I.W.W. meeting place, Malgren's Hall,[73] where William Chance remembered often seeing Hill playing the piano, banjo, and violin. The strike ended within a few days, but the police persisted in rounding up and deporting or jailing Wobblies.[74] As secretary of the San Pedro local, Joe Hill was undoubtedly a source of irritation to the police, who tried to deport him as a foreigner and an I.W.W. agitator.[75]*

As a direct result of the San Pedro strike, Hill, according to his own story, was arrested and spent thirty days in the city jail on a charge of vagrancy, simply because he was "a little too active to suit the chief of the burg."[76] The San Pedro police gave a decidedly different version of this incident, reporting that Hill was arrested as a suspect in a streetcar holdup in June 1913, but as no one could identify him, he was jailed for thirty days for vagrancy. (See the letter from the San Pedro police chief to the Salt Lake City police in Chapter 6.)

In contrast to his I.W.W. activity and the time he spent at Malgren's Hall, Joe Hill was also attracted to the markedly different atmosphere of the Sailors' Rest Mission, a Christian organization located at Fourth and Beacon streets in San Pedro. Aside from the questionable report of Ralph Chaplin that Hill wrote "Casey Jones—The Union Scab" at the mission,[77] proof that Hill knew the place and used the piano is found in a short sketch, "The Two Roads," by John Makins, superintendent of the mission.

> Last July Charles A. Nethery, a young man converted in our mission in 1912, was ordained a minister of the Gospel, and called to a pastorate in the town of Ferndale, Wash. Before going there he married Miss Amy Kay. Letters from them show they are enthusiastic in their work, and are having good results.
>
> Contrast Mr. Nethery's course with that of a young man [Joe Hill] who came to San Pedro and to our mission about the same time Nethery came and who had the same opportunities to help himself. He used our piano a great deal, for he was a musician, he refused to be a Christian, but listened attentively to the teaching of the I.W.W. and joined their ranks. He came to his end in Salt Lake City three years later, and was executed for the murder of a groceryman. These two men knew each other, came under the same influence but traveled different roads.[78]

---

* The attempt apparently collapsed when the federal government failed to provide the necessary funds to deport Hill.

"A typical scene at the gospel service," the Sailors' Rest Mission at
Fourth and Beacon streets, San Pedro.

Mr. Makins, who apparently tried to convert Hill and lure him away from the I.W.W., reportedly wrote him many times while he was in prison in Utah, but received only one letter from Hill in response. The letter, the last written by Hill before his execution, refers to their friendship in these words: "You will find me the same Joe—as in days of yore."[79]

The foregoing account of the whereabouts and activities of Joe Hill during the decade 1902 to 1912 leaves us with a paucity of fact and an abundance of speculation. But even less is known about him from early 1913 until the late summer of that same year when he left San Pedro and moved toward the day in early January of 1914—the day that began a twenty-two month period during which his life would become a part of the public domain, and interest much of the newspaper-reading population of America.

In light of the difficulties encountered in pinpointing Joe Hill in time and space during the years prior to his arrest in Utah, can we hope for any greater success in delving into the personality of the man? Possibly, because, in contrast to the obscure trail of his journeys across the land, we have the relatively complete record—in the form of his songs, articles, and letters and the comments of those who knew him—of what he thought, felt, and apparently was.

Joel Hägglund left his native Sweden for America where he believed prosperity would be his merely for the asking and where equality of opportunity was a reality. But, for Joe Hill, America turned out to be a land specializing in the oppression of foreigners and migrant workers. It could have been nothing less than an embittering experience. Certainly, it changed a young man raised in a conservative Christian home which taught him loyalty to "God, King and all authority" into a "rebel true-blue," opposed to the existing social and economic inequalities, to the authority of the law when it sanctioned injustice, and, apparently, to Christianity. There was clearly a distinct difference between the boy, Joel Hägglund, and the man, Joe Hill, who wrote "The Preacher and the Slave."

And yet much of Hill's later behavior seems to be a carry-over from his conservative upbringing, and the transition appears to have occurred in his reappraisal of the world rather than in fundamental traits of his personality.

Before he achieved notoriety with his arrest and conviction, "fellow worker Hill" was known to most Wobblies only as a signature under the titles of his songs in the "Little Red Song Book." Those few who knew him personally agree on several traits which seem to characterize both the boy and the man. He was reported to be meticulous and neat in his personal habits. He ". . . never smoked in his life nor drank intoxicating liquor. . . ." "He was well dressed and had . . . that fresh-scrubbed, immaculate look. . . ." Although legend portrays him as a prominent I.W.W. organizer, those who knew him best describe him as quiet and withdrawn—a "lone wolf." Not inclined toward oratory nor possessing the gregariousness of an organizer, Hill became known primarily through his songs and his long day in court. Alluding to his role in matters of organization, he wrote from prison:

> I think the organization should use all its resources to keep the "live wires" on the outside. I mean the organizers and the orators. When they are locked up they are dead as far as the organization [is] concern[ed]. A fellow like myself, for instance, can do just as well in jail. I can dope out my music and "poems" in here and slip them out through the bars and the world will never know the difference.[80]

It was said that he preferred staying in his own "shack" to going out on the town. He was reportedly adept at oriental cooking, sharing gladly with pals who dropped in. Confirming his preference for the "quiet life," he wrote Sam Murray while in prison:

> Friend and fellow worker. Yours of March 13th at hand. I note that you have gone "back to nature" again and I must confess that it is making me a little homesick when you mention that "little cabin in the hills" stuff. You can talk about your dances, picnics and blowouts, and it won't affect me, but the "little cabin" stuff always gets my goat. That's the only life I know.[81]

Hill was said to be courteous to women, but by the same report he was no ladies' man and never had a steady girl, and this impression of him has been widely accepted. "Mac" McClintock stated, however, that he was somewhat more adventurous with women: "Women were a push over for him—and he frequently made use of them. In fact, his sojourn in Hilo was due to a jam he got into with a certain rich-bitch in Portland, Oregon."[82]

Although little is directly expressed by the available facts about Hill's relationship with women, it is implicit in the letters written in his defense after his arrest and in the concern shown in his plight by such women as Theodora Pollok, Virginia Snow Stephen, and Elizabeth Gurley Flynn that their interest was in Hill the man as well as Hill the Wobbly on trial for his life.

His personality seems to have fit his independent pattern of living. According to one report, he was not an idler, but worked hard and kept his union dues paid up. Another report, while agreeing that his dues were always paid, stated that he seldom worked. The *Los Angeles Times* reported that "When he first arrived, he worked steadily and lived quietly. . . . Then he fell in with the

I.W.W. . . ." It is probable that he worked when necessary to earn money with which to live, but preferred occasional work to a steady job because he wanted free time for composing songs and poetry and for traveling.

Although his bent was toward the literary, physically he was well equipped for the rigors of the "hobo life."

> Tall and lean, he moved with the sinewy ease of a panther and could go into explosive action with almost incredible speed. I know that this sounds like the hero of a pulp western—but it's true. I was a railroader for a lot of years but I don't believe I ever saw a man who could board, or drop off, a faster train than Joe Hill.[83]

Philosophically, Hill became, during his wandering years, a man far different from the youth from Gävle. He developed a keen hatred for the inequities of American society which allowed business to prosper while segments of labor were impoverished. "Mac" McClintock claimed his hatred found vent in lawlessness.

> Here's another thought on Joe Hill. In most things he was as anti-social as any yegg—I believe that he was a crook and that he made a lot of scores. He had a code of his own about such matters; the old Robin Hood stuff. He wouldn't have stuck up a streetcar conductor for his personal dough—but it was okeh to snag the company's coin. The fact that he might have to shoot the conductor in a getaway didn't bother Joe. If the poor sap wanted to be heroic in defense of his master's property he'd just have himself to blame if he got hurt.
>
> And you can figure that there was no police dossier on Joe because, regarding most crooks as a bunch of rats, he never frequented their hangouts nor made any friends among them. . . .
>
> Joe Hill, in my book, was half Wob—with an ideal of economic justice to shoot at and a Social War to fight before the ideal could be obtained. The other half was plain crook—take what you can when you can. A "lone ganger" against society.[84]

In the same vein, novelist Stewart Holbrook wrote to Wallace Stegner: "Years ago a Wobbly editor [probably McClintock] told me that all Wobs in the know, knew that Hill was a stick-up man, that they [the I.W.W.] blew him up into a Martyr for the sake of the Cause."[85]

But "all Wobs in the know" did not agree; in fact, the statement is clearly a minority viewpoint. Louis Moreau, for example, mentions nothing about a criminal side to Hill. William Chance emphatically denies it.[86] H. M. Edwards, an acquaintance of Hill's close friend, Sam Murray, when asked whether Murray ever mentioned Hill's being a criminal, said:

> At Vallejo [California] we [Sam Murray and Edwards] would often be together . . . and usually celebrated the occasion with stew and dago-red. Since we trusted each other implicitly and swapped stories about past experience, including Sam's trip into Mexico with Joe Hill during the revolution, it is safe to assume that Sam would have told me about Joe Hill being a two-bit gunman who went around sticking up people had that been the truth. Instead of that Sam Murray showed me letters and original bits of poetry he had received over the years from Joe Hill. . . .[87]

In agreement with these later statements, and in contradiction to McClintock's, is the fact that Hill had no known criminal record before his arrest in

59

Utah in 1914. The only other known incident involving him with the police was his arrest for vagrancy in San Pedro.

More likely is the claim that Hill vented his hostility and desire for social change almost exclusively through his writing. Words became effective weapons as he railed at the hypocrisy of authority.

> "The People's flag is deepest red." Who are the people?
>
> "God knows" Taft stands for "the people." If you don't believe it just read the "Los Angeles Crimes" and you will find out that, next to General Debility Otis, Taft is the greatest man in the country. Yes, Fatty stands for the people all right—when he is standing, but he is sitting down most of the time.
>
> And "Teddy da Roos," who used to peddle the Bull Moose, is also very strong for "the people." Some time ago he wasn't so strong and then it was that he invented a policeman's riot club filled with spikes. It would crush the skull of a wage slave with one blow. Yes, "Teddy da Roos," he is strong for "the people."
>
> And Woodhead Wilson, he is for "the people" too. This is what he said in one of his speeches: "Why shouldn't the children of the working-class be taught to do the work their parents are now doing?" Of course, he meant to say "Why shouldn't the children of the rich be taught to rob the class their parents are now robbing?" And he is going to give "the people" free silver, he says, but if a working stiff wants any silver he has to peel off his coat and hop to the stormy end of a No. 2.[88]

In Hill's earliest writings it is clear that he despised inequities sanctioned by the law. It is also evident that, although he was a "loner" according to almost all available accounts, he viewed organization—the concentration of power—as the working man's only real protection against those who would exploit him. In his 1910 letter from Portland he stated simply that "organizing" was the answer, but in later years he developed sophisticated ideas for utilizing organization.

Cognizant of the fact that ". . . as a rule a fellow don't bother his head much about unions and theories of the class struggle when his belly is flopping up against his spine,"[89] he proposed a plan to create more jobs.

> Much has been written lately about various new ways and tactics of carrying on the class struggle to emancipate the workers from wage slavery.
>
> Some writers propose to "organize with the unemployed"; that is, to feed and house them in order to keep them from taking the jobs away from the employed workers. Others again want to organize a Gunmen Defense Fund to purchase machine guns and high-powered rifles for all union men, miners especially, that they may protect themselves from the murderous onslaughts of the private armies of the master class. Very well; these tactics MAY be perfectly good, but the question arises: Who is going to pay for all this?
>
> Estimating the unemployed army to be about five millions in number and the board bill of one individual to be five dollars a week, we find that the total board bill of the whole unemployed army would be twenty-five million dollars per week.
>
> The price of a machine gun is about $600 and a modern high-power rifle costs from $20 to $30. By doing a little figuring we find that fifty million dollars would not be sufficient to buy arms for the miners, let alone the rest of the organized workers. Every workingman and woman knows that, after all the bills are paid on pay day, there is not much left to feed the unemployed army or to buy war supplies with.
>
> What the working class needs today is an inexpensive method by which to fight the powerful capitalist class and they have just such a weapon in their own hands.
>
> This weapon is without expense to the working class and if intelligently and sys-

tematically used, it will not only reduce the profits of the exploiters, but also create more work for the wage earners. If thoroughly understood and used more extensively it may entirely eliminate the unemployed army, the army used by the employed class to keep the workers in submission and slavery.

In order to illustrate the efficacy of this new method of warfare, I will cite a little incident. Some time ago the writer was working in a big lumber yard on the west coast. On the coast nearly all the work around the water fronts and lumber yards is temporary.

When a boat comes in a large number of men are hired and when the boat is unloaded these men are "laid off." Consequently, it is to the interest of the workers "to make the job last" as long as possible.

The writer and three others got ordered to load up five box cars with shingles. When we commenced the work we found, to our surprise, that every shingle bundle had been cut open. That is, the little strip of sheet iron that holds the shingles tightly together in a bundle had been cut with a knife or a pair of shears, on every bundle in the pile—about three thousand bundles in all.

When the boss came around we notified him about the accident and, after exhausting his supply of profanity, he ordered us to get the shingle press and re-bundle the whole batch. It took the four of us ten whole days to put the shingle pile into shape again. And our wages for that time, at the rate of 32 cents per hour, amounted to $134.00. By adding the loss on account of delay in shipment, the "holding money" for the five box cars, etc., we found that the company's profit for that day had been reduced about $300.

So there you are. In less than half an hour's time somebody had created ten days' work for four men who would have been otherwise unemployed, and at the same time cut a big chunk off the boss's profit. No lives were lost, no property was destroyed, there were no law suits, nothing that would drain the resources of the organized workers. But there WERE results. That's all.

This same method of fighting can be used in a thousand different ways by the skilled mechanic or machine hand as well as by the common laborer. This weapon is always at the finger tips of the worker, employed or unemployed.

If every worker would devote ten or fifteen minutes every day to the interests of himself and his class, after devoting eight hours or more to the interests of his employer, it would not be long before the unemployed army would be a thing of the past and the profit of the bosses would melt away so fast that they would not be able to afford to hire professional man-killers to murder the workers and their families in a case of strike.

The best way to strike, however, is to "strike on the job." First present your demands to the boss. If he should refuse to grant them, don't walk out and give the scabs a chance to take your places. No, just go back to work as though nothing had happened and try the new method of warfare.

When things begin to happen be careful not to "fix the blame" on any certain individual unless that individual is an "undesirable" from a working class point of view.

The boss will soon find that the cheapest way out of it is to grant your demands. This is not mere theory; it has been successfully tried more than once to the writer's personal knowledge.

Striking on the job is a science and should be taught as such. It is extremely interesting on account of its many possibilities. It develops mental keenness and inventive genius in the working class and is the only known antidote for the infamous "Taylor System."

The aim of the "Taylor System" seems to be to work one-half the workers to death and starve the other half to death. The strike on the job will give every worker a chance to make an honest living. It will enable us to take the child slaves out of the mill and sweatshop and give their unemployed fathers a chance to work. It will stop the butchering of the workers in time of peace as well as in time of war.

If you imagine "Making Work for the Unemployed" is unfair, just remember Ludlow and Calumet and don't forget Sacramento where the men who were unable to get work had their brains beaten out by the Hessians of the law and were knocked down and drenched to the skin with streams of ice-cold water manipulated by the city fire department, where the unemployed were driven out of the city and in the rain only to meet the pitchforks of the farmers. And, what for? For the horrible crime of asking the governor of California—for A JOB!

This is the way the capitalist class uses the working class when they can no longer exploit them—in the name of Law and Order. Remember this when you MAKE WORK FOR THE UNEMPLOYED![90]

Once a worker's immediate basic needs were being met, Hill urged militancy in the rebel ranks. The majority of his songs stress in some way the advantages inherent in I.W.W. membership. And, just before his execution, he left as his epitaph the famous injunction, "Don't waste any time in mourning: Organize!" However even while urging organization, Hill could see that the I.W.W.'s characteristically haphazard spurts of activity which so often poured massive union effort into areas of slight industrial importance prevented the effective use of the organization's power. Accordingly, he expressed to a friend his ideas for increasing the effectiveness of union effort.

There is too much energy going to waste organizing locals in "jerkwater towns" of no industrial importance. A town like San Diego for instance where the main "industry" consists of "catching suckers" is not worth a whoop in Hell from a rebel's point of view. Still there has been more money spent on that place than there ever was on Pittsburgh, Detroit and other manufacturing towns of great importance. Organization is just like dripping water on a blotter—if you drip enough of it in the center it will soak through clean to the edges.[91]

There is not the slightest doubt that Hill, when he arrived in Utah in 1913, had become, by his own definition, a "rebel true-blue," dedicated to changing conditions in America. But there was, and is, considerable doubt that the rebel who was ready and willing to help overturn the established social and economic system, or to help sabotage an employer's business for the benefit of the workers, was also capable of gunning down the owner of a small grocery store and his son in Salt Lake City, Utah, in January 1914. Twelve important men in Joe Hill's life, however, thought he was.

Charged
with
murder

3 Joe Hill left San Pedro, California,
late in the summer of 1913 and traveled to Los Angeles to visit his friend Oscar
Westergren who was ill in a hospital there.[1] With Chicago as his destination, Hill
then left Los Angeles and continued as far as Salt Lake City, Utah. In Salt Lake
City his journey was delayed for two years, but he eventually arrived in Chicago
in November 1915—the occasion being his funeral.

Hill had stopped in Salt Lake City to earn a "stake" for the trip to Chicago
and, according to an account by Ralph Chaplin, to visit a distant relative named
Mohn.[2] He found work in Park City, Utah—a small mining town located in the
mountains about thirty miles southeast of Salt Lake—in a mine owned by the
Silver King Coalition Mining Company.[3] Also employed at the mine was Hill's
friend Otto Applequist, whom he had probably met while working in San
Pedro.[4]

Hill became ill while working in Park City and was hospitalized for two
weeks, during which time he lost his job. After his illness he was taken to
Sandy, Utah, a suburb of Salt Lake City, by Applequist, also jobless, who introduced him to several Swedish families. Arriving during the festive Christmas
season, Hill quickly became popular with his countrymen because of his ability
to sing and play the piano and was often invited to their homes to perform
Swedish songs.[5]

Hill and Applequist spent the first weeks in January of 1914 as guests of
the Eselius brothers who lived in Murray, Utah. Since Hill's arrival in Utah, he
and Applequist had been frequent guests at the Eselius home, visiting there for
two weeks in August and a week in September of 1913.[6] Hill had become acquainted with Edward and John Eselius earlier that year while all were working
on the San Pedro waterfront and living nearby in a hobo jungle known as "Happy Hollow."[7]

On Saturday night, January 10, 1914, Joe Hill left the Eselius home sometime between six and nine p.m. and did not return until about one a.m. the
following morning.[8] His actions between the time of his departure from the
house and 11:30 p.m. that Saturday evening have never been satisfactorily explained either by Hill or his accusers.

It is known that Joe Hill visited a physician, Dr. Frank M. McHugh, shortly after 11:30 p.m. Saturday night, January 10, 1914. Dr. McHugh maintained
an office in his home at Fourteenth South and State streets in Salt Lake City.

McHugh, in bed at the time, heard a knock on his door, got up, and asked what his visitor wanted. According to McHugh: "A husky voice said that he had been injured. . . . I turned on the lights and a man walked in whom I recognized as Joe Hill, who I remembered was staying at the Eselius home in Murray." [9] (McHugh was at the time treating one of the Eselius brothers for pneumonia.) Hill said, "Doctor, I've been shot. I got into a stew with a friend of mine who thought I had insulted his wife. When he told me I had insulted his wife I knocked him down, but he got up and pulled a gun on me and shot me. I have walked away up here and I guess it isn't serious. Because this fellow that shot me didn't really know what he was doing, I want to have nothing said about it. If there's a chance to get over it, it will be O.K. with my friend." [10] *

Hill's friend Otto Applequist.

Despite many requests and the pleas of his friends, Hill refused to provide details to corroborate his story. He never revealed the names of the other persons allegedly involved or the location of the quarrel. An anonymous letter sent from Buffalo, New York, which tended to substantiate Hill's story concerning his wound, was received by his attorney, O. N. Hilton, shortly before Hill's execution in November 1915 and represents the best support for Hill's story which came to light:

---

* The story of Hill's wound was reported differently in the *Deseret Evening News* of January 14, 1914, which quotes McHugh as saying, "I asked him how he came to be shot and he told me that he and another fellow had quarrelled over a girl and that he had struck the other man, who retaliated by shooting him."

January 10, 1914, 10 o'clock p.m., at the home of the Eselius; Joe Hillstrom re-membered having an appointment with a woman acquaintance in Murray thereupon Joe Hillstrom left the house alone and walked to the house of said acquaintance and upon arrival He came in contact with a man how was in a great state of excitement and before they recognized each other the other man drew a gun and fired the shot through Joes body and in the struggle that followed Joe Hillstrom rested the gun from the man Whereupon Joe remarked that it would be a suvenir in case He Joe lived through it, and from there he went to Dr. McHugh's office. This is all I can say at present, Yours truly, Buffalo, New York[11]

Although this letter contains some information that is consistent with Hill's explanation of his wound, it is significant that it arrived almost two years after the shooting and contains many facts made generally available in Salt Lake City papers—considerations which impair its corroborative value.

65

Dr. McHugh removed Hill's clothing to his waist. His shirt and undershirt were soaked with blood; there was a bullet hole in his chest and a ragged exit hole in his back. The doctor later described the wounds in some detail: "The bullet entered a little below and a little to the outer side of the nipple line, ranging upward, backward and outward, and emerged a little below the interior angle of the scapula."[12] He noted also that the bullet grazed Hill's left lung, causing slight hemorrhaging in the lung.[13]

While McHugh was examining Hill, Dr. A. A. Bird, a friend of McHugh's, noticed the light in the office window and stopped for a visit. McHugh proceeded to dress Hill's wound while Dr. Bird visited. After the wound was dressed, McHugh helped Hill into his clothes. As he was pulling a sweater jacket over Hill's head, a gun in a shoulder holster fell from the clothing. Because the gun was in a holster, both doctors saw only the handle.[14] McHugh then put the holstered gun into a pocket of the light gray overcoat Hill had been wearing when he came into the office. He noticed that the coat did not have a bullet hole in it,[15] although the other clothing did, indicating that Hill was not wearing the coat when he was shot.

The gun Hill carried into Dr. McHugh's office is the source of some unre-solved confusion as well as incriminating evidence against Hill, supportive of the accusations that were later to be made against him. In contradiction to the "souvenir" explanation proffered in the letter from Buffalo is a statement writ-ten by Hill in 1915 that he owned the gun, a 30-caliber Luger, having bought it at a second-hand store on December 15, 1913.*

---

* Hill said of the gun:

It was bought less than a month before my arrest in a second hand store on west South Temple Street, near the depot. I was brought down there in an automobile by three officers and the record of the sale was found on the books: price, date of sale, and everything just as I had stated. The books did not show what kind of gun it was, how-ever, and as the clerk who had sold it was in Chicago at the time a telegram was sent to him to which he sent this answer: Remember selling Luger gun at that time. What's the trouble? I bought the pistol on Dec. 15, 1913, for $16.50. Anybody may go to the store and see the books.

For Hill's complete statement see Appendix B.

In the same statement Hill claimed he was unarmed at the time he was shot and offered no explanation as to why he had the gun when he arrived at McHugh's. These disparate statements can be reconciled only by assuming that he acquired the gun and the gray overcoat between the time he was wounded and the time he arrived at the doctor's office. While it is possible, in light of the facts, to accept this, there is no evidence that Hill acquired the overcoat and gun after being wounded except for the fact that the overcoat appeared to have no bullet holes in it.

Hill, after his wound was dressed, requested that he be permitted to go to the Eselius home to recuperate. Dr. McHugh acceded to this request, and did not insist that Hill go to a hospital because he reasoned that a man who is shot through the chest and can walk to a doctor's office ". . . is not in too bad of shape."[16]

McHugh did ask Dr. Bird to drive Hill to the Eselius house, however, since it was not out of his way. He also requested Dr. Bird not to inquire into how Hill was shot, explaining that Hill wanted the matter kept secret. Consequently, Hill and Bird talked very little.[17] En route to the Eselius house Dr. Bird's auto developed engine trouble, forcing him to get out and crank. With Bird thus engaged, Joe Hill, as Hill reported later, threw the gun he was carrying from the car window to the side of the street.[18] Hill never explained why he got rid of his gun, and the weapon was never located despite repeated searches by the police. Eventually, Dr. Bird managed to get the car started and the journey continued.

As they approached the Eselius house, Hill asked Dr. Bird to turn off his headlamps, and Bird complied.[19] As the car stopped, Hill gave two shrill whistles—apparently as a warning. The two men entered the house through the back door. Inside were several men, including two Eselius brothers and two of their nephews, the Erickson brothers. These four had returned from the Utah Theatre just fifteen minutes before Hill and Bird arrived.[20] They expressed surprise at seeing Hill and the doctor and asked if Hill was hurt. A few minutes later, Hill and Bird went into a back room where a cot was located for the wounded man.

The instances of Hill's carrying a gun into Dr. McHugh's office, his throwing a gun from Dr. Bird's automobile, his asking Dr. Bird to turn off his headlamps, and the two shrill whistles were later construed by Salt Lake City police and the Utah courts to substantiate his involvement in criminal activity that night. Certainly, these were suspicious actions.

There are also conflicting accounts of Otto Applequist's activities and whereabouts that evening. One of the Eselius brothers was quoted as saying that Applequist was in bed but not asleep when Dr. Bird brought Hill in. After Bird left, Applequist got out of bed, had a brief talk with Hill, and a short while later left the house. When asked where he was going, he is reported to have said that he was going to get an early start looking for a job.[21] (Another account claimed that Hill and Applequist left the Eselius house at the same time but that Applequist never returned.[22] This seems to be in error, however, because later it became clear that Applequist was there when Hill returned.)[23] One fact is certain: Despite an intensive police search for him, Otto Applequist has not been seen or heard of since that night.

On the same night, January 10, 1914, shortly before 10 p.m., John G. Morrison and two of his sons, Merlin and Arling, were in the process of closing the Morrison grocery store located on West Temple and Eighth South streets in Salt Lake City. (The store's glass front faced east on West Temple Street, which runs north and south. One half block to the west was a cross-street known as Jefferson Street, and midway between Jefferson and West Temple was an alley.) Arling, a youth in his late teens, was sweeping; Mr. Morrison was pulling a sack of potatoes across the floor, and thirteen-year-old Merlin was moving toward the entrance to a storeroom, when two men wearing red bandana handkerchiefs over their faces and soft felt hats entered. One was tall, the other short, and each carried a pistol. As they entered, they shouted "We have got you now!"[24] Merlin, the only living witness of the ensuing events, explained that upon hearing the men, he turned to see what was happening. As the men advanced toward his father, Merlin heard one shot. He did not see his father at that instant, but immediately after the shot he saw his father's back just rising up from behind the counter. At that moment Merlin saw the taller of the two men, with an automatic pistol in his hand, lean over the corner of the counter and fire a second shot. Mr. Morrison fell behind the counter out of Merlin's view. Immediately after the second shot came several more, then the men ran from the store. Merlin did not see his brother Arling during the shooting. When the men left the store, Merlin went to his father. Mr. Morrison was still alive but was unable to speak. Merlin then saw his brother lying dead on his side with his right hand outstretched. Near Arling's hand was a pistol which Merlin had seen his father load and place in the ice-box earlier that evening. The boy ran to the telephone and called the police.[25]

By the time the police arrived, many spectators had gathered at the store. Hearing shots from across the street, Mr. Holt, a neighbor, ran to the Morrison grocery to see what was happening and saw two men making their exit from the store. He noticed that one of the men moved more slowly than the other and held his hands to his chest as he ran. Holt later surmised that the man had been wounded.[26]

Mrs. Vera Hansen, who lived almost directly across from the store at 773 South West Temple, heard the shots and went to her front door. She saw a man coming out of the front door of the grocery.[27] She immediately walked out to the sidewalk in front of her house, which was about twenty-five feet from the store. It was a bright moonlit night, and there was an arc light at the intersection. While Mrs. Hansen was standing on the sidewalk watching the man, she thought she heard him say "Oh Bob" in a voice that sounded full of pain. As the man came out of the store, he was slightly stooped with his hands drawn up toward his chest. He followed the sidewalk to the intersection where two men were apparently waiting for him. When he reached them, all three disappeared into the alley behind the Mahans' house.

Nellie Mahan lived across the street to the south of the Morrison store.

* *

Masked Murderers Fled Through Its Front Door

STORE of J. G. Morrison wherein occurred the tragedy of Saturday night when Mr. Morrison and his son Arling were killed by two masked men, who gave the father no chance to surrender and who shot the boy after he had fired at them.

J. G. Morrison's grocery.

Between 9:30 and 10 p.m. she heard a series of shots and hurried to her front room. Looking out the window to see if there was a light in the store, she saw a man wearing a dark coat and a soft hat run from the store to the corner of the curb on Eighth South. The man uttered some words which she did not understand, then reportedly said "I'm shot." He stopped briefly on the corner, then ran toward the alley in back of her house. Nellie Mahan did not see any other men, but she heard voices coming from the rear of her house.[28]

The first policemen to arrive at the scene took Mr. Morrison to the police station hospital where he died a short time later without making a statement about the killers.[29] The police and the neighbors made a thorough search of the area around the store—a search which yielded four suspects who were duly arrested and some rather curious evidence.

Policemen Crosby and Hendrickson had to "empty their guns" to apprehend two suspects who were trying to board a freight train that was slowly leaving a railroad station not far from the store. The men, C. E. Christensen and Joe Woods, were jailed. The police discovered that they were wanted in Prescott, Arizona, for a $300 robbery, but, curiously, they were not held as suspects in the Morrison killings.[30]

A man later identified as W. J. Williams who was found walking near the Morrison grocery soon after the shooting was also arrested. A bloody handkerchief was found in his pocket, and the newspapers reported that the police sus-

69

All Day Search Without Any Results

INTERIOR of Morrison grocery store at Eighth South and West Temple, scene of the double murder Saturday night, when John G. Morrison, the proprietor, and his son J. Arling Morrison were shot down by two masked highwaymen. The father fell behind the counter at the end of the glass showcase to the right. The son was standing behind counter to the left opposite scales and near cash register when the desperadoes entered and opened fire on his father.

Scene of the double murder.

pected he was one of the killers and was looking for his companion when arrested. Williams told police that he was living at the Salvation Army House, but inquiries proved he was not known there. The only statement Williams made was that he was innocent. Apparently the police believed him, for he was eventually released.[31]

Just as the police returned to the grocery after apprehending Williams, a taxicab moving at high speed approached the store and stopped abruptly. The driver asked a policeman if he had requested a cab, saying that a man with a gruff voice had called, ordering him ". . . to use all speed to get to the Morrison grocery store."[32] The *Salt Lake Herald-Republican* reported that the police believed one of the murderers was wounded and the taxi was summoned by the wounded man's companion to aid in his friend's escape.[33]

Nineteen-year-old Oran Anderson became a suspect when, on the night of the Morrison murders, he walked into the police station with a 38-caliber bullet wound in his arm. He claimed that he had been held up and shot by two gunmen in the vicinity of Eighth South and Sixth West streets. Anderson was questioned extensively because of the possibility that he might have been wounded in Morrison's store, but apparently the police accepted his story, and he, too, was released.[34]

It is not clear from available records just when these suspects were released. It is evident, however, that Hill monopolized police interest after his arrest, and it is probable that the other suspects were released shortly thereafter.

As the investigation continued into the early hours of Sunday morning, Perry Morrison, oldest son of the murdered man (who was not in the store at the time of the shooting), found some blood in an alley near the store.[35] The police theorized that Arling Morrison had wounded one of the assailants with the gun found near his body, and that the blood found in the alley was that of the wounded man. The location of the stains led police to believe that the wounded man was hiding in an unoccupied house near the alley. A search of the house revealed nothing, but discovery of the bloodstain touched off many separate searches for more bloodstains in the vicinity.

After the blood in the alley led to nothing, a fresh trail was followed farther to the south and led the searchers to a warehouse located near Jefferson Street. At the northwest corner of the building a large amount of blood was discovered and a sample was taken. The police surmised that the suspect had found it necessary to stop there and clear his lungs of blood. From the warehouse, police followed the trail along a zigzag course back and forth across Jefferson Street and into a vacant lot where it ended.

Another blood trail, which a Salt Lake City newspaper described as "even more prominent than the former one," was picked up on First West Street. This trail led to the railroad tracks near Tenth South Street where it, too, was lost.

A final trail was located by Arthur Gardiner, a soda fountain clerk. Mounted police managed to follow it to a small ditch near a crossing of the Oregon Short Line Railroad tracks at Twelfth South Street. The police found what appeared to be a bloody hand mark in the snow, and they believed that the person who left the trail washed blood from his hands at the ditch. Following the blood to the Denver and Rio Grande Railroad yard, they discovered the charred coals of a recent fire. Beside the coals, Patrolman Crosby found two empty 38-caliber revolver cartridges, one of which was apparently blood-stained.[36]

It was never proved that the samples taken from the various trails were human blood. A dog with a bleeding paw was found in the area, which probably explains several of the "trails."

While searching the neighborhood, Captain V. A. Vance found a red bandana at the rear of a nearby residence. Merlin Morrison later said the bandana resembled the ones worn by the killers.[37]

By midday Sunday, the eleventh of January, 1914, the police had searched the entire area surrounding the Morrison store. The investigation had unearthed no evidence pointing to any individual suspect. The *Salt Lake Herald-Republican* reported Monday morning that it was admitted at police headquarters that descriptions of the two persons who killed the Morrisons ". . . are not only incomplete as regards to color and style of clothing, but also as to height and weight as well."[38]

Two new developments in the case occurred Monday, January 12. A streetcar conductor, J. R. Usher, reported that a suspicious-looking man had boarded his car at Tenth South at 11:26 the night of the murders. At that time Usher did not know of the Morrison killings.[39] Usher described the man as raw-boned, wearing a dark suit and black hat, and he said his attention was drawn to the man because he boarded on the exit step and appeared to be unfamiliar with the area. Usher learned from other passengers that the man asked which car to take to get downtown. Usher reported that the man sat hunched over in his seat all the way downtown, and then, as the car neared Second West and Second South, he rang the bell but did not get off until the car reached Main Street. The man appeared to be drunk when he boarded the car but not when he got off. He was later identified by Usher from a police photograph as ex-convict Frank Z. Wilson.[40]

The second development, which probably also related to the man Usher had seen, was reported by Peter Rhengren, who claimed he saw a man lying in a ditch at Eighth West and Eighth South at about 11:30 Saturday night. When Rhengren offered help, the man got out of the ditch and ran to an approaching streetcar.[41]

Revenge was the motive most often ascribed to the killings in the first few days following the incident. Two groups of facts lent validity to this assumption. First, the murderers made no attempt to rob the store—instead, they entered, called out "We have got you now!" and started shooting. Second, there was reason to believe Morrison may have become the object of someone's hatred while employed as a policeman in Salt Lake City for a five-year period prior to becoming a businessman. The police considered it possible that ex-convict Frank Z. Wilson, the man Usher reportedly saw, and who had originally been arrested by Morrison, might have sought revenge on January 10, 1914.

It was widely known that John Morrison regretted his employment on the police force and that he constantly feared retaliation. He voiced his fear to a friend and former colleague, Police Captain John Hemple, on the very afternoon of the day he was murdered, "John I have got just five hundred dollars left of the money I have made in this city by mighty hard work, and I would gladly give it all up if I could have my name blotted out of the police department's record. I have lived to regret that I ever was a member of the force."[42] Hemple told the press that "Morrison was in constant dread of men he had arrested when he was a policeman."[43]

71

It was also known that Morrison had been violently attacked on two occasions in the previous twelve years. Both times he miraculously saved himself through his courage and his skill with a gun. On both occasions he wounded his attackers, giving them more than sufficient motive to return and conclude their violent business with him.

The first attack on Morrison occurred on the evening of February 2, 1903.[44] The Morrison family was eating dinner in their living quarters behind the store when they heard someone enter the store. Morrison stepped from the dining room into the rear of the store where he surprised three masked men. When ordered to put his hands up, Morrison dropped down behind the counter, crawled back to the dining room, and picked up a new double-barreled shotgun which he had never before fired. Returning to the store, he stood up in full view of the three men, who immediately began firing at him with their revolvers. Morrison triggered the first barrel of his shotgun; it failed to fire. He pulled the second trigger and again nothing happened. Morrison discarded the shotgun and, once again, returned to the living area—amidst a hail of bullets—located his revolver, returned, and exchanged shots with the men. He wounded one; the other two lost courage, and all three escaped.

The police who investigated this shooting said that twenty shots were fired at Morrison, but only two found their mark, wounding him in the hand and leg.[45] They also said that four men were involved in the attack—one man standing guard outside.[46] Apparently the motive for this attack was robbery, as an unsuccessful attempt had been made to break open the store's cash register.[47]

After this attempt a trail of blood believed to have been left by the man Morrison wounded was found and traced to the Garfield Beach Train Station, but was lost there.[48]

Later the same evening, police officer Horace Heath saw three suspicious-looking men enter a saloon at South Temple and First West streets. He followed to investigate, and as he entered the front door, the three men fled through the back.[49] Seeing the men run down First West Street, Heath hailed a ride in a buggy and soon caught up with them. He jumped from the buggy and ordered them to halt, but instead they began shooting and Heath returned the fire. For a time Heath and the three men engaged in a running gun fight. Then one man stopped behind a tree. Heath shot him and he sank to the ground. As Heath approached, the wounded man raised himself and shot point blank, shattering the officer's ankle. With only one bullet left in his gun, Heath aimed from a distance of six feet, killing the man with a shot through the head.[50] The other gunmen ran through the yards of several homes and disappeared. The dead man was taken to the mortuary and was positively identified by Morrison as one of his assailants.[51]

After Morrison's death, the police speculated that the companions of the man killed by Officer Heath after their attack on Morrison returned on January 10, 1914—eleven years later—to exact their revenge.[52]

The second attack on Morrison prior to the fatal attempt in 1914 occurred on the evening of September 20, 1913. Morrison, who had subsequently moved his living quarters from the rear of the store, was walking home with the Saturday receipts. At First West and Eighth South streets two men with drawn guns ordered him to raise his hands, and, once again, John Morrison reacted in the same courageous manner. He drew his own gun and exchanged shots with the would-be robbers. One of the attackers was wounded, but both made their escape—one of them on a bicycle.[53]

Many who knew Morrison believed that these second attackers were the ones who succeeded in killing him. The *Salt Lake Herald-Republican* reported on January 11, 1914, the day after the murders, that "John G. Morrison lived in daily fear of violence since September 20, 1913, when a desperate attempt was made to rob him."[54]

Morrison told at least four people other than Police Captain Hemple of his fear of reprisal. Steven Davis reported to the police on January 11, 1914, that Morrison had told him a few days earlier that he was "reasonably sure" he knew who the men were who tried to rob him the second time,[55] but no names were mentioned because Morrison was waiting to act until he was positive of his theory.

To Herbert Steele, Morrison said, "I believe the man who tried to hold me up last September is living right here in this neighborhood and posing as a normal citizen. He even comes in this store, I'm positive of this, too, although I know I cannot prove it for I only saw him in the dark that night. What's more, this fellow knows I suspect him and he will get me the next time."[56]

Newsman Hardy K. Downing, who interviewed Morrison after the 1913 attack, was also told of Morrison's fear of another attack.

Morrison had often described the bandits to his wife and instructed her to have police question a neighbor (who was never named publicly) if anything happened to him. The police did question the man after the murder, but released him after they apprehended Joe Hill.

Before the arrest of Joe Hill, the police did not hesitate to link the murder with the earlier attacks. By Monday, January 12, the police had released stories to the press stating their belief that the killers were the same men who had tried to rob Morrison in September 1913.[57]

On that Monday, Joe Hill was in bed at the Eselius house in Murray, Utah, recovering from his gunshot wound. By the following evening, Tuesday, January 13, he was in jail, charged with the Morrison murders.

The events of Monday and Tuesday following the murders which culminated in Hill's arrest now appear confused because of conflicting accounts. Adding to the confusion is a belated report that either on Monday or Tuesday Joe Hill confessed to Dr. McHugh that he had killed the Morrisons. Dr. McHugh made the details of the alleged confession public in 1946—more than thirty years after the murder—in an interview with Vernon Jensen, a student of the Hill case.[58] At that time, McHugh said that he was out of town on Sunday, the day after he had treated Hill; his first knowledge of the Morrison murders came from the Monday morning newspaper. Jensen reports that "As soon as he

[McHugh] read the headlines of the killing of Morrison and his son, he surmised that Hill might have been involved."[59] * Jensen continues:

> Thereupon he visited the Eselius home to see Hillstrom, who, when confronted, said, as nearly as Dr. McHugh could remember, "I'm not such a bad fellow as you think. I shot in self-defense. The older man reached for the gun and I shot him and the younger boy grabbed the gun and shot me and I shot him to save my own life." He also added, "I wanted some money to get out of town."[60]

McHugh then told Jensen that he went "immediately" to Police Chief Fred Peters of Murray and told him of treating Hill (but not of the confession). He advised Peters that Hill ". . . was a cool fellow with lots of nerve" who might shoot it out if the police tried to take him. McHugh further told Peters that he was going to give Hill a shot of morphine as a part of his treatment and suggested that after the morphine had taken effect an investigation could be made without injury to the investigating officers.[61]

The interview between Jensen and Dr. McHugh is the only source of information available concerning the alleged confession by Hill. However, evidence is available from varied sources which, while failing to prove Hill did not make the confession, casts serious doubt on the allegation that he did so.

The Salt Lake City press of January 1914 named Dr. Bird, not Dr. McHugh, as the man who told the police of Joe Hill.[62] Available official records do not indicate who made the report. Philip Foner, in his study of the Hill case, says Dr. McHugh informed the authorities.[63] Barrie Stavis, in the introduction to his play on Hill, says both doctors did.[64] Regrettably, neither account cites the source of information, but Stavis has reportedly seen letters McHugh wrote to Utah officials claiming the reward offered for the capture of the Morrisons' killers.[65]

Since the press reports appeared just several hours after Hill was arrested, it seems reasonable to assume that the police told the press Dr. Bird was the informer. The press report, if correct, casts doubt on the validity of Dr. McHugh's story.

---

*Mr. Jensen explains in two articles (see fn. 58) and two letters to the author (April 24 and May 24, 1967) how he learned of the Hill confession. While doing research in Utah, he became interested in the Hill case and was advised by James H. Wolf of the Utah State Supreme Court to interview Dr. McHugh about his experience with Hill. This Mr. Jensen did, and thereby the alleged Hill confession came to light.

The only record made of the interview with McHugh was compiled from notes which Jensen made following the meeting. In 1948, having prepared a draft of the article later printed in *Industrial and Labor Relations Review*, Jensen sent a copy to McHugh who, according to Jensen, confirmed in a letter ". . . that what I had written was correct."

The author began researching the Hill case in 1964, by which time Dr. McHugh had died, making further firsthand information on the Hill confession unobtainable. The author did interview Mrs. McHugh, who remembered her husband treating Joe Hill for a wound but knew nothing about a confession.

Mr. Jensen has since misplaced the notes he took of the interview and the confirming letter from McHugh, but he has assured the author that they would not add to the information in the aforementioned articles.

As a witness for the prosecution at Hill's trial in 1914, McHugh had the opportunity and the obligation to divulge the story of the confession, but he offered no information concerning it to the state's attorneys, nor did he mention it on the witness stand. He did, however, testify concerning his treatment of Hill's wound, the location of the wound, and the gun Hill was carrying. When asked what he knew about how Hill was wounded, he reported only Hill's claim that he had been wounded in a fight over a woman. Also in contradiction to his 1946 statement to Vernon Jensen, McHugh testified in 1914 that he had been told by the police that Hill was to be arrested before he offered to administer a sedative to make the suspect safe to apprehend.[66]

Explaining McHugh's actions in withholding information about the confession, Jensen says, "As a socialist and a disbeliever in capital punishment, he [McHugh] did not want to see Hill executed. Since he was never asked if he had received any other explanation of Hill's wound, McHugh chose not to tell all he knew."[67]

There is further reason to challenge the validity of McHugh's claim that Hill confessed. Hill's alleged confession as related by McHugh does not coincide with known facts of what occurred in the Morrison store during the murder. There is no evidence that Mr. Morrison reached for the gun as Hill was said to have claimed. When the killers entered the store, Morrison was leaning over pulling a sack of potatoes across the floor; he was shot while still leaning over. Also, there was no evidence that the assailants intended to rob Morrison, because they immediately called out, "We have got you now!" This is difficult to reconcile with McHugh's contention that Hill intended to rob Morrison.

McHugh's belated assertion that Joe Hill confessed the murders to him must be relegated to a place alongside the "remaining mysteries" of the Joe Hill case because of lack of definite evidence to either prove or disprove it.

It is, however, a matter of official record that McHugh did visit Hill on Monday to dress the wound and that he returned Tuesday to change the dressing and administer a shot of morphine. Sometime during Monday or Tuesday the police were apprised of Hill's whereabouts and decided to apprehend him. Tuesday evening, Chief Peters, accompanied by deputies Ed Larson and Joseph Newlands, went to the Eselius home to arrest Hill. They encountered no opposition from the Eselius family and were shown to the room where Hill lay in bed,[68] weak from his wound and drowsy from morphine. As Chief Peters entered the room, Hill made a movement to reach for a handkerchief, and Peters drew his gun and fired at him. The shot, barely missing Hill's chest, struck his hand, shattering the knuckles. Peters failed to report the shooting, and the police in Salt Lake City were puzzled as to the origin of the wound.[69] They were developing a theory that it was the hand wound that had caused the curious trails of blood found on the night of the murder when, finally, Peters admitted that he had shot Hill when he made a move that looked as if ". . . he was reaching for a gun."[70] Later investigation proved there was no gun in Hill's room.

Tuesday night Joe Hill was taken to the Salt Lake County jail where he was put to bed, so weak he could not speak.[71]

**Murray officers Fred Peters, Ed Larson, and Joseph Newlands (left to right)
were congratulated by Salt Lake City police for apprehending Hill.**

Consistent with their belief that Morrison had been killed for revenge, the police told the press that Joe Hill was actually Frank Z. Wilson, the former Utah State Prison convict who was seen on the streetcar, and who had been a prime object of police search for several days in connection with the Morrison killings.[72] But after the police learned Hill's true identity, their interest in Wilson as a suspect evidently faded, as the *Salt Lake Tribune* stated that "The police are elated over the capture of Hill, whom they feel certain is one of the men wanted for the murder of the Morrisons."[73]

The *Deseret Evening News* of January 14, 1914, reported that the police investigation following Hill's arrest ". . . tended to strengthen the net of circumstantial evidence which is being woven around Hillstrom and to gather loose ends of evidence and scattered clues which have been unearthed since the case began early Sunday morning."[74]

The *Salt Lake Herald-Republican* claimed that thirteen-year-old Merlin Morrison, the only eyewitness to the shooting of his father and brother, identified Joe Hill as "the man my brother shot."[75] The newspaper's statement falls somewhat short of the facts, for it was not proved that Arling Morrison had shot one of his assailants. The newspaper was also mistaken in saying that Merlin identified Hill positively as one of the killers. Actually, Merlin went to the Salt Lake County jail Wednesday, January 14, and said of Joe Hill: "Hillstrom is about the same size and height as one of the men who entered my father's store Saturday night. As the light was bad I could not get a lasting impression of the man's features, but Hillstrom appears to be very much the same build as the man who entered the store first and whom I saw fire at my father."[76]

These two photographs of Joe Hill, taken shortly after his arrest, show a real
Wobbly migrant worker and contrast sharply with the gaunt prisoner of later pictures.

After the arrest, the police made a search of the Eselius house and of Hill's
clothing, but found nothing which would connect him with the crime except
his bullet-torn clothes. After Hill told the police that he had thrown the gun
seen by Drs. Bird and McHugh from Dr. Bird's car, they searched for the gun
but never found it. They found $5.60 in Hill's pockets and a note which read:
"Hilda and Christina were here. We went to the Empress. Tried to find you.
Otto."[77] The signer was probably Hill's friend Otto Applequist.

Otto Applequist became the object of an extensive police search when
they learned from the Eselius brothers of his mysterious behavior following
Hill's return to the house with Dr. Bird. Believing that Applequist was the second man involved in the murder of the Morrisons, the police offered a reward
for his capture and printed and distributed nationally circulars bearing his picture.[78] Applequist was reported in towns in western Utah during the days immediately after the circular was released, but he was never located and his
whereabouts and possible involvement in the affair remain unknown.

Robert Erickson, a nephew of the Eselius brothers, was arrested because
of his friendship with Hill.[79] Police thought he might be the man the killer referred to as he ran from the store crying, "Oh Bob."[80] Robert Erickson claimed
he had attended the Utah Theatre with the Eselius brothers on the night of the
murders,[81] and his alibi was accepted by the police when the theater ticket
stubs were located.

The police apparently detained Erickson in the hope of obtaining a confession from Hill. His mother, Mrs. Betty Eselius Olsen, was told that her son
would be released if she would obtain a statement of confession from Hill. Mrs.

Olsen went to the jail and spoke with Hill in Swedish, encouraging him to confess, but he told her, as he had told McHugh and the police, that he was wounded in a fight over a woman.[82] Robert Erickson was subsequently released from jail.

Despite their failure to get a confession, the police remained confident they had the killer. The *Salt Lake Herald-Republican* announced on January 15 that ". . . strand after strand of circumstantial evidence is slowly being woven about Joseph Hillstrom, alias Joe Hill. Acting Sheriff Atha Williams says, 'it will be virtually impossible for Hillstrom to establish an alibi.' "[83]

The certainty with which the police believed Hill guilty does not seem warranted by the circumstances and facts connected with the murders and with Hill's arrest. That Hill was one of the men who had previously attacked Morrison was never suggested by the police. They seem to have completely discarded their original theory of revenge as the motive for the killings. It is true that Hill had stayed with the Eselius brothers for a week in September 1913 and, therefore, could conceivably have been involved in the second attack on Morrison. But the exact date of Hill's stay at the Eselius home during September was never established, and no proof of Hill's having had any contact with Morrison—other than circumstantial evidence connecting him with the murder—was ever presented, either before, during, or after his trial.

The police based their case against Hill on the possibility that one of the assailants may have been wounded at Morrison's store, and the further possibility that the same man appeared nearly two hours after the shooting with a fresh-bleeding wound at a doctor's office 4.9 miles distant from the scene of the crime. (Salt Lake City streets have been renumbered since 1914; what was then Fourteenth South is now Thirty-ninth South.) And they based their case on these possibilities despite the indications and their previous theory that John Morrison had been murdered for revenge; despite Morrison's widely known fear that he might be attacked by people whom he thought he knew and whom he had named to his wife; and despite the lack of a motive on the part of Joe Hill. In short, the entire police case seems to have been based on the fact that Joe Hill received a gunshot wound on the same night as the murder.

He was formally charged with first-degree murder on January 20, 1914.

A
guilty
man?

On January 27, 1914, Joe Hill ap-
peared before Precinct Justice Harry S. Harper for arraignment and entered a
plea of "not guilty." A reporter describing the scene noted that Hill was apparently weak from loss of blood, ". . . but was cool and collected in mind."[1]

"When the justice called upon Hillstrom to answer to the murder charge
he rose to his feet slowly and walked to the desk of the justice unassisted. Supporting himself by resting one hand on the desk, he listened to the reading of
the complaint."

"You are entitled to twenty-four hours to enter your pleading," said
Harper.

"I will enter my pleading now; it is not guilty," Hill replied.

"Also you are entitled to counsel," Harper advised.

"I have no money to pay counsel," answered Hill. "I will act as my own
counsel."[2]

Hill then agreed with the assistant county attorney to set the preliminary
hearing for January 28, 1914.[3]

The records of the preliminary hearing have not been preserved by Salt
Lake County officials, but what occurred can be reconstructed from two
sources: (1) the accounts reported in the Salt Lake City press (the coverage in
the *Salt Lake Herald-Republican* is the most complete); (2) Joe Hill's own version of his struggle with the Utah courts. His statement, prepared in September
1915, was submitted to the Utah Board of Pardons at that time.

> When the time came for my preliminary hearing, I decided to be my own attorney,
> knowing that it could be nothing against me. I thought I'd let them have it all their
> own way, and did not ask any questions. When the court went into session, I was asked
> if I objected to having the witnesses remain in the courtroom during the trial, and I
> replied that it was immaterial to me who remained in the courtroom. All the witnesses
> then remained inside, and I noted that there was a steady stream of "messengers"
> going back and forth between the witnesses and the county attorney during the whole
> trial, delivering their messages in a whisper. When the trial commenced, there were
> first some witnesses of little importance, but then a man came up that made me sit up
> and take notice. He put up his hand and swore that he positively recognized me and
> that he had seen me in the Morrison store in the afternoon of the same day that Morri-
> son was shot. I did not say anything, but I thought something. This man was a tall lean
> man with a thin pale face, black hair and eyes, and a very conspicuous black shiny
> mustache. I don't know his name and have never been able to find out. (Keep this man
> in mind, please.) The little boy, Merlin Morrison, was the next witness that attracted

my attention. He was the first one to come up and look at me in the morning of the day after my arrest. Being only a little boy, he spoke his mind right out in my presence, and this is what he said: "No, that is not the man at all. The ones I saw were shorter and heavier set."

When he testified at the preliminary hearing, I asked him if he did not make that statement, but he then denied it.

I accidentally found a description of the bandit in a newspaper, however, and the description says that the bandit was 5 feet 9 inches tall and weighed about 155 pounds. That description seems to tally pretty well with Merlin Morrison's statement, "The ones I saw were shorter and heavier set." My own height is six feet and I am of a slender built.

The next witness of importance was Mrs. Phoebe Seeley. She said she was coming home from the Empress Theatre with her husband and she met two men in a back street in the vicinity of Morrison's store. One of them had "small features and light bushy hair." This description did not suit the county attorney, so he helped her along a little by saying, "You mean medium colored hair like Mr. Hillstrom's, don't you?" After leading her along that way for a while, he asked her this question: "Is the general appearance of Mr. Hillstrom anything like the man you saw?" She answered, "No, I won't, I can't say that."

This is the very same woman who at the district court proved to be the star witness for the prosecution. She did not only describe me into the smallest details, but she also told the jury that the man she saw had scars on both sides of his face, on his nose, and on his neck. I have such scars on my face, and that was practically the testimony that convicted me. . . .

The next witness was Mr. Zeese, detective. When I was sick in bed at the Eselius house in Murray, the lady gave me a red bandana handkerchief to blow my nose on. At the trial she told that she had several dozen bandana handkerchiefs that were used by her boys and brothers when they worked in the smelter. After my arrest Mr. Zeese went to the Eselius house looking for clues. He found this handkerchief, and with his keen, eagle eyes he soon discovered some "creases at the corners." With the intelligence of a super-man, he then easily drew the conclusion that this handkerchief had been used for a mask by some "bandit." Then he capped the climax by going on the stand and telling his marvellous discovery to the judge. Mr. Zeese is well known in Salt Lake City, and comments are unnecessary.

The next witness at the preliminary hearing, Mrs. Vera Hansen, said she saw two or three men outside of the Morrison store shortly after the shooting. She heard one of the men exclaim "Bob," or "Oh Bob," and she thought that my voice sounded the same as the voice she heard on the street. I then asked Mrs. Hansen this question: "Do you mean to tell me that you, through that single word Bob, were able to recognize my voice?" Now I am coming to the point.

After the preliminary hearing I got a record of the hearings and took it to my cell in the county jail. I immediately discovered that it had been tampered with, that everything I had said had been misconstrued in a malicious way. It was a little hard to prove it at first but on page 47, I found the questions that I had put to Mrs. Vera Hansen, and there the tampering was so clumsy that a little child could see it. In the records the question reads like this, "Do you mean to tell me that you through the single word (mark 'single word') 'Oh, Bob, I'm shot,' " four or five words. Here anyone can see that the official court records were altered for the express purpose of "proving" that someone was shot in the Morrison store. I then started to look for testimony of a man with a black shiny mustache but to my great surprise I could not find it anywhere in the records in spite of the fact that this man had positively recognized me at the preliminary hearing. No wonder that this very dignified stenographer, Mr. Rollo, who is also stenographer for the United States supreme court, was shaking like a leaf when he put up his hand and swore that the records were "correct" in every detail.[4]

Hill correctly noted a mistake in the record of Mrs. Hansen's testimony at the preliminary hearing. The trial record shows that Mrs. Hansen heard the man say only, "Oh Bob."[5] Another witness, Miss Nellie Mahan, claimed she heard the man say, "I'm shot."[6] As for the tall man with the black mustache who, according to Hill, identified him, the press mentioned nothing; at the trial, the prosecution called no such witness.

The author of the account of the preliminary hearing in the *Salt Lake Herald-Republican* described Hill's strategy. He was ". . . letting them have it their own way" because "he knew he was innocent." This attitude—that his innocence somehow protected him against a possible judicial misstep—is paradoxical in light of Hill's expressed skepticism about the equal dispensing of justice in America. Perhaps it reflected certain attitudes acquired in his boyhood. Surely a just God, even if one no longer had a conscious need for Him, might be seen in an unguarded moment as One who would not permit the execution of an innocent man. Thus Hill may have thought, and if he did—if there was this much residue of earlier religious attitudes in him—then his frequent visits to the Sailors' Rest Mission in San Pedro are more understandable. And perhaps the sentimental songs are also more understandable; there is nothing in all their wishful dreaming, certainly, that exceeds the sentimental idealism of this notion of Hill's that innocence is automatically its own protection.

On the other hand, this protestation of innocence, the public expression of his belief that justice would prevail, is equally compatible with the picture of Hill as a guilty man, pretending innocence and seeking martyrdom to further the sacred cause of uniting the workers against the exploiting class.

We are left, then, with the enigma of just exactly what Hill did hope to accomplish by his "letting them have it their own way." But one thing we know: his attitude was to prove detrimental to his legal defense.

The newspaper listed witnesses at the preliminary hearing who were involved in some way with events associated with the murder.[7]

1. Mr. and Mrs. Frank Seeley, passersby, saw two suspicious-looking men near the Morrison store just prior to the murder.

2. John Edgar Thompson and Margaret E. Kessler, passersby, also saw suspicious-looking men in Morrison's neighborhood prior to the murder.

3. Merlin Morrison was taken to the county jail where he attempted to identify Hill as one of his father's murderers.

4. A. S. Thompson and William Hooper, patrolmen, were responsible for investigating and reporting on the positions of the bodies in Morrison's store.

5. Dr. H. B. Sprague, coroner, made an examination of Morrison's wounds.

6. Vera Hansen, a neighbor of Morrison's saw men running from the store after the shooting.

7. Nellie Mahan, another neighbor, also saw two men leave Morrison's store after the shooting.

8. Harry Hall, streetcar conductor, saw a man who resembled Hill board a streetcar the night of the murder.

9. George Cleveland, detective, examined the trails of blood and other objects of the police investigation connected with the murder.

81

10. Drs. McHugh and Bird dressed Hill's wound and drove him to the Eselius home after the treatment.

11. George Albert Vance found a red bandana near the Morrison store.

12. Mr. Zeese, detective, also found a red bandana.

Joe Hill directed only three questions to the witnesses. He asked Merlin Morrison if he had said that Hill was not one of J. G. Morrison's murderers when he had seen him in the county jail.[8] Merlin replied "no," he had never said that Hill was *not* one of the men.[9] Hill later told newsmen that a man he had never met before came to the county jail and told him that Merlin, after seeing him in the jail, was unable to identify him as the murderer.[10] Hill's claim that Merlin's opinion as to his involvement in the crime changed between the visit to the jail and the preliminary hearing is apparently based on this second-hand information.

The second question was directed to Mrs. Vera Hansen, who testified that she saw a man running from the store crying, "Oh Bob." Hill asked if she could determine by those words alone whether it was he who killed Morrison.[11] She said she could not do that. Hill ". . . waved his hand slowly much in the fashion of a veteran criminal lawyer and said 'that's all.' "[12]

Hill then attempted to cross-examine Harry Hall, the streetcar conductor, who testified that on the night of the murder a man with Hill's features had boarded a southbound Murray streetcar at Twelfth South and State Street. Hall said that the man had a sharp nose, but that he didn't see his eyes.[13] "Squaring his shoulders and leaning forward, Hillstrom cleared his voice in a manner which appeared to indicate that he intended putting Hall through severe cross-examination." He said to Hall, "When one individual notices another he sees the person's eyes before his nose."[14] This sort of anti-climactic amateurism was characteristic of Hill's efforts in his defense.

His closing statement further disclosed how ill prepared Hill was to defend himself.

> I have only this to say. I fail utterly to understand what significance there is in the finding of a red handkerchief [the handkerchief found in his bedding at the Eselius house by Detective Zeese]. There are many people who have red handkerchiefs. . . . I have no witnesses in favor of my case at the present time and I have no further statements to offer at the present time. My case will be presented when it comes before the district court.[15]

In spite of his poor performance at the preliminary hearing, Hill had not significantly damaged his case. Since the purpose of a preliminary hearing is to determine whether there is evidence to show "probable cause" that the defendant committed a crime, and since it usually requires little evidence for the prosecution to establish this, the defense normally presents little of its case at that time. The defense, as a rule, is concerned with determining the scope of the prosecution's evidence and with cross-examining the prosecution's witnesses to elicit information which may be helpful at the trial. Therefore, while Hill's cross-examination was ineffective at best, it was damaging primarily in the sense that it failed to provide him with information he might have used to his advantage in the trial.

The hearing resulted in Justice Harper's ruling that there was sufficient evidence against Hill to warrant a trial. The trial was set for June 17, 1914.

The growth of the Joe Hill legend was facilitated by controversies arising from his trial before Judge Morris L. Ritchie of the Utah Third Judicial Court. Many have charged that an organized conspiracy—consisting of persons variously labeled as "the copperbosses," "the Utah officials," "the establishment" in Utah, and the Mormon church—was instrumental in obtaining Hill's conviction. On the other hand, there are those who believe that his trial in the district court was eminently fair. Neither view seems to be correct. While there is no evidence of a conspiracy masterminding Hill's conviction, there *are* good reasons for believing that the trial was not as fair as it might have been. But this raises the question of whether *any* homeless migrant, Wobbly or not, would have received a fairer trial anywhere in America in 1914. The answer is probably not. The Hill case, it seems, serves well as an example of a weakness in the judicial procedures of 1914 as they dealt with those in the lower socioeconomic levels. The question must be considered in light of the disparity between the resources available to Hill in defending himself and those of the state in his prosecution.

The prosecutor for the state was District Attorney E. O. Leatherwood. Defense attorneys were E. D. McDougall and F. B. Scott, whose services Hill had obtained in a rather unusual manner. Shortly after the preliminary hearing,

83

**District Attorney E. O. Leatherwood,
prosecuting attorney at Hill's trial.**

McDougall visited Hill and explained that he was an attorney, a stranger in town, and interested in the case. He offered to handle Hill's defense without fee. Hill accepted. Shortly thereafter, McDougall and Scott became partners. [16]

Selection of the jury for the trial took three days because of the lengthy questioning of prospective jurymen by Hill's attorneys. For example, after

McDougall and Scott had exhausted their peremptory challenges, John G. Ryan was questioned at length to determine his suitability as a juryman. In the course of the questioning it was disclosed that Ryan's father had been murdered in much the same manner as J. G. Morrison. The defense contended that this should disqualify Ryan on the grounds of possible prejudice. In their effort to convince Judge Ritchie, both McDougall and Scott questioned Ryan vigorously. Although Ritchie did disqualify Ryan, he criticized the defense methods, saying that the keenest of men or the most impartial could be ". . . confused and forced to answer unsatisfactorily by the metaphysical subtleties of the counsel."[17] (In its subsequent appeal, the defense claimed Judge Ritchie's remarks indicated prejudice against Hill.)

The following members of the jury were finally selected:

Ernest K. Alder (*teamster*)	John Garbett (*coal dealer*)
H. C. McDonough (*bill collector*)	T. H. Owen (*motorman*)
Joseph Kimball (*real estate agent*)	Robert McDowell (*salesman*)
Rudolph Boss (*farmer*)	Joseph M. Green (*farmer*)
John A. Hillstead (*clerk*)	Fred R. Robinson (*blacksmith*)
H. E. Thomas (*laborer*)	George E. Nicholes (*building contractor*)[18]

The trial began at two p.m. on Wednesday, June 17, 1914.[19] Hill was to be tried for only one of the murders, that of J. G. Morrison.*

In his opening statement, District Attorney Leatherwood indicated that the state's evidence was only circumstantial and that he, therefore, would not prove directly that Hill had killed Morrison, but would submit a chain of circumstances from which guilt would be inferred.[20] The first witnesses for the state were policemen who introduced routine evidence concerning location of Morrison's store, position of the bodies, bullet holes, and other physical details.

Merlin Morrison testified on Thursday, June 18. Prior to the boy's appearance, the press considered him to be the state's key witness.[21] But his testimony, while not detracting from the state's case, did not positively identify Hill as the murderer.

Merlin gave an account of the killing and was then questioned by Leatherwood as to Hill's physical appearance compared with the taller of the murderers. Merlin stated that Hill's height was ". . . about the same as that of the man who fired the shot at my father."

Leatherwood then asked, "Does the general appearance of Mr. Hillstrom resemble that of the tall man?"

MERLIN: *He looks the same.*

---

* Volume I of the trial transcript, evidence introduced by the prosecution, has been lost by the Salt Lake County Clerk's office. Information concerning the prosecution's case has been taken from the press accounts.

LEATHERWOOD: *Does this man's general appearance*
correspond with that of the man who shot your father?

MERLIN: *Yes, sir.*[22]

Merlin admitted in cross-examination that the killers wore hats and bandana handkerchiefs which covered their faces except for the eyes. Since he could not see their features, he could not identify the defendant as one of the men.[23] In light of this failure to positively identify Hill, the *Salt Lake Herald-Republican* probably over-dramatized its description of his actions during Merlin's testimony. "Hillstrom who sat restlessly in his chair listening to the vivid picture of the scenes in the store on the fatal night drawn by the witness, cringed under the final statements of the boy in identification, dropped his head forward and held his eyes riveted on the floor."[24]

The third day of the trial proved to be one of the most dramatic. The session opened with Herman Harms, the state chemist, testifying that the blood found in the alley on the night of the murder was definitely of mammalian origin but that he could not determine whether or not it was human. At this point, Hill stood up and addressed the court.[25]

HILL: *May I say a few words?*

JUDGE: *You have a right to be heard in your*
own behalf.

HILL: *I have three prosecuting attorneys here,*
and I intend to get rid of two of them. [Addressing
his counsel] *You sit over there, you are fired,*
too, see. And there is something I don't
understand . . .

JUDGE [interrupting]: *You need not carry out in*
detail any difference you may have with counsel if any.

HILL: *I wish to announce I have discharged my*
counsel, my two lawyers.

COUNSEL: *If you have discharged us, that is all*
there is to it.

HILL: *If the court will permit, I will act as my own*
attorney after this, and cross-examine all the witnesses,
and I think I will make a good job of it. As far as the
district attorney is concerned, I think we will get
along fine; he comes right out in the middle of the
road. I know where he is at. These fellows here
[indicating counsel], *I think I can get along*
very nicely without them; they are dismissed. Can I
act as my own attorney in this case, and cross-
examine all the witnesses, and will I have the right
to withdraw any witness who has been on the stand

85

here? Bring buckets of blood for all I care, I
intend to prove a whole lot of things here; I will
prove these records here of the preliminary hearing
are the rankest kind of fake. That is what I will
prove. And I will prove a whole lot of other things.
I will prove I was not at that store.[26]

The court directed the defense counsel to remain and proceed with the cross-examination. Hill asked again if he had the right to discharge his counsel. The judge replied that he would consider the matter. If he decided that Hill was serious, the right would be granted. Again Hill insisted that he wanted to conduct his own defense, and, finally, the judge allowed him to question witnesses after his counsel had finished with them. When his counsel resumed questioning Harms, Hill exclaimed, "I told you to get out of that door." One of them replied, "I am acting under the court's instruction; I think you are a little beside yourself at present."[27] The questioning continued. Hill did not interrupt again but exercised his right to question the witness after his counsel had finished. At the conclusion of Harms's testimony, the court requested Scott and McDougall to remain, giving them the status of *amicus curiae* (friend of the court)[28] and instructing them to do all they could to help the defendant.

Mrs. Seeley, who proved to be the state's most effective witness in its attempt to identify Hill as the taller of the killers, was called to testify. During her testimony Hill continued to protest that he wanted to conduct his own defense; after requesting Judge Ritchie to clarify the role the attorneys were to assume, he once again asked Scott and McDougall to leave. The judge finally decided to retire the jury and settle the matter.

After the jury left, the judge spoke to Hill.

JUDGE: *. . . you realize it is a remarkable*
proceeding, at least, to get up in the midst of a
trial and discharge your counsel?

HILL: *Yes, sir.*

JUDGE: *You realize that if there is not sufficient*
reason for discharging them that it would be quite
difficult to get other counsel to go on with the
case at this time; you know that do you not?

HILL: *I will act as my own counsel, and I am going*
to win this case without counsel.[29]

The court then allowed Hill and his attorneys time to discuss their differences. Afterward, Hill announced that he did not mind if they stayed in the courtroom and questioned witnesses on their own, but he made it clear that he would act as his own counsel and that he would examine all witnesses himself.[30] (See Appendix B for Hill's description of the firing episode.)

F. B. Scott, still bitter about the incident more than a year later, wrote the *Salt Lake Telegram* in August 1915:

> The foreman of the jury and several other jurymen tell me that we were conducting the defense so well that they were inclined to believe Hillstrom innocent until the uncalled for outbreak when he said, "There are too many attorneys for the state here. I am going to get rid of them."
>
> The jurymen say that had all the earmarks of guilt to their minds—that in their judgment it was perfectly uncalled for.
>
> I am certain that if it had not been for this outbreak and its effect on the minds of the jury Hillstrom would never have been convicted.[31]

The jury was recalled, and the examination of Mrs. Seeley proceeded.

Mrs. Seeley testified that she and her husband walked home from the Empress Theatre on the night of the murder. As they passed the Morrison store, they saw Mr. Morrison, Arling, and Merlin inside. When they reached the cobblestone crossing of Jefferson Street, two men walking shoulder to shoulder crowded the Seeleys off the sidewalk. Leatherwood questioned her concerning this encounter:

Did this man that turned, the taller of the two,
did he look directly at you?

Yes.

And did you look directly at him?

Yes.

Did you notice anything peculiar about the features
of the face of the man. . . ?

Yes.

I wish you would just tell in your own way, Mrs. Seeley,
what there was about the face of that man that attracted you.

Well, his face was real thin; he had a sharp nose,
and rather large nostrils. He had a defect on the side
of his face or neck.

On the side of the face or neck?

Right here on his face.

What do you mean by that—apparently a scar?

Yes, it looked as though it might be a scar.

And you observed that?

Yes, sir. . .

Did the nose appear to be particularly sharp that you
saw on the tall man there at that time?

Yes.

And the nostrils were peculiar?

Yes, the gentleman that I met was a sharp faced man with a real sharp nose, and his nostrils were rather large.

* * *

How does the height of the defendant, Mr. Hillstrom, compare with the height of the man that turned and looked at you there at that time?

Very much the same . . .

As to build?

Yes, they were slender built, both of them . . .

How does Mr. Hillstrom, as he sits here, compare in regard to thinness with the man that you saw that day?

His thinness is just about the same . . . but his hair is entirely different.

In what respect is his hair different?

His hair has been cut . . .

Did you state whether or not the appearance of the defendant's hair is anything like the hair you saw on this man that night?

He had light hair; yes; the one I saw.

Light hair?

Yes; medium complexioned, like this man.

* * *

How does the nose of Mr. Hillstrom compare with the nose of the man you looked at there?

Very much the same.

How do the marks, especially upon the lefthand side of his face and neck, that you have had an opportunity to observe, correspond with the marks on the man that you saw there on that night?

Well, they look a great deal alike to me . . .[32]

At this point F. B. Scott cross-examined Mrs. Seeley and extracted from her the statement that, even though she saw the man's face in a very detailed way, she still had an honest doubt that Hill was the man she saw.[33] Hill, according to the press, was obviously pleased with Scott's performance in the cross-examination.[34]

After Mrs. Seeley's testimony, Judge Ritchie called for the noon recess. Hill conferred with his attorneys and talked with some of his friends. When one friend, Hilda Erickson, was seen speaking with Hill, the press speculated that she might prove to be the woman who could provide his alibi.[35]

Although it was known that Hill was a member of the I.W.W., and although members of the organization had filled the courtroom during the first two days of the trial, it was apparently not known publicly until June 19 that the Wobblies were planning an active campaign in Hill's defense. On the afternoon of that day, Soren X. Christensen, prominent Salt Lake attorney, showed Hill, Scott, and McDougall a telegram from Orrin N. Hilton, who had been retained by the union's Salt Lake branch, Local Sixty-nine.

> Sit in Hillstrom case now in trial in Ritchie's court, saving all exceptions possible with view to taking to supreme court. Judge Hilton makes this request, see letter Virginia Stephen.[36]

Judge Orrin N. Hilton, Joe Hill's attorney.

The background of the I.W.W.'s involvement in the case has been explained by William Chance, an acquaintance of Hill's from San Pedro. In early January 1914, Chance had seen Hill in the Wobbly hall in Salt Lake City. A few days after this meeting, Chance and Ed Rowan, the leader of the union in Salt Lake City, saw the headlines and a picture of Joseph Hillstrom in the press announcing his arrest as a suspect in the Morrison murder. According to Chance, the picture was of very poor quality and he had never before heard the name Joseph Hillstrom. But the picture resembled his friend Joe Hill enough to cause Chance and Rowan to visit the jail to find out if Hillstrom and Hill were one and the same. After talking with Hill, they offered to do anything to help him and to organize I.W.W. support. Hill told them emphatically that he did not want the union involved and indicated that he thought he would soon be released. Chance and Rowan respected Hill's wish and did not immediately initiate organization of Wobbly support. A few days later, Chance left Salt Lake City and never saw Hill again.[37]

However, when Rowan learned that Hill was to stand trial for the murder, he immediately organized the Joe Hill Defense Committee. The committee originally consisted of Rowan as chairman and George Child as treasurer. Fred Ritter, Sam Scarlett, Meyer Friedkin, and Philip Engle were also active in the effort to organize support for Hill.

The I.W.W.'s first official call for help appeared in the April 18, 1914, issue of its publication, *Solidarity*. Headlined, "THE MAN WHO WROTE 'MR. BLOCK' AND 'CASEY JONES' CAUGHT AND HELD ON TRUMPED UP CHARGES,"[38] the article cited Hill's devotion to I.W.W. principles and the contribution he made through his songs, then urged all members to raise money for his defense. (See Chapter 6 for complete article.) The second official entreaty for support appeared in the May 23, 1914, issue of *Solidarity*. It was a letter from Ed Rowan explaining the charges against Hill and announcing that a defense committee had been established.[39] Both articles maintained that Hill was being framed because of his radical songs and his Wobbly affiliation.

**Virginia Snow Stephen, a leader
in the fight to save Hill.**

Virginia Snow Stephen, an instructor of art at the University of Utah in Salt Lake City and daughter of former Mormon church president Lorenzo Snow, became involved through her friendship with Ed Rowan, her opposition to capital punishment, her sympathy for the working class, and her exposure to Hill's songs. Mrs. Stephen, a socialist, expressed her views in a letter to a friend. "Do you believe there is justice for the poor working factory girl, or for the ill-paid person in other employment? If you knew and had seen right here in Salt Lake City what I have seen with my own eyes, you might change your view."[40]

Mrs. Stephen visited Hill in jail during the spring of 1914 and came away convinced that a man who could write songs like "Come and Take a Joy-ride in

My Aeroplane" and "Oh Please Let Me Dance this Waltz with You" was incapable of committing murder.[41] Because he knew that Mrs. Stephen was traveling east to attend summer school at Columbia University, Ed Rowan persuaded her to stop in Denver, Colorado, to ask O. N. Hilton to join Hill's defense.

At the time Mrs. Stephen contacted Hilton he was involved in a court case in Michigan and was unable to go to Salt Lake City immediately. He and Mrs. Stephen, however, sent the telegram to his friend and colleague S. X. Christensen, asking Christensen to intercede in Hill's behalf. Hilton was a very capable attorney. In 1912 he re-edited *Warton's Criminal Evidence* and had written a volume entitled *Due Process of Law*. He was retained by the United Mine Workers and had been counsel for twenty years for the Western Federation of Miners.[42] Hilton traveled to Salt Lake City later to represent Hill in his appeal to the Utah Supreme Court.

Even though the I.W.W. announced publicly in April of 1914 its intention to support Hill, it was not until the intervention of S. X. Christensen on June 19 that most people in Salt Lake City became fully aware that Hill was a Wobbly and that he had strong I.W.W. support. Mrs. Stephen's participation in the affair served to heighten local interest, and the press reflected its surprise at the involvement of a member of such a prominent Utah family.[43]

On the day after Christensen's intervention, the press began to emphasize Hill's Wobbly affiliation. The *Salt Lake Tribune* announced: "Hillstrom is the author of a score of poems and songs, many of which have been adopted by the I.W.W. organization and the Socialist party and have been sung all over the country . . . . That is why the I.W.W. is financing his defense and why so many I.W.W. and socialists are present at the trial."[44] The newspaper also reported that Ed Rowan of the Salt Lake local ". . . declared that the organization would stand by the accused man until his case had been carried to the highest court in the land, or until he had been freed."[45]

As the afternoon session of June 19 commenced, Hill—who had begun with two attorneys that morning and had voiced his desire to be rid of them—had three defense attorneys. The breach between Hill and his two original attorneys had apparently been mended during the recess.

Margaret Davis testified during the afternoon session that Joe Hill resembled in body size the taller of the two men she had seen near Morrison's store a few minutes prior to the murder. She could not, however, identify Hill as the man she had seen.[46]

Witnesses for the state were still being questioned on Saturday, June 20, 1914. Mrs. Athana Saccoss—presumed to be the author of the anonymous letter published in the *Arbetarbladet* in Gävle, Sweden, on December 18, 1915 (See Appendix B for complete letter)—testified that she had known Hill as a child but had not seen him since he left Sweden until she met him in a Salt Lake City cafeteria just before Christmas in 1913.[47] She met him again two days before the murder and invited him to her house on Saturday, January 10—the night of the murder. She said Hill replied that, "He might come and that he would if he could, but that he might not be able to." She then asked him to come on Sunday, and he replied that he ". . . might go to California that day."[48] This information was used by the prosecution in an attempt to prove that Hill was planning the murder for Saturday night, January 10.

The next witness for the prosecution, Mrs. Vera Hansen, testified, as she had at the preliminary hearing, that she heard Hill cry out, "Oh Bob." She also said, apparently without objection from the defense counsel, that Hill's voice, which she had gone to the county jail to hear a few days after his arrest, sounded "exactly" the same as the voice she had heard on the night of the murder. Further, despite the fact that the man she saw was stooped over, Mrs. Hansen said that Hill's height was the same as that of the man she had seen. [49]

Miss Nellie Mahan, who told in her preliminary hearing testimony of the man she saw running from the store and crying out "I'm shot," now added that the man was very tall and thin. When asked how that man compared with Joe Hill, she said, "Well all I can say is that the man I saw running was very tall and thin and Mr. Hillstrom is very tall and thin."[50]

The doctors McHugh and Bird appeared for the state on Monday, June 22, and described the treatment of Hill's wound. Dr. Bird answered questions about the drive to the Eselius house. Leatherwood asked the doctors to describe the gun which had fallen from Hill's clothing that night—the handle of which they had seen. They were shown Colt and Luger automatic pistols and were asked if either resembled Hill's gun. (Morrison was killed with a 38-caliber automatic, and it had been proved that Hill had bought a Luger a few weeks before the murder.) Dr. McHugh could not say whether or not the guns shown to him resembled the one Hill had on the night of the murder.[51] Dr. Bird said that the gun in question looked like the 38-caliber Colt shown him by the prosecution.[52]

McHugh was then asked to state the caliber of the gun with which Hill had been wounded. (Morrison owned a 38-caliber Colt.) McHugh could not be certain but said it was larger than a 32-caliber.[53] He made no mention during his testimony of the confession he later claimed to have received from Hill.

Other state witnesses appeared on Monday.

B. H. Seager, a deputy sheriff, said he was told by Hill that he had thrown his gun away while riding with Dr. Bird to the Eselius house.

Thomas Higgs, the newsman who recovered Morrison's gun in the store, was not an expert on firearms but testified that the gun smelled as if it had been recently fired.

Mrs. J. G. Morrison testified that her son, Arling, had been five feet four inches tall.

Merlin Morrison was recalled and testified that after the murder he saw his father's gun beside the right hand of his dead brother.

The state concluded its case in the afternoon of Monday, June 22, 1914, and the defense immediately moved that the court instruct the jury to find the defendant not guilty. Judge Ritchie denied the motion.[54]

At this point the *Salt Lake Herald-Republican* reported:

> The state feels that it has made an exceptionally strong case in the line of circum-

stantial evidence and feels that the identification by Mrs. Phoebe Seeley of Hillstrom by his nose, nostrils, and the scar on his neck and face is clinching in its effect of establishing the sameness of identity between Hillstrom and the taller of the two men encountered near the store by Mrs. Seeley.[55]

At the midway point of the trial, the Salt Lake County sheriff reported that his department had received information that Hill's sympathizers were planning to abduct him from the courtroom. He added that he had several deputies stationed in the courtroom and any trouble could be handled by his department.[56]

The defense* began the presentation of its case Tuesday, June 23. By then it was apparent to Hill's attorneys that Joe Hill himself would be of little help in their efforts to obtain his acquittal. They complained that Hill ". . . is assuming the attitude that he would rather die than reveal his exact whereabouts and the identity of those who he was with on the night of the murder."[57] They told the press that Joe Hill ". . . is a man of the nature that would rather face death than divulge the secrets of an affair of this sort."[58]

Because of Hill's refusal to explain in detail his actions on the night of the murder, his attorneys were forced to devise a defense which would not depend on that testimony. Their plan was divulged by F. B. Scott in his introductory remarks.

> We expect to meet circumstance with circumstance, suspicion with suspicion.
> We expect to prove that other men answering the general description of Mr. Hillstrom have been and still are under suspicion of having committed this murder.
> We expect to prove that Mr. Hillstrom was shot with a steel bullet and not with a lead bullet.
> We expect to prove that he could not have been shot in Morrison's store by Arling Morrison.
> We expect to prove that the man who was shot in Morrison's store that night, if any man was shot, of which there is grave doubt, carried the bullet from the store in his body, whereas the bullet with which Mr. Hillstrom was shot went clean through his body and was not carried away by him.
> We expect to prove that the gun which Mr. Hillstrom had on him when examined by the physicians was not a gun that could shoot the kind of bullets that have been introduced here in evidence as found in Morrison's store, that it was not a Colt automatic, nor any other kind of an automatic gun that could shoot such bullets.
> We expect to show that undue influence has been used attempting to get a confession from this defendant of something that he never committed, and we expect to prove that witnesses for the defense that have been subpoenaed have been approached by the state with an attempt to get them to change their testimony so as to favor the cause of the state; and we further expect to prove that witnesses for the state have altered their testimony from the time they were first examined at the preliminary hearing in order to make the facts fit Mr. Hillstrom in this case.[59]

The first defense witness was Mrs. Betty Eselius Olsen, a sister to the Eselius brothers, who lived in their home and served as housekeeper. Mrs. Olsen

93

---

* Volume II of the trial transcript, evidence presented by the defense, is available and has been used for reference.

testified that she had given Joe Hill a red bandana handkerchief the day *after* he was wounded and that the family had several such handkerchiefs for use by the Eselius men, who worked in a smelter.[60] The defense claimed that the handkerchief which the prosecution had claimed was worn by Morrison's killer was the one Mrs. Olsen had given Hill after he was wounded and the one found in the Eselius home by detective Zeese. The defense, through Mrs. Olsen's testimony, also attempted to show that the state had used undue influence to try to extract a confession from Hill. Mrs. Olsen had been told that her son, Robert Erickson, who had been arrested as a suspect in the killings, would be released if she could induce Hill to confess.[61] Mrs. Olsen said that the police repeatedly came to her home to search for Hill's gun and other evidence. She informed the court that the investigating officers had told her Joe Hill had confessed to the police that he had given the gun to her. This she maintained was a lie; Joe Hill had not given her a gun. The defense contended that the police resorted to lies to obtain evidence against Hill.[62]

The defense then endeavored to prove that Arling Morrison did not fire his father's gun at the assailants and that Hill, therefore, could not have been wounded at the scene of the murder. Lester Wire, a policeman, testified that it was common practice for a policeman to leave an empty chamber in his revolver for the hammer to rest on.[63] Riley M. Beckstead, another policeman, testified that he and John G. Morrison had been colleagues on the police force in Salt Lake City.[64] Since Morrison had been a policeman, and since one chamber of his gun contained a spent cartridge, as brought out in evidence introduced by the state, the defense drew the inference that the gun had not been fired on the night of the murder. The defense contended that the spent cartridge on which the hammer rested served a safety purpose. This position was weakened for want of evidence that policemen customarily let the hammers of their revolvers rest on a spent cartridge instead of an empty chamber.

The defense's next tactic was to produce evidence that Joe Hill had no known motive for killing Morrison but that there were other persons known to Morrison who had considerable provocation to seek revenge. They called Hardy K. Downing, an ex-newspaper reporter, to testify concerning his interview with Morrison after the September 1913 attack.[65] District Attorney Leatherwood objected to his testimony, and the court sustained the objection on the questionable grounds that Hill would have to be claiming "self-defense" to make the evidence of a previous attack relevant.[66] The court's second reason for sustaining the objection was that the testimony was based on a conversation with a man who was no longer living. Therefore, the jury was not permitted to consider the relevant evidence that the victim had sustained two attempts on his life prior to the final, successful one.

Emerson John Miller, an employee of the Western Arms and Sporting Goods Company, testified for the defense as an expert on guns. The only expert opinion the court allowed him was the observation that when semismokeless or smokeless gunpowder—the type used by Morrison—is used in a cartridge it cannot be determined by smell when the gun was fired.[67] This was an impor-

94

tant link in the defense argument that Arling did not fire his father's gun[68] and served to counteract the testimony given by newsman Thomas Higgs for the prosecution that the gun found near Arling Morrison's body smelled as though it had been recently fired. Miller also testified, but not as an expert, as to the direction in which the bullets were fired by Morrison's assailants.[69] He said the bullet indentations found in the walls and floor proved there were two series of shots fired from different positions, and the defense inferred from this that Arling had not exchanged shots—if he had fired at all—with the tall man who attacked J. G. Morrison, but with the man nearest him who was thought to be the shorter man. Hill's attorneys thus hoped to demonstrate that Hill could not have been wounded in the store and that he was not the tall man who shot Morrison. The inference, however, was vague and apparently failed to convince the jury. There was no evidence presented that the men had not shifted positions during the shooting.

With Miller's testimony the defense also tried to prove that Hill was wounded by a steel bullet, while the bullets in Morrison's gun were lead. Judge Ritchie repeatedly refused to allow Miller to state his opinion as to the type of bullet that wounded Hill. The judge held that too much time had passed between the night when Hill was wounded and the time Miller examined the wound, a few days prior to the trial, to obtain valid evidence.[70] Miller admitted that both steel and lead bullets cause discoloration of the flesh, but he implied that lead causes greater discoloration than steel. He also stated that the bullet which wounded Joe Hill "key-holed" rather than "mushroomed."[71] The defense contended that steel bullets were more likely to "key-hole" than were lead ones.

In cross-examining Miller, Leatherwood forced him to admit that he did not actually know what caused the discoloration of the skin and that he was not sure he could tell the difference between lead and steel bullet wounds without having several comparisons.[72]

Robert Erickson, originally thought by the police to have been the "Bob" called to by the man who ran from the store, testified that he and his brother Oliver had gone to the Utah Theatre on the evening of January 10, 1914, with their uncles John and Victor Eselius. They returned home just fifteen minutes before Joe Hill arrived with Dr. Bird.[73]

Leatherwood, in cross-examination, asked Erickson if he had seen Otto Applequist after returning from the theater. The defense counsel objected to the question, but the court overruled the objection. Leatherwood again asked the question. Erickson did not answer immediately, but after some hesitation said, yes, he had seen Applequist after he returned home.

Dr. Beer, who had examined Hill's wound and the jacket he had worn on the night he was shot, testified that the bullet hole in the jacket did not match the wound in Hill's chest. The hole in the jacket—when worn normally—was four inches lower than the wound. Dr. Beer explained that when Hill raised his arms "to extreme length" above his head, the hole in the jacket matched perfectly with the location of the wound.[74] The defense inferred from this that

Hill was shot while holding his hands over his head and there was no evidence that Morrison's killers had held their hands in this position at any time during the encounter. Dr. Beer was then asked whether, in his opinion, Hill could have been wounded while in any position other than standing with his arms above his head. Leatherwood objected and the objection was sustained.[75] The defense argument that Hill was wounded while his hands were raised over his head was never satisfactorily accounted for by the state.*

The next three witnesses for the defense introduced testimony concerning persons who behaved suspiciously in the general area of the killings on the night of January 10. The defense alleged that these persons were more logical suspects than Hill. The first of these witnesses was Peter Rhengren, a machinist who worked the night shift in the Denver and Rio Grande Railroad shops. Walking to work on Saturday night, January 10, at 11:20 p.m., approximately eight blocks from the scene of the murders[76] he encountered two men. As he approached, one of the men turned and walked away, the other fell to the ground and lay resting in the snow, propped up on one elbow.[77] Rhengren went up and looked directly into the man's face, but neither of them said anything. The man appeared to be hurt rather than drunk, and Rhengren candidly stated that he did not help him because he was afraid. He planned, rather, to meet a friend with whom he customarily walked to work and then return and help the fallen man. However, when Rhengren left to meet his friend, the man rose, walked to a streetcar and boarded it. Rhengren testified that the man was wearing a black coat, dark pants, and a black hat, but that he definitely was not the defendant, Joe Hill.[78]

James R. Usher, the conductor of the streetcar, testified that the man attracted his attention because he acted as if something were wrong and he boarded on the wrong side of the car.[79] The man did not smell of alcohol or appear drunk and was about six feet one inch tall, raw-boned and thin. He rode in the streetcar hunched over in his seat, until he got off at Second South and Main streets in downtown Salt Lake City.[80] During the investigation of the murder in January 1914, Usher had identified the man from a police photograph as ex-convict Frank Z. Wilson.[81] He submitted this information to the court. Until Hill's arrest, the police were seeking the recently released Wilson as the most likely suspect in the murders.

Carl A. Carlson, a policeman, was questioned about suspects apprehended

---

* James O. Morris in "The Joe Hill Case" (unpublished thesis, 1950, in the Labadie Collection, University of Michigan Library) presents an interpretation of how Hill could have been wounded in Morrison's store. He contends Hill reached over a counter to shoot Arling who was lying wounded on the other side. In reaching over, Hill's coat moved up on his body. While the upper part of Hill's body extended over the counter, Arling fired his father's gun, wounding Hill in the chest. Morris believes the bullet from Arling's shot went through Hill's body and lodged in the ceiling. Hill then fired at Arling, pointing his gun down toward the floor.

There is no evidence concerning a police search of the ceiling for bullets. They did, however, find a bullet lodged in the floor where Arling's body lay.

during the investigation. Carlson testified that Oran Anderson, who claimed he had been wounded by two gunmen on January 10 near Eighth South and Sixth West streets, had been arrested in connection with the murder but was released because the police thought he had a good alibi.[82] It is not known why no mention was made of the other persons arrested in connection with the murder.

Policeman George E. Cleveland was the last witness for the defense. He stated that police had found six bullet holes in the interior of Morrison's store after the murder, and that six spent bullets were found during the investigation. But no bullet was found that could have come from Morrison's gun.[83] This fact is one of the strongest points in the case for the defense. Conceivably, the bullet that wounded Hill and then passed through his body could have remained in the store, undiscovered by repeated police searches, but it remains damaging to the prosecution's case that all bullets were located except the one that allegedly wounded Hill.

97

At that point in the trial, according to the *Salt Lake Herald-Republican*, "... abruptly and unexpectedly the defense ceased introducing evidence... and after a lengthy conference with the defendant rested its case without placing the accused man on the stand." The "lengthy conference," during which a difference of opinion arose between the original attorneys and Christensen, dealt with the advisability of Hill's taking the stand. Scott and McDougall advised that he should. Christensen, perhaps thinking that his testimony would not help but might harm the case, given Hill's refusal to further explain his wound, advised against his taking the stand. Hill decided not to testify.[84] In a letter written afterward to the *Salt Lake Telegram*, F. B. Scott complained, "Hillstrom, from the beginning of the trial, insisted that he was going to take the witness chair. ... Owing to bad advice from someone else, at the eleventh hour he changed his mind and refused to take the witness chair. ..."[85]

The trial concluded with summations by both sides and with the judge's instruction to the jury. Though not recorded in the transcript, the summations were reported in considerable detail by the local press.

The prosecution had shown that on the night of the murder someone of Hill's general appearance had been in the vicinity of the Morrison store just prior to ten p.m., that there was reason to suppose he might have been wounded in the store, and that Hill had arrived at Dr. McHugh's office at 11:30 with a fresh wound. The prosecution, however, had been unable to secure a positive identification of Hill as the murderer. Lacking the link to prove that Joe Hill was the man involved in the chain of circumstances testified to by the state's witnesses, the district attorney attempted to provide the needed connective in his summation which began on June 24. Leatherwood began with a review of the circumstances that tended to incriminate Hill.

> Mr. Morrison was shot down in cold blood without cause or reason. And a child—I may call him a child—was shot down by some brutal monster because he dared raise a hand in protection of the father, whose life was being shot out of him just across the store.
>
> Gentlemen, it is for such as you to say how long this sort of thing shall go on. It is

for you in the performance of the high duty you are called upon to perform to put a stop to the making of widows and orphans in this manner by enforcing the penalty of the law on such men as go about shooting down peaceable and law abiding citizens. I ask you to do your duty to the state and to Joseph Hillstrom. Extend to him all the presumptions given him by the law. Be fair in all things to him, but be mindful of your duty to the public. I am proud to say there is no spirit of revenge in the framing of the laws of this state and there is not and never shall be any spirit of revenge in the conduct of any case in any court of this state. But the law says that he who unlawfully sheds the blood of his fellowmen shall be punished according to the law for the protection of our homes and families.

Against Joseph Hillstrom as an individual I bear no personal feeling, no malice. [86]

98

Leatherwood then turned to a review of the evidence. Ignoring the controversial intricacies argued by the defense—the type of material from which the bullets were made and the direction from which they came—the prosecuting attorney created a verbal picture of the murderer.

It is clear from the evidence that some brute—I repeat brute—not satisfied with shooting down that child Arling Morrison, went to the counter, reached over it and shot that child once, twice, and perhaps three times until he shot out every spark of life. If I had a picture drawn by an artist of the murderer of that child it would not be a picture of a cyclops with a distorted face and blood shot eye, but that of a cold, cruel, bloodless brute.[87]

Of the alleged shot fired by Arling, Leatherwood said, "Oh, how the defense has tried to get away from the firing of that gun; but they can't. It seems that fate directed that shot of Arling's for it placed the indelible mark on the murderer of his father, and (pointing to Hill) he bears that mark today."[88]

The *Salt Lake Tribune* expressed its admiration for Leatherwood's oratorical ability. "It was with a veritable sledge hammer of eloquence and logic that the District Attorney welded together the links in the chain of circumstantial evidence."[89]

As the defense rose to its summation, it was faced with making up for its misfortunes in the early days of the trial: Hill's attempt to discharge his counsel; the failure to prove important points in the testimony of witnesses Beer, Downing, and Miller; and the unfortunate implication of Hill's refusal to explain his wound. The three defense attorneys occupied the entire day, Thursday, June 25, in presenting their summation. They stressed a theory of circumstantial evidence which maintained that the circumstances in a case such as Hill's could be compared to a chain—ruined when a single link is broken.[90]

In reviewing the case, McDougall told the jury several times that if it ruled against Hill the case would be taken to the supreme court.[91] Stressing this point was probably unwise, for it tended to remove from the jury the pressure of final responsibility for a man's life. S. X. Christensen then spoke of the prosecution's failure to prove Hill's motive for killing Morrison. The earlier attacks on Morrison in 1903 and 1913 were mentioned for the first time in the trial when Christensen claimed that these attackers had a motive while Joe Hill had not. Christensen also stressed the failure of the police to find the bullet that wounded Hill and contended that it was not even proved beyond reasonable doubt that

Arling had fired the gun. He criticized the testimony of Mrs. Seeley, saying that if she could describe in detail Joe Hill's face, and yet would not say it was Joe Hill she had seen, her identification was not credible.[92]

F. B. Scott took over the defense summation after Christensen finished. Scott said Hill's outburst in firing his counsel was "striking evidence" of his innocence. The outburst showed him to be a highly temperamental man with the sensitive nature of a musician and the picture Leatherwood had drawn of the killer did not fit him.[93]

McDougall, speaking for the second time, concluded the summation with a series of inflammatory statements. Bluntly, he stated that he believed Mrs. Seeley had lied, saying, "I believe her testimony was a frame up."[94] McDougall then attacked the whole system of judicial procedure in Utah, charging that the presumption of innocence was a mere fiction to prosecuting attorneys. He said that courts and juries in Utah were tools used by prosecuting attorneys to build their reputations. Leatherwood, McDougall stated, did not care about justice; he was only trying to ". . . make a record before the people."[95] McDougall told the jury that it seemed reasonable to him that a man in Hill's position would be willing to testify to clear himself. He said he had pleaded vainly with Hill to tell how he was wounded. "He would have gone to the gallows to spite me. He hated me so for trying to get him to tell how he was wounded. He's that sort of man. He won't tell. What his reason is I don't know. This I do know, he wasn't shot in Morrison's store. That has been proved conclusively."[96]

McDougall's criticisms of the witness Mrs. Seeley and the Utah courts were ammunition for Leatherwood's final summation. The press reported that Leatherwood ". . . called down the wrath of heaven upon the heads of the defense attorneys for daring to lift the finger of criticism at a woman as a witness in a court of justice."[97] He continued, saying it was with pride that he ". . . realized that the women of Utah are shoulder to shoulder with men in the great accomplishments in every line of life."[98] A hopeful candidate for the United States Congress, Leatherwood also defended the honor of judicial procedure in Utah from McDougall's untimely attack.

> When a man charges the courts are tools, that juries are corrupt, and public officers are false to their trust and intimates that Utah's a state where a man cannot procure a fair trial, when he strikes at the very root of our American institutions of justice and freedom, I resent it. I care not whether such criticism comes from the pulpit or the soapbox, I resent it.[99]

Leatherwood's increasingly irrelevant statements brought an objection from the defense counsel, but Judge Ritchie allowed the prosecution to continue.[100]

> My blood boils with keen resentment, gentlemen, when I hear such unwarranted attacks on American institutions, institutions which are the foundation stones of our glorious concepts of liberty, equality, and justice, and I tell you that when any considerable number of our fellow beings subscribe to the doctrine you heard enunciated here this morning then liberty flees the confines of our fair land and anarchy begins its sway.[101]

99

Leatherwood, mirroring the popular 1914 stereotype of the I.W.W. member, then made the most direct inference in the trial to Joe Hill's membership in the organization.

> We must enforce the majesty of the law as framed by the people of this great state; enforce it so that anarchy and murder and crime shall be pushed back another step beyond the pale of civilization, enforce it so that you and yours and all upright men shall walk the earth free from the danger of those parasites on society who murder and rob rather than make an honest living.[102]

Still to come were Leatherwood's concluding remarks, which may have constituted reversible error when the case was appealed in 1915 and certainly would today. Leatherwood implied that not testifying in his own behalf proved Hill's guilt and thus flouted the guarantee that no presumption of guilt shall be made from a defendant's refusal to so testify. Turning, Leatherwood pointed his finger at Hill and said,

> If you were an innocent man, Joe Hillstrom, when Seager [a deputy sheriff] asked you for an explanation of your wound and told you if you would tell where and how you were wounded and if the story could be corroborated, you would be freed, why in God's name did you not tell him the story and clear your name from the stain upon it? Because you were a guilty man and you couldn't tell a story that could be corroborated. That is why.[103]

Leatherwood then asked the jury to find Hill guilty.

The summations completed, Judge Ritchie instructed the jury. If they were to find Joe Hill guilty of first degree murder as charged, they must determine beyond a reasonable doubt that the defendant, according to the information, had ". . . unlawfully, willfully, feloniously, deliberately, maliciously, premeditatively, and with specific intent," taken the life of John G. Morrison. He informed them that the lesser offenses of second degree murder and manslaughter could be found under the same stipulations.[104]

Other instructions covered presumption of innocence, the right of the accused to refrain from testifying, the presence or absence of motive, false testimony, tests for judging the credibility of witnesses, and instructions for determining the degree of murder committed.[105]

The most controversial instruction given by Ritchie, the one upon which Hill's guilt or innocence directly depended, dealt with the nature of circumstantial evidence. The defense, in summation, argued that circumstantial evidence alone is no stronger than its weakest part. Consistent with this theory, the defense had requested that Judge Ritchie instruct the jury that, ". . . when circumstances which succeed and depend on each other as a chain, alone are relied on for conviction, each link must be proven beyond a reasonable doubt."[106] Ritchie, however, rejected this concept of circumstantial evidence, insisting instead that all circumstances should be considered together. In his instructions he implied that circumstantial evidence was of the nature of a cable, which could have several broken strands and still support the weight of a conviction.

> This kind of evidence is the proof of such facts and circumstances connected with

or surrounding the perpetration of the crime charged, as to tend to show the guilt or innocence of the person accused; and if these facts and circumstances when considered all together are sufficient to satisfy the minds of the jury of the guilt of the defendant beyond reasonable doubt, then such evidence is sufficient to authorize a conviction. But if such facts and circumstances, when considered together, are explainable upon any other reasonable hypothesis, then the defendant is innocent, and such evidence will not warrant a verdict of guilty. [107]

The case went to the jury at 4:20 p.m. on Friday, June 27. The *Salt Lake Tribune* reported that a decision was reached by 11:00 p.m. that same night, but the jury decided to adjourn and poll themselves again on Saturday morning. [108] At 10:00 a.m. Saturday morning, the court clerk read the verdict. Joe Hill was guilty as charged. [109]

Hill listened to the reading of the verdict with no sign of emotion. The *Deseret Evening News* reported that "... there was not even a change of color in his cheeks." [110] The police, expecting a demonstration by Hill's I.W.W. supporters, had plenty of lawmen on hand. But no disturbance occurred. [111]

The trial of Joe Hill was marked by at least three issues from which error could be argued.

1. Judge Ritchie's appointment of Hill's attorneys as *amici curiae* was technically incorrect. But after Hill's inept performance at cross-examination during the preliminary hearing, it was clear he would have been incapable of conducting his own defense at the trial. Ritchie probably realized this when he requested that Hill's attorneys remain after Hill fired them. Nevertheless, by naming them friends of the court, Ritchie opened himself to criticism. *Black's Law Dictionary* defines *amicus curiae* as, "... a by-stander (usually a counselor) who interposes and volunteers information upon some matter of law in regard to which the judge is doubtful or mistaken. Implies friendly intervention of counsel to remind court of a legal matter which has escaped its notice and regarding which it appears to be in danger of doing wrong." [112]

Precedent not established in Hill's day but since provided by cases containing an *amicus curiae* issue supports Black's definition of the limited role of one appointed to that position. [113] There was, in 1914, precedent supporting the position that a judge cannot force counsel upon a defendant not wanting it. [114] It is arguable, therefore, that Judge Ritchie abridged Hill's right as granted by the laws of Utah "... to appear and defend in person and by counsel." [115]

2. Exception can be taken to Judge Ritchie's instruction to the jury in reference to circumstantial evidence. The defense's conception of such evidence was more nearly in line with Utah precedent.

In a case such as Hill's, where there is no direct evidence connecting the defendant with the crime, the Utah code stated: "Where the state seeks to convict a defendant upon circumstantial evidence, it must show by a preponderance of the evidence that the alleged facts and circumstances are true. . . .

[T]he chain of evidence must be complete and unbroken and established beyond reasonable doubt."[116]

The above view was enunciated by the Utah Supreme Court in 1894.[117] In 1896, the Utah courts again said, "The chain of circumstances must be complete and unbroken and should be established beyond a reasonable doubt,"[118] and the same view was reiterated in 1898: "When circumstances which succeed and depend upon each other as a chain alone are relied on for conviction, each link must be proven beyond a reasonable doubt. . . ." The only condition made by the Utah court in the 1898 situation was that in cases involving some direct evidence of guilt, the chain of circumstances could be impaired without making acquittal necessary.[119]

The instruction on circumstantial evidence asked for by Hill's attorneys appears to have been taken verbatim from the words of the Utah Supreme Court in the above case. If Judge Ritchie's instruction was also based on that case and given on the premise that there was direct evidence of guilt in the Hill case, he failed to refer to such evidence.

Despite this apparent error in Judge Ritchie's instruction to the jury, the defense, for reasons unknown, made no protest in its appeal.

3. The prosecution, in implying that Hill's refusal to testify was evidence of his guilt, made an error that would certainly be grounds for reversal today in light of recent Supreme Court decisions. The matter was not clearly defined in 1915, however, and in various jurisdictions prosecutors were able to mention the defendant's refusal to testify without violating his rights under the fifth amendment to the Constitution of the United States.[120] In Utah, in 1915, since there were no judicial decisions pertaining to this matter, the basic guideline was contained in paragraph 5015 of the *Compiled Laws of Utah* which stated that "A defendant's neglect or refusal to be a witness shall not in any manner prejudice him, nor be used against him in the trial or proceeding." In addition, there was precedent in several western states indicating that in his remarks to the jury a prosecutor cannot mention the defendant's refusal to testify.[121] Given the legal conditions existing in Utah in 1915, then, it appears that a reasonably strong case could have been made for reversal on the grounds of prejudicial error.

During the sentencing on July 8, 1914, under the Utah statutes defining the penalty for first degree murder, Joe Hill was given the option by Judge Ritchie of being hanged or shot to death. Hill replied, "I'll take shooting. I'm used to that. I have been shot a few times in the past and I guess I can stand it again."[122]

Following the jury's verdict, the defense attorneys filed a motion for a new trial. A hearing on this motion was held by Judge Ritchie on September 1, 1914, with Soren X. Christensen arguing for Hill and District Attorney Leatherwood representing the state.[123] Christensen contended that the state had failed to establish beyond reasonable doubt the identification of Joe Hill as the murderer of Morrison. He argued further that the incident in which Hill fired his lawyers prejudiced the jury against him, and he claimed that the method of selecting the jury had made a fair trial for Hillstrom almost hopeless. "That jury," he said, "was selected by a science at which the District Attorney is a past master and the defendant's attorneys were unskilled."[124]

After studying the arguments for four hours, Judge Ritchie rendered his decision. He denied the motion for a new trial. The defense immediately took steps to have the case appealed.[125]

Unexplained
gunshot
wound

5 "May it please the court: A careful
study of the record in this case warrants the assertion, made with the certainty
of absolute conviction, that no case appealed to this court in recent years is so
utterly lacking in the essential fundamentals of proof to sustain a conviction."[1]
With these words, Orrin N. Hilton opened his argument for Joe Hill before the
Utah Supreme Court. Assisting Hilton was Soren X. Christensen.

Hill's attorneys claimed that there had been several errors in the trial. First
mentioned in the brief, and clearly the argument they relied on most heavily,
was the prosecution's failure to identify Hill as Morrison's murderer. They emphasized that Merlin Morrison, the only eyewitness to the killing, had not been
able to identify Hill as one of the murderers, but rather could only say Hill was
about as tall and about the same size as one of the killers. The defense also
maintained that Phoebe Seeley, who described in detail the facial characteristics of the man she saw near the store just prior to the murder, had an "honest
doubt" that Hill was that man.[2] They challenged the accuracy of the comparisons made by Vera Hansen and Nellie Mahan between the man they saw on the
night of the murder and Joe Hill and contended that the "actual experience of
mankind" argues against the validity of comparisons made between a stooped-
over man running across a street at night, calling out in pain, and a man seen and
heard several days later under completely different circumstances.[3] Miss
Mahan's testimony that the man near Morrison's store was ". . . very tall and
thin and so is Mr. Hillstrom" was criticized as utterly failing to identify Hill.[4]

The alleged failure of the state's witnesses to identify Hill was argued in
the appellant's brief.

> There is nothing in any way to connect the defendant Hillstrom with the "taller
> man" who ran from Morrison's store. Not only that, but one witness says the taller
> man "wore the cap. . . ." Two other witnesses say he wore a hat but could not distin-
> guish the color. It must happen whenever two men meet, no matter where, when or
> how often, that one is always the taller, that fact is universal, for to find two men of
> exactly the same height in a casual meeting, is almost impossible, for where they are of
> the same size, the difference in hats or dress will often cause one of them to be de-
> scribed as the taller. And that is all that the state has to rest on. The witness makes no
> further claim than that Hillstrom was "about as tall as the taller of the two men."[5]

Hilton and Christensen referred the court to a case on which it had previously ruled, wherein it had condemned identification consisting of "about

the size" and "looked like him" as wholly insufficient to connect the defendant with the crime.[6] In that case the court had held that the evidence failed to establish the defendant's identity.[7] They concluded:

> It is essential that the identification be complete and convincing. Human experience is, that disconnected matters, matters helped out by the imagination, matters depending largely on inferences and comparisons, are so frequently wrong, in the absence of the genuine standard of comparison, that they are not to be relied upon. Size, figure, actions under pain, actions under imprisonment, are so much alike that the most accurate observer is more often mistaken than correct.[8]

Another error in the trial, according to Hilton and Christensen, was Judge Ritchie's failure to grant a directed verdict as moved by Hill's original attorneys. Arguing that there was insufficient evidence presented at the trial to identify Hill as the murderer and that therefore the case should never have been given to the jury, they referred the supreme court to several decisions in which various courts had held that the judge has a duty to decide if there is sufficient evidence to support the verdict for the plaintiff. If there is not, the judge must rule for the defendant, regardless of whether there is a scintilla of evidence against him.[9]

At the center of this contention was the elusive question of what is sufficient evidence to give a case to the jury. Citing previous cases in Utah and New York, Hilton and Christensen attempted to show that Judge Ritchie had been in error in submitting the case to the jury.* This, they claimed, was reason enough to reverse the verdict.[10]

Insufficient evidence identifying Hill as the murderer and failure to grant a directed verdict were but two of the errors Hill's attorneys argued existed in the trial. They also noted seven others.

1. Since a motive was not proved by the prosecution, the defendant should have been presumed innocent.[11]

---

* Utah statute provides the following standard of proof to be used in criminal cases: "A defendant in a criminal action shall be presumed to be innocent until the contrary is proved; and in case of a reasonable doubt whether his guilt is satisfactorily shown, he shall be entitled to an acquittal." (*Compiled Laws of Utah* [1907], tit. 91, ch. 33, §4848.) Interpreting this statute in a previous case, the supreme court had said that where the state seeks to convict a defendant upon circumstantial evidence, it must:

> ... show by a preponderance of the evidence that the alleged facts and circumstances which complete the chain are true, and it must also show that such facts and circumstances are not compatible upon any reasonable hypothesis with the innocence of the accused, and incapable of explanation upon any reasonable hypothesis other than that of the defendant's guilt. The chain of evidence must be complete and unbroken and established beyond a reasonable doubt. [Brief for the Appellant, p. 23.]

Hill's attorneys cited a case decided in New York in which that court had ruled that, since the "burden of proof is upon the people of not only removing the presumption of innocence, but of establishing the guilt of the accused beyond a reasonable doubt, the mere scintilla, or even some proof is not sufficient to warrant the submission of the case to the jury." [Brief for the Appellant, p. 24.]

2. The court should have allowed the defense witness Hardy K. Downing to give testimony concerning the previous attempts on Morrison's life.[12]

3. There were errors in the admission of expert testimony. The testimony of Dr. Sprague concerning Morrison's wounds was objected to because it had been entered from the preliminary hearing record (Sprague was out of town during the trial), and newsman Thomas Higgs's testimony as to when Morrison's gun was fired was rejected on the grounds that he was not an expert on guns.[13]

4. The judge erred in making critical comments on the manner in which the defense attorneys questioned prospective jurors.[14]

5. For a period of time Hill had been without counsel and this was alleged to be contrary to the provisions of the Constitution of the United States. In the right to appear and defend in person and by counsel, argued the attorneys, the word *and* is a substantive part of the right and does not mean *or*.[15]

6. The judge made an error in instructing the jury, because his wording of the instruction concerning circumstantial evidence ". . . wrongly dignified mere suspicion as 'circumstances,' and placed 'mere suspicion' in a class with 'circumstantial evidence.' "[16] According to Hilton and Christensen, this was particularly damaging because the whole case rested on "mere suspicion."

7. The court erred in failing to give the jury proper instructions on judging the credibility of the witnesses.[17]

Hill's attorneys concluded with the statement that the case presented by the defense at the trial had effectively challenged all the testimony given on behalf of the state. According to Hilton and Christensen, there was not a suspicious circumstance left unanswered when the defense rested its case.[18]

The case for the state was argued before the supreme court by Attorney General A. R. Barnes and his assistants, E. V. Higgins and G. A. Iverson. They began their argument with a pointed criticism of Hill's attorneys for neglecting to file a writ of error on insufficiency of evidence as required by the Utah Constitution.[19] Then, assuming that the court would overlook that technicality, they began their rebuttal against the contention of insufficiency of evidence. Arguing that there was no reasonable doubt that Hill and the tall man described by the prosecution's witnesses were the same person, they cited the witnesses' testimony and concluded that ". . . all the facts and circumstances proven throughout the case are consistent with the defendant's guilt and inconsistent with his innocence."[20] In so doing, they did not counter the contention of insufficient evidence with logical argument, but merely reaffirmed the jury's decision that Hill was guilty.

Judge Ritchie's decision not to grant a directed verdict was argued to be correct from two standpoints. First, they maintained, the request was, in effect, a motion for nonsuit, and such a motion must specify precisely where it is claimed proof is deficient so that the plaintiff may supply such proof if able. They then pointed out that the Utah Supreme Court had, in the past, refused to sustain a motion for nonsuit which did not meet these requirements. Therefore, the defense's request, in failing to specify any alleged insufficiency, became invalid.[21] Second, although they agreed that the law had established a standard of proof in criminal cases and that this standard must be met to have legal conviction, the state nevertheless contended that only when there is absolute lack of evidence to sustain a verdict should a case not be given to the jury. According to the attorney general, when the prosecution rested its case in the Hill trial, there was ample evidence against the defendant and, thus, no cause to grant a directed verdict.[22]

As to the lack of proof that Hill had a motive for killing Morrison, the state asserted that ". . . from all the circumstances in the case, a motive is clearly discernible." What the motive had been was not specifically determined— only that it may have been robbery or revenge.[23] According to the state, the determination of motive was a question for the jury. Concerning the alleged error that Joe Hill was tried for a time without benefit of counsel, the state pointed out that a defendant may waive the right of counsel and try his case himself. When this right is waived, no constitutional provision or statutory law is broken.[24] The contention that the examination of jurors was in error was answered simply by stating that Judge Ritchie was not in error and referring the court to the trial record.[25]

After each side had presented its arguments to the supreme court both orally and as written briefs, the case was studied by three men, Chief Justice Straup, Justice Frick, and Justice McCarty.

Joe Hill and his attorneys were confident that the supreme court would reverse the trial court's decision. In a letter to his friend Sam Murray in California, written just after the case was presented, Hill said: "My case was argued on the twenty-eighth of May [1915], and according to Judge Hilton, the results were satisfactory. He says he is sure of securing a reversal, and if so, there hardly will be another trial, for the simple reason that there won't be anything to try. . . ."[26]

However, following six days of private deliberation, the three justices announced their decision that there was no cause to grant a new trial or to reverse the jury's verdict. Hill reacted to this disappointment in another letter to Sam Murray: "We were all very much surprised at the decision, because we thought that I would be granted a new trial anyway. But as Judge Hilton says, 'the records of the lower court are so rotten they had to be covered somehow.' "[27] Hill and his supporters continued to hold this opinion, and, in choosing to ignore the legal position of the supreme court, probably aided the myth-building process.

Because of the limitations on its jurisdiction imposed by the Utah Constitution,* the Utah Supreme Court felt itself unable to consider the central argu-

---

* Utah's constitution limited the supreme court's authority in cases of appeal to questions of law, which means that the credibility of witnesses and the weight given their testimony are matters exclusively for the jury to decide. Neither could the supreme court weigh evidence or determine fact. When presented with conflicting evidence, the court was required to assume that testimony introduced on behalf of the prevailing party was true. Utah

ment of Hill's attorneys—lack of sufficient identification—and insisted that this was a question not for the supreme court, but for the jury:

> To do what counsel, both by brief and in oral argument, in effect have asked us to do, to place ourselves in the jury box, weigh the evidence, determine the credibility of witnesses, consider their opportunity and means of observation, and the reliability and worthiness of their testimony, is to ignore the law and to usurp a function not possessed by us.[28]

By adhering strictly to this line of reasoning the court disposed of the bulk of Hilton and Christensen's arguments as matters also for the jury to decide. It refused to consider any of the following contentions—important in Hill's appeal—on the grounds that they did not fall within its jurisdiction.

1. There were discrepancies between witnesses' statements as to the apparel worn by the assailants.

2. The defendant was not shot in the store, as proven by the fact that the bullet hole in his jacket was four inches lower than the wound in his body.

3. The defendant was not shot in the store because no bullet from the gun found near Arling Morrison's hand was ever located.

4. Because of a police officer's custom of leaving an empty chamber for the hammer of his revolver to rest on, and because of a defense witness's statement that it could not be determined when the gun was last fired, the gun found near the young Morrison's body was not fired by him.

5. The blood trails found on the street near the store were from a dog, not a human being.

6. The man seen lying on the ground near Eighth West may have been the man who was shot by Arling Morrison.

7. The handkerchief found in Hill's room was given him by Mrs. Olsen the day after he was shot.

8. No motive was proved as to why Hill would kill Morrison.[29]

Constitution, Art. 8, §9; State v. Benson, 46 Utah 74, 148 P. 445 (1915); United States v. Harris, 5 Utah 436 (1888).

The Sacco and Vanzetti case, which ended with the execution of the two defendants in 1927, has many parallels to the Hill case. One similarity between the two is the limited scope of authority of the appellate courts in both Utah and Massachusetts. As Felix Frankfurter states in *The Case of Sacco and Vanzetti* (Boston: Little, Brown and Co., 1961), p. 89, the Massachusetts Supreme Court could not retry guilt or innocence, nor could it inquire as to whether the facts as printed in the record justified the verdict.

These restrictions on the Utah Supreme Court's authority were, however, subject to a qualification which could conceivably have been used in the Hill case to reverse the jury's verdict if the court had been disposed to issue a reversal. While prohibited from passing judgment on the weight of evidence in a criminal case, it could determine whether or not the jury had entirely ignored the evidence. Legal precedent decreed that if the great preponderance of the evidence was against the verdict, the decision of the lower court might be reversed; but if there was "substantial" evidence in favor of the verdict, it should not be disturbed. Traditionally, this qualification was seldom employed, as the term "substantial" could be variously interpreted. State v. Brown, 36 Utah 46, 102 P. 641 (1909); State v. Lachall, 28 Utah 80, 77 P. 3 (1904); State v. Montgomery, 37 Utah 515, 109 P. 815 (1910).

Hilton and Christensen had argued that when these factors were properly considered there would remain no evidence to connect Hill with the murder. But the court, defining its role as determined by law, dismissed all the above contentions by simply stating, "It is apparent all this was for the jury."[30] This vividly shows the damage done to Joe Hill's case on the trial level.

After the supreme court had excised the heart of the defense's argument, it still had to establish its own opinion as to whether or not there was error in the trial and to find arguments with which to support the jury's verdict and the judge's decisions. The opinion was written by Chief Justice Straup.

The court conceded that the testimony given by Merlin Morrison, that one of the killers was about the same size as Joe Hill, was alone not sufficient to prove Hill was the murderer. But the court noted the additional testimony given by the lady witnesses who testified that Joe Hill was comparable in size to the taller of the killers and that Hill's voice was the same as that of the assailant who called out. However, the court said, even with this additional testimony, there was still insufficient proof of Hill's guilt.[31] It then cited Mrs. Seeley's statement that the man she saw and the defendant were alike in size, features, slim face, sharp nose, and scar on the face and neck. It contended that her detailed description connecting Hill with the man she saw, even though she had an honest doubt that Hill was the man, should be given more weight than a straightforward statement that Hill was the man, without the description.[32]

Straup next discussed what was, in the court's opinion, the clinching and necessary fact that proved Hill's guilt—the unsatisfactorily explained bullet wound. In context with the other evidence, the wound was a relevant mark identifying Hill as one of the killers. The court said Hill's unexplained wound was ". . . quite as much a distinguishing mark as though one of the assailants in the assault had had one of his ears chopped off."[33] Drawing a further analogy, the court stated:

> With other evidence in the case, that unexplained or unsatisfactorily explained wound might, to the triers of facts, point with as much certainty to the defendant as one of the perpetrators of the offense as though that night at 11:30 or 11 o'clock some stolen and identified article from the store had been found in his unexplained or unsatisfactorily explained possession.[34]

Clearly, the court felt that without the unexplained gunshot wound, all the testimony against Hill would not have been enough to convict him. The wound represented the significant and clinching factor which transformed the otherwise circumstantial evidence into direct evidence. But then the court, in a devious bit of circumlocution, reaffirmed Hill's constitutional right to be silent about his wound, saying that this could not be held to be an admission of guilt, that it did not prejudice his case in any way, and that the state was required to prove the defendant's guilt beyond all reasonable doubt. However, Hill could not, it claimed, ". . . avoid the natural and reasonable inferences deductible from proven facts by merely declining to take the stand."[35]

But what did the court consider the proven facts to be? It properly tried to put the burden of determining the facts on the jury, and the jury apparently accepted the testimony of the witnesses who testified that Hill and the murderer might be the same person. This the jury had the right to do. But according to the supreme court, the testimony that connected Hill with the murder and the inferences which could be drawn from that testimony were not enough to convict him. It was the unexplained gunshot wound that, when added to the testimony of witnesses, clinched the case against Joe Hill. The fault of the court's reasoning is that in making "natural and reasonable inferences" from the proven fact that Hill was wounded, the court inferred more than was natural and reasonable. The natural and reasonable inference that could be drawn from Hill's wound did not prove that he was wounded by Arling in Morrison's store. There was no evidence to show that Hill was not wounded at some other location, and it had never been conclusively proved that the gun found in the store had actually been fired. If there had been evidence such as the finding of a "chopped-off ear" in the store and the apprehension of a man with a recently chopped-off ear, a reasonable inference could have been made that the man had his ear chopped off in the store. In the Hill case, however, there was no such significant evidence connecting Hill with the murder. In fact the bullet that allegedly came from Arling's gun and passed through Hill's body was never found in the store. The court had to assume more than was warranted by the facts when it maintained that because Hill had an unexplained wound he was wounded during the killings; and, as the court itself said, this assumption had to be made to convict Hill.

The court disposed of the remaining issues with relative ease. As to the question of motive, it said: "Since the evidence is sufficient to show that the defendant was one of the perpetrators who, with his face masked and gun in hand, entered the store and deliberately shot his victim to death, it is immaterial to inquire whether the motive was assassination or robbery."[36]

Concerning the allegation that Hill was deprived of his right to choose his own counsel, the court said that he did have the right to discharge his counsel with or without cause. However, since he discharged them just before the examination of the important state witness, Mrs. Seeley, it would have been cruel to allow Hill to "stumble along" on his own without help. The cross-examination of Mrs. Seeley by Hill's discharged attorneys, the "friends of the court," aided Hill, argued the court, and thus justified Judge Ritchie's decision to have them continue as amici curiae.[37]

The alleged error of admitting testimony of Dr. Sprague from the preliminary hearing because proper diligence had not been used to subpoena him for the trial was dismissed when the court ruled that proper diligence had been used.[38]

The court also ruled that there were not improper restrictions on the examination of prospective jurors, and that the instructions given by the judge to the jury had not been in error.[39]

Justice Straup concluded the opinion by saying: "Thus on review of the record we are satisfied that there is sufficient evidence to support the verdict;

111

that the record is free from error; and that the defendant had a fair and impartial trial, in which he was granted every right and privilege vouchsafed by the law."[40]

Justice Frick and Justice McCarty wrote concurring opinions. Frick argued that Joe Hill's bullet wound was the differentiating factor between his case and the case referred to by Hill's attorneys in which a defendant was acquitted because of insufficient evidence identifying him as the criminal. Frick set forth some factors which he believed the jury had a right to assume when deciding the case. The first was that the jury could reasonably believe that if Hill had been shot as he claimed, someone would have heard the shot and reported it. Also, Frick believed the jury could justifiably hold that any reasonable human being would be willing to suffer almost any humiliation rather than indict an innocent man, ". . . and that any woman Hill was allegedly protecting would come forth if there were such a woman." He stated that a reasonable man, situated as was Joe Hill, would have told the authorities the circumstances of how he had been wounded.[41]

**Utah Supreme Court Justice
W. M. McCarty.**

Justice McCarty recounted the testimony of Mrs. Seeley, Nellie Mahan, and Vera Hansen, and argued that their testimony identified Joe Hill as the killer—an argument contrary to Straup's opinion that the testimony of these witnesses could not alone convict Hill.[42]

After the appeal had been denied, those supporting Joe Hill urged that his case be taken to the United States Supreme Court. Hill agreed. Writing to Elizabeth Gurley Flynn, he said, ". . . I am only a drop in the bucket and this is a fight where individuals don't count. My right hand was shot all to splinters anyway when I was arrested and it doesn't matter much where I go to but to tell you the truth I hate to lay down as long as there is a fighting chance."[43]

The case, however, was never appealed to the United States Supreme Court. Since there was no federal consideration in the case, his attorneys apparently thought it would be useless to attempt an appeal.

The question of Joe Hill's guilt or innocence is no more certain today than it was in 1915. After reviewing all available records, however, there is considerable reason to believe that Hill was denied justice in the courts of Utah, and that there was still reasonable doubt as to his guilt after the district court and the supreme court had consigned him to the firing squad. Although there was a climate of opinion in Salt Lake City hostile to the I.W.W. and Hill, it does not seem that prejudice appreciably affected the trial court or the supreme court in their respective decisions. Rather, it seems that injustice resulted from a breakdown of the adversary system of trying law cases. Hill's case was almost certainly a fluke turned out by the judicial machinery.

The reason for the breakdown can be found partly in the difficulty facing a financially and socially inconsequential migrant worker who had to conduct an adequate defense at trial in 1914. In Hill's case, this handicap was compounded by ideological and personal characteristics of the man. While imbued with the I.W.W. desire to radically change society, Hill paradoxically seemed to have naïve faith in the abstract concept of justice.

It seems, in retrospect, that one who was considered by his friends to be a "prisoner of the class war," given the handicaps of his situation and his skeptical attitude about being dealt with fairly by his presumed enemies, should have taken it upon himself to be resourceful and to present the best case possible in his defense. Hill, however, seems to have believed that he would be dealt with justly, regardless of what he did as a defendant. He continually presented his worst side, making mistakes from the beginning. In the preliminary hearing he was his own counsel; he asked only three questions in cross-examination; he had no witnesses of his own. In the district court, with two shy and inexperienced attorneys, he was obstinate and uncooperative. He attempted to dismiss his lawyers and argued with the court while the jurors looked on. His counsel made a serious mistake in summation. Thus, when the case reached the supreme court, irreparable damage to Hill's chances of being found innocent under the evidence had already been done by the jury's decision against him on important matters of fact. Limited by the statute governing its authority, the supreme court reaffirmed the jury's decision using the specious argument that, given the various circumstances of the case, a natural inference to be made from Hill's wound was that he had been wounded in Morrison's store.

The difficult thing to understand, if Hill was innocent, is why he did not exert every effort to save himself by allowing his friends to secure competent counsel, beginning with the preliminary hearing, and by accounting for his wound. Instead, Hill made sardonic comments about the injustice of his treatment and statements about the righteousness of his cause, while at the same time he seems to have viewed justice as existing quite apart from the practical

113

necessity of presenting a convincing case before the jury. Hill may have been a guilty man seeking to create for himself a martyr image, or an idealistic and unusually stubborn man who insisted upon taking literally the doctrine that a man is presumed innocent until he is beyond all reasonable doubt proved guilty.

Utah
the Wobblies
and
Joe Hill

6 To understand the controversy and
bitterness surrounding Hill's case as it moved through the Utah courts, it is important to know something of the tradition of conflict into which Hill was thrust when, shortly after his arrest, it was discovered that he was a member of the Industrial Workers of the World.

The I.W.W. aroused inordinate animosity in Utah as throughout the rest of the nation. Although the organization did not advocate violence, its goal to radically change the existing political and economic structure resulted in the condemnation of the Wobblies as undesirable revolutionaries. Across America, as Max Eastman wrote in 1914, "The church, the press, the state, the host of the people in this country hate the I.W.W., and they rejoice in every occasion when they can spit upon it. They hate it with a hatred beyond all proportion to its menace against privilege, or against property, or against law and order."[1]

The contention that Joe Hill was framed on a murder charge by the business, political, and religious establishment of Utah flourished after his death. This contention gains meaning from the underlying and overt bitterness toward the I.W.W. and Hill existing in Utah, for by 1914, when Joe Hill was on trial for his life, previous conflicts between business and labor had created an environment so filled with suspicion and hatred that it was possible for the Wobblies to interpret his conviction as nothing less than a direct conspiracy to rid Utah of Hill and to strike a blow at the organization he represented.

The labor disputes that did the most to create the acrimony surrounding Hill's case began in 1912 when miners struck in Bingham Canyon, a mining camp located in the Oquirrh Mountains west of Salt Lake City. At that time the great majority of Bingham miners were recent immigrants, with Greeks the largest nationality group. Because of the hostility of the mine owners, labor organizers worked undercover and union membership was not large. I.W.W. power was negligible, and the Western Federation of Miners claimed only 250 members in the summer of 1912 shortly before the strike began.

Conditions at Bingham were ripe for spontaneous protest, however. Greek miners worked under the "padrone" system in which a labor agent supplied jobs to immigrants for an initial fee and often an added monthly fee. The agent for the copper companies, Leonidas Skliris, whose contacts throughout the West could have men traveling to a job upon his command, was especially hated. For two years the Greeks had tried to expose Skliris, but mine officials denied the existence of the padrone system, saying that no one had to pay to get a job at Bingham. Then, in May 1912, the W.F.M. called a strike at a nearby Murray, Utah, smelter which idled more than eight hundred men for six weeks and which was eventually broken by strikebreakers supplied by Skliris. This strikebreaking incident enraged the Bingham miners and left them emotionally ready for a strike. Membership in the W.F.M. reportedly jumped from 250 in July 1912 to 2,500 in October because the union offered the Greek miners promise of release from Skliris.[2]

In September 1912, the W.F.M. asked the Bingham copper companies for a fifty cent per day pay increase and recognition of the union as a bargaining agent. W.F.M. president Charles Moyer, opposing an immediate strike, traveled to Utah to confer with company officials, who refused to see him. However, the miners voted an immediate strike which affected 4,800 men, and Moyer remained to press the union's demands.

Strikers equipped themselves with guns and blankets and took up positions on the mountain across from the mine where they could forcibly repel strikebreakers the company threatened to import. Mine owners reacted by offering an immediate twenty-five cent a day pay increase, but refused to negotiate with the union, charging union leaders with precipitating the strike. In Salt Lake City, Governor William Spry threatened violence if the miners did not surrender their position on the mountain. He and seventy-five armed deputies descended on Bingham to enforce the threat, but the miners stood firm.

Finally, the Greek miners were persuaded to meet with Spry and company officials and said they would return to work at existing wages if Utah Copper would agree not to deal with Skliris. The company responded by again denying the existence of the padrone system and defending Skliris. Governor Spry was unable to offer any comfort and the miners angrily left to continue the strike.[3]

Additional deputies were brought in from Salt Lake City, and Skliris began recruiting strikebreakers, who, in spite of the efforts of the strikers to keep them out, began filtering into town. Responding to the charges against him, Skliris publicly offered to pay 5,000 dollars to anyone who could prove charges of extortion. When a spokesman for the Greek miners responded to this offer, Skliris suddenly fled to Mexico. At this point the overjoyed Greeks were ready to return to work, but Moyer persuaded them to stand behind the union's demands—so the strike continued.[4]

By October 10, work had resumed at the largest mines, using strikebreakers protected by company deputies led by Axel Steele. The strike dragged unsuccessfully on—with several outbreaks of violence between strikers and company deputies—toward the November 15 expiration date of the strikebreakers' contracts, at which time the workers hoped the company would capitulate. But November 15 arrived with no change in the company's attitude. The workers gradually returned to work without having achieved recognition for the union. The strike was not a complete failure, however, because the company granted pay raises of from twenty to twenty-five cents a day, the hated padrone system was gone, and the W.F.M. had gained considerable membership at Bingham.[5]

There is no evidence that the Industrial Workers of the World were involved in this strike, even though the I.W.W. was beginning to organize in Bingham and a man named Louis Theodoropoulos was reportedly known among Greek miners as an I.W.W. organizer.[6] A. S. Embree, a minister turned I.W.W. organizer, claimed that, ". . . if the Bingham strike had been taken in hand by the I.W.W. the advantage seized at the start would not have been thrown away."[7]

It is almost certain that Joe Hill was not involved at Bingham, although later, during the campaign to save him from execution, it was claimed by some of his supporters that he was "framed on a murder charge" because of his organizing activities at Bingham and because his songs incited miners there to strike. A verse of the song "I Dreamed I Saw Joe Hill Last Night," written after his death, keeps that story alive today:

> "The copper bosses killed you, Joe,
> They shot you Joe," says I.
> "Takes more than guns to kill a man."
> Says Joe, "I didn't die."
> Says Joe, "I didn't die."[8]

Although it was not responsible for the Bingham strike of 1912, the I.W.W. did extend its influence into the Utah mining towns of Park City and Eureka, and later into Bingham in competition with the W.F.M. Critical of the inability of the W.F.M. to organize a strike for higher wages in Park City, Lee Pratt of Salt Lake City I.W.W. Local Sixty-nine complained that underpaid workers couldn't strike for fear that unemployed workers would take their jobs. Claiming that the W.F.M. divided the "slaves" in Park City by making contracts with the "bosses," he advised: "Don't fight among yourselves, let the workers as a class fight the bosses as a class."[9]

In 1913 the I.W.W. instigated a strike near the small central Utah town of Tucker against railroad track-laying operations of the Utah Construction Company. Again, there is no evidence that Joe Hill was involved. The strike was called because working conditions were bad and pay was low. The workers had several demands: a twenty-five cent per day increase in pay, a shorter working day of nine rather than twelve hours, improvement of bathing and laundry facilities, free bunks and bedding, and abolishment of monthly hospital fees since Utah Construction had no hospital at Tucker.[10] The company reacted to the strike by sending fifty armed "guards" to Tucker led by Axel Steele, the same man who led the company deputies at Bingham.[11] The company gunmen removed 160 supposed agitators led by James Morgan. These men were taken by special train to jail in Provo, Utah. Morgan and a few other leaders were kept in jail; the others were sent to Salt Lake City where, with other I.W.W. members and sympathizers, they held a protest meeting which culminated in a parade and speeches at a public park.[12] "Mutterings of a general strike" filled the air.[13]

Officials of Utah Construction Company maintained that conditions in the Tucker camp were not as bad as the Wobblies claimed and that over a thousand men were satisfied ". . . until this I.W.W. agitation."[14] The *Salt Lake Tribune* reported on conditions in Tucker after the "guards" had deported the agitators. "With the dove of peace hovering over the strike district at Tucker, and a sufficient force of deputy sheriffs to insure its not being frightened into flight, the scene of official operations was shifted to Salt Lake City."[15]

Many viewed this outburst of I.W.W. activity with hostility, but the strike did not collapse when it met resistance. The *Salt Lake Tribune*, interviewing a group of strikers, quoted Hill's acquaintance, Mac McClintock.

118

> . . . The fight has only begun. We are accused of having precipitated the strike with only one hundred and fifty men. If we did that, it speaks well for our effectiveness. We can easily command one thousand men for use in the Tucker strike who are dyed-in-the-wool I.W.W. They have learned how to win by going to jail and will cheerfully take the jail route to victory.[16]

Mac McClintock (wearing beret),
a leading agitator at the Tucker strike.

The *Industrial Worker*, an I.W.W. newspaper published in Spokane, Washington, gave its version of the strike: "Five hundred slaves under the banner of the I.W.W. have revolted against unbearable conditions existing in camps of the Utah Construction Company and their subcontractors at Tucker, Utah. The men have put up with bad food and unsanitary conditions for a year and have now turned to the I.W.W. as the only means of improving their living conditions."[17] Later, the *Industrial Worker* called for all "Wobs" in the West to migrate to Tucker to help the cause, admonishing them to "Wear your wooden shoes to Tucker."[18]

Solidarity, in statements similar to those made two years later in denouncing Utah's treatment of Joe Hill, charged that the Wobbly strikers were being "... railroaded into jail on trumped-up false charges and framed-up evidence," and that Utah Construction Company was a "robber corporation," and "another name for the Mormon Church."[19]

The Tucker strike was ended by midsummer of 1913. The I.W.W. was able to gain a twenty-five cent a day pay raise and some improvement in camp conditions, including beds and blankets for the workers. *Solidarity* claimed the Tucker strike as a clear victory for the I.W.W., a proof of the value of "direct action" in the war against the capitalists.[20] Conversely, many Utahns viewed the Wobblies' success with alarm, fearing further union activity.

A by-product of the Tucker strike which considerably heightened animosity between the organization's supporters and detractors was an attack made on Wobbly leader James Morgan in downtown Salt Lake City by Axel Steele. At the time of the attack, Tuesday night, August 12, 1913, Steele was again employed as a special deputy for the Utah Copper Company. Morgan, released from jail in Provo the day before, arrived in Salt Lake City on the night of August 12 and organized an I.W.W. street meeting in which he planned to denounce the role of Steele and his company deputies in the Tucker strike. Learning of the meeting, Steele and several comrades gathered in a saloon across the street from where it was to be held and plotted revenge. They drew lots for the privilege of striking Morgan first and decided on a signal—the waving of the American flag by Steele—to begin their attack.[21]

The meeting began with the assembled Wobs singing Joe Hill's song, "Mr. Block." Morgan then mounted a soapbox and began his oration. As he spoke, Axel Steele pushed to the center of the crowd, tore the I.W.W. banner from its mooring, and unfurled the American flag.[22] At this signal, the man who had won the right to assault Morgan first hit him from the rear, knocking him from the box. Six men jumped on Morgan's attacker and began beating him. More of Steele's men began attacking I.W.W. members in the audience. Wobbly Thomas Murphy drew a gun and fired—in self-defense as he said—at four of his assailants. Murphy was later prosecuted and convicted on a charge of assault with intent to commit murder.[23]

According to a newsman at the scene, Morgan, with blood streaming from his face and the back of his head, remounted the soapbox and resumed his speech, although he was forced to stop every few moments to wipe the blood from his mouth and eyes. When the police arrived, Axel Steele dragged Morgan from the platform and forced him into a police car. Morgan reportedly continued his oration all the way to the police station. The fire department dispersed the crowd by spraying them with streams of water.[24]

The reaction of the police, the Salt Lake City press, and the citizenry to Steele's attack on Morgan shows that a professional "deputy" like Axel Steele could break the law and receive the sympathy, if not the sanction, of many in Salt Lake City by literally wrapping his actions in the American flag and claiming that his attack on the I.W.W. was an act of patriotism. No charges were filed against Steele even though he was known to be the instigator of the riot. Morgan was arrested and held on charges arising from the incident, as were six other Wobblies.[25] Police Chief Grant said he would allow no more I.W.W. street meetings in Salt Lake City.[26] An editorial in the *Salt Lake Tribune*, while identifying Steele as the aggressor, excused his actions as only "natural" in view of I.W.W. provocation.

> Mr. Steele was clearly the aggressor in this riot, and was aided and abetted by a number of personal friends. The streets of Salt Lake City are no place for the violent pursuit of private animosities.
>
> As for the I.W.W., that organization is fast getting to be a universal menace to the public peace, a standing threat against the good order of the community everywhere. Wherever its membership appears there are riots and fighting. Secretary Haywood in his speech in this city distinctly stated that his organization was at war with the government. Nothing is more natural than that an organization that is at war with the government should provoke condemnation from loyal citizens and incite riot and bloodshed.[27]

The conflict between Steele and Morgan occasioned comment from *Solidarity*, which claimed that Morgan arrived in Salt Lake City from Provo after ". . . having satisfied the powerful interests responsible for his arrest." Upon arrival, he was assaulted by Axel Steele, a ". . . notorious gunman and the principal hireling of the largest Utah corporations in their unrelenting attempt to humiliate and crush the workmen in Utah."[28]

Local Sixty-nine of the I.W.W., drawing impetus from the success of the Tucker strike, increased its agitation in the Salt Lake City area during 1913. Its secretary and leader, Ed Rowan, expressed the organization's view of conditions in Utah in a *Solidarity* article published just a few days before Joe Hill was arrested for murder. "The glorious west," said Rowan, "is pictured in glowing colors by advertising the beauties, freedom, and prosperity of Utah." However, he claimed, recent events involving labor had exposed the fact that in Utah, just as in other states, ". . . the moment the workers organize for material benefits on the job, not a stone is left unturned to use any means violent or otherwise to thwart them." Concluding, he cautioned, ". . . concerted action is now going on all over the country to imprison members of our organization."[29]

Judging from their later statements, the Wobblies considered Joe Hill's arrest to be part of such a "concerted action" to imprison I.W.W. members. It seems very doubtful, however, that the Salt Lake police could have known of Hill's I.W.W. connection at the time he was arrested, although they learned of it shortly thereafter when they received an answer from the San Pedro police to their letter inquiring about Otto Applequist.

> I see by the papers that you have under arrest one Joe Hillstrom, a partner of Applequist's, held on suspicion. You have the right man. They held up a street car here in San Pedro last May and left town the same night. Hillstrom returned and on June 4, 1913, I arrested him, but neither the car crew nor any of the passengers were able to identify him as he had his face covered with a black veil.
>
> I recovered the veil, hat and overcoat which Hillstrom wore at the time of the holdup, which was identified by the conductor.
>
> Hillstrom pleaded guilty to a charge of vagrancy and served thirty days in city jail.

He is certainly an undesirable citizen, and is in the United States unlawfully. He is somewhat of a musician and is a writer of songs for the I.W.W. song book.[30]

Once his connections with the I.W.W. became known, Hill was cast into the tradition of conflict which had been created by the Bingham strike, the Tucker strike, and the attack on Morgan. The letter from the San Pedro police also indicated he had a criminal background—an unfortunate implication, as no evidence was ever found to support it. Hill later explained his San Pedro arrest in a letter to the *Salt Lake Telegram*.

In spite of all the hideous pictures and all the bad things said and printed about me, I had only been arrested once before in my life, and that was in San Pedro, Cal. At the time of the stevedores' and dockworkers' strike I was secretary of the strike committee, and I suppose I was a little too active to suit the chief of that burg, so he arrested me and gave me thirty days in the city jail for "vagrancy"—and there you have the full extent of my "criminal record."[31]

During and after his trial Hill was vilified by the many who considered him a criminal and his organization anathema, while he was supported and eulogized by the Wobblies, who considered his arrest a farce designed to harass the union. Once Joe Hill's reluctance to accept I.W.W. aid had been overcome, the organization, believing him innocent of all crimes except that of "helping the cause of the worker," threw its influence into his defense. On April 18, 1914, two months before the trial began, a public appeal for help appeared in *Solidarity*. Prior to this, Ed Rowan had written Hill's friends in San Francisco asking for financial assistance to obtain a competent lawyer.[32] The San Francisco Wobblies established a Joe Hill Defense Committee and issued the April 18 appeal jointly with Salt Lake City Local Sixty-nine.

**The man who wrote "Mr. Block" and "Casey Jones"
caught and held on trumped-up charges**

The master class have again shown their hand, in a dastardly attempt to railroad to the gallows in a deal such as the hirelings of the master class know how to frame up, one of the best known men in the movement. They have picked for their victim a man who is beloved by all who know him; one who at all times has worked untiringly for the cause of industrial freedom; who has contributed his time and energy and to our knowledge has never received anything for his services to this organization.

Time has always found him on the job wherever there was need for active rebels, and ever ready to come to the aid of his fellow workers. That his efforts have brought results is proven beyond a doubt, and can be measured in terms of dollars and cents for those who measure the accomplishments of their fellow men in these terms; but who will attempt to calculate the benefits or the members attracted by the propaganda of industrial unionism? The only way we can estimate it is through the storm of abuse and the gallons of ink spilled by the prostitutes of the press in the criticisms and abuse heaped on the author of "Mr. Block." Now there is not one in this organization who can say he does not know this man. For wherever rebels meet, the name of fellow worker Joe Hill is known. Though we may not know him personally, what one among us can say he is not on speaking terms with "Scissor Bill," "Mr. Block," or who has not heard the "White Slave," or listened to the rendering of the famous "Casey Jones" song, and many others in the little red song book.

The time has come to show that we appreciate the work of this fellow worker. Fellow worker Hill has been active in the Salt Lake area among the slaves of the Utah Copper Company and the Utah Construction Company, who we all know are merely adjuncts to the Mormon church. The I.W.W. has been a thorn in the side of the masters in the Salt Lake district. The latter are still smarting under the sting of the publicity they received during the Tucker fight, and desiring to rid themselves of a man they consider a dangerous agitator they have taken the opportunity to attempt to fasten the murder of an ex-policeman on to fellow worker Joe Hill.

They have bent every effort since January 10 to weave a chain of evidence around him, but so far all they have is a flimsy bunch of circumstantial dope cooked up in the office of the hirelings of the Mormon church. The son of the dead man, who was present when the killing took place, has failed to identify Hill as the man who killed his father, and has in many other ways strengthened the defense.

Now when the police failed to connect him directly, they attempted to blacken the name of fellow worker Hill and prejudice the public against him. They wrote to San Pedro, California, where Hill worked among the transport workers, in an endeavor to get something against him. The Chief of Police informed them that Hill was an undesirable character. To prove that, the Chief stated that Hill was an I.W.W. agitator and the author of the I.W.W. songs. What more is needed to convict him?

Fellow workers it is up to us to get busy; form choruses to sing Hill's songs on the streets and take up collections, give away song books, and send fifty percent to the defense of Joe Hill. Let every rebel who feels that the movement will lose heavily should the masters succeed in sending Joe Hill to the gallows get busy.[33]

It was recommended that all funds be sent to Ed Rowan in Salt Lake City; songbooks were to be ordered from the San Francisco Joe Hill Defense Committee, composed of Al Hall, Frank Buncman, and Harry Blehr.

Years later, Ralph Chaplin described his reaction to this first public announcement of Hill's arrest.

My weekly copy of *Solidarity* carried a small but devastating headline announcing the arrest of Joe Hill in Salt Lake City. He was charged with the murder of a local grocery man named Morrison. The story as presented was rather muddled, but it was taken for granted that this was another "capitalist frame up," a statement with which I was strongly inclined to agree. Joe Hill, in addition to being my exemplar in the field of proletarian song, was a dreamer, an artist, an idealist—the last person in the world anyone could suspect of wanting to kill anybody. For me the news of his arrest during an I.W.W. organizational drive was bitter medicine. I could not shake from my mind the picture of Joe Hill sitting behind bars in a prison cell. Was there no end to capitalist atrocities?[34]

In the second public appeal for help, printed in the May 23, 1914, issue of *Solidarity*, Ed Rowan reported that he had already received two hundred dollars in Hill's behalf. Appearing with Rowan's statement was a letter from Hill's two original attorneys, Scott and McDougall, who said:

The main thing the state has against Hill is that he is an I.W.W. and therefore sure to be guilty. Hill tried to keep the I.W.W. out of it and denied it, but the papers fastened it on him. For this reason he is entitled to be helped and not allowed to hang for being an I.W.W. Every man is presumed innocent until proven guilty. It should not be necessary for him to prove his innocence and it would not be if he were not an I.W.W.[35]

After Hill was found guilty, *Solidarity* reviewed the state's evidence and, concluding that his conviction was unjust, asked ". . . the many thousands who know Joe through his songs" to respond with aid in his behalf.[36] The appeals for help appearing in *Solidarity* were the forerunners of a deluge of articles, songs, poems, letters, and petitions seeking to help Hill.

Before the filing of an appeal to the supreme court invalidated the original execution date of September 4, 1914, William D. Haywood, general secretary of the I.W.W., wrote an essay graphically depicting the tragedy that would occur when Joe Hill was "judicially murdered."

> On that morning as dawn breaks behind the Wasatch mountains, Joe will be led from the condemned cell into the yard. Surrounded by guards he will be seated upon a rough pine box—his coffin—a bandage will be placed over his eyes, a heart shaped target will be pinned on his left breast over his pulsing, joyful, strong, young heart. A firing squad of six men with five loaded rifles will take their places, with guns to their shoulders. At a signal from the warden, the six hired executioners will pull the trigger, five bullets will tear through the heart of Joe Hill, his tuneful tongue will be silenced forever. No more will his voice be heard in the jungle, in the hall, or on the job.
>
> They are going to kill Joe Hill; he was convicted of murder on the flimsiest kind of circumstantial evidence. If the state takes his life there will be no extenuating circumstances in its favor, except to have killed a man who had done much to solidify the working class.

Haywood urged his readers to raise funds to finance Hill's appeal for a new trial and to write to Governor Spry of Utah.[37]

Ralph Chaplin's "Joe Hill," which appeared in the September 12, 1914, issue of *Solidarity*, was the first of many poems about Hill.

A rebel we have known for long,
Who's thrilled us often with his song,
Has fallen on an evil day—
They seek to take his life away!

They'd fill his warrior heart with lead
And gloat to see him safely dead—
His voice for ever hushed and still,
Our singing, fighting brave Joe Hill!

His spirit glorified in the fight—
In labor's sure resistless might;
And one big union, staunch and strong,
This was the burden of his song.

His heart was hot with burning hate
Against the bosses, small and great;
He told what haughty Sab-cats do,
And all about the wooden-shoe.

The "Long-haired preachers" feared his name.
He filled apologies with shame;
While "Mr. Block" so bland and meek
With "Scissor-Bill" did take a sneak.

Now boys, we've known this rebel long—
In every land we've sung his song—
Let's get him free and he may see
The day of our great victory!

123

He made them hate him high and low,
They feared his tuneful message so;
He'd fight for us while he had breath—
We'll save him from the jaws of death.

    No harm to him can we allow,
    He needs our help and needs it now;
    He's in their dungeon, dark and grim—
    He fought for us; we'll stand by him.[38]

The September 26, 1914, issue of *Solidarity* carried the argument of the I.W.W. in Salt Lake City that Joe Hill's arrest was part of a series of retaliatory acts against Wobblies by the capitalists of Utah. Stressing that 1913 had been a "banner year" for the organization, the article explained that a membership of over three hundred, "all militants," had made the I.W.W.'s influence increasingly felt in agitation on the job and in the Labor Council. "Then came the Tucker strike, in which two thousand of the despised 'shovel stiffs,' American and foreign, threw down their tools and walked out. The M. and M. [Merchants and Manufacturers] were thunderstruck." After that ". . . steps were taken to smash the I.W.W.'s solidarity." First came the attack on James Morgan, then the periodic arrests of members of Local Sixty-nine on various "trumped-up" charges. Throughout Utah, bosses employed the blacklist system against organization members. Viewing the arrest of Joe Hill as another instance of persecution, the article charged, "Joe Hill's case is a clear attempt on the part of the police to have him shot without a shadow of evidence to connect him with the crime."[39]

Throughout America there was a sympathetic reaction to the appeals for help. On August 29, 1914, a protest meeting was held in Union Square in New York City. A resolution adopted by the assembly and sent to Governor William Spry of Utah expressed the opinion that Joe Hill had been "railroaded on flimsy evidence" and that Governor Spry would be "considered the agent of a reactionary state" if he did not act to free Hill.[40] In Minneapolis, Minnesota, a meeting was held at which "every chair was taken in a large hall" and "all went home rejoicing in the fact that they had done their share toward liberating the innocent victim Joe Hill who is lying in the dungeon of the Salt Lake City jail with the tentacles of capitalism wound tightly around him."[41] In December 1914, a British branch of the I.W.W. met in London to collect funds for Hill's defense. The audience was told that Joe Hill had been arrested in Salt Lake City in retribution for the Wobbly-inspired strike at Tucker, Utah. Several of Hill's songs were sung, money was collected for the defense, and a resolution was adopted which ". . . demanded the unconditional release of Joe Hill."[42] Late in 1914, *Solidarity* began advertising a new edition of the "Little Red Song Book," which was to be the Joe Hill edition.[43]

I.W.W. agitation continued into 1915, reaching a climax in November of that year. Early in 1915, the Salt Lake City Wobblies, in conjunction with the Salt Lake League for the Unemployed, conducted a demonstration which was probably detrimental to Hill's cause as it served only to keep the "I.W.W. issue"

124

before the citizens of Utah. The Utah legislature was considering an appropria-
tion bill to provide public works jobs for the state's unemployed; the demonstration was held to encourage its passage. A parade of about seven hundred
persons carrying signs reading "We Want Work, Not Charity" and "We Will Not
Work on the Chain Gang" was stopped by police on its way to the state capitol.
A police van was summoned. When one man was put inside, others, both men
and women, insisted on filling the wagon. The remainder of the marchers
changed course and paraded to the jail, where the police decided to free them

One of three pictures of Joe Hill
appearing in the "Little Red Song Book."

all. The parade then continued to the steps of the state capitol where several
songs were sung, including "Red Flag," "The Tramp," "One Big Industrial Union," and "Hallelujah! I'm a Bum." These efforts evidently did not have much
influence on the legislature for, as *Solidarity* reported, "the slimy politicians"
voted the bill down.[44]

In the spring of 1915, Elizabeth Gurley Flynn* arrived in Salt Lake City
to visit Joe Hill who was in the county jail awaiting the Utah Supreme Court's
hearing of his case. Her visit was a significant milestone in the I.W.W.'s support
of Hill; after the account of their conversation was published in *Solidarity*,
there was little doubt that the I.W.W. would expend unlimited effort to sup-

---

* Miss Flynn, the foremost woman organizer in the I.W.W. and an influential leader in
that organization, subsequently joined the American Communist Party and was serving as an
officer at the time of her death in 1964.

port Hill and herald him as a symbol of courage, idealism, and exemplary radical spirit. Poetically, Miss Flynn recorded her impressions of the meeting.

126

> Salt Lake City is a garden city, encircled by great mountains, crowned with eternal snows. In the springtime its green shimmer, high altitude, clear, pure air and leisurely moving people should be ennobling and inspiring to one [and a place] from whence the easterner is not pleased to terminate. . . .
>
> But this superficial impression is rapidly dispelled by a visit to that cornerstone of civilization the county jail.
>
> At the doorway of the low-visaged structure, squatted in behind residences, the familiar, fetid jail odor assails the nostrils and the clang of the keys, the surly permission to enter, the damp, tomblike air within, welcomes us to the compulsory abode of the free spirit under capitalism.
>
> It was indeed a free spirit that drew us there—Joe Hill, the inimitable songster and poet of the I.W.W. . . . They have accused him of an ignoble act, murder for petty theft, and they lied and lied until they've hypnotized themselves into believing it. So when he came to us he was guarded on all sides by deputies, he came with a smile and a cheery greeting, with the cleareyed look of one who cannot be crushed. He is tall, good looking, but naturally thin after sixteen months in a dark narrow cell, with a corridor and another row of cells between him and daylight, and nourished by the soup and bean diet of a prison. Yet he writes constantly and his latest jail product "The Rebel Girl" is judged by many as his most beautiful. . . . Joe Hill had nothing to say about his case, or himself, but wanted to know about the I.W.W., its growth, outlook, its contemplated work in the harvest, *Solidarity*, and Margaret Sanger's case, etc. And so the hour was spent in giving him the news of the movement, and a few words of encouragement about his fight for life. I've seen men more worried about a six month's sentence than Joe Hill apparently worries about his life. He only said: "I'm not afraid of death, but I'd like to be in the fight a little longer."
>
> He's a true soldier in the army of labor, philosophically accepting the status of a prisoner of war and the possibility of death. But, shall we fellow workers accept it with him so lightly?
>
> When I came out into the blinding sunshine, a cold hand gripped my heart. Was I leaving a tomb? Would he ever "be in the fight a little longer?" Nor is this concern for the individual exclusively, although I see no reason why we shouldn't exhaust our defense resources for every individual; but it's the realization that Joe Hill typifies to the employer the I.W.W. and if he can be murdered legally, so can every other agitator and organizer out here in short order.
>
> Can we afford to give up our Joe Hill without a struggle? While I was in Salt Lake City, I saw a telegram from the attorneys pressing the committee for funds, $660 is still due, half of which the committee has. A stupid, sentimental story was published that "a woman of unlimited means" is backing the case. There is no truth in this, it is merely the fabrication of a romantic reporter. But I was surprised to know that members throughout the country believe it and are under the delusion that the committee has plenty of money. Three hundred dollars is needed quickly and fellow workers should realize that even if the appeal is granted it will not mean necessarily his release, but a new trial, the expense of which will have to be met.
>
> Joe Hill didn't ask the I.W.W. to fight for him; he was in jail months before he'd consent to the local's taking up his case. So this appeal is not from him, but in the spirit of:
>
> > "He's in their dungeon, dark and grim;
> > He stood by us, we'll stand by him!"
>
> As a matter of fact he hasn't been told how low the funds actually are, and it's up to us to make it unnecessary.
>
> I appeal to you—help Joe Hill to fan the flames of discontent, "to fight and sing a little longer!"[45]

When the Utah Supreme Court upheld the verdict of the district court, the admonitions and protests in support of Hill increased. On July 17, 1915, *Solidarity* expressed the sense of urgency Hill's supporters must have felt. "Do something and do it quick. Hold protest meetings, send resolutions of protest to Governor Spry. Raise funds and give the case the utmost publicity. Act now before it's too late."[46]

The belief that Joe Hill was unjustly convicted spread to non-I.W.W. liberal and radical organizations and publications. Reflecting the Wobbly propaganda, *Appeal to Reason*, a socialist newspaper printed in Girard, Kansas, which claimed the largest circulation of any socialist publication at the time, carried an article which declared, "The persecution of Joe Hill is a clear case of infamous injustice. He was boldly railroaded by an unfair, farcical trial in a community where public sentiment was inflamed against him because he had been a conspicuous leader of local strikes."[47]

During the summer of 1915, several meetings were held in cities across America to rally support for Hill and collect funds for his defense. At a meeting in Chicago chaired by Vincent St. John, a prominent I.W.W. leader, Meyer Friedkin of the Hill Defense Committee in Salt Lake City proclaimed that Hill's ability to "... inspire the mob with songs, poetry, and prose which raise the spirit of rebellion" was the reason for the "... blood-thirsty desire of the capitalist class to do away with fellow-worker Hill."[48] At a meeting in San Francisco, Austin Lewis, a lawyer and writer on syndicalism, recited the facts of the Joe Hill case and concluded he was unjustly convicted. A resolution was then adopted and sent to the governor of Utah.

> We working men and women of San Francisco in mass meeting assembled, hereby notify you that we hold you personally responsible for the life and freedom of Joe Hill now under sentence of death in Utah, and we hereby promise him our moral, financial, and physical support.

Solidarity, reporting on the meeting, recommended the spirit of the resolution to all its readers.

> If all locals would do the same we would find that the Governor and Supreme Court judges who have so ignominiously refused to recognize us in the past on account of our inferior strength would be more willing to consider our demands, because what they dread is the destruction of that which makes them our economic masters. Consequently, if such resolutions are carried out to the letter the masters may have a rather peculiar emotional reverberation through their spinal columns, and will be more apt to listen and consider the advisability of quitting the slaughter of men for that very rash offense of belonging to a radical organization.[49]

The foregoing statements are examples of the significant body of literature and spoken opinion which argued that Hill was innocent, the victim of unjust treatment. As other organizations, publications, and individuals became aware of his plight and were convinced he was innocent, the original I.W.W. interpretation of the facts of the case was transmitted throughout the world. Eventually this interpretation—an innocent worker, unjustly convicted by cap-

127

italist bosses because of his radical activities—became a significant element in the folk hero image of Joe Hill.

The I.W.W. further protested that it was being persecuted by Utah law when on October 30, 1915, during the height of the "Save Joe Hill" campaign, a member of the organization, R. J. Horton, was shot and killed in downtown Salt Lake City by Police Major H. P. Myton.

Myton had arrested Horton in the past and there was hostility between them. The two men were quarreling, and as he testified at his trial, Myton went angrily to his room, pocketed his revolver, and returned to the street. Witnesses reported that Myton and Horton were arguing; Myton had his gun pointed at Horton, who told the officer to put the gun away, saying, "A man who would pack a star is no good and that goes for you."

128

> MYTON: *What do you mean by these insinuations?*
>
> HORTON: *That is meant for you and any other son-of-a-bitch who will wear a star.*
>
> MYTON: *I'll kill you for that.*

Then, as Horton reportedly moved to strike the policeman, Myton fired three times, killing him.[50]

Myton was charged with first degree murder by the county attorney, with Patrolman J. C. Anderson signing the complaint. Habeas corpus proceedings were initiated immediately by Myton's attorney to have his client released on bail. District Attorney Leatherwood, again the prosecutor, opposed the proceedings, saying that although Major Myton was a good friend of his, before the law he ". . . is no better than the humblest citizen, and I must insist that the law be carried out in regular procedure." Leatherwood added, "There is an element here preaching on the streets that the laws are not enforced impartially toward all men," and insisted that a preliminary hearing be held before the question of bail was discussed.[51]

At the preliminary hearing presided over by Justice L. R. Martineau, it was decided that Myton should stand trial on a charge of voluntary manslaughter, not first degree murder. Bail set at 3,500 dollars was paid, and Myton was released.

The press reported that Myton then went to the Elks Club where he received congratulations from his friends.[52]

Leatherwood charged that the preliminary hearing was irregular, claiming that since Myton had been charged with first degree murder, Martineau had no authority to bind him over on a charge of voluntary manslaughter. The charge of voluntary manslaughter, he insisted, dismissed the original charge of murder which included all degrees of homicide.[53]

The matter was referred to Judge Ritchie for his consideration, and it was decided that Justice Martineau should hold another hearing. As a result of the second hearing, Major Myton was bound over to the Third District Court to stand trial for the further reduced charge of involuntary manslaughter. Because

Myton had for many years been bailiff in the Third District Court and was well known, the district judges asked to be excused from sitting in the case. The matter was finally brought to trial before Judge Call of the First District on February 16, 1916. Myton testified in his own behalf, claiming self-defense, and was acquitted by the jury after three hours' deliberation.[54]

The I.W.W. presided over Horton's funeral. Songs were sung, and several speakers, among them Ed Rowan and Virginia Snow Stephen, gave eulogies.[55]

With the limited records available it is impossible to prove whether the reduction of charges against Myton—from first degree murder to voluntary manslaughter to involuntary manslaughter—was at all justified. But Utah law, it seems, was more lenient with Myton than with Hill, and the situation invites speculation on just how much the unpopularity of the I.W.W. contributed to this disparity.

There was merit in the I.W.W. claim that public opinion in Utah was against the organization. Generally, Utahns viewed the union's activities with aversion and distrust, as implied in a *Deseret Evening News* editorial:

> A few years ago it [the I.W.W.] was not known. All of a sudden it came into promi-
> nence, as mushrooms that grow overnight.
>
> A great deal has been said about them, most of which is justified by the vehement
> specimens of oratory their street meetings offer. They are revolutionaries. They be-
> lieve in a violent overturning of the established institutions. Their ethical standards are
> in many respects different from those generally accepted.[56]

Undeniably, there existed in Utah at that time an anti-I.W.W. and Joe Hill senti-
ment which intensified during the months prior to Hill's execution. This feeling is described by Miss Theodora Pollok, a member of the California Suffrage Association, in a telegram and letter to Swedish Minister to the United States W. A. F. Ekengren. (The telegram is quoted within the letter.)

> Under the date of September 27, I sent you the following telegram, with reference
> to Joseph Hillstrom:
>
>> Representing a group of club women and social workers I went recently to Salt
>> Lake to investigate Joseph Hillstrom case. His trial was irregular and prejudicial and
>> procedure was unprecedented in criminal cases. Circumstantial evidence with im-
>> portant links missing convicted him. Utah's ironbound conservatism and prejudice
>> against his labor affiliation was so great that otherwise stern disbelievers in capital
>> punishment refused to ask commutation and sympathetic professional men feared
>> assisting me. Petition you request reprieve pending your investigation.
>
> T. Pollok
>
> The stay of execution granted to Hillstrom through your instrumentality gives me
> time to write an explanation of my telegram, while explanations are of any avail to
> Hillstrom.
>
> *   *   *
>
> The group of people for whom I acted in going to Salt Lake was composed largely
> of women, all of them actively interested in social work, prison reform, the abolition
> of capital punishment. . . . However, the matter of real importance which developed
> from my trip to Salt Lake City was, to my mind, the discovery of the feeling of the
> community in this case, a feeling directed not so much against Hillstrom as against his

129

organization, which made a fair trial for Hillstrom (in a human not merely technical sense) impossible in Salt Lake. Only a person coming quietly into Salt Lake and as it were, incognito, sounding the sentiment would possibly be able to discover this. Most of us are not conscious of our prejudices, and the people of Utah on account of their past history, are peculiarly adept in concealing even their conscious prejudices.

I went to Salt Lake with no intention of trying to convince people there of Hillstrom's innocence. I have indeed no conviction myself, save that he seemed not to have been convicted on evidence but on coincidence, not to have been proven guilty but to have been obliged to prove his innocence, and I thought the death penalty very extreme under the circumstances. . . .

I found in Salt Lake City that even the prosecuting attorney and the Supreme Court judges had a great deal of feeling against capital punishment, especially on circumstantial evidence. . . .

But practically none of the prominent people whom I consulted would ask that the death penalty be set aside in the case of Joseph Hillstrom, sentenced to death on evidence purely circumstantial. I believe this lack of logic to be traceable almost invariably not so much to the evidence in the case as to the community feeling about Hillstrom's organization—their childish bugaboo, the I.W.W., although all with one voice disclaimed of course any enmity toward labor organizations.

I might have been mistaken about this, however; I might have misread the papers; I might have been misinformed. But the feeling was finally voiced to me by a lawyer in town, who, sitting in a public hall felt that it was necessary to lower his voice to a whisper when he said to me: "I tell you you have a hard job ahead of you if you are trying to do anything for the man [Hillstrom]. Innocent or guilty, there's a tremendous undercurrent against him." And when I asked him "why," he replied, "Because of the organization he is connected with," still whispering. Then he added, "I'll be glad to give you any help and tips I can which won't endanger my own business interests," and thereafter, with great kindness, did so.[57]

Miss Pollok's attempt to discover the attitudes of prominent Salt Lake City citizens may have met with rebuffs in some cases because of their understandable reluctance to divulge personal views to strangers. Despite the possible challenges to the credibility of her conclusions, however, her letter to Minister Ekengren remains the best available contemporary document in which an attempt was made to discuss the topic of prejudice toward Joe Hill in Utah.

But there is no evidence to indicate an organized movement against Joe Hill. While most political and business leaders in Utah encouraged Governor Spry to resist the pressure to save Hill's life, there is nothing to suggest they engaged in an illegal conspiracy.

There is also no support for the I.W.W. allegation that the Mormon church sought to have Hill executed, and the organization appears to recognize this today. It was perhaps natural for the I.W.W. to link Hill's arrest with the Mormon church, the single most powerful institution in Utah and clearly part of the state power structure. The worker who felt he was abused in "Mormon territory" probably felt he was abused by the most dominant authority, and was likely to speak of it as Mormon. At Joe Hill's Chicago funeral, O. N. Hilton specifically charged the Mormon church with controlling the judge, jury, and police in Salt Lake City and being therefore responsible for Hill's death. Elizabeth Gurley Flynn made similar charges just before Hill's death.

That the Mormon church as an organization was involved in the Hill case in any direct way is unlikely for several reasons. The officials responsible for dealing with Hill were mostly non-Mormon. Harry Harper, the precinct justice who ruled against Hill, was a Mason; trial judge M. L. Ritchie was a vestryman at St. Mark's Episcopal Cathedral; all three supreme court justices—Straup, Frick, and McCarty—were non-Mormons; the jury that decided Hill's guilt was composed of six Mormons and six non-Mormons; District Attorney Leatherwood and Attorney General Barnes were also non-Mormons.[58]

Perhaps the strongest indication that the Mormon church was not involved comes from the I.W.W. itself. In 1948, that organization officially reviewed the case, once again deciding that Hill was innocent and that he had been framed and unjustly executed. Missing from this review, however, is any mention that the Mormon church was involved.[59] Explaining the shift in I.W.W. viewpoint, Ralph Chaplin, in a personal letter written many years after Hill's death, said: "In those days it was fashionable in radical circles to blame the Mormons. But I've changed my mind about it. The religious beliefs of the men who killed Joe Hill are no more important than those of the men who lynched Frank Little."[60]

However, to say that there is no evidence of an organized conspiracy against Hill is not to say that the people of Utah, and particularly Utah officials, can be held blameless in the handling of the case. Following the discovery that Hill was a Wobbly songwriter, he became the central figure in a conflict the character of which was governed largely by events that preceded his arrest. He became the focal point of the hatred engendered by labor conflicts in a state hostile to labor agitation—particularly that of the radical I.W.W. As will be shown later, there are indications that some Utah officials, whose special job it should have been to guarantee Hill justice since public opinion was against him, actually took steps to further aggravate that opinion. As the effort to prevent his execution stirred widespread support and finally brought appeals from President Woodrow Wilson, resistance in Utah stiffened.

Plunged into a situation governed to a considerable extent by events gone before, Hill fit perfectly into the role in which he was cast. Letters by and about him illustrate the unique personality which, combined with his talent and his stony insistence on a "new trial or die trying," brought a local murder case to nationwide attention and a "common Pacific Coast wharfrat" into the ranks of the heroes of labor.

Charlotte Anita Whitney, Theodora Pollok, and Mrs. A. C. Pollok wrote to Frank P. Walsh of the Federal Industrial Relations Commission asking for his help in the Hill defense effort. After explaining Hill's refusal to divulge any information about how he received his wound—other than the fight-over-a-woman story—the women said:

> Such coolness, the I.W.W. boys say, is entirely characteristic of Hill . . . whom they idolize not only because of his songs (which are certainly the cleverest satires on the industrial situation in America) but because of his coolness, courage and quiet determination under all circumstances.
>
>   *   *   *
>
> You know enough of the labor war to know that without proof in black and white

131

to the contrary, every spirited laboring man will believe that Hill was a martyr to the worker's cause. Every time that one of Hill's songs is sung (and as I understand, they have gone as far as South Africa and Australia) the hatred engendered by the injustice and the insult of Hill's death will flame up anew. It may be that Hill is one of the martyrs for whom we of the human race seem to lust. But we can not in honor accept that, until we *must*.

Hill is a man of unusually exemplary life. He did not drink or even smoke, and had no prison record, even in labor troubles—he is six foot one or so and of remarkable strength, I understand![61]

After Judge Ritchie decided on September 1, 1914, to deny the petition to grant a new trial, the necessary papers were filed to have Hill's case appealed, thus invalidating the September 4, 1914, execution date. On the day his execution had been scheduled, Hill, appearing full of humor and remarkably disarming, wrote to E. W. Vanderleith, a friend in San Francisco:

Dear Friend and Fellow Worker:

Well, Van, this is Sept. 4 which was supposed to be my last day on earth—but I am still wriggling my old lead pencil and I might live a long time yet, if I don't die from "Beanasitis" (that's a brand new disease).

I was up before Hisonor Sept. 1st. My attorney, Soren X. Christensen, made a motion to postpone all proceedings until Judge Hilton arrived from the East. The motion was denied. Then he had to make the argument alone right then and there. He made a pretty good argument although he was not prepared for it.

Among other things he pointed out the fact that no human being can tell by the smell if a gun loaded with smokeless powder has been shot one year, one month, one hour or ten minutes before examination, as our expert had testified; but the "Court" *proved* by the European war news that the soldiers smelled the guns in Brussels to find out if they had been recently shot. And in the face of such proofs Christensen had to shut up like a clam. What else could he do, Van? What else could *anybody* do?

Well, I was denied a new trial on account of them countrymen of yours going round smelling the end of guns and then sending telegrams about it. Well, I don't wish them anything bad but—I hope they'll all choke themselves with sauercraut.

Well, Van, all joking aside, I guess I have a long wait ahead of me and I think the best you all can do is to forget me for awhile. I know *you* would do anything for me, Van, and I will never forget the untiring fellowship that you boys showed me during my trial. I don't thank you for it and I make no promises but I'll *always* remember it. But the best you boys can do is to forget me and use your energies and your financial resources for the One Big Union.

I think some of you are making too much fuss about me anyway. I wish you would tell those who are writing poems about me that there is no poetry about my personality. I am just one of the rank and file—just a common Pacific Coast wharfrat—that's all. I have always tried to be true to my friends and to my class. What any outsider may think about me is no concern of mine.[62]

Writing to Elizabeth Gurley Flynn on January 18, 1915, Hill expressed modest surprise over the efforts being made to help him.

Friend and F. W.

Saw your address in the "Sol" and am enclosing a letter for Jos. J. Ettor and if you would try to locate him for me I would appreciate it very much. It is a receipt for some money and that's why I am anxious to locate him. While I am at it I want to thank you for what you have done for me and for the interest you have taken in my welfare, but on the square I'll tell you that all the notoriety stuff is making me dizzy in the head and I am afraid I am getting more glory than I really am entitled to. I put in most of the later years among the wharf-rats on the Pacific Coast and am not there with the lime light stuff at all. I am feeling well under the circumstances and the boys and girls here are taking care of me like a mother would her first born babe—

> With best regards to all
> I am yours for the O.B.U.
> Joe Hill [63]

As it became apparent that, if executed, Joe Hill would become a martyr to the cause of the working class, he reacted in a letter to Elizabeth Gurley Flynn during August 1915:

> ... I have absolutely no desire to be one of them what-ye-call-em-martyrs and if there is any way of carrying the case to the U.S. Sup. Court, it is of course O.K. with me. ...
> Well I guess I must admit that I am absolutely helpless and unable to do anything for myself.
> ... I am getting along fairly well here—Being the air is purer and not so hot as down in the Co. jail. Well I don't know anything new, and will close for this time. Take good care of your throat and, what ever you do—don't try to overthrow the "system" all alone.

> With best wishes I am
> Fraternally yours
> Joe Hill [64]

133

The Utah State Penitentiary in 1915.

Later, Hill would make statements indicating that he accepted the idea of becoming a martyr. He came to feel that his case was symbolic of the struggle of working class people to receive justice in the courts. But perhaps an accurate expression of his true feelings toward his predicament, as well as of his dauntless personality, is the following excerpt from a letter he wrote to E. W. Vanderleith:

> No, Van, I don't dislike the poems of . . . and . . . and the others, I know they mean well, and the poems are swell, but it kind of gets my goat to be mushed up that way. You know I always intended to go it alone, but somebody on the coast started the ball rolling, and here I am a martyr, a Tin-Jesu. Well honestly, wouldn't that jar ye. [65]

134

"My dear Governor Spry...

7

On August 2, 1915, for the second time, Judge M. L. Ritchie sentenced Joe Hill to die. The execution was set for October 1, 1915. Hill described the event and his thoughts on his future in a letter to Elizabeth Gurley Flynn.

> I was resentenced to be shot on the first day of Oct. and according to the local press the only hope for me is the Board of Pardons. That means, I suppose that they are going to give me life if I beg for it real nice. Now I'll tell you Gurley, I never did like the ring of the word "pardon" and I think I'd rather be buried dead, than buried alive. I never "licked the hand that holds the whip" yet and I don't see why I should have to start it now.[1]

Nevertheless, Hill's attorneys applied to the Utah Board of Pardons for a commutation of the sentence to life imprisonment. The application for commutation was heard at the Board's regularly scheduled meeting on September 18, 1915.

The Board of Pardons was composed of the three Utah Supreme Court justices who had already decided Hill was guilty: Straup, McCarty, and Frick, together with the governor of Utah, William Spry, and Attorney General A. R. Barnes, the Board secretary (a non-voting member).

For several weeks the Board had been receiving letters and petitions from individuals and groups who requested, and in some cases demanded, that Hill be given a commutation, a new trial, or a pardon. On August 21, *Solidarity* had printed a sample petition which Wobblies were urged to submit.

> This appeal is directed to the Board of Pardons in behalf of Joseph Hillstrom, a member of the Industrial Workers of the World, under sentence of death in the Utah Penitentiary. We have read and heard something of the case:
>
> 1st. We do not believe Joseph Hillstrom guilty of the crime for which he has been convicted.
> 2nd. We do not believe that he had a fair trial.
> 3rd. We have learned that the jurors were not selected in the usual way.
> 4th. The defendant was practically without counsel when he was on trial for his life.
> 5th. No motive was shown for the crime of which he was convicted.
> 6th. The conviction was found upon the flimsiest kind of circumstantial evidence. Believing these to be the facts, we the undersigned, demand that the death sentence in the case of Joseph Hillstrom be set aside and clemency extended.[2]

Salt Lake City, Utah, _____September 1,____ 191**5**

Application of _____Joseph Hillstrom_____

To the Honorable Board of Pardons of the State of Utah:

commutation
I hereby apply to your Honorable Body for a .... and respectfully represent as follows:

First—That I am serving a term of imprisonment in...... Utah State Prison

under conviction and sentence on a charge of........ Murder in the First Degree

Second—I was convicted and sentenced on the .... *2nd* day of *Aug. 1915*

A. D. ...., at .... Salt Lake City, ... County of ..... Salt Lake

and State of Utah, in ...... Third Judicial District .... Court, in and for the

County and State aforesaid, Honorable .... M. L. Ritchie, ... presiding.

Third—I was sentenced to ..be shot.. *on Oct 1, 1915*

and thereafter was imprisoned in the........ Utah State Prison

Fourth—Honorable .... E. O. Leatherwood .... prosecuted the case.

Fifth—My true name in full is ...... Joseph Hillstrom

I was convicted under the name of .... Joseph Hillstrom

Sixth—The names of persons charged to have been connected with the same offense are as

follows: _____

Seventh—I have never been convicted of any offense except _____

Respectfully submitted,

Joseph Hillstrom

Joe Hill's application for commutation
of his sentence to life imprisonment.

Ed Rowan told the readers of *Solidarity* that since Hill had been resentenced to die on October 1, his ". . . defense is now in full blast." He then appealed to all persons to write letters to Governor Spry and the Board of Pardons, asking for clemency for Hill.[3] Among thousands of letters and petitions received during the next few weeks were the following:

Workers in Boulder City, Australia, threatened to boycott American-made products if Hill was executed.[4]

Frank Caurll, Clara K. Schade, and John F. C. Holler of San Francisco wrote:

> His Honor Governor William Spry and the Board of Pardons of the State of Utah.
>
> I hereby respectfully petition your clemency in the case of Joseph Hillstrom, now condemned to die on October 1, 1915, for his supposed murder of J. G. Morrison.
>
> The facts of the trial of this case are now traveling far and wide, and are such as to call forth protest from every justice-loving man and woman.
>
> From authentic sources I learn that the evidence in Hillstrom's case was flimsy and entirely circumstantial; the identifications of Hillstrom insufficient and trivial; no motive was shown for his committing the murder; the proceedings of the court in the matter of the dismissal of Hillstrom's attorneys was irregular and prejudicial to the defendant's cause, and the community in which he was tried was prejudiced.
>
> No man should die on such a showing. For a state, through its officials, to administer the penalty of death where the slightest chance of innocence remains, is a blot upon the honor of the state. Such brutalities committed by a state undermine the strength of government and bring contempt upon the law.
>
> It is your duty and your privilege to guard the honor of your state. Therefore I petition you for a commutation of the sentence of Joseph Hillstrom.[5]

Emil S. Lund, a member of the Utah State House of Representatives, requested that Joe Hill's sentence be commuted to life imprisonment. He cited as his reason his belief that capital punishment was immoral and made it clear that he had no sympathy with the I.W.W.[6]

The Board received several petitions of the exact type recommended by *Solidarity*.[7]

Telegrams were received from I.W.W. locals, private individuals, and leagues for the abolishment of capital punishment.[8]

A letter from Buffalo, New York, dated August 10, 1915, and signed by Otto J. Guosa, is of particular interest since Guosa claimed to have lived with Hill at one time and was obviously acquainted with some of the events of Hill's life. It is possible that Guosa also wrote the anonymous letter O. N. Hilton later received from Buffalo, New York, which tended to corroborate Joe Hill's statement that his gunshot wound was inflicted during a fight over a woman.

> We the under singed do hereby hopefully beg Your Honner to intersced for clemency of one Joe Hillstrom a prisnor of the State of Utha and sentensted to die for a crime for witch He stands inocent and for witch the State has failed to prove any direct evedence or even a motive for said crime, and as the writer of this letter I have known Joe Hilstrom for three Years and Worked with Him at different times and even lived in the same house with Him in San Pedro Cal. and I always found Him to be a good Worker When employed in the Dock and Lumber Yards of said City, and When not ocupied there He always found a great demand for His musical tallents as an violenest or pianest Was always of sober habits and a good caractor, and even in one case He

partisepated With Me in giving chase to a holdup in San Pedro Cal. at a time When police methods were very lax in said City, and in reguards to His prescent diffeculty I do remember that He had some trouble of ver a Woemen how was from Salt Lake City and how shortly afterwards left for Salt Lake City, and in a short time Joe Hillstrom left San Pedro Cal. and the next I heard of Him was of His prescent trouble in Salt Lake City, and it is at all posible that his prescent diffeculty is over this self same Woemen, and rather than to expose Her secrets to the World He Would rather die a victim to her friendship.

So We the undersinged do Most sincerly hope You May give Clemency to Joe Hill-strom,

> We do hereby offer our greatest
> thanks in advance of Clemency[9]

138

The letter was signed by fifteen people besides Guosa, apparently to lend credence to its contents. Judging from the information revealed by the letter, the author could very well have been Otto Applequist.

Paul Jones, Episcopal Bishop of the Salt Lake City diocese, sent a form petition.

TO THE BOARD OF PARDONS
OF THE STATE OF UTAH,

We hereby respectfully petition for the commutation of sentence of Joseph Hill-strom, now condemned to die on October 1st, 1915.

We make this petition for the following reasons, all of which we believe to be of substantial importance in upholding respect for the Courts in the State of Utah.

1. Conviction in this case was based on purely circumstantial evidence.
2. No motive for the crime on the part of Joseph Hillstrom was shown.
3. No previous connection of the doomed man with the late J. G. Morrison was shown.

On evidence purely circumstantial, lacking such important links and therefore leaving so many possible doubts as to the guilt of the condemned man, we believe that

Under our law which, remembering the sacredness of human life, humanely provides that a man shall be considered innocent until proven beyond a doubt to be guilty,

The infliction of the death penalty on Joseph Hillstrom may at some later date prove the State of Utah to have been the murderer of this man rather than the administrator of justice and thus mar the honor of our State and become a burden upon the consciences of our administrators of justice.

Signed: Paul Jones[10]

Among the letters asking for clemency was one from Eugene V. Debs.

Please allow me to say a word in behalf of Joseph Hillstrom (also known as Joe Hill). From the reports that have come to me from those in position to know the facts and whom I regard as entirely trustworthy, I am convinced that there is more than a reasonable doubt as to the guilt of this unfortunate brother of ours in the cause of labor. He was convicted upon circumstantial evidence, denied the right to choose his own counsel, while at the same time there was unquestionably a strong prejudice against him on account of his activity in the labor movement.

Joe Hill is a poet, a writer of songs, a man of soul, a tender and sympathetic nature and the crime of murder is as foreign to him and as unthinkable as it would be to any other man of like temperament. For this reason and others I will not trouble you with, I beg you to give serious consideration to the case of Joe Hill and if you do I am confident you will grant him executive clemency. Joe Hill is not a murderer; he is a man and the great state of Utah where murder is so abhorred cannot afford to take his life.

Thanking you sincerely for myself and for the working people in whose behalf Joe Hill has labored and suffered and made many sacrifices I remain,

Yours very truly,
Eugene V. Debs[11]

The Board of Pardons had received several hundred letters before its September 18 meeting; thousands more would be sent before the fight to save Hill came to an end.

Joe Hill was present when the Board heard his case. He was accompanied by his attorneys O. N. Hilton and Soren X. Christensen, and by Ed Rowan,

**Joe Hill in handcuffs—
thinner and more dapper
than at his arrest.**

139

secretary of the Salt Lake Joe Hill Defense Committee. Hill's attorneys made the following points in arguing for a commutation:

1. That there was insufficient evidence connecting Hill with the crime to prove his guilt and to warrant his execution.

2. That Hill had had "a legal trial but not a fair trial."

3. That the case rested solely on circumstantial evidence and that a life should not be taken on that kind of evidence.

4. That the infliction of the death penalty was barbarous and ought not to be imposed in any case.[12]

The Board's attitude as it considered the case is revealed in a statement Justice McCarty made to the press at the close of the meeting. "All of the talk concerning what should have been done in the trial of the case has no place here."[13]

In a prepared statement released a few days following the meeting which explained its reasoning in denying a commutation, the Board stated that the presumption of innocence, which existed before the verdict in the trial, ceased to exist after the jury found Hill guilty. The Board claimed that Hill, after the verdict, had ". . . the burden to show, or bring forward, or point out, something to justify a commutation of sentence or clemency in his favor,"[14] and explained that neither Hill nor his lawyers had attempted to point out any reasons which would justify the demand for commutation or clemency.[15] All that was offered in support of the applicant's case, according to the Board, was an argument that circumstantial evidence should not be used as the basis for a man's execution, together with mention of several cases in which persons convicted solely on circumstantial evidence were later proved to be innocent.[16] This argument did not appear relevant to the Board because the Board did not accept the claim that Hill's conviction rested on circumstantial evidence. It is not surprising that the Board agreed with the supreme court that there was direct evidence against Hill since three of the four voting Board members were the supreme court.[17] The supreme court had already ruled that the evidence against Hill ceased to be circumstantial and became direct when the following factors were considered in combination: (1) the testimony of the women witnesses who saw someone of Hill's general appearance near Morrison's store but who could not identify Hill as that man; (2) Hill's unexplained gunshot wound; (3) the unproven theory that Arling shot the gun found near him. The conclusion that there was direct evidence may have been a question open to review by another Board of Pardons, but it was clearly not debatable with a Board composed of these four men, three of whom had already decided in an official capacity that there was direct evidence.

Hill's attorneys complained to the Board that the supreme court had been prejudiced because Hill failed to testify at the trial. The Board answered that it had no power to review alleged mistakes of the supreme court and said that since no petition for a rehearing had been filed, it could only assume that there were no grounds on which to seek a rehearing.[18] Hill's attorneys explained that the petition was not filed because Hilton had been in Denver at the time it should have been submitted, and Christensen, who was supposed to file, failed to do so.[19] This serious oversight by Hill's attorneys, which, if properly initiated, might have provided a slim means to keep the case alive, was an unfortunate instance of negligence.

It was too late now for either the attorneys or Hill to say—as they should have said at the trial—that the burden of proving Hill's guilt still remained with the state, even if his story that he had been wounded in a quarrel over a woman was a complete hoax. When Hill faced the Board of Pardons, the burden of proof was his. The Board told Hill he could not

> . . . ask anyone to believe his claim with no evidence whatever to support it and with no effort or attempt even to produce or furnish any—hence it is time enough to consider the applicant's alleged attitude in protecting the honor of some woman when there is some evidence to show that he received his wound at some place other than at the place of the homicide.[20] *

Justice McCarty of the Board of Pardons offered Joe Hill a bargain, making it easy for him to reveal the circumstances in which he was wounded. He promised the condemned man that if he would tell his attorneys in confidence the name of the woman and the place and circumstances surrounding the shooting, and if the story could then be substantiated by an investigation to be conducted by prison warden Arthur Pratt, Hill could go free. It was part of the promise that Hill's attorneys and Warden Pratt would be the only persons who would know the name of the woman, and it would never be made public. Thus, McCarty concluded, Hill would be saved from death if he were innocent, and the honor of the woman would be preserved.

141

Hilton and Christensen urged him to accept the bargain[21] but, according to a telegram (probably sent by Ed Rowan) to *Solidarity*, Hill declined, replying, "I don't want a commutation, if you can't give me a new trial that is all there is to it. I don't want the humiliation of a pardon or a commutation. What I want is an acquittal."[22] He said that only at a new trial before a jury would he prove his innocence and send ". . . several perjurers to the penitentiary where they belong."[23]

Hill restated his position a few days following the Board of Pardons' meeting in a letter to Jerome B. Sabath of the National Association for the Abolition of Capital Punishment, who was endeavoring to have the sentence commuted to life imprisonment. "I do not want my death sentence commuted to life imprisonment and I am not clamoring for a pardon; I do, however, want a new trial—a fair trial. If I cannot have a new trial, I am willing to give my blood as a martyr that others may be afforded fair trials."[24]

These statements indicate a basic disagreement or misunderstanding between Hill and his attorneys. Although the attorneys had petitioned for a commutation, Hill was not asking the Board for a commutation, and if his statements are believed literally, he would not have accepted one.

The Board of Pardons explained to Hill that it had no power to grant him a new trial; it could only grant him a pardon or commute his sentence.[25] Hill, however, continued to demand the acquittal of a jury.[26] The Board asked him

---

* It seems that the Board, by insisting that Hill would have to divulge specific details of how he was wounded before any favorable action could be taken, was, in effect, denying any possibility of granting him a commutation. A commutation is given on some basis other than proven innocence; if Hill had proved he was shot while in some location other than Morrison's store, he probably would have been granted a full pardon.

why he had not offered his evidence at the trial. He replied that he thought the "law presumed him innocent," and that he believed he would not be convicted on the evidence presented against him.[27] The Board then asked him if he would answer questions that it might ask. Hill replied that he would answer no questions until he was granted a new trial.[28] The Board reiterated its limitations and asked Hill's attorneys if their client understood that the Board had no power to grant a new trial. The attorneys replied that Hill had been so informed but that he refused to give any information until he was before a jury.[29] Finally, the Board asked Ed Rowan if he would encourage Hill to give some new evidence. Rowan replied that Hill knew his own mind and was quite capable of determining for himself his desires in the matter; therefore, he did not want to advise his friend.[30] With no new information forthcoming and discussion at an impasse, the Board denied Hill's petition.

In the report stating its reasons for refusing the petition (for complete statement, see Appendix B), the Board mentioned the letters received from all over America in support of Hill but dismissed them by saying that the writers had been "misguided and misdirected" and were "misinformed as to the real facts."[31] If the people who wrote the letters had read the records, claimed the Board, they would have agreed with the decision to deny the petition. Concluding, it branded as completely false the suggestion that Hill had been convicted because of his membership in the Industrial Workers of the World.[32]

After the meeting, Justice McCarty told the press:

> If I were convinced in the least that Hillstrom is not rightfully convicted, I would vote to give him a full pardon, but when he did not take the opportunity offered him he practically confessed that the conviction is legal and right. . . . It is a terrible thing to send an innocent man to his death, but when every opportunity has been given that man and his attorneys to raise even the suspicion of doubt in the minds of any member of the Board of Pardons and the offers have been cast aside we cannot do anything further.[33]

O. N. Hilton, after failing to convince the Board of Pardons to act favorably toward Hill, explained to the press his feelings concerning the meeting.

> This result, the denial of Hill's petition, is only an exemplification of the iniquitous system of having a pardoning board constituted of four members, all but one of whom have already prejudged the case and solemnly announced that the accused was guilty. Judges are only human, after all, and having once made up their minds it is but natural that they should not only be tenacious of their opinions but insistent in their defense of such preconceived judgments. I found them all unusually so except, perhaps, the governor, and I had not spoken five minutes before they were all after me in violent and frequently raucous disputation and dissent. At one time three of them were talking all at once. What else could be expected than they should find against Hillstrom?
> . . . As to the merits of Hillstrom's contention, I can only say that his complaint has always been earnest and consistent—that he was deprived of an honest and fair trial, and in that contention I most heartily concur.
> I say without the slightest hesitation that the trial which resulted in Hillstrom's conviction was the most unjust, wicked and farcical travesty on justice that has ever occurred in the west. . . . I was much impressed by Hillstrom's attitude and what he said before the board. His language was classic. The board offered to pardon him if he would state all the facts which might be later verified as the truth, but Hillstrom re-

fused because, as he reasoned, a pardon presupposed a crime committed and he was innocent of all crime and so demanded a new trial when his vindication, as he believed, would be sure to come.[34]

The press denounced Hilton's statement, charging that even though Hilton—with the able help of Christensen—had ample opportunity to convince the Board that Hill's conviction was unjust, he had failed to do so and that his subsequent criticism of the Board was an attempt to vindicate himself.[35] The press attack on Hilton was the first in a series of incidents in which the attorney and various Utah officials, newspapers, and agencies denounced one another. The conflict eventually resulted in Hilton's disbarment in Utah.

Consistent with its anti-Hill attitude throughout, the local press strongly supported the Board of Pardons in its decision. Calling Hill's stand "perfectly irrational," one writer inferred "Hillstrom had no evidence of his innocence; he could produce none and, therefore, resorted to the role of 'martyr.' "[36] An editorial commenting on Hill's claim that he was protecting a woman's honor acknowledged the emotional appeal of his stand, saying, ". . . if it is more than a hackneyed invention, it will save Hillstrom's life provided he uses it in the simple, and secret way suggested by the Board of Pardons." Terming the Board ". . . more than ready to temper justice with mercy," the writer concluded: "If Joseph Hillstrom goes to his death, it will be because he ought to go and because the Board of Pardons can find no excuse to save him."[37]

On the other hand, the I.W.W. journals and other elements of the radical press strongly condemned the decision and called for renewed effort to save Joe Hill by appealing directly to Governor Spry. The *International Socialist Review* urged that thousands of letters, telegrams, and petitions be sent to the governor, as he was now the only one who could save Hill—by exercising executive clemency.[38]

Declaring that since the Board of Pardons refused Hill a commutation and since Hill apparently was not going to save himself, the ". . . I.W.W. must accept responsibility for demanding a pardon or a commutation,"[39] *Solidarity* admonished its readers to ". . . turn on the search light. Let the white livered, legalized, would be murderers know that a million workers have them in their gaze."[40]

In a spirited *Solidarity* editorial, Emma B. Little exhorted the working class to act to save Hill.

> Another crime is about to be perpetrated by the capitalist class against the workers. Our song bird is about to be executed—before he ever has a chance to sing for us the glorious songs of freedom—the freedom of the white slaves from wage slavery.
>
> Will we permit him to be executed? Only we can prevent his execution. We, the great working class, are the ones to say when the lives of the people shall go out into the unknown.
>
> We say Joe Hill shall not go out. Altogether we say he shall not go. We need him in our business. The singing of songs and the writing of books is an important work in civilizing the world. This is Joe's work and we say he shall do this work and no damnable capitalist court shall railroad him to the other side.
>
> We say he shall not go out, and now boys it's up to you. Get busy on this job.

143

Circulate petitions, flood the governor's office. You won't have any trouble to get signers, even those who do not know anything about the case will sign a petition that asks the death sentence be set aside, in a case of circumstantial evidence—point out the fact that the sentence was hurried so as to give the accused no time to obtain help—point out the fact that the accused is a common workingman, that he is unusually intelligent—a poet, a song-writer. You will be surprised to find how many will sign your petition. Don't wait to get acquainted with a man before you ask him to sign—most everybody is human, just ask everyone you meet, that's a good way to get acquainted, and you can do some propaganda work for the I.W.W. at the same time. This is hard on Joe Hill but it is excellent propaganda for the I.W.W.—and don't forget to ask the women to sign, most of them know how to sign their names and very few will refuse. You'll be surprised to find how many people are anxious to sign. The working class are getting tired of having their fellow workers railroaded, and even non working class are tired and they will sign too. More than ninety nine out of every hundred will sign if they are only asked. The case is so rotten, it smells all over the USA.

Hold mass meetings. Show up this capitalist conspiracy to murder a common working man like yourselves! Why? Because he has always been active in the working class movement. Because he has done everything in his power to better the conditions of the workers. Because he has always made every possible effort to educate the workers as to the necessity for organization on the job in order that they may free themselves from wage slavery.

Sing Joe's songs in your union hall, on the streets everywhere two or three are gathered.

Also if convenient use a little sabotage in your business. The Bible says a tooth for a tooth an eye for an eye a life for a life—and Joe Hill's life is worth more to us of the great working class than are the lives of all the courts in Utah.

> We demand this life!
> We are going to enforce our demands!
> Get busy boys, boys get busy,
> Emma B. Little[41]

Because Hill was a Swedish citizen, his supporters decided to ask the Swedish government to apply diplomatic pressure on the State Department in Washington to encourage Governor Spry to grant a reprieve. Mrs. Virginia Snow Stephen—who had helped bring O. N. Hilton into the case—and Sigrid Bolin of Salt Lake City sent a plea to the Swedish Minister to the United States, W. A. F. Ekengren, asking him to aid Joe Hill. Bill Haywood telegraphed Ekengren on September 20:

Joseph Hillstrom a Swedish subject has been sentenced to be shot to death October first at Salt Lake City, Utah. Will you request Secretary of State Lansing to delay execution pending investigation.[42]

Ekengren responded two days later, sending the following message to Oscar W. Carlson, Swedish vice consul in Salt Lake City and former Salt Lake County commissioner, instructing him to look into the Hill case.

Virginia Stephen and Sigrid Bolin of your city ask intervention for Hillstrom. Please ascertain whether there are any grounds on which stay of execution could be asked. Also state your opinion about Hillstrom's guilt or whether the circumstances under which eventual crime was committed were such as to warrant protest against court's judgement. Please telegraph.[43]

Two days later, Carlson replied:

Have ascertained no substantial grounds on which to ask for stay of execution. Defendant has been extended rights and privileges accorded him by the law. The circumstances under which the crime was committed as disclosed by the evidence in the case do not warrant a protest against the courts. Judgment all proceedings have been lawful and regular. The Board of Pardons afforded defendant opportunity to make any additional showing before acting on his application. I mailed copy of Supreme Court's decision to you at Washington.

Swedish Vice Consul Carlson[44]

Carlson also informed the Utah Board of Pardons of his findings.

William D. Haywood,
General Secretary of the I.W.W.

145

Tom Mooney, a labor organizer who was to be accused of murder after a bombing incident in a San Francisco War Preparedness parade less than a year after Hill's execution, protested to Ekengren that Carlson was biased against Hill and urged him to help.

The International Workers defense league San Francisco in mass meeting this day instructed the undersigned its secretary to telegraph our protest in behalf of Joseph Hillstrom a citizen of Sweden to you the highest legal diplomat of the government in this country. We protest against the statement of the Swedish Vice Consul at Salt Lake City saying Hillstrom received fair impartial trial. Consul is influenced by his business associations in that community. We protest against Hillstrom's conviction and execution secured on circumstantial evidence brought about by fraud and prejudice. We ask you to call this matter to the attention of Secretary of State Lansing and by all means secure stay of execution and commutation of sentence in the interest of international justice.[45]

Ekengren, apparently not convinced by Carlson's opinion, remained concerned. He studied the available documents relating to the case and concluded that Hill was not fairly tried and should not be executed.

After his initial inquiries, Ekengren received many requests that he help. Professor Thorild Arnoldson of the University of Utah and Oscar W. Larson, president of the Salt Lake City branch of Verdandi, requested Ekengren to assist Hill. Arnoldson and Larson also cabled Carl Lindhoden, the burgomaster of Stockholm, and several members of the Swedish parliament soliciting support for Hill.[46]

Jane Addams, of Hull House in Chicago, wrote urging Ekengren to act, saying that the circumstances in the case were tragic.[47]

Many Swedish-Americans, who had no apparent connection with the I.W.W., wrote Ekengren on behalf of their countryman.[48] One such letter was signed by sixteen Swedish-Americans from San Francisco, among them Ragnar Johanson, one of the persons who in 1949 publicized the fact that Hill was Joel Hägglund. These men, convinced that Hill was convicted on insufficient evidence, asked the Minister to use his influence on Governor Spry.[49] Another letter was received from the Swedish employees of a laundry in Minnesota.

> Having a countryman's welfare at heart, who upon the flimsiest pretext has been convicted in Utah and sentenced to die on the first of October 1915 for no other reason than that his big Swedish heart could not submit to the cruelties to the working class perpetrated by the master class, but sang out to arouse them from their lethargy and to tell them of the danger threatening them if not solidly united to help one another, we the undersigned of Swedish soil and parentage beseech you to use all your influence and power to save this our beloved countryman from death. Save Joe Hillstrom (Joe Hill) the working class poet.[50]

Attorney Frank B. Scott, asked by the Eastern Swedish Club to send his opinion concerning Hill's conviction to Ekengren, telegraphed that the evidence against Hill did not prove guilt beyond a reasonable doubt and that, in his opinion, Hill was innocent of the crime. Scott advised Ekengren to encourage Hill to take advantage of the Board of Pardons' offer to vindicate himself by divulging the name of the woman he was allegedly protecting.[51] Upon receiving Scott's message, Ekengren telegraphed Vice Consul Carlson in Salt Lake City, instructing him to confer with Scott and to try to induce Hill to name the woman. After twice visiting Hill and conferring with Scott, Carlson again reported to Ekengren and the Utah Board of Pardons that he could still see no reason why sentence should not be carried out.[52]

During the period when the Swedish government—through Ekengren—was being apprised of Hill's plight, the number of letters and petitions to Governor Spry greatly increased. The press of September 21, 1915, reported that ". . . letters and telegrams from all parts of the world, demanding a pardon for Hill, poured into the office of Governor Spry yesterday. Most are from lawyers and professional men who are not affiliated with the I.W.W."[53] During the last several days of September, the governor's office received an average of two hundred letters and telegrams a day.[54]

As the execution date neared, the protest increased in emotional fervor. Speculating on the reason why so many thousands would write letters in Hill's behalf, the *Salt Lake Herald-Republican* guessed that Hill's choice of death by shooting rather than by hanging had contributed to the unusual notoriety of his case. Continuing, the editorial stated that the eastern press, which opposed Hill's execution, ". . . probably fancy that circumstance [shooting] gives the whole affair an aspect delightfully western and murderous."[55]

In the meantime, Governor Spry had received a number of letters threatening his life and the lives of other members of his family. Some of these letters were signed by agent number seven of the mysterious and unknown order of K.O.D. A copy of one of these lurid threats, printed in the Salt Lake City press, informed Spry that under orders of the headquarters of K.O.D., the warning was given him that he must commute Hill's sentence on or before September 30, 1915, or suffer the death penalty himself. The threat read in part: "We work silently but when the time comes for a reckoning it will be swift, sure and terrible, for the revenge of the K.O.D. is silent, swift, sure, and terrible. We never fail." Governor Spry was warned that if he received the jack of spades in the mail, he was to consider himself condemned to death.[56] The press reported that other prominent Utah leaders had also received K.O.D. threats.

After printing the lurid threat to Governor Spry, the *Los Angeles Times* claimed, without substantiation, that the K.O.D. ". . . is a secret organization of members of the I.W.W. It corresponds in many respects to the Mafia."[57]

A letter printed in the Salt Lake City press, postmarked Seattle, Washington, threatened that a ". . . state of siege and destruction will be declared in Utah if Joe Hill is executed. The siege will extend to all churches, banks, ranches, and state buildings in Utah."[58] This and similar threats on public buildings prompted officials to assign special state guards and Pinkerton detectives to guard the Hotel Utah, Newhouse Hotel, Salt Lake City and County Building, Mormon Temple, and Utah State Capitol during the last weeks of September.[59]

Utah officials feared that an "army" of Joe Hill sympathizers from all over the West would mass in Salt Lake City and march on the state prison in an attempt to free Joe Hill. As a result, no visitors were allowed to enter the prison without written permission from the governor.[60] According to author Curt Gentry, Warran Billings (co-defendant with Tom Mooney in the San Francisco 1916 Preparedness Day bombing case) had concocted a plan to free Joe Hill from prison by force. While in Denver, Billings heard a rumor that miners had cached guns and ammunition in a cave during the Ludlow strike in Colorado. Reportedly, it was Billings' plan to arm men with these weapons and storm the Utah State Prison to free Hill. The plan failed to materialize when he was unable to locate the cave.[61] If other insurrectionist ideas existed in the minds of Hill's supporters, they remained only ideas; no organized movement appeared.

There is no direct proof that the threatening letters received by Utah officials came from Hill's supporters. Proof exists, however, that at least some of the letters may have been written by persons who hoped to profit from the fear they might generate. After Hill's execution, *Solidarity* published an article claiming that many of the threatening letters were written by a private detective agency in Salt Lake City to arouse fear and thereby create protection work for themselves.[62] This accusation was substantiated by a report in the *Deseret Evening News* stating that Paul Riley and Harry McDonald, employees, and H. F. Gerry, head of the Intermountain Detective Service, were arrested for threatening to bomb the governor's house during the excitement over the Joe Hill case.[63] A statement by Salt Lake City Postmaster Noble Warrum indirectly indicates that some threatening letters may have been given to the press by Utah officials to unite the citizens behind Governor Spry in opposition to the mounting appeal to save Hill. Concerning the letters Warrum said:

> I have never seen one of the letters claimed to have been written to or received by the governor or his secretary. Mr. C. M. Christensen, the post office inspector now here, told me Thursday morning before leaving for Provo, that no one has ever shown him such a letter or asked him to investigate anything in relation to it. As it is not his business to go and ask people to submit cases to him he has no knowledge that such threats ever passed through the mails. In any event when people really want matters investigated they are not supposed to publish them in the newspapers first and turn them over to secret servicemen ten days later.[64]

Governor Spry reacted to the threats in a manner apparently calculated to build confidence in the office of the governor. Reporting that he felt the threats were part of a campaign to frighten state officials, he said,

> I am not afraid of any threats that may be made by any man or organization of men, when they resort to the unprincipled tactics of sending anonymous letters through the mails. I am going about my business as I always have gone about it and am not frightened by the threats of death to myself or my family. I do not want any police officers around me, for I am afraid of none of those who have made threats. I am not carrying a gun nor do I want anyone to carry a gun to protect me. . . .[65]

In the same issue of the newspaper containing the governor's statement, there appeared an article telling of the arrival in Salt Lake City of William A. Pinkerton, head of the Pinkerton Detective Agency, who had come from Chicago to formulate plans for the protection of Governor Spry and other state officials.[66]

On Saturday, September 25, six days before the scheduled execution, the Board of Pardons met in emergency session under protection of armed guards. Minister Ekengren had telegraphed Frank L. Polk, acting Secretary of State, requesting that he ask Governor Spry to have Hill's execution postponed. Ekengren explained that he had not had an opportunity to thoroughly study the record and that although Hill's case seemed to have been ". . . regularly tried before all the instances of the state," he felt the need of requesting a postponement because ". . . numerous applications have been addressed to me to intercede in his behalf on the ground that evidence of his guilt is insufficient and that an execution of the sentence would be a gross injustice." Ekengren further explained that he desired time to study the court records. Polk conveyed the request to the governor, commenting, "I shall be glad if you give this request of the Swedish Minister careful attention."[67]

It was reported in Salt Lake City that the Board of Pardons considered these messages and decided that a reprieve would not be granted unless the State Department directly requested it.[68] Governor Spry answered Polk with a review of the appeal, including Vice Consul Carlson's investigation, and forwarded a copy of the Board of Pardons' report. He pointed out that so far nothing had appeared to justify clemency or commutation, but, indicating the Board's willingness to heed a direct request from the State Department, he closed, "We respectfully await any further request you may deem proper."[69]

Acting Secretary of State Polk forwarded the reply and the enclosed report to the Swedish Minister.

Governor Spry also sent a personal letter to Ekengren in which he informed the Minister that although Hill and his attorneys had been given ample time to produce new evidence they had failed to do so. He reaffirmed his belief that Hill's trial had been fair and, regarding postponement of the execution, explained that such matters were decided on the facts presented, not by appeals from people misinformed or uninformed as to the real facts of the case. In conclusion, Spry offered: "If you know anything or are able to direct us to any one who possesses knowledge of any matter of fact or thing tending to justify commutation we will be pleased to consider the question of postponement."[70]

At the September 25 meeting, the Board also reviewed a statement prepared by Chief Justice Straup at Governor Spry's request which stated the official position of Utah concerning Hill's guilt and his treatment in Utah courts (see Appendix B). The lengthy statement reviewed the arguments the Utah Supreme Court and Board of Pardons had already enunciated. After the meeting the Board decided to release it for publication, apparently in an attempt to counteract I.W.W. propaganda. After the statement appeared in the press, a *Salt Lake Herald-Republican* editorial commented that it showed the Hill case was an ". . . ordinary homicide case, with the guilt of the condemned clearly proven." Concerning the public protest to prevent Hill's execution, the editorial stated ". . . the furor, where it affects the intelligent and the sincere, is based upon misinformation; with others, it is merely an effort of the lawless to protect another equally lawless."[71]

On September 28, after reading the supreme court's decision and reflecting on Joe Hill's plight, Minister Ekengren repeated his request to Polk that the execution be postponed[72] and also wired directly to Governor Spry his opinion that even if Hill had entered the Morrison store the trial had not proved he did the shooting. He expressed serious doubt as to any motive Hill could have had, since robbery did not appear to be the reason for the attack, and certainly, during Hill's short stay in Salt Lake City, he could ". . . hardly have made such enemies that he would shoot and kill them out of pure malice." Bringing diplomatic pressure to bear, he informed Spry, "Today I have been telegraphically instructed by my Government to endeavor to secure a new investigation in the case and in their behalf and in my own I ask you again very earnestly to consider at least a postponement of the execution."[73]

Upon receipt of Ekengren's message, the Board of Pardons was once again convened under armed guard. The Board subpoenaed Oscar W. Larson, Sigrid Bolin, Virginia Snow Stephen, and Thorild Arnoldson, seeking an explanation of what they knew about the case and of why they had helped to involve the Swedish government in Hill's behalf.[74] The police could locate only Miss Bolin and Professor Arnoldson. Arnoldson explained that he did not have any facts to offer concerning the case and that he involved himself because of his belief that capital punishment was wrong.[75] Miss Bolin told the Board that she had read the transcript of the trial and was convinced that Hill was innocent.[76] A statement prepared by Joe Hill, in answer to the Board's statement written by Justice Straup, was also introduced at this meeting. Hill's main points were the same as were argued in his defense in court (for complete statement see Appendix B). In conclusion, he reiterated his now familiar stand.

> Now, anyone can readily understand that I am not in a position where I could afford to make any false statements. I have stated the facts as I know them in my own simple way. I think I shall be able to convince every fair-minded man and woman who reads these lines that I did not have a fair and impartial trial in spite of what the learned jurists may say to the contrary. Now if you don't like to see perjurers and dignified crooks go unpunished, if you don't like to see human life being sold like a commodity on the market, then give me a hand. I am going to stick to my principles no matter what may come. I am going to have a new trial or die trying.
>
> Yours for fair play,
Joseph Hillstrom [77]

The Board of Pardons met again the next day, September 29, and questioned Virginia Snow Stephen and Oscar W. Larson. Mrs. Stephen said she became involved because of reports from "reliable sources" that police officers put Hill through the "third degree" at the county jail in an attempt to extract a confession from him. Also, she said that accounts of the preliminary hearing in the Salt Lake City press had convinced her that Hill was not being given a fair trial.[78] She appealed to the Swedish government because the Board of Pardons was not ". . . listening to the voice of the people." While Mrs. Stephen was before the Board, Chief Justice Straup accused her of being ". . . hostile to the courts of the land and the constituted authority of government."[79]

Oscar W. Larson, while explaining to the Board his belief that Hill was innocent, was himself questioned about his political beliefs. He reportedly told the Board he was a socialist and that he wanted a change in the form of government in America.[80]

After listening to Stephen's and Larson's statements, Governor Spry answered Minister Ekengren's message. Opening with a curt statement that the supreme court and Board of Pardons were in a much better position to judge the case than ". . . one unfamiliar with the record or the real facts,"[81] he again summarized the events of the night of the murder and the evidence presented concerning those events, stating, "Against that proof Hillstrom offered nothing." Continuing, he insisted that even though Hill and his friends had ample opportunity, they had furnished nothing in rebuttal, either at the trial or in the appeals to the supreme court and the Board of Pardons, in addition to which

Hill ". . . has since declined to give any [explanation] but has stated that it was 'no one's business' how or where he was shot." Spry went on:

> In pursuance to your prior telegrams that a Mrs. Stephen and a Miss Bolin claiming to know something about the case had wired you for intervention and of a cablegram sent by Arnoldson and Larson of this city to the Burgomaster of Stockholm, we caused them to appear before the Board and on inquiries made of them they stated they did not know Hillstrom, knew nothing of his past life and nothing that could be presented by them or anyone else in Hillstrom's favor on a further hearing of the case. All stated they had not heard evidence nor read it, except one who claimed to have read a portion of it and the briefs of Hillstrom's counsel.

Spry again reminded Ekengren that Vice Consul Carlson had reviewed the evidence and that Carlson and every ". . . disinterested person familiar with the record and the evidence" were convinced Hill was guilty. He then suggested that Ekengren appeal directly to Hill and his friends for further information.[82]

On September 29, Elizabeth Gurley Flynn and a friend, Mrs. J. Sargent Cram, traveled to Washington, D.C., to ask President Woodrow Wilson to intervene and obtain a reprieve for Hill. Mrs. Cram's husband had led the New York state delegation in voting for Wilson at the Democratic National Convention in 1912 and had access to the White House.[83] Mrs. Cram, a liberal and a pacifist, was the sister-in-law of Gifford Pinchot, who went with them to the White House meeting.

Joseph Tumulty, the President's secretary, met with the women and heard their story. Already that day, Tumulty had received the following wire from O. N. Hilton.

> Please say to President that Hillstrom's execution in Salt Lake City means judicial murder. It is a case of weak circumstantial evidence at best and the trial was marked by flagrant disregard of his constitutional rights. An investigation will show it is a conviction condemned by all here who are familiar with the facts.[84]

Frank B. Scott was also to wire Tumulty later that day after Tumulty suggested that Mrs. Cram ask Scott, as Hill's former attorney, to appeal to the President. Scott's message read:

> Response your suggestion, I appeal to the President to request thirty days reprieve for Joe Hill; absolutely no evidence connecting Hill with murder except his unexplained bullet wound. Three others with unexplained bullet wounds same night. Hillstrom frantically makes no attempt to save life; insists his wound no one's business. Believe but for threats sentence would have been commuted, should be.[85]

Tumulty explained to his visitors that the President had no authority to intervene in state murder cases, but suggested, nevertheless, that the Swedish Minister send ". . . a stronger and direct appeal to the President." Mrs. Cram contacted Ekengren, expressing her hope that ". . . you will feel empowered to [do] this most important office for your unfortunate countryman."[86]

At 11:24 p.m. on September 29, 1915, Ekengren sent his appeal to President Woodrow Wilson.

> A Swedish subject named Joseph Hillstrom has been sentenced by the Courts of

151

Utah to be shot October 1st for murder in the first degree. I have only had a short time to study the case. However, I have come to the conclusion that the evidence, which is only circumstantial, is insufficient to warrant capital punishment, and that the prisoner's insolent behavior during trial and refusal to take the stand in his own behalf prejudiced both jury and Court against him. I have already through the Department of State, as well as directly appealed to Utah's Governor for a stay of execution in order that the case might be reopened but so far have received only an answer that if any new facts can be shown in favor of the accused he will listen to this appeal.

As the insufficiency of evidence is the reason for my appeal, I cannot feel satisfied with such an answer. My opinion as to the injustice of the sentence considering the evidence presented at the trial is shared by several men of legal profession as well as by a great number of prominent citizens in different parts of this country and I have received numerous applications to try to intercede in behalf of the condemned. Also my government which has from several sources received information about the case, has instructed me to do my utmost.

In order to exhaust every possible means to at least postpone the execution of the sentence, I venture to most respectfully lay the case before you, Mr. President, for your benevolent consideration.

W. A. F. Ekengren, Swedish Minister[87]

Early on the morning of September 30, 1915—the day before the scheduled execution—Ekengren, apparently following Governor Spry's advice, sent a telegram to Joe Hill requesting that he divulge the details of how he was wounded.

Governor Spry willing to consider question of postponement of execution if anything new as matter of fact can be presented. Won't you give some indication of where and how you received the wound you had dressed the night of the murder or at least won't you indicate where you were. I am doing all I can to head off the execution but without your co-operation I fear the results will not be good. Please wire me collect.[88]

Then, in a final attempt, Ekengren appealed for the third time to Governor Spry. Undoubtedly alluding to Spry's suggestion that persons ". . . unfamiliar with the record" were not in a position to judge the case accurately, he specified, "I have the honor to state I have gained knowledge of the case not only from Hillstrom's lawyers and friends but from the opinion rendered in the case by Utah's Supreme Court as published in the *Pacific Reporter* and still fail to see that the evidence is anything but circumstantial." Again he raised the question of motive, pointing out that while it had not been established that Hill ever knew Morrison, the assailants evidently knew him, as they cried "We have got you now!" before opening fire. Regarding the lack of direct identification of Hill, Ekengren reiterated his belief that Hill should not have had to prove anything until a clearcut case was established against him. Of Hill's failure to testify he said, "It is not my intention to justify or excuse Hillstrom's insolence and stubbornness throughout the procedure, nevertheless I cannot see any connection between that and the case, though I doubt not that it unduly influenced those who had to do with the trial."[89]

By the afternoon of September 30, it appeared as if none of the appeals to save Joe Hill was having any effect. President Wilson had not acted. Governor Spry refused to act until new evidence was presented by Hill. Hill stubbornly refused to accept the Board of Pardons' offer of freedom if he would explain his wound to his attorneys.

Utah State Prison officials began preparations for the execution. Warden Pratt posted a death watch over Hill, and the prison blacksmith shop was converted into chambers for the firing squad.[90] Joe Hill wrote farewell letters, a few of which have been preserved. To Sam Murray he wrote:

Well, Sam, I received your letter, but you shouldn't feel so sentimental about it. This dying business is not quite so bad as it is cracked up to be. I have always said "a new trial or die trying," and I'll show that I meant it. I was moved to another cell last night and have an armed guard in front of my cell. I was also given a swell feed for the first time in God knows how long, and that is one of the surest signs.

Well, Sam, you and me had a little pleasure at one time that few rebels have had the privilege of having, and I guess I've had my share of the fun after all. Now, just forget me, and say goodby to the bunch.

Yours for the OBU
Joe Hill[91]

To Oscar W. Larson he wrote the following letter which has been translated from Swedish.

Dear Comrade—

I have received your welcome letter.

The Swedish consul has told me that you are worried about me. This you need not be. I am sure you understand my position. I have always said that I would get a new trial because I know I have the right to demand one. Whatever is said is said. I have told all my friends, it's been in the papers, and a man must stay with his word. I am right, and, as they say in Old Sweden, "I'll split a yard before I give one inch."

Biography you say? No. Let's not spoil good writing paper with such nonsense— Only the here and now is of concern to me. I am "a citizen of the world" and I was born on a planet called the earth. The exact spot where first I saw the light of day is of such slight importance that it deserves no comment—My best song and "Girl" is "The Rebel Girl" and my next favorite is "Old Man Noah."

I haven't much to say about myself. Will only say that I have done what little I could to bring the Flag of Freedom closer to its goal. I also once had the great honor to do my part on the field of battle under the Red Flag and I must say that I am very proud about it—I will close now with the Warmest greetings to all the Swedish revolutionaries and Verdandi members.

I have been and am yours for
Freedom & Brotherhood
Joe Hill[92]

To Ben Williams, editor of *Solidarity*, he wrote:

Dear Friends and fellow workers:

"John Law" has given me his last and final order to get off the earth and stay off. He has told me that lots of times before, but this time it seems as if he is meaning business.

I have said time and again that I was going to get a new trial or die trying. I have told it to my friends. It has been printed in the newspapers, and I don't see why I should "eat my own crow" just because I happen to be up against a firing squad. I have stated my position plainly to everybody, and I won't budge an inch, because I know I am right. Tomorrow I expect to take a trip to the planet Mars and if so, will immediately commence to organize the Mars canal workers into the I.W.W., and we will sing the good old songs so loud that the learned star gazers on earth will once and for all get

153

positive proofs that the planet Mars really is inhabited. In the mean time I hope you'll keep the ball a-rolling here. You are on the right track, and you are bound to get there. I have nothing to say about myself, only that I have always tried to do what little I could to make this earth a little better for the great producing class, and I can pass off into the great unknown with the pleasure of knowing that I have never in my life, doublecrossed man, woman or child.

With a last fond farewell to all true rebels and a hearty thanks for the noble support you have given me in this unequal fight, I remain,

> Yours for International Solidarity,
> Joe Hill[93]

And, to Elizabeth Gurley Flynn,

Dear Friend and F.W.

Well Gurley I guess I am off for the great unknown tomorrow morning. I have said that I'd have a trial or die trying. They can kill me I know, but they can never make me "eat my own crow." I consider myself lucky anyway because I have managed to get some of the facts out, but not all of them by any means. Well I had the pleasure to fight under the Red Flag once, anyway, so I guess I've had my share of the fun. I would like to kiss you Good-bye Gurley, not because you are a girl but because you are the original Rebel Girl.

> Good Bye
> Yours for the OBU
> Joe Hill[94]

As the day progressed and it appeared that Hill was resigned to his fate, Governor Spry received the following message from the President of the United States:

Respectfully ask if it would not be possible to postpone execution of Joseph Hillstrom, who I understand is a Swedish subject, until the Swedish minister has an opportunity to present his view of the case fully to your Excellency.

> Woodrow Wilson[95]

Hurriedly, Governor Spry called a meeting of the Board of Pardons in the chambers of the supreme court. Following the meeting, which lasted an hour, Warden Pratt was instructed to remove the death watch.[96]

Hill said nothing when he was told he would not die the next morning. "A suggestion of a smile about his mouth" was the only sign of emotion he displayed.[97]

Later that evening, the Board of Pardons met again. Following this meeting Governor Spry sent a message to President Wilson explaining that he was granting Hill a reprieve. Clearly indicating that the reprieve was being granted only because the President had requested it, Spry advised that Hill was guilty and had had a fair trial, and that the President should encourage Ekengren to travel to Salt Lake City to make his investigation prior to the next Board of Pardons meeting on October 16.[98] Spry then issued an order of respite.[99]

Joe Hill was granted a sixteen-day reprieve by the unprecedented intervention of the President of the United States to save a man condemned to death by a state. Ironically, he was saved from death by the man he had depicted in his writings as "woodhead Wilson."[100]

The following day, October 1, President Wilson sent a second message to

Governor Spry in an apparent attempt to lessen the degree of any possible offense the governor may have felt at his request for postponement. Wilson emphasized that he had acted only in consideration of ". . . the representative of a foreign nation."[101]

The President also instructed Acting Secretary of State Polk to inform the Swedish Minister of Spry's request. Accordingly, Polk told Ekengren of the reprieve and that Governor Spry urged him to travel to Salt Lake City to conduct his personal investigation prior to the October 16 Board meeting. Polk explained that Spry wanted him to investigate personally because Vice Consul Carlson had already ". . . gone thoroughly into the case" and "assured the Board that he knows no reason why the Board should change its decision."[102]

Also, on October 1, Joe Hill replied to the Swedish Minister's request of the previous day.

> Wire received have written for publication full statement of facts now in hands of Governor. After you receive and read said statement I am certain you will understand me better. Stay granted until October 16. Thank you for your noble efforts. I remain yours
>
> Joseph Hillstrom
>
> Pay no attention to attorney Scott. Deal with Soren X. Christensen Salt Lake City or O. N. Hilton Denver.[103]

While the I.W.W. and other pro-Hill factions were elated by the President's action, Utah was shocked that the President of the United States would interfere in the affairs of a state—especially to save a condemned Wobbly. The extent to which Utah's official pride and prestige had become involved is indicated in the following excerpt from an editorial in a Salt Lake City paper on September 30, following the President's request for a postponement.

> There should be no misunderstanding of the fundamental principle involved in the case of Joseph Hillstrom. He is no longer a factor in the equation. It is the State of Utah that now stands before the bar, and the issue is whether law shall continue to be law or whether a hue and cry may suspend or even destroy it.[104]

When they learned of his intervention, it must have seemed absurd to Utahns that the President would use his office—which to many Americans symbolized the efforts of civilized man to order his society by law—to help an individual who was, to them, the embodiment of the spirit of anarchism.

Justice McCarty feared that the President's action would give confidence to the I.W.W. and that a reign of terror might prevail in Utah. He predicted that

> . . . [the I.W.W.] may, and no doubt will, construe the President's action as a tacit approval of their course and methods. Should my fears in this regard be well founded, and I believe they are, in the meantime hundreds of this undesirable element will swarm to this state and, using Hillstrom as an excuse, will undoubtedly attempt to create a reign of terror such as existed in the Coeur d'Alene country, at San Diego, and at Goldfield, Nevada. Should this happen—and it is entirely within the range of probabilities—President Wilson, more than any other individual or factor connected with the Hillstrom case, will be responsible for the results.[105]

Reaction of the local press ranged from acceptance to anger. The *Deseret Evening News* editorialized on the living drama of the last-minute reprieve, complaining that ". . . the case throughout has been given importance to which it is not entitled."[106] The *Salt Lake Tribune*, reasoning that President Wilson could not have acted otherwise in the face of Ekengren's request, added that the reprieve ". . . will serve a good purpose in acquainting the American people with the facts before Hillstrom is sent to his death."[107] More hostile, the *Salt Lake Herald-Republican* charged that the President's action could only intensify bitterness and encourage lawlessness and continued agitation. "This state will indeed be fortunate," it claimed, "if an army of these gentlemen of leisure and of vicious tendencies do not encamp within its borders to terrify and to occupy the commonwealth they have temporarily conquered." Critical of President Wilson for interfering in a situation he did not understand, the writer concluded:

> Joseph Hillstrom and his crime are no longer an issue. The question has become whether Utah's laws for the protection of Utah's citizens can and shall be enforced. It has become a question whether an organized effort to interfere with law and its purposes shall succeed or whether the officials to whom the people of Utah delegate the power and authority of government are honest enough and capable enough to use that power and authority without unjustified interference from beyond the state borders.[108]

Although Utah experienced no "reign of terror," Joe Hill's reprieve did have the effect, as Justice McCarty had feared, of giving the I.W.W. confidence in its power and methods. Charles Ashleigh, who adapted Joe Hill's soupline song for use in New York City, expressed this feeling in a *Solidarity* article entitled "Reflections on Joe Hill's Reprieve." Congratulating the Wobblies for their "indomitable energy" in wresting a working man from the very jaws of death, he exulted, "Without using economic weapons, by sheer massed publicity and pressure of opinion, we have gained a point." The fact that a victory had been won ensured, for Ashleigh, the eventual success of the I.W.W. in transforming ". . . a crowd of malcontents into a self disciplined army of fighting producers," in order that the working class might gain "not just the amelioration of a few evils but the whole world."[109]

Solidarity also editorialized on the role played by Joe Hill in obtaining the reprieve.

> . . . Possibly very few workers knew the magnificent role played by Joe Hill himself, in this desperate struggle for his life. No victim of class injustice in modern times has exhibited such unswerving courage under fire. Accustomed to an outdoor life, and chafing under prison confinement, Hill nevertheless refused to yield an inch. Before the Board of Pardons he said: "I do not want a pardon or a commutation, I want a new trial or nothing." To the press he wrote: "I have lived like an artist and I shall die like an artist." At Hill's very last when asked by the Swedish Consul to name the woman he said: "It's nobody's business who she is—I am innocent." Even the cold blooded impersonal upholders of the law must have been shaken at the thought of killing such a man.[110]

"Don't waste time in mourning: organize!"

8 Because Joe Hill's fate was again to be decided on October sixteenth, his attorneys had just sixteen days in which to provide an acceptable reason for Utah authorities to commute his sentence to life imprisonment. On October third, O. N. Hilton traveled to Washington, D.C., to consult with Minister Ekengren.

Before meeting with Hilton, Ekengren had not decided whether or not he would travel to Utah to make a personal investigation. He was also undecided about whether to retain another attorney to review the evidence with 1,500 dollars provided by the Foreign Minister of Sweden. Ekengren consulted Isaac B. Reinhardt, an attorney and president of the National Association for the Abolition of Capital Punishment, about investigating the case, but after meeting with Hilton decided neither to retain another attorney nor to travel to Utah himself.[1]

Hilton was responsible for this decision as Ekengren explained to Reinhardt on October 8:

> Have been in conference today and yesterday with O. N. Hilton. . . . He strongly advised me not to send anybody to Utah as my representative neither to go there myself as for the present nothing can be done for obtaining new trial. . . . We agreed on another way of action will explain later.[2]

To a legal advisor to the Swedish Legation, Henry G. Gray, Ekengren sent a similar message, again indicating that another course of action had been agreed upon.[3] Gray answered the following day, concurring with Ekengren's decision not to go to Salt Lake City and expressing his view that it would be very difficult to obtain even a commutation as no new evidence had been introduced.[4]

The Swedish Minister's plan of action was revealed when, in answer to a request from Mrs. J. Sargent Cram for information concerning his preparation for the Board of Pardons meeting, he replied:

> Have appealed to the President asking him if possible to use his influence with Governor of Utah for a commutation of sentence which is all I can do for the present. Have also tried private influence to same effect. When answer obtained will telegraph immediately. This is strictly confidential.[5]

Ekengren, on Hilton's advice, had committed himself to appeal to Governor Spry through intermediaries rather than to investigate personally.

The private attempt to influence Spry was made through Utah Senator Reed Smoot. Hilton probably advised this, believing that Smoot would be willing to help. While traveling back to Denver from their Washington meeting, Hilton wrote to Ekengren that he was preparing a draft of a letter which Ekengren might need to send to the President, but added, "I hope you received assurances from Senator Smoot as will not render such a course imperative. . . ."[6]

Senator Smoot apparently suggested that Ekengren submit to him a memorandum requesting that he intercede with the governor. However, entries in the senator's diaries during this period show that he fully believed Hill to be guilty and resented President Wilson's (and presumably Ekengren's) interference. Accordingly, he refused to intercede and instead of answering Ekengren's memorandum, released it to the press. Although Smoot received numerous letters requesting his help, he would not be swayed. (On November 19, Hill's execution day, Smoot, who was staying in New York City, was awakened by a 2 a.m. telephone call from Mrs. Cram, who pleaded that he ask Governor Spry to stay the execution. Smoot voiced his final refusal to become involved, replying that he could not and would not do so.)[7]

Hilton, writing to Ekengren concerning Smoot's refusal to cooperate, said: "I am at a loss to understand how Senator Smoot could be so unmindful of professional ethics and so impolite as to neglect to reply to your telegram solicited by him, and then give it to the papers for publication."[8]

Between the granting of the reprieve and the October 16 Board meeting, Joe Hill asked Ekengren not to act until he received the statement Hill had submitted to the Board of Pardons.[9] However, Ekengren told Jerome Sabath, secretary of the National Association for the Abolition of Capital Punishment, "I do not think the convicted's statement will alter the situation."[10]

As the first part of Hilton's plan had obviously failed, it became evident that another personal appeal to the President was the only course of action remaining to the Swedish Minister. On October 13, Ekengren received a telegram from Bill Haywood supporting the decision to try to influence Governor Spry to grant a commutation.[11] Hilton also wrote Ekengren reiterating his view that to execute Hill would be nothing less than judicial murder.[12] Later that day, Ekengren sent the following message to the President of the United States:

My dear Mr. President,

As a result of your representation to the Governor of Utah, Joseph Hillstrom, who is under death sentence, was granted a respite until the next meeting of the Board of Pardons which convenes on the 16th instant, when, as I understand it, a new date will be fixed for the execution.

This delay has afforded me an opportunity to investigate carefully the facts in the case and the course of the trial. The result of that is that I am more firmly of the opinion that the evidence and the course of the trial do not warrant the execution of a death sentence, nevertheless there seems now to be but one way to prevent this, i.e., to secure a commutation. I cannot see how it would be possible to obtain a new trial. The records show numerous instances where exceptions might have been noted that would have made a new trial almost imperative, at least easy to obtain, but they were not made; and now one cannot take advantage of errors and irregularities as a means to reopen the case. The legally trained men whom I have consulted are of the same opin-

ion. As the experience I have already had with the authorities of Utah leads me to fear
that representations made by me to the Board of Pardons will be unavailing and wish-
ing to do all that possibly can be done, I venture to once more address you, Mr. President, directly in this matter. This time I would most respectfully ask whether you
could consistently recommend to the Board of Pardons of the State of Utah that the
death sentence be commuted. I am, my dear Mr. President,

Most respectfully yours,
W. A. F. Ekengren[13]

For two days Ekengren waited for the President's answer. Finally, on
October 15, he telephoned the President's office and, expressing concern over
the impending Board meeting, asked the President's secretary if Wilson intended to request a commutation. In the absence of presidential action, Ekengren explained that, following instructions from his government, he would wire
Governor Spry a final request for commutation.[14] Shortly thereafter, the President informed Ekengren of his decision not to further involve himself in the
Hill case.[15]

Ekengren then contacted Hill, pleading with him to give ". . . some indication of where and how" he received his wound, concluding, "I am doing all I
can to head off the execution but without your cooperation I fear the results
will not be good."[16] Clearly unable to understand why Hill would not relent
and explain how he was wounded, the Minister expressed his feelings to journalist Timothy Walsh of the *New York World*, who was supporting the save Joe
Hill campaign. "Of course he may have his own grave reasons for remaining
silent, but as his life is at stake it seems that such reasons whatever they may be
could be waived."[17] Later that day, Ekengren notified Hilton, "All other resources having failed, I have today as the only way still open addressed to the
Governor an appeal as strong as capacity of foreign diplomat and the present
circumstances of the case permit. . . . Have very little hope for success."[18]

As Ekengren had indicated, his appeal was as strongly worded as he could
properly make it.

> Through your courtesy of granting a postponement of the execution of Joseph
> Hillstrom, sentenced by the courts of your state to be executed for murder in the first
> degree, I have had the opportunity to carefully study not only the opinion of the
> Supreme Court but also the stenographic records of the proceedings before the lower
> court together with other available documents in the case and through the informa-
> tion thus obtained I have only been further confirmed in my opinion that the evidence
> against the convicted does not warrant a capital punishment.
>
> I am well aware that from a technical point of view a new trial is out of the question
> as the matter now stands but considering the weakness of the evidence which at best is
> only circumstantial I herewith venture not only on my own but on my Government's
> behalf to address a most earnest appeal to you, Mr. Governor, and through you the
> entire Board of Pardons, with a view to obtain a commutation of sentence for my
> unfortunate countryman if for no other reason—at least for the sake of humanity and
> comity usually practiced between friendly nations.
>
> W. A. F. Ekengren[19]

Later, in a complaint concerning the treatment Utah authorities gave this
request, Ekengren told Hilton, "In publication of that protest, probably given

to the press by Utah authorities, the last lines containing the chief point were striken out."[20] To Timothy Walsh, he said the appeal as it appeared in the press was "incomplete and as such misleading."[21]

Hilton replied that he was "not surprised" at the way Ekengren's request was handled. "It is the same tactics they are pursuing about these alleged threats, as every indication is that they are writing these letters themselves addressed to themselves, or procuring it to be done."[22]

As the Board of Pardons met on October 16, unsubstantiated information was released to the Salt Lake City press that Joe Hill had shot a police officer in San Pedro, California; that he had been involved in a streetcar robbery in Long Beach and in the dynamiting of the Los Angeles Times Building; that he had shot a deputy sheriff in Layton, Utah, while robbing the Layton Hardware Company in 1911; and that he had been imprisoned in Butte, Montana, for an undisclosed crime.[23] Hill's involvement in any of these crimes was never proved.

Prison officials and the Board of Pardons claimed to have taken "every precaution" to keep the information secret and protested that it was ". . . much to the chagrin of the state authorities" that it leaked out. All Governor Spry would say concerning the source of the information was that it was ". . . gleaned from a prisoner at the Utah State Prison." (Prison officials had reportedly intercepted a letter from Hill to Bill Haywood in which he mentioned seeing a certain man in prison. After questioning by prison officers, the unnamed man allegedly gave the information that Hill had a criminal record.)[24]

This news leak on the day of the Board meeting, considered in light of the fact that the charges were never substantiated, suggests that Utah officials were using the information to build support for their position and to detract from Hill's appeal to public sympathy. Later—on the day before Hill's execution—more unfounded and damaging information "leaked out."

The meeting of the Board of Pardons convened at 10 a.m. on October 16 in a room guarded by fourteen armed men. Hill's case was not heard until 3 p.m. The actual meeting seemed anti-climactic in comparison to the behind-the-scenes maneuvering of the preceding two weeks. Joe Hill, represented by Soren X. Christensen, refused to attend the meeting as he felt he had adequately stated his position in his previous appearance before the Board. The Board dismissed Ekengren's appeal, demanding "tangible facts" before it would consider a commutation. Christensen, after explaining that he had tried many times to convince Hill to disclose the details of how he was wounded, told them he had nothing new to present.[25] Thereupon, the Board terminated the reprieve and referred Hill back to Judge Ritchie for resentencing.[26]

On October 17, 1915, Salt Lakers read: HILLSTROM MUST DIE, PARDONS BOARD DECIDES: SWEDISH MINISTER APPEAL IS FRUITLESS.[27]

In retrospect, it seems that Ekengren should have gone to Salt Lake City. Since the Board had made it clear that no favorable action would be taken without the presentation of some new evidence, and since Hill's refusal to explain his wound made the presentation of new evidence almost impossible, Ekengren's best chance would probably have been to show his willingness to do everything possible by visiting Salt Lake City. It is evident that the Board fully expected him to investigate personally, as Jerome Sabath had told the Swedish Minister on October 11 that the Board was demanding a report on his investigation and was dissatisfied with his delay.[28]

After the decision, O. N. Hilton, who did not attend the meeting on October 16, issued an "Open Letter to the Board of Pardons of Utah," challenging its members to public debate. The letter appeared in several newspapers.

To Board of Pardons of the State of Utah

Gentlemen:

Assuming that your reasons for denying clemency to Joseph Hillstrom are correctly set forth in the public press this morning and for the purpose of showing that they are not founded on either the law or the facts in the case, but are intended to and do delude and deceive the public, I respectfully make the offer to publicly discuss the facts at any time in any city in the USA with any member of your board, or all of them; such discussion to be before the date assigned for his execution.

I make this request to afford an opportunity to refute, as I feel I can among other things, the false, wicked and cowardly aspersion of his character—that Hill has heretofore committed any crime or that he has now, or ever has had, any criminal record—now for the first time so bravely urged as a sufficient justification for taking his life.

This matter, as you must realize, is one now of national if not international importance, and has excited intense interest from New York to San Francisco; and I would be, as the attorney for the condemned man, of "meaner stuff than men are made of" if I did not, in the brief time of life now allotted him, challenge you to the proofs.

I am only anxious and determined if Hillstrom is judicially murdered that the people of the country—the great jury to whom we must all go at last—shall fully understand just where rests the full measure of responsibility for "the deep damnation of his taking off."

Any communication will reach me addressed to this city [Denver, Colorado].

Very respectfully,
O. N. Hilton[29]

That Hilton did not expect his challenge to be accepted is evident from a telegram he sent to Ekengren.

I sent you a copy of my "open letter." I do not expect any reply to it, but if I get one, I shall be delighted, as I can rout them on every contention. They cannot defend their action, and they know it.[30]

On October 18, Joe Hill was sentenced to die for the third time. The execution date was set by Judge Ritchie for November 19, 1915. The press commented that when he was sentenced Hill tried to make a statement, but the court silenced him. Hill reportedly said, as he was being escorted from the courtroom, "The judge didn't want to hear what I had to say and I don't blame him."[31] Writing to O. N. Hilton, Hill explained his resentencing and his thoughts on the case.

Dear Judge:

. . . I did not know how the Board had decided until the Judge told me in Court. When I found out that it was another death sentence, I stood up and asked for permission to make a statement, but was taken out, and what I had to say was never said, and never will be. Well Judge, I guess the legal part of the case is done now, and I am glad of it. I've had a lawful trial, they say, and as I don't think there is much danger of any-body accepting your challenge, we might as well consider the case closed. Now there is only one more thing I'll ask you to do. I know it will be done right when you do it. I would like to have all records of the case sent to Chicago Headquarters, to be kept on file for future reference—a copy of the preliminary records; copy of the District Court records; the two to be kept for comparisons; the original of my statement (not copy— Mr. Christensen has the originals). I think Ed Rowan has a copy of the preliminary records, but am not sure of it. I have made some quotations in my statement from the preliminary records, and I wish to see if I made a mistake. If so, you might correct it, and have it typewritten. Now that's all I want done, Judge—you have always kept every promise you made to me, and that's why I want you to do this. In case someone, in the future, should want to learn the details of my case, from beginning to end, I would like to have it all together, and as you are my attorney, I wish to have it sent from your office. With best wishes for your Health and Welfare, I remain Respectfully your Client.

Joe Hill[32]

Although Hill may have considered his case closed after the resentencing, those leading the attempt to prevent the execution still hoped for success. In-creased pressure was applied to persuade Hill to disclose the details of his wound. Isaac Reinhardt expressed to Ekengren his hope that the appeals of Hill's supporters would yet ". . . succeed in convincing him that his false notion of chivalry is detrimental to all concerned, not even excepting the woman whom he says he seeks to shield."[33]

At this point, Hilton received the previously mentioned anonymous letter from Buffalo, New York, which offered an explanation of the circumstances surrounding the condemned man's wound. He apparently considered this letter the best remaining chance to save Hill. After the Board's decision, Hilton had confided to Ekengren, "I am much distressed at the plight of this young man and feel like fighting for him to the last ditch."[34] But he also commented to Reinhardt that without an explanation of his wound, Hill would ". . . be exe-cuted no matter how many petitions are filed."[35] Now, after reading the letter from Buffalo, Hilton earnestly sought Hill's permission to release its contents.

On yesterday I received a letter from Buffalo, which at the writer's request I have forwarded to the Swedish Minister. This letter gives me for the first time knowledge of the real facts in your case. I will continue to respect your wish if you so insist and will not divulge its contents if you so request me, but it would be most satisfying to me if I could and so save you from your impending fate. If the details are shown to be true, the Governor assured me personally that he would issue a respite up to the last mo-ment if he was assured a mistake had been made, and your story was substantiated.

Now Joe, if I have ever deserved the full confidence of a client, it is in your case. I most earnestly beseech you to tell me truly. I will take such action as will result in your vindication. I am fully persuaded without this you will be executed and while you say your life is of no importance, nevertheless no one wishes wantonly to shed your blood, and while I believe the authorities are misled and have deprived you of a manifest right in denying you a fair trial, still you must realize that all human judgments are fallible and are sometimes honestly executed, though found in error.

No cause has ever been helped by violence, tumult or disorder and the community in which you are has a right to know the actual truth. These, my last words to you, express the hope that you may be guided and helped in your decision by a realization of the awful responsibility that rests on all and that in this supreme moment I may hear from you that I am at liberty to make the facts public if they are true.[36]

There is no record of a reply from Hill. It is clear, however, that he disregarded Hilton's plea.

While Hilton was meeting failure in his attempt to pursuade Hill, Ekengren continued to search for a way to prevent the execution. Ever since the granting of the reprieve, Ekengren had considered sending an attorney to Salt Lake City to investigate the case, and several attorneys were anxious to offer their help. A Kansas City, Missouri, lawyer, Franz Lindquist, had asked to help, but Ekengren rejected his repeated offers. Isaac Reinhardt was prepared to confer with Hilton in Denver, then continue to Salt Lake City to investigate, but Hilton had advised against retaining Reinhardt.[37] From Ekengren's correspondence it is apparent that after failing to sway the Board, he increasingly sought the advice of Marcel A. Viti, a personal friend and attorney who was Swedish Vice Consul in Philadelphia. Following Viti's advice, Ekengren finally decided that rather than send an outsider, he would retain a competent attorney in Salt Lake City. He reasoned that a local man would be more familiar with Utah procedure and laws.

Joe Hill opposed Ekengren's idea of retaining another attorney. On October 28 he wired Ekengren, "Please send Hilton if finances allow."[38] On November 12 he again wired:

> Judge Hilton is the best attorney in the world. Please don't expend any more money on others. The case is closed. Now my friends know I am innocent and I don't care what the rest think. Hearty thanks to you and the whole Swedish nation for your noble support.
>
> Remain yours
Joseph Hillstrom[39]

However, Ekengren had available the 1,500 dollars authorized by his government, and since he had been instructed to do all within his power to prevent the execution, he disregarded Hill's request and proceeded to enlist the help of a Salt Lake City attorney.

He first solicited the firm of VanCott, Allison and Ritter, having dealt with VanCott before. But the firm declined to look at the evidence, declaring that the case was hopeless.[40] Ekengren then wired the office of Pierce, Critchlow, and Barrette, offering them 1,500 dollars to make the review. E. B. Critchlow visited Hill in prison and informed him he had been asked to look into his case, meanwhile assuring Hill that he was "strongly opposed" to the I.W.W. Hill said it was "all right with him" if Critchlow investigated the case.[41] The attorney asked Hill to disclose any new facts about his wound that he might remember, and Hill replied that he regarded it a private matter. Critchlow countered that he was mistaken because his wound was a material fact shown at the trial which had a bearing on his guilt or innocence; therefore, he had no right to regard it as a purely private matter. After the interview, Critchlow accepted the offer to review the case, concluding his letter to Ekengren with, "Mr. Hillstrom is not an unintelligent man, and apparently realized fully the force of our observation."[42]

On November 10, Critchlow informed Ekengren that he had completed the investigation and review. He reported that he had found "no reason" to think the verdict of "murder in the first degree" not warranted by all the testimony introduced. "We find no error or information in the record which, in our judgment, should cause you to suspect that any injustice is in fact being done in sentencing him to death." Critchlow did add, however, that there was a technical error that possibly could be used to reopen the case. Under the statutes of Utah, Dr. McHugh's testimony was incompetent, because he should not have been allowed to testify concerning information he received as a result of his professional treatment of Hill's wound. Critchlow explained that Hill's attorneys had not objected to the doctor's testimony, but they should have done so. If they had objected and that matter had been relied upon in appeal, he claimed, the supreme court would have ruled that the testimony was incompetent. Speculating that Hill's attorneys did not object possibly because they thought the doctor's declaration that Hill suffered his wound ". . . in an argument over a woman" would help his case, Critchlow nevertheless stated his opinion that this technicality would provide the only chance to have the case reopened.[43]

Critchlow wrote again to Ekengren on November 12, "We are extremely anxious to avoid sensational publicity, or to disclose to the disadvantage of the defendant our personal opinion in this case." Concluding, he said, "Permit us to say that we dislike very much to be called upon to act in this matter, but felt that under the ethics of our profession we were not quite at liberty to refuse."[44]

After reviewing with Viti the suggestion that a rehearing could possibly be obtained on the basis of the incompetency of McHugh's testimony, Ekengren sent two telegrams to Critchlow on November 17. In the first, he explained that since his government had instructed him to do all he could, he, in turn, instructed Critchlow to do his best to get a rehearing.[45] The second telegram, sent to insure that Critchlow would act, said, "Do all you can."[46] The same day, Critchlow wired Ekengren to say that his firm "declined further action in the case." He explained that he had talked to F. B. Scott, who told him that Hill personally requested that the testimony of Dr. McHugh be admitted to add weight to his contention that he was shot in a fight over a woman. Because of this, Critchlow claimed that he could not, in propriety, make an application for a rehearing.[47]

While Ekengren's last efforts to save Hill were failing, the I.W.W.—its wrath fanned by the Salt Lake killing of A. J. Horton by Police Major H. P. Myton—maintained and even increased its high pitch of excitement and agitation demanding Hill's release. Three thousand people in Minneapolis, Minnesota, marched in protest of the execution.[48] On November 5, *Solidarity* reprinted an editorial which had appeared in the *New York Globe* a few days earlier, supporting the view that Joe Hill was not a victim of a class war, that there was no capitalist conspiracy against him, and that Hill was not to be executed for his political ideas.[49] In rebuttal to the *Globe*'s editorial, *Solidarity* offered a statement by Elizabeth Gurley Flynn reviewing the evidence against Joe Hill and concluding that he was the innocent victim of a conspiracy. Miss Flynn said, "If Joe Hill had not been known as a prominent figure in the I.W.W., certainly if he had been a Mormon, the Mormon judge and jury would have released him on the flimsy showing made by the prosecution." She concluded by saying:

> The day Joe Hill's brave strong heart is torn with bullets, his fruitful pen is stilled, and we take his body forth to the music of his own songs, the stigma of murder will be stamped on every cowardly member of this Mormon Board. Utah will never be permitted to forget her second "Mountain Meadow" disgrace. Labor again turns for justice elsewhere than the courts of law.[50]

A mammoth "Joe Hill Protest Meeting" was held in the Manhattan Lyceum in New York City on November 8. Blazoned on a canvas banner overhanging the speaker's podium were the words, "On November 19, Joseph Hillstrom will be shot through the heart by six hired gunmen of the State of Utah. Shall we let him die?" *Solidarity* declared that "Not in recent times has there been a meeting of workers so thoroughly supercharged with protest as was this."[51] Many persons of radical left sympathies spoke at the meeting. Elizabeth Gurley Flynn admonished the audience to act to prevent Hill's execution by making their belief in his innocence known to Utah officials. John Reed, author, radical, and editor of *Metropolitan Magazine*, spoke of the importance of Hill to the labor movement in America. Ann Strunsky Walling poetically eulogized the condemned man. James Larkin, the Irish labor organizer, charged that Joe Hill's death would erect a monument to ". . . the weakness of class union and the failure of Solidarity. . . . But let the monument of failure and shame not be erected. Let the case of Joseph Hillstrom go to the greatest jury of all—the jury of the workers. Let the working class pass judgment and liberate Joe Hill. If we but say the word nothing can stop us."[52] At the conclusion of the meeting, motions were made and unanimously adopted to have an appeal for help sent to President Wilson and a "message of good cheer" to Joe Hill.[53]

On November 13 *Solidarity* carried an article by John Sandgren, an I.W.W. editor and the man leading the effort to arouse Swedish-Americans on Hill's behalf. He explained his activities, saying that Joe Hill's account of his trial had been translated into Swedish and that several thousand copies had been circulated across America. Resolutions demanding Hill's release had been printed and distributed. They were to be sent to President Wilson, Governor Spry and the Utah Board of Pardons. Three mass meetings of Swedish-Americans were held in the New York City area in one week, all demanding Hill's release. Sandgren, stating his philosophy of protest, said, "We, for our part, hold that the only safe method to adopt is to stir up the people of this country to a realization of the dastardly act almost to be committed against an innocent man. Only by shaking the country to the foundations will we prevail over the evil powers that control the fate of our beloved fellow worker, Joe Hill."[54]

As the execution date approached, it became clear that petitions and emotion-filled speeches would not save the condemned man and that the only chance remaining (barring an offer by Hill to explain his wound) would be President Wilson's intervention. Elizabeth Gurley Flynn and Mrs. J. Sargent Cram, together with O. N. Hilton, persuaded Mr. Cram to arrange an interview with the President. As mentioned earlier, a previous attempt by the two women to see the President on September 28 had been unsuccessful.

On November 11, the two women traveled to Washington. Mrs. Cram had asked Minister Ekengren to accompany them, but he declined. They breakfasted with Gifford Pinchot, Mrs. Cram's brother-in-law, who then escorted the women to the White House. Miss Flynn reported that they were greeted by the President's secretary, Mr. Tumulty, when they arrived, and a few moments later the President came in and greeted them cordially. The President listened to the women's plea, but said that although he had intervened once at the request of the Swedish Minister, he feared that his further involvement might do more harm than good. Miss Flynn later reported that she bluntly said to the President, "He's sentenced to death. You can't make it worse, Mr. President." The President reportedly smiled, said, "Well, that's true," and promised to consider the matter. After the meeting, both Miss Flynn and Mrs. Cram felt they had failed in their final attempt to save Hill.[55]

On November 15, four days before the scheduled execution, the American Federation of Labor was holding its thirty-fifth annual convention in San Francisco, California. Tom Mooney, secretary of the International Workers Defense League, received permission to present Hill's case to the convention in the hope that a resolution of protest would result and be sent to President Wilson and Governor Spry. Following Mooney's presentation the matter was referred to the committee on ways and means. The Utah delegation to the convention, headed by D. A. Camomile, supported the Mooney resolution. However, when news of Camomile's action reached Salt Lake City, the Salt Lake Federation of Labor was outraged. The local leaders met and issued a statement expressing their opinion that Joe Hill's trial had been fair and impartial. They advised the American Federation not to be "dragged" into the Joe Hill affair.[56] Nevertheless, on November 16 the convention's committee on ways and means recommended that American Federation of Labor President Samuel Gompers wire the committee's resolution to the President of the United States and to the Governor of Utah. The resolution was adopted by the delegates assembled.

THE PRESIDENT:

The Convention of the American Federation of Labor assembled here unanimously adopted the subjoined preambles and resolutions:

To the Officers and Delegates of the Thirty-Fifth Annual Convention of the American Federation of Labor: We, your Committee on Ways and Means, to whom was referred the appeal affecting Joseph Hillstrom, report as follows: That we have examined this case as thoroughly as time would permit and have listened to lengthy statements from persons who claim to be conversant with the facts and we beg leave to offer the following resolution for immediate consideration and action:

WHEREAS Joseph Hillstrom, a workingman of the State of Utah, and active in the cause of labor, has been sentenced to death by shooting by a Utah court and the date of his execution has been fixed for the nineteenth day of November, nineteen fifteen, and

WHEREAS the circumstances surrounding the said conviction and sentence are such as to make the grounds for this conviction and sentence appear to be utterly inadequate and matters of the gravest doubt in that the evidence was of a purely circumstantial nature and highly improbable and the rights of the said Joseph Hillstrom do not appear to have been sufficiently or at all safeguarded, but on the contrary seem to have been violated to such an extent that the said Joseph Hillstrom did not have a fair and impartial trial and

WHEREAS the feeling against the said Joseph Hillstrom as a labor agitator was such as to have militated against him with the jury greatly to his detriment and

WHEREAS we are of the opinion that the said Joseph Hillstrom did not have a fair and impartial trial, therefore be it

RESOLVED by the Thirty-Fifth Annual Convention of the American Federation of Labor that we urge the governor of the State of Utah to exercise his prerogative of clemency in this case and to stop the execution of the said Joseph Hillstrom and that he be given a new and fair trial and be it further

RESOLVED that the President of the American Federation of Labor is hereby authorized to forward at once copies of these resolutions to the Governor of Utah, to the Board of Pardons of the State of Utah, to the Swedish Ambassador and to the President of the United States and that they be published in the American Federationist and in the official publications of the affiliated unions.

May I now prevail upon you to exercise your great influence to at least help in saving the life of Joseph Hillstrom, particularly when there is so much doubt concerning his case.

> Samuel Gompers, President
> American Federation of Labor[57]

On November 16, along with Gompers' telegram, President Wilson received a message from Helen Keller.

THE PRESIDENT

Your excellency: I believe that Joseph Hillstrom has not had a fair trial and the sentence passed upon him is unjust. I appeal to you as official father of all the people to use your great power and influence to save one of the nation's helpless sons. The stay of execution will give time to investigate. New trial will give the man justice to which the laws of the land entitle him.

> Helen Keller[58]

President Wilson replied to her the next morning.

My dear Miss Keller:

I was very much touched by your telegram of November sixteenth with regard to Joseph Hillstrom and wish most sincerely that it were within my power to do something, but unhappily, there is nothing that I can do. The matter lies entirely beyond my jurisdiction and power. I have been deeply interested in the case but am balked of all opportunity.

> With sincere regard,
> Very truly yours,
> Woodrow Wilson[59]

However, between the time he sent the telegram to Helen Keller and the late afternoon of November 17, Wilson apparently changed his mind about not interfering. That afternoon he instructed Mr. Tumulty to send a message in reply to Samuel Gompers' telegram.

> The President has received your telegram embodying resolutions of the Convention of the American Federation of Labor concerning the case of Joseph Hillstrom, and has this morning again telegraphed the Governor of Utah urging the justice and advisability of a thorough reconsideration of the case.
>
> J. P. Tumulty[60]

For the second time, the President of the United States appealed directly to the Governor of Utah on Joe Hill's behalf.

> Hon. William Spry
> Salt Lake City, Utah
>
> With unaffected hesitation but with a very earnest conviction of the importance of the case, I again venture to urge upon your Excellency the justice and advisability, if it be possible, of a thorough reconsideration of the case of Joseph Hillstrom.
>
> Woodrow Wilson[61]

Why President Wilson should have changed his mind at this time can only be speculated upon. The Swedish Minister had not recently requested the President to act. Most probably, Wilson made the decision out of sympathy for Joe Hill's plight and in deference to the political power of a united working class.

Upon receipt of the President's telegram, the Board of Pardons called an emergency meeting to consider the request, and on November 18, the day before the scheduled execution, Governor Spry, with the Board of Pardons' sanction, replied to the President, making little effort to conceal his bitterness and dislike for the chief executive's intervention. After reviewing the previous appeals and the fact that in spite of the reprieve granted Hill no new evidence had been forthcoming, Spry charged:

> Forty six days after the granting of the respite and at the eleventh hour you as the President without stating any reasons therefore again wire urging a thorough reconsideration of the case because of its importance and the justice and advisability of such a course. Your interference in the case may have elevated it to an undue importance and the receipt of thousands of threatening letters demanding the release of Hillstrom regardless of his guilt or innocence may attach peculiar importance to it, but the case is important in Utah only as establishing after a fair and impartial trial the guilt of one of the perpetrators of one of the most atrocious murders ever committed in this State. It is also important by reason of the fact that this case has had more careful and painstaking consideration at the hands of the proper officials of Utah than any other like case in the history of the State.

Stressing the efforts that had been made in Hill's behalf, including his representation by three groups of attorneys and the Board of Pardons' offer of immediate clemency if his wound could be satisfactorily explained, Spry closed, "Tangible facts must be presented before I will further interfere in this case."[62]

The reaction in Utah to President Wilson's request and Governor Spry's refusal was, as before, almost unanimously in support of the governor. Justice McCarty, claiming that President Wilson interfered for political reasons, commented bitterly that: "President Wilson's conduct . . . will undoubtedly insure him not only the vote but the active support of practically every thug, yeggman and ex-convict in the land as well as those of that class who are now doing time in various state prisons."[63]

The *Deseret Evening News*, in an editorial, stood firmly behind Governor Spry's message of refusal to President Wilson. "Governor Spry will win the applause of his constituents and of all people who entertain the view that justice must be even handed, dispensed without fear, favor, and affection, if he pays no heed to the President's plea."[64] The *Salt Lake Tribune* added: "From the Utah point of view it is impossible to exaggerate the enormity of the President's blunder and his only excuse appears to be that he blundered through misinformation and neglect to make proper inquiry into the case."[65] The *Salt Lake Herald-Republican* also reacted with indignation, charging that the President

> . . . stooped from the dignity of his high office to pander to the class consciousness that takes no account of facts but only of prejudice. He lent the weight of his mighty authority to question the integrity of Utah courts and the humanity of Utah people. He has pilloried Utah, as he would dare pillory no other state in the union, without warrant in law or privilege. Utah will not forget.[66]

The *Ogden Standard-Examiner*, while believing Joe Hill guilty, argued that Governor Spry should have paid more respect to the ". . . exalted office of President of the United States." The writer reasoned that because there exists in America a class of dissatisfied people who feel they are being ". . . crushed beneath the iron heel of commercialism," the government and courts should extend themselves to reassure the discontented class ". . . that, in the crucial test, the law is not disregardful of possible error and is administered without prejudice; and that mandates of the courts are tempered with mercy."[67]

Not only the newspapers in Utah but also most leading citizens supported Governor Spry in saying that outside interference was not warranted.[68] Even the principals of Salt Lake City schools forwarded resolutions to the governor pledging their support and loyalty to him in his efforts to carry out the court's decree.[69]

Spry had the support of businessmen, as exemplified by Spencer Penrose, secretary of the Utah Copper Company, who sent a telegram from Colorado Springs.

> Please allow me to congratulate you most heartily on the manly and sane stand you have taken on the Hillstrom case notwithstanding the pressure brought to bear on you by those whose nerves are so easily affected by cheap sentimentality. You deserve all honor and gratitude from your fellow citizens of the United States.[70]

On November 18 Utah state officials made a blunder matched only by their lack of acumen on October 16 when, just prior to the Board of Pardons' consideration of Hill's case, they had released the unproved claim that he had a criminal record. As preparations were being made for the execution, prison officials located a black suit that Hill had asked to be allowed to wear to the execution. The suit, worn by Hill during his trial, had been stored in a closet in the prison during his months of confinement. When prison officials inspected it on November 18, they reportedly found the name "Morrison" written with indelible pencil in three different places in the suit. The news was released to the press, which immediately announced that dramatic new evidence had been found that connected Joe Hill with the Morrison murder. The allegation was that Hill had stolen the suit from J. G. Morrison. When Hill was confronted with it, he speculated, probably correctly, that a deputy sheriff had printed the name in the suit while it was closeted in the county jail.[71] That the prison officials, press, and police would attach such importance to the situation indicates the extent to which they had allowed reason to be overcome by emotion.

With the execution now only twenty-four hours away, tension gripped Salt Lake City. There was widespread fear that the I.W.W. would make some desperate last-minute attempt to free Hill and that the threats allegedly made to life and property would be carried out. The University of Utah, the state capitol, the governor's home, and several large business and commercial buildings in Salt Lake City had been lighted with arc lights for several nights and guarded by armed men twenty-four hours a day to protect them against expected Wobbly sabotage.[72] The *New York Tribune* reported to the nation that

SALT LAKE IS TERROR STRICKEN BY I.W.W. THREATS AS APPEAL IS DENIED.

Ten armed men are guarding the Governor's house. The homes of other state officials are also being guarded. All of the city's large buildings are under guard. Threats have been made to dynamite the Hotel Utah, the Mormon Temple and other buildings owned by the Mormon Church. The entire city is terror stricken. I.W.W. members have made threats against the city and state and secret servicemen said tonight they expect an attempt to dynamite the Governor's home.[73]

Adding to the tension were several emotion-filled public meetings held during the last two days of Hill's life. On the evening of November 17, the Liberal and Verdandi clubs of Salt Lake City, denied the use of Unity Hall, held an outdoor meeting in support of Hill and resolved to send telegraphic messages urging that Ekengren and President Wilson make one last appeal.[74] Speaking at the Newhouse Hotel on the eve of the execution, Isaac A. Hourwich of the *New York Review* claimed that Hill had not been proved guilty and should not be executed.[75] President Wilson's successful postponement of the October 1 execution date seemed to give Hill's supporters reason to believe he would once more escape death. All during the day and evening of November 18, the I.W.W. held meetings. In the evening, at an outdoor mass meeting in downtown Salt Lake City, several local leaders spoke. Ed Rowan reviewed the case and claimed that Hill was innocent. Following Rowan, Fred Ritter of the defense committee proclaimed:

We hold no animosity against the Governor or any member of the State Board of Pardons. The Governor is not responsible and he cannot help what is to be done. It is the law, and there is no personal feeling against the Governor nor anyone else. Joseph Hillstrom must die, a victim of the system under which we live.[76]

After the speeches, Hill's songs were sung by the large audience. Many stayed late into the night, chanting "And Joe Hill will be shot in the morning," then loudly answering themselves with "Not if we can help it."[77] During the chanting, one speaker reportedly voiced the phrase, recorded by a reporter for the *Los Angeles Times*, that subsequently became part of the Joe Hill lore, adapted as the title of a play and the theme of a song about him. The speaker called out, "Something is going to happen. Joe Hillstrom will never die, do you hear it everybody, Joe Hillstrom will never die."[78]

However, as time ran out, there remained no real reason for believing that Joe Hill would never die. The only question still to be answered was whether he would maintain his composure and nerve to the last or perhaps confess to the Morrison murder or break down under the strain. Hill's belief that the manner in which he died mattered to the workingmen of America apparently sustained him to the last, and the twenty-four hours preceding his execution evoked his final acts of defiance.

On November 18, the *Salt Lake Herald-Republican* expressed the opinion that all the stories circulated about Joe Hill's remarkable nerve were false and that he was a man of little or no spine.[79] Stories appeared in the Salt Lake press that Hill had "   become exceedingly nervous and could hardly talk to those who have visited him."[80] Another account said he had to ". . . place a pencil in his mouth to steady his lip movements" when he spoke.[81] When asked about Hill's bravery, Warden Pratt answered, "Hillstrom is just like all other condemned men—when the time comes he will weaken."[82]

That the reports of Hill's lack of nerve were nothing more than rumors is clearly shown by a remarkable interview between Hill and a *Salt Lake Herald-Republican* reporter on the afternoon of November 18. Hill was in his cell; the reporter talked to him through two sets of iron bars. The interview shows Hill to have been stoically reserved and calm on the eve of his execution—able to reason and to think clearly, and maintaining a sense of humor. Although the *Salt Lake Herald-Republican* had been decidedly anti-Joe Hill in its editorial statements throughout, the reporter who interviewed the condemned man unashamedly showed his respect for his courage and will power.

Hill stood and leaned against the door of his cell during the interview, resting his arms on one set of crossbars. He wore a dark blue soft shirt of coarse material, a coat made of overall material, dark blue pants and white canvas shoes. Around his neck was a neatly knotted white silk handkerchief. A green celluloid eye shade helped accommodate his eyes to the difference between the darkness of his cell and the white corridor outside, and also shaded his eyes when he did his "scribbling."[83] He showed no signs of nervousness. His hands, protruding through the bars, hung down in a relaxed manner.[84] His voice was clear except for an occasional moment when evidence of a slight cold was noticeable. He frequently smiled in reply to some particularly stimulating question. The newsman reported:

> Altogether the impression Hillstrom gave was one of a mentally clear, self-assured personality raised above the pall of the doom he knew he was approaching. There was

171

nothing to indicate vindictiveness, braggadocia or penitence in the man's demeanor. He seemed obsessed with a spirit of confidence and optimism. Although given every opportunity by leading questions he made no appeal for pity, his mental attitude was absolutely beyond the possibility of being surprised and he specifically stated that he had no worries.[85]

Concerning his trial and his handling by Utah courts and officials, Hill is reported to have said:

> I am not vindictive. I nurse no hard feelings, but I do sense a very real feeling of being the victim of an unfair trial and injustice. I have throughout my life done what was right to everybody. I can sincerely say that never in my life have I done anything for which I now should be sorry. Whatever comes will take care of itself; there is neither sense nor use in worrying. . . .
>
> What do I think I could accomplish if I had a new trial? This, which is everything, my innocence. . . .
>
> Why didn't I go on the stand before? Because the case was so badly mishandled and mismanaged and confused that I was disgusted. I felt certain that sufficient error had crept in to assure a new trial when I could make my defense properly and advantageously.
>
> Why should I at this time go into a statement concerning my whereabouts that night? Why should I now drag in a woman's name? Even if I would, the statement would be worthless as it would be uncorroborated, but even if it would help I have not the slightest intention or desire of going into that matter. . . .
>
> Why should I call in involved parties? I have never in my life asked anybody to help me and I won't now.
>
> What do I expect to accomplish by my situation? Well, it won't do the I.W.W. any harm and it won't do the State of Utah any good.[86]

Hill had other visitors than the newsman. Soren X. Christensen visited him to say goodbye and to inform him he was entitled by law to invite five persons to witness the execution. Hill replied he wanted only three: Ed Rowan, Fred Ritter, and George Child. Hill requested that Christensen not let the University of Utah medical school have his body and said he did not want to be buried in Utah.[87] Later that afternoon, Rowan, Ritter, and Child arrived to bid farewell. Hill waved goodbye to his visitors; he could not grasp their hands because the distance between the two sets of bars around his cell was too great.

That evening, the Warden sent a "death watch" to stay with Hill through his last night. Hill reportedly said that the watch was unnecessary. "I am not the kind of man who would commit suicide. If they decide to execute me they will find me ready. They know this, for they let me have a razor to shave this morning. I could have drawn this razor over my throat and committed suicide, but I am not the kind who believes in taking one's own life.[88]

When Hill was asked if he had any last requests, he replied that he wanted a bottle of grape juice, which was provided, along with a hearty meal.[89]

After eating, he settled down to write farewell messages to several persons as he had done once before. To Bill Haywood he wrote:

> Goodbye Bill: I die like a true rebel. Don't waste any time mourning—organize! It is a hundred miles from here to Wyoming. Could you arrange to have my body hauled to the state line to be buried? I don't want to be found dead in Utah.
>
> Joe Hill[90]

172

Diagram sketch of the Utah state prison ward, showing how Hillstrom, poet and song writer of the Industrial Workers of the World, will be put to death—From the Cleveland Press.

Solidarity published this description of the planned execution.

Haywood sent a farewell telegram.

> Goodbye Joe: You will live long in the hearts of the working class. Your songs will be sung wherever the workers toil, urging them to organize.
>
> W. D. Haywood[91]

Hill sent a second message to Haywood. "I will die like a true-blue rebel. Don't waste any time in mourning—organize."[92]

To Elizabeth Gurley Flynn Hill wrote: "Composed new song last week, with music, dedicated to the 'Dove of Peace.' It's coming. And now, good-bye, Gurley dear, I have lived like a rebel and I shall die like a rebel."[93]

To James Rohn in Minneapolis, Minnesota, Hill wrote: "Wire received. I will die like a rebel. Composed new song last week dedicated to the 'Dove of Peace.' It's coming your way. My best to everybody. Good-bye."[94] Hill was replying to a message that Rohn had sent earlier in the day: "Joseph Hillstrom we the members of No. 400 I.W.W. decide you shall die of old age. Four thousand of us stand back of you, farewell."[95]

To the San Francisco local of the Industrial Workers of the World, Hill wrote: "Goodbye fellow workers. Forget me and march right on to emancipation."[96]

Hill then sent a second message to Elizabeth Gurley Flynn.

Dear Friend Gurley:

I have been saying Goodbye so much now that it is becoming monotonous but I just cannot help to send you a few more lines because you have been more to me than a fellow worker. You have been an inspiration and when I composed the Rebel Girl you was right there and helped me all the time. As you furnished the idea I will now that I am gone give you all the credit for that song, and be sure to locate a few more Rebel Girls like yourself, because they are needed and needed badly. I gave Buster's picture to Hilda and she will watch so his pony doesn't run away. With a warm handshake across the continent and a last fond Goodbye to all I remain

Yours as Ever
Joe Hill[97]

The "Buster" referred to in the letter was Miss Flynn's young son. A few weeks before, Hill had written a poem about Buster after receiving a picture of the boy on a horse, and had sent it to him in care of his mother.

Joe Hill's last farewell message was sent to his friend John Makins of the Sailors' Rest Mission in San Pedro, California. The message hints of their close relationship in the past. It is reported that Makins, hearing of Hill's conviction, had sent him several telegrams, but the following note was Hill's only reply.

John Makins
Sailors Rest
San Pedro, Cal.

Your telegram received. Good-bye. Why should I be afraid to die? You will find me the same Joe as in days of yore, in disposition and in ideas. When you get to heaven you will find me on a front seat.

Joe Hill[98]

A guard reported that at about 10 p.m. Hill handed him a poem through the bars of his cell. It was his last will, which has become a prized piece of poetry in the heritage of the American labor movement.[99]

My Last Will

My will is easy to decide
For there is nothing to divide
My kin don't need to fuss and moan
"Moss does not cling to a rolling stone."
My body?—Oh!—If I could choose
I would to ashes it reduce
And let the merry breezes blow
My dust to where some flowers grow.
Perhaps some fading flower then
Would come to life and bloom again.
This is my Last and Final Will.
Good luck to All of you

Joe Hill[100]

During the night of November 18, O. N. Hilton received a notarized statement from William Busky of Seattle, Washington. Busky claimed that he was with Joe Hill on the night of January 10, 1914, and that Hill did not commit the Morrison murder. Busky further claimed that he and Joe Hill were together between the hours of 2 p.m. and 10 p.m. in Murray, Utah, and that during this time they had both gone to the smelter and received jobs rustling cards from a foreman named Hines.[101] Busky had reportedly explained the matter to Seattle police and a Seattle newspaper before sending the sworn statement to Hilton.[102] He allegedly left Hill at 10 p.m. on January 10 in downtown Salt Lake City, at which time Hill had not been wounded. He claimed that the next day he heard of Hill's arrest and said that he was also arrested by Salt Lake City police after they overheard him tell a friend that Hill was not guilty. Continuing his story, Busky said he testified at Hill's preliminary hearing, but was not allowed to testify at the trial. He claimed that after being held in jail for forty-one days, he was told to leave town.

Hilton forwarded Busky's telegram to Governor Spry. A hasty investigation disclosed that there was no foreman at the smelter named Hines. Spry was convinced that if Busky knew anything about Hill's actions on January 10, 1914, he must have been implicated in the murder himself. Accordingly, he telegraphed the Seattle police requesting that Busky be arrested for suspicion of murder. The Seattle police replied that they would not arrest Busky unless Utah sent a warrant.[103] Early in the morning of November 19, prison officials asked Hill if he knew William Busky. Hill replied that he did not.[104] This convinced Governor Spry that Busky was not telling the truth, and he decided the execution should be held on schedule.

It seems likely that the Busky telegram was a desperate last-minute attempt by the Seattle I.W.W. to halt the execution. The Seattle local had been sending telegrams every hour since 5 p.m. November 18 to President Wilson and Governor Spry demanding that Hill not be executed.[105] Evidence presented at the trial shows that Hill was at the Eselius home during the early evening of January 10, and there is no evidence that Busky was there also. There is no record of Busky having testified at the preliminary hearing, and his claim that Hill was arrested the day after the murder is certainly in error. Hill was not arrested until three days later.

About 5 a.m. on Friday, November 19, Joe Hill awoke. His actions that morning provided drama to match the rest of the last few months of his life. The day before, Hill had been given a broom with which to clean his cell. When he awoke on Friday morning, he broke the handle of the broom in half, tore up the blankets from his bed, twisted the blanket strips through the bars of his cell door so it could not be opened, then put his mattress against the door.[106] When the guards tried to remove the barrier from the door, Hill jabbed at them with the sharp point of the broken broom handle. The guards broke some brooms and began jabbing at Hill. One guard punched at Hill's stomach with his weapon in an attempt to force him to the rear of the cell while another attempted to remove the barricade from the door. Hill wrested the stick from the guard and was then armed with two weapons. According to the *Salt Lake Herald-*

175

Joe Hill's prison record sheet with the date of his
execution noted across the upper right-hand corner.

176

Mary Latham painted this twelve-by-twelve-foot
mural in vivid colors on a wall of the old Joe Hill
Hospitality House in Salt Lake City.

Republican, the strange duel lasted long enough for Hill to bloody the two guards. The duel was still going on when Sheriff Corless arrived to take Hill from his cell.[107]

When the sheriff approached, Hill quit fighting. Corless, who had developed a friendship with Hill, said, "Joe this is all nonsense."

Hill replied, "What do you mean?"

Corless answered, "You professed to die like a man."

Hill hesitated, then said, "Well I'm through but you can't blame a man for fighting for his life."[108]

The condemned man was taken from his cell and led out into the prison yard. The firing squad was already in the blacksmith's shop, concealed behind a canvas drape cut with five holes for the rifle barrels. Four of the rifles contained bullets—one held a blank. Hill was placed on a chair located twenty feet in front of the canvas drape. When he sat in the chair, he said rapidly, "I will show you how to die. I will show you how to die, I have a clear conscience."[109] He was strapped into the chair and a mask was placed over his eyes.

A doctor held a stethoscope over Hill's heart and located its exact position in his chest. A paper target was put over the spot.

When these preparatory actions were completed, the attending guards stepped back. Joe Hill tossed back his head and tried to see from underneath the mask. He shouted, "I am going now boys. Good-by!"[110] There was no response from anyone. The three men Hill had invited to the execution—Ed Rowan, George Child, and Fred Ritter—were not allowed into the prison on orders of the warden.[111] Hill again shouted, "Good-by Boys!"

Deputy Shettler, in charge of the firing squad, began the sequence of commands, preparatory to firing. "Ready, aim," he called out.

Joe Hill shouted, "Fire—go on and fire," a smile spreading over his face.

Shettler commanded "fire" and the rifles cracked.[112] A newsman witnessing the scene reported: "Before the sound of the officer's voice had died, there were five reports, almost in unison, puffs of white smoke came from the curtained window and Hillstrom's chest sank in as though he had been hit with a mighty weight."[113]

The smile faded from Hill's face, his muscles spasmodically contracted, his body stiffened, then relaxed and hung limp in the straps.

Shortly afterward, one member of the firing squad said:

It seemed like shooting an animal. How my thoughts wandered! It seemed an age waiting for the command to fire. And then, when it came from Hillstrom himself, I almost fell to my knees. We fired. I wanted to close my eyes, but they stared at the white paper heart, scorched and torn by four lead balls. Four blackened circles began to turn crimson, then a spurt and the paper heart was red.[114]

Three of the four bullets went directly into Hill's heart. At sixteen minutes before 8 a.m. on November 19, 1915, Joe Hill was pronounced dead.[115]

"I don't want to be found dead in Utah"

9 Throughout the intermountain area,
most rural and mining town newspapers applauded the execution.[1] Across the United States, major city newspapers were almost unanimous in their support of Governor Spry.[2] In Salt Lake City the *Deseret Evening News* editorialized:

> The law has been enforced and justice has been satisfied. For this result every good citizen should be profoundly grateful. The state by the firmness of its executive and other officials has happily escaped any reputation for weakness, sentimentality or cowardice. The integrity of the courts and the intelligence of the people have been vindicated. . . . The case may still persist in prominence in some quarters, but it can be nothing more than a "nine day wonder." So far as the law and the state are concerned it is ended.[3]

The error of this opinion was soon obvious. More astute in its prediction was the *New York Times*, which commented: ". . . presumably there will grow up in the revolutionary group of which he was a prominent member a more or less sincere conviction that he died a hero as well as a martyr. . . . This is the regrettable feature of the episode, for it may make Hillstrom dead much more dangerous to social stability than he was when alive."[4]

Governor Spry reacted by declaring, "We did our duty with Joe Hillstrom, and we expect to do it with his lawless colleagues that have recently infested the city with their threats and their presence."

He ordered that all "inflammatory" street speaking be stopped[5] and threatened that if regular peace officers did not take action he would "bring to bear a force that will do so."[6] Harper J. Dininny, a Salt Lake attorney, thought the governor overzealous in calling for such drastic measures. Dininny said there were only thirty Wobblies in Salt Lake City and the sheriff could "handle them with ease."[7]

The Wobblies were not the only ones to feel Utah's wrath after the execution. In headlines stating "Hillstrom Champion To Be Dropped by University of Utah by End of School Year," it was announced that Virginia Snow Stephen would be fired from her university teaching position. The school's Board of Regents had decided to dismiss Mrs. Stephen on October 7, but did not disclose that fact until after the execution because of threats that university buildings would be dynamited if she were fired.[8] She left Salt Lake City and married Constantine Filigno, a former member of the I.W.W. They moved to Willow Creek, California, where they homesteaded forty acres of land in 1916.[9]

180

The Firing Squad With The Screen Removed

ɔn't Waste any Time in Mourning–Organize

This cartoon by Ralph Chaplin appeared in *Solidarity*
with a description of the execution and Hill's "Last Will."

Because of the series of angry statements which had passed between O. N. Hilton and various representatives of Utah, and because of the funeral oration Hilton delivered for Joe Hill, the attorney was disbarred in Utah. As an example of the feeling toward Hilton, the Park City newspaper, the *Park Record*, reported: "His looks alone should debar him from practice in the courts of Utah—to say nothing of his slanderous attack on the Supreme Court of Utah and the vile epithets hurled at the state officials in his funeral oration of the murderer, Hillstrom, in Chicago recently."[10] Hilton expressed his feelings about disbarment, saying, "I cannot be disgraced or humiliated by being disbarred from the practice of my profession in that State...."[11] He was formally disbarred on July 1, 1916.[12]

In Utah politics, Republican Senator Reed Smoot, campaigning in 1916, criticized Woodrow Wilson for his "unwarranted interference" in trying to prevent Hill's execution. Utah Democrats wrote to Wilson, informing him of Smoot's attacks and urging him to respond.[13] There is no evidence that Wilson replied.

While those who thought Hill justly executed were trying to make sure that his posthumous notoriety would only be a "nine day wonder," his advocates were determined that Joe Hill would not be forgotten. Prior to his arrest, his songs, his membership in the I.W.W., and his being alive or dead were of importance primarily to himself and his fellow workers. With the notoriety of his trial, his conviction, and his execution, it was apparent that Joe Hill was becoming more widely known. But not until his two funerals did it become massively evident just how many people had been touched by Hill and his "martyr's death." There, the most eloquent and moving sentiments rendered in Hill's behalf to that time were spoken. The myth-building process had begun to produce results.

The first funeral was held in Salt Lake City on Sunday, November 21, 1915, the second in Chicago on Thanksgiving Day, November 25.

The day after the execution, November 20, Joe Hill's body lay in state at the O'Donnell Mortuary in Salt Lake City, dressed in a black suit.[14] In the right lapel was an I.W.W. membership button, put there by Wobbly S. P. Wise, who used the front half of his own button while a companion contributed the back half.[15] In the left lapel was a boutonniere composed of one red and one white rose. The desire of the public to view the body was so great that the mortuary made special arrangements to stay open late into the night. The *Salt Lake Herald-Republican* reported that those who visited the bier included "... newsboys, workingmen with their lunch boxes beneath their arms, business and professional men and women, people who were both well dressed and poorly clad. The expressions of opinion were as various as the appearance of the visitors."[16]

On Sunday, November 21, two hundred persons filled the chapel of the O'Donnell Mortuary early in the day. By 3 p.m., when the funeral was scheduled to begin, several thousand people were gathered outside, unable to gain entrance.[17] The men attending the funeral wore bows of red ribbon in their lapels and some wore red ribbon armbands. Hill's coffin, enveloped in a red covering, was piled high with floral offerings.

George Child, secretary of Local Sixty-nine's Joe Hill Defense Committee, opened the funeral services and set the tone for the speakers who followed him, both in Salt Lake City and Chicago, when he said Hill was killed to please the ruling class. Referring to the shooting of R. J. Horton in downtown Salt Lake City, Child reminded the audience that Major Myton was out on bail, whereas Joe Hill had had to spend two years in jail and could not even shake hands with his friends on his last day. "We are indignant when we see such inequality." He continued, saying that the I.W.W. was trying to bring about better working and living conditions in the world and "... poor Joe understood those things. He had been in the lumber and construction camps; had traveled in box cars and knew the sufferings of the workers. He wrote with feeling because he knew conditions." Child concluded: "Joe was simply an earnest workingman trying to bring about better conditions. His aim was for organization, so you folks could become a power for better conditions. His spirit will live on. He was an optimist. He believed the workers would come together and triumph over the tyranny of the master class."

The other speakers at the services were George Falcon, a Wobbly from Denver, who read several selections from *Cry for Justice* by Upton Sinclair; Oscar W. Larson, a local Swedish leader and Hill's friend; M. Brennan, who said, "Joe Hill lived and died for these ideals: shorter hours, more pay, more of the good things of life for the workers"; Philip Engle, who proclaimed, "The hanging of the so-called Chicago anarchists did not stop the tide of emancipation and neither will the killing of Hillstrom"; Emil S. Lund of the Utah House of

181

The procession escorting Joe Hill's body to the train.

Representatives, who spoke against capital punishment; and Ed Rowan, who concluded the services with the following sentiments: "Hill was working for elimination of wage slavery, work slavery, child slavery. . . . Time will tell, and time will show the sterling qualities of the man."[18] Music for the services was rendered by the Swedish Temperance Society choir.

After the funeral services, Joe Hill's body was placed in an open auto-hearse. A procession formed and traveled slowly to the Union Pacific Railroad Station. Six women pallbearers, dressed in white gowns with red sashes over their shoulders, walked along with the hearse, three on each side. Two hundred marchers followed behind. As the procession moved slowly through the main thoroughfare, the marchers sang some of Joe Hill's songs—"There Is Power in a Union" among them.[19]

When the procession reached the station, Hill's coffin was placed in a traveling box, the floral offerings were packed around it, and a letter to Bill Haywood was placed on top of the box. The women pallbearers cried as they took off their red sashes and laid them over the casket. Bert Lorton, an I.W.W. member, accompanied Joe Hill's body to Chicago.[20]

In Chicago, on November 23, a committee of Wobblies headed by Ralph Chaplin and Bill Haywood met the train and took the body to the Florence Funeral Parlor, where a viewing similar to the one in Salt Lake City was held under the supervision of an I.W.W. "death watch." Thousands of people again filed past Joe Hill's remains. Ralph Chaplin described the event.

> Through that little dim-lit room passed a constant stream of workingmen and women of all ages and nationalities—Bare-headed and reverently they tiptoed in single file, gazing briefly at Hill's clearcut sensitive features, made doubly delicate and life-like by the soft candle light that played upon them, and from which imprisonment, torture and death had been unable to efface the fearless, half-ironical smile of a "rebel true blue . . . ." Many touching scenes took place here. Strong weather-beaten men

who were not afraid of anything, were ashamed of their own swimming eyes when they found themselves once more in the hard glare of the street; foreign workers of both sexes who gazed with timid horror as though surprised at seeing, here in "the land of the free" the same inexorably bloody hand of despotism that had driven them from their native lands; stern-faced, dark-haired shop girls who placed tiny bouquets and single crimson carnations or roses upon the dead body of the man whose songs they knew and whose death they admired; social workers, reporters, magazine writers, musicians, and artists—all united in honoring the memory of the murdered minstrel of toil.[21]

The I.W.W. had difficulty obtaining a large hall in which to hold the funeral, but was finally able to rent the West Side Auditorium.* Leaflets imprinted: " 'He died that men might live,' workingmen and women attend in mass—we never forget," and announcing that O. N. Hilton would deliver the funeral oration were distributed throughout Chicago.[22] The covers of programs at the funeral read: "In Memoriam Joe Hill, We Never Forget, Murdered by the Authorities of the State of Utah, November 19, 1915."[23]

The *Chicago Daily Tribune* disparaged the sentiment prevalent among those in Chicago who mourned Joe Hill on Thanksgiving Day.

> They're burying Joe Hill today. It's a big event in Chicago's "rebel" ranks. The ghetto, the slums, the lodging house quarters, and the manufacturing districts are buzzing with preparation for the funeral of the I.W.W. song writer who was executed in Utah, after conviction of murder.
>
> Anarchists, Industrial Workers of the World, Nihilists, Sabotagists, and secret organizations, whose existence is based on opposition to a permanent social and economic system, are taking part in the rites.[24]

Early on the morning of the funeral, throngs of people began moving into the West Side Auditorium. By 8:30 a.m., all 5,000 seats were filled. Ralph Chaplin reported that ". . . by 10:30 a.m. the streets were clogged for blocks in all directions; streetcars could not run and all traffic was suspended."[25]

---

* B. Yelensky, one of those who helped the I.W.W. arrange for the West Side Auditorium, wrote an account of how the organization obtained use of the hall.

Before the body of Joe Hill arrived in Chicago, some of my fellow friends from the I.W.W. asked me if I knew of some large hall for the funeral of Joe Hill because at every suitable hall the H.Q. [I.W.W. headquarters] went to they refused to rent the hall for such a funeral and demonstration. I told the fellow workers that one hall that I knew which I think will rent to them is the West Side Auditorium on Taylor and Racine Avenue, as we had there all our radical meetings and entertainments, but the fellow workers didn't tell me for which date the funeral was planned.

At the time no one of us had a telephone so a few days later a committee of two fellow workers came to me and said that fellow worker Bill Haywood would urgently like to see a committee from the Anarchist Red Cross. I went to see the recording secretary Jack Goodman, and we went to see Bill Haywood. I think the H.Q. at that time was somewhere on Chicago Avenue near Lake Michigan. When we arrived in the H.Q. we find there Bill Haywood, Thompson, and a few other fellow workers.

Bill Haywood told us the story that they decided to have Joe Hill's funeral on Thanksgiving Day, and the only hall willing to rent for the funeral is the West Side

184

The West Side Auditorium in Chicago during Hill's funeral.

On the stage inside, the casket was covered with a huge red flag and surrounded by myriad floral decorations. Those attending wore red streamers around their necks, and many wore buttons inscribed, "He died a martyr."[26]

When the services began, the crowd took advantage of the opportunity to vent its emotion with the singing of several of Hill's songs. The audience sang "Workers of the World Awaken." A young Polish girl, Jennie Wosczyuska, sang Hill's "Rebel Girl." "Stung Right" and "The Preacher and the Slave" were then

---

Auditorium, but on the same day the Anarchist Red Cross has the yearly Bauern Ball [harvest festival] which starts around 2 p.m. So Bill Haywood and the other fellow workers there appealed to us that we should start the Ball a little later, and give enough time for Joe Hill's funeral. We were willing to cooperate but the trouble was that for this Ball we used to decorate the hall with all kinds of fruit and decorations for which we used special wiring across the hall. So we told Bill Haywood and the others that we would call a special meeting of the Anarchist Red Cross and take up this matter.

We had that meeting, and after many pro and against arguments, on account that this Ball used to bring in the most amount of money for the political prisoners in Russia, the Anarchist Red Cross decided to cooperate with the I.W.W. with a provision that the funeral had to be through not later than 1 p.m. and that the I.W.W. would supply a strong committee to help remove the chairs from the hall and clean up. Our conditions were accepted, and Joe Hill's funeral went through on time, and we in one hour prepared the hall for the Bauern Ball which started somewhat late, but went through with a success as usually.

—B. Yelensky

I.W.W. officials at the Chicago funeral.

sung by the audience,[27] and mass singing in the street outside echoed that in the auditorium.[28] The press noted that these songs, set to popular tunes, made strange dirges.[29]

Bill Haywood made a short speech introducing the main speaker, O. N. Hilton,[30] who delivered the most articulate enunciation to that date of Hill's martyr image. Besides eulogizing Hill, Hilton spent almost two hours castigating and defaming Utah and the Mormons. He made a complete and thorough review of the evidence presented in the various courts, and conveyed the distinct impression that Hill had been victimized, as were other "gentiles" in Utah, because he was not a Mormon.[31] Hilton then discussed his views on President Wilson's intervention, quoting from a speech given by Wilson to a group of European immigrants.

> "A man enriches the Country to which he brings dreams, and you have brought them and have enriched America in so doing. A man does not go out and seek the thing that is not in him. A man does not hope for the thing that he does not believe in, and if some of us have forgotten what America believed in, you at any rate imparted in your own hearts a renewal of that belief. Each of you, I am sure, brought a dream, a glorious shining dream, a dream worth more than gold or silver, and that is the reason why I welcome you here."
>
> Those are President Wilson's words, and, my friends, that was why this man, speaking as he did, that was why this mighty man stretched his hands to poor Joe Hill, this dreamer of dreams, this singer of songs, this player of music, who sought to lighten the dreary gray and unrelieved blackness of the lives of his fellow workmen, and he sang in a crude yet heartfelt way his verses of a better and brighter day, such as he, the President, had in mind. . . .[32]

Bitterly, Hilton recalled that Governor Spry had refused President Wilson's second "sacred request for a delay of Hill's execution." He emphasized the fact that a person convicted of murder in Utah could choose between being hanged or shot, interpreting this as an example of the "... humanity of Salt Lake City in this enlightened age."[33]

Continuing his oration, the attorney portrayed Joe Hill as a saint and a martyr of the working class.

> I studied the man and I felt if there was anything in the way of consciousness of guilt he would tell me of it before the Supreme end came. They always do. I never knew it to fail in my life. There are two men they will always be honest with if they are guilty, and that is the doctor and the lawyer. I looked to see if any such consciousness of guilt would display itself by a furtive look, an expression, some uneasy apprehension, some element of fear, but nothing of the kind. He was always clear eyed, fearless and unafraid. He said to me one day, he said, "Judge, duty is the principal thing. There is always some sweetness sooner or later in doing that, but without it the best things will turn to ashes and to dust. ...."
>
> If you can find a midnight assassin with such an exposition of the principles of right doing, then I confess that the entire fabric of our nature is false and untrue.
>
> Joe Hill had an obsession, an obsession to duty. He was not learned, and his years were too few to give him experience, but he knew, men and women, that great wrongs stalked unchecked through the land, and that the workingmen bore the brunt of it all. He had no quarrel with Society as it is organized. He did not wish to seize the scheme of things into his own hands and remold it to make for his individual desires; not at all; but his protest always was against those who seize and misapply the privileges that should be distributed with even handed justice to the rich and to the poor alike. He could not write upon the principles of sociology, but he could and did know that power and greed were using these practices to oppress and grind down scores of his fellow men, the small merchant, the small shop keeper, the small man who stood nearest to the great forces of labor, and that unworking and unearned greed would never willingly lessen its grip upon mankind. Joe knew all of that. Joe lived it, and in this way he protested against it. He lived a wholesome, clean life. He wrote his earnest, if crude, verses as embodying his thoughts, and he had sublime faith that justice and integrity must triumph, and a heart of loving tenderness toward all of God's oppressed and unhappy children, a boundless charity, even towards his slanderers. And this is the life story of this man who lies before us today, whose calm dead face looks back at us today wreathed in the unfading calm of immortality, a memory for us all, and an inspiration to better thoughts and a more steadfast course.[34]

Hilton's conclusion was filled with sentiments which persisted in ensuing eulogies of Hill.

> And so, men and women, we delight today to drop a tear upon this coffin and a flower into this grave. I think there is one thought that comes to us all on an occasion of this kind, and that is that our beloved dead do not ever wholly die; ... So it will be, men and women, with Joe Hill. As you read his inspiring poems, and as your hearts beat in unison with him, when you sing his sweet songs, so ever in tenderest memory he will come to us again a sweet, gentle, musical echo of the ripple of that eternal tide upon the shore of time.
>
> And so we say, rest softly, kind mother earth, over this poor mutilated form, and to you, soldier poet, martyr and hero, with the flush of this magnificent oncoming industrial freedom upon your brow, all hail and all hail![35]

After the oration, the large crowd slowly filed out as pianist Rudolf Von Liebich played Chopin's "Funeral March."[36] Outside the auditorium, the crowd was so tightly packed that Hill's casket could not be removed to the hearse. When the Rockford, Illinois, I.W.W. band began playing, the committee in charge of the funeral asked the band to lead part of the crowd around the block so that room could be made and Hill's body brought out to the hearse.[37] A procession of marchers followed the hearse as it moved slowly on its way to the streetcar station at VanBuren and Halsted streets.

The committee in charge of the funeral, who helped clear the streets, led the procession followed by twelve pallbearers with the casket and the hearse, flower bearers, the band, and the crowd of marchers.[38] Onlookers, who covered the rooftops and jammed the windows, looked down on the flower bearers who formed a walking garden almost a block long. A giant red flag made from crimson-colored silk was carried by the representatives of the Rockford I.W.W. As they moved slowly along, taking possession of the streets they traveled, the mourners sang Joe Hill's songs. When a song from one section of the giant human serpent died down, the same song or another would be taken up by other voices along the line. Ralph Chaplin recalled that "The whole street seemed to move and sing as the throng inched through the west side streets."[39]

187

Pallbearers leaving the Florence Funeral Parlor with the casket.

Mary Gallagher, whose husband, Douglas Robson, wrote and published songs for the I.W.W., attended the funeral and followed the cortege to the cemetery. She said it was "... a cold winter day but there was a very long funeral procession. One thing which struck me, the Irish policemen on the streets who were directing the procession always took off their hats as the hearse passed."[40]

When the hearse reached the station, the casket was put aboard the train and taken to Graceland Cemetery, located in the suburbs of Chicago.[41] Many of the marchers followed to the graveside where another long memorial service was held. Vincent St. John, Bill Haywood, and Irish labor leader James Larkin spoke. Eulogies for Hill were given in Swedish, Russian, Hungarian, Polish, Spanish, Italian, German, Yiddish, and Lithuanian.[42] Joe Hill's friends stayed at the cemetery, singing his songs late into the night.[43]

The day after the funeral, the I.W.W. committee in charge of the arrangements returned to Graceland Cemetery to witness the cremation. The body was photographed and identified for the last time on the morning of November 26, then the casket was put on a slab of stone and pushed into a blast furnace. Chaplin relates:

> Through a small hole in the side of the furnace, each committeeman viewed the flame-lashed casket containing the fine body and placid features of Joe Hill, dreamer, poet, artist, and agitator, which had four purple bullet holes in his young chest as punishment for the crime of being "true blue" to his class—and to himself.[44]

Hill's ashes were placed in envelopes and distributed to I.W.W. locals in every state but Utah. Envelopes were also sent to South America, Europe, Asia, South Africa, New Zealand, and Australia. On May 1, 1916, according to Chaplin, the ashes were released to the wind.[45] Joe Hill's last will was fulfilled. *

---

* A letter sent to Miss Agnes Inglis, the librarian in charge of the Labadie Collection at the University of Michigan Library, describes how Joe Hill's last wish was actually carried to completion in 1950. The writer of the letter, Wobbly George Carey, described his role in the distribution of a packet of Hill's ashes in 1916. Later, about 1919, he found another packet in a Toledo, Ohio, I.W.W. hall which had been raided and wrecked. For many years he tried to deliver the ashes to someone in the organization who could dispose of them, but was unable to find anyone. Finally, as described in the letter, he took the job into his own hands.

> It was June 26, 1950, that I finally decided to try and carry out Joe's last wish to the best of my ability. . . .
>
> On this early June morning I awoke to one of the most beautiful June days that I have ever known anywhere. Nature seemed to have outdone herself that day when I awoke to the realization that I was grown old and that I had an obligation to carry out. The thought came to me. I was all alone. Why not do as he requested? Here was a spot. The grass was green, there was a yard covered with flowers and trees. Birds were singing all over the place. No place could be more fitting. I arose and walked out into the garden and with no more ceremony than a murmured "Good Bye, Joe," I carefully scattered the contents of the little envelope over the soil. I felt at ease. My pledge had been kept.

Printed on the envelope that contained the ashes was the following:

Fellow Worker:

> In compliance with the last will of Joe Hill, his body was cremated at Graceland Cemetery, Chicago, Illinois, Nov. 26, 1915.
>
> It was his request that his ashes be distributed.
>
> This package has been confined to your care for the fulfillment of this last will.
>
> You will kindly address a letter to Wm. D. Haywood, Room 307, 164 W. Washington St., Chicago, Ill., telling the circumstances and where the ashes were distributed.

WE NEVER FORGET
JOE HILL MEMORIAL COMMITTEE

The foregoing material can be found in the Labadie Collection at the University of Michigan or in Joyce L. Kornbluh, ed., *Rebel Voices: An I.W.W. Anthology* (Ann Arbor, Michigan: University of Michigan Press, 1964), pp. 156-57.

Graceland Cemetery with a "small section of the rebels."

Reaction to the funerals by the press in Salt Lake City and elsewhere was hostile. A *New York Times* reporter claimed that those who attended Hill's funeral were anarchists, nihilists, socialists, "bums," and hobos; only ten percent were "native born Americans."[46] The *Los Angeles Times* gave a caustic account of the funeral.

> Los Angeles is to be congratulated on the fact that it is two thousand miles from Chicago where three thousand I.W.W.'s attended the mortuary services which preceded the cremation and interment of the body of Hillstrom who was eulogized as a "poet comrade" by speakers who denounced his execution as "a willful cold-blooded murder by powerful Utah money interests."
>
> In being cursed by I.W.W. orators in ten different languages, Governor Spry received a high compliment for his manliness in refusing to grant the ill-considered request of President Wilson to pardon Hillstrom.[47]

The *Ogden Standard-Examiner* (Ogden, Utah) vilified Joe Hill's funeral in the following words:

> On a day when every honest American in the land was offering prayers of thanksgiving for the flag that had led the United States to the highest pinnacle of republics, we are told that the red flag of anarchy floated undisturbed at every turn, and that ninety percent of the murderous mob were low-grade foreigners, who not having taken the oath of allegiance, have no respect for the American flag or the law it represents. This scum of the earth offered no prayer for the soul of Joseph Hillstrom. There was no touch of religion in the ceremony. The laws of God were ignored with the laws of men. Murder, hatred and revenge formed the theme of this funeral service over a man who had paid the penalty for a double murder.[48]

The *Salt Lake Herald-Republican* concentrated its attack on O. N. Hilton.

> Attorney Hilton's disgraceful appeal from the orderly process of the courts to the violent prejudices of an unlawful mob is not the concern of Utah alone. Today he is defying Utah law, Utah tolerance and Utah justice. Tomorrow he may be carrying the

**Irish labor leader Jim Larkin (left) and Big Bill
Haywood (right) giving orations at the cemetery.**

190

red flag of anarchy elsewhere. He is an enemy of everything civilization holds dear, champion of the unlawful passion the transitory vagaries of a dangerous hour may bring forth. How long shall the borrowed respectability of the profession he disgraces be permitted to shield him.

From the moment he entered the case of Joseph Hillstrom, until its final curtain in Chicago on Thursday when he raved over the body of the client he so inefficiently served, Hilton has indulged in sharp practices the veriest shyster would have scorned.[49]

In contrast to the foregoing, W. S. VanValkenburgh, in an article published a month after the execution, captured the spirit of Joe Hill's life that is perpetuated in legend today.

He was a genius in the rough. A poet who . . . wrote prose and verse that stirred his fellows like the gale an aspen leaf. Homeless, moneyless, friendless—in the larger sense—the undaunted champion of an unpopular cause, framed up, convicted on flimsy circumstantial evidence; fore-doomed to destruction, and yet true to himself to the very last. Such a man was Joseph Hillstrom.[50]

Joe Hill
will never die

10 The Joe Hill case aroused interest
and concern throughout the nation and beyond—products primarily of the volatile combination of anti-I.W.W. sentiment in Utah and the inconclusive circumstantial evidence at his trial. Hill personally contributed to his notoriety as a martyr with several memorable statements of purpose and principle. "I have lived like an artist, and I shall die like an artist"; "I am going to get a new trial or die trying"; "I will die like a true blue rebel"; "I don't want to be found dead in Utah"; and "Don't waste any time in mourning—organize!" became the basis of his forming legend.

In addition to Hill's own dramatization of his cause, the environment in which the legend first grew was particularly conducive to its development. I.W.W. historian Fred Thompson has analyzed the social context in which Hill's plight first received sympathetic attention.

> The concern for Joe Hill's legend seems to have been strongest among either drifters or those who had spent earlier years of their life drifting and who knew what tremors run through a skid road when the local press reports the sort of crime they know requires the cops to select a skid road suspect; the content of his songs hit them, but even more his stand for the importance of the doctrine of burden of proof. The hobo is practically helpless at proving an alibi.[1]

Labor historian Vernon Jensen further observes: "That such a legend could grow and be so powerful is a sad commentary on our industrial relations practices, for such a legend feeds on the despair and frustration of workers."[2]

But Hill and the social environment alone did not create the legend. A primary factor in the evolution of his story was supplied by the imaginations of other men, acting individually or within the framework of an organization.

The group most responsible for creating the martyr image was the I.W.W. The spirit of the Wobblies contained what economist Robert F. Hoxie has described as

> a strong force of romantic idealism which, strange as it may seem, exists in the minds and hearts of the down trodden constituency of the I.W.W. In spite of the fact that these men will have none of the regularly constituted authority when it makes for strength, they are hero-worshippers and are easily led for the moment by the "heroes of labor." These heroes are momentary leaders of strikes and of the battles with the police and militia, those especially who have gone on trial and suffered imprisonment. . . . Such men grip the imagination of the rank and file.[3]

This tendency of the "rank and file" to admire persons who symbolized rebellion made Hill a great asset. Few members so cleverly ridiculed constituted authority in seeking to bring the American "wage slave" to an awareness of his class position. His message, directed to those inhabiting the mission-studded skid roads across America, was the simple but powerful assertion that "There Is Power in a Union." Since Hill had become a lyrical spokesman for the Wobblies, his conviction and execution came to symbolize the injustices they saw in American society. Alerted by the Joe Hill defense campaign, the Wobblies united solidly behind him, and although failing to gain his freedom, did help him to achieve widespread notoriety.

The I.W.W. tenderly preserved its martyrs within the pages of the "Little Red Song Book." Pictures and a few words about Joe Hill, Wesley Everest, and Frank Little still appear in the songbooks printed today, with Hill's picture and his "Last Will" regularly occupying the opening pages.

One poem and one song—Ralph Chaplin's "Joe Hill" and John Nordquist's "November Nineteenth"—survivors of a group of eulogies written about Hill at the time of his death, also regularly appear in the songbook.*

JOE HILL

Murdered by the Authorities of the State of Utah, November 19, 1915.

High head and back unbending—fearless and true,
Into the night unending; why was it you?
Heart that was quick with song, torn with their lead;
Life that was young and strong, shattered and dead.

Singer of manly songs, laughter and tears;
Singer of Labor's wrongs, joys, hope and fears.
Though you were one of us, what could we do?
Joe, there was none of us needed like you.

We gave, however small, what life could give;
We would have given all that you might live.
Your death you held as naught, slander and shame;
We from the very thought shrank as from flame.

Each of us held his breath, tense with despair,
You, who were close to death, seemed not to care.
White-handed loathsome power, knowing no pause,
Sinking in labor's flower murderous claws;

---

*Other eulogies not included in the "Little Red Song Book" but published in *Solidarity* include Joseph O'Carrol's "To the Governor of the Sovereign State of Utah" (*Solidarity*, 13 November 1915, p. 1), Richard Brazier's "Joe Hill—A Tribute" (*Solidarity*, 14 August 1915, p. 2), and W. H. Lewis' "Our Martyr" (*Solidarity*, 11 December 1915, p. 4). A later poem, written by Covington Hall (Covami) and entitled "A Fair Trial," appeared in *Battle Hymns of Toil* (collected poems of Covington Hall, Oklahoma City: General Welfare Reporter, n.d., p. 30).

Boastful with leering eyes, blood-dripping jaws . . .
Accurst be the cowardice hidden in laws!
Utah has drained your blood; white hands are wet;
We of the "surging flood" NEVER FORGET!

Our songster! have your laws now had their fill?
Know ye, his songs and cause ye cannot kill.
High head and back unbending—"rebel true blue"
Into the night unending; why was it you?[4]

NOVEMBER NINETEENTH
(Tune—"The Red Flag")

They've shot Joe Hill, his life has fled,
They've filled his manly heart with lead;
But his brave spirit hovers near
And bids each fellow worker cheer.

　　On high the blood red banners wave!
　　The flag for which his life he gave;
　　The master class shall rue the day
　　They took Joe Hillstrom's life away.

Now, fellow workers shed no tear,
For Joe Hill died without fear;
He told the bosses' gunmen, low:
"I'm ready; fire! Let her go!"

No more Joe Hill shall pen the songs
That pictured all the workers' wrongs;
His mighty pen shall rust away,
But all his songs are here to stay.

Now Salt Lake City's Mormon throngs
Must list to Joe Hill's rebel songs
While rebel workers press the fight
And show the One Big Union's might.

March on, march on, you mighty host,
And organize from coast to coast;
And Joe Hill's spirit soon shall see
Triumphant Labor's victory.[5]

With the entrance of the United States into World War I, the I.W.W. suffered serious reductions in membership. In the chauvinistic atmosphere that affected American public opinion during the war years, the Wobblies' antiwar position was considered treasonable. Subsequent persecution during the "red scare" precipitated a decline of the organization from which it has never recovered. With the weakening of the I.W.W., organizations such as the American Communist Party began to recognize Hill's propaganda value and to use his story for their purposes. But the primary organizational support for Hill was reduced, and since the end of World War I the legend has been perpetuated mainly by individuals.

Literary interest in proletarian subjects has led writers to Joe Hill because his life and songs provide a usable prototype of the twentieth-century proletarian hero. Early in the present century men such as Jack London and John Reed were exploring and revitalizing through their lives and writings the workers' hero. Hill is a complete and authentic American embodiment of such a vagabond social revolutionary—a working class intellectual existing on the fringe of society yet able to see into its center with dissatisfaction and demand change.

194

The 1920's—Ralph Chaplin, apparently in a conscious effort to keep Hill's name alive, wrote several articles which appeared in left-oriented publications during the 1920's. Foremost among these was "Joe Hill: A Biography," based on information from John Holland and providing the only biographical material available for many years.[6] In December 1923, one month after publishing the biography, the *Industrial Pioneer* printed "The Last Letters of Joe Hill."[7] In 1925, a young poet, Alfred Hayes, wrote "I Dreamed I Saw Joe Hill Last Night." Several years later Earl Robinson set the words to music and the song became one of the major factors in the perpetuation of Hill's story.[8] When Paul Robeson sang it before a group of unemployed Welsh miners in London in the 1930's, a listener remembers that the audience was ". . . thunderstruck by the power and beauty of Robeson's rendition of the song."[9] There are other notable accounts of the ballad's impact on people who learned of Hill for the first time through these words:

I dreamed I saw Joe Hill last night,
Alive as you and me.
Says I, "But Joe you're ten years dead,"
"I never died," says he,
"I never died," says he.

"In Salt Lake, Joe," says I to him,
Him standing by my bed,
"They framed you on a murder charge,"
Says Joe, "But I ain't dead,"
Says Joe, "But I ain't dead."

"The copper bosses killed you, Joe,
They shot you, Joe," says I.
"Takes more than guns to kill a man,"
Says Joe, "I didn't die,"
Says Joe, "I didn't die."

And standing there as big as life
And smiling with his eyes,
Joe says, "What they forgot to kill
Went on to organize,
Went on to organize."

"Joe Hill ain't dead," he says to me,
"Joe Hill ain't never died.
  Where workingmen are out on strike
  Joe Hill is at their side,
  Joe Hill is at their side."

"From San Diego up to Maine,
  In every mine and mill,
  Where workers strike and organize,"
  Says he, "You'll find Joe Hill,"
  Says he, "You'll find Joe Hill."

  I dreamed I saw Joe Hill last night,
  Alive as you or me.
  Says I, "But Joe, you're ten years dead,"
  "I never died," says he,
  "I never died," says he.[10]

195

The ballad, widely printed in songbooks, has been recorded by Michael Loring and Paul Robeson, among others.[11]

In 1924 Upton Sinclair published a short play, *Singing Jailbirds*. The "jailbirds" are Wobblies and their singing revolves around such Hill songs as "The Preacher and the Slave," "Scissor Bill," and "The Rebel Girl." The Wobbly hero of the play, Red Adams, jailed and beaten to death for refusing to cooperate with the law, is almost certainly drawn from the Hill prototype. *Singing Jailbirds* was first produced in the late 1920's in Greenwich Village by a group of four young writers, among them Eugene O'Neill and John Dos Passos, and ran for six weeks.[12]

Articles by Ralph Chaplin in 1926 and 1929[13] and Carl Sandburg's mention of Hill in *The American Songbag* in 1927 also aided the legend's growth.[14]

The 1930's—Carl Sandburg, who had praised Hill's songs, referred again to Hill in his long poem, *The People, Yes* (1936): " 'Don't mourn for me but organize,' said the Utah I.W.W. before a firing squad executed sentence of death on him. His last words running, 'Let her go!' "[15]

The new generation of militant industrial unionists who fought to create the Congress of Industrial Organizations (C.I.O.) learned the story of Joe Hill and sang his verses. As the Depression of the 1930's deepened, Hill's songs and his idealistic protest gained renewed meaning. "Pie in the Sky" ("The Preacher and the Slave"), according to novelist Wallace Stegner, became the ". . . theme song of the generation of the thirties." Commenting that he heard the phrase all through the Depression years, Stegner said, "For my money, that one mordant, ironical phrase is the principal basis for the legend, or at least for the lasting of Hill's legend."[16] Folklorist Archie Green sees the phrase as ". . . the most significant Wobbly contribution to the American vocabulary,"[17] while Pete Seeger stated, " 'Pie in the Sky' is the [Hill] phrase and the song which has most entered American folklore."[18]

During the 1930's Hill's songs were sung by radical and left-oriented

American students. Archie Green remembers hearing student groups in California between 1935 and 1939 singing Hill's "Casey Jones," "The Preacher and the Slave," "Mr. Block," and other radical union songs.[19]

Joe Hill's appeal to left-oriented groups and the defection of an element of the I.W.W. to communism led to efforts by the American Communist Party to appropriate his legend, though it is difficult to imagine the individualistic Hill as a subject for communist discipline. Despite this incongruity, he has been frequently mentioned in the Swedish communist newspaper *Ny Dag* and scattered reports indicate that he is admired in Russia.*

The body of poetry about Hill was expanded during the thirties with Kenneth Patchen's "Joe Hill Listens to the Praying," expressing the feeling of romantic adventure and idealism that radicals of those years must have found appealing in Hill and the I.W.W.

JOE HILL LISTENS TO THE PRAYING

Look at the steady rifles, Joe.
It's all over now—"Murder, first degree,"
The jury said. It's too late now
To go back. Listen Joe, the chaplain is reading:

Lord Jesus Christ who didst
So mercifully promise heaven
To the thief that humbly confessed
His injustice
     throw back your head

Joe; remember that song of yours
We used to sing in jails all over
These United States—tell it to him:
"I'll introduce to you
 A man that is a credit to our Red,
  White and Blue,
 His head is made of lumber and
  solid as a rock;
 He is a Christian Father and his
  name is Mr. Block."
     Remember, Joe—

"You take the cake
 You make me ache
 Tie a rock on your block and
  jump in the lake,
 Kindly do that for Liberty's sake."

---

* In a *Salt Lake Tribune* article (6 March 1966, sec. A, p. 16), journalist Theodore Long said he was told by a woman guide in Russia how thrilled she was on hearing Paul Robeson sing ". . . that old American folk song, 'I Dreamed I Saw Joe Hill Last Night.' " An instance of Communist efforts to use Joe Hill comes from a *Washington Post* article (8 February 1960, referring to a dispatch from London to the *Baltimore Sun*). According to the article, some of Hill's songs, or approximations of them, were being taught to Russian school children to illustrate the frustration of working men in capitalist countries.

JOE HILL WILL NEVER DIE

Behold me, I beseech Thee, with
The same eyes of mercy that
                                    on the other

Hand we're driftin' into Jungles
From Kansas to the coast, wrapped
    round brake beams on a thousand
    freights; San Joaquin and Omaha
    brush under the wheels—"God made the summer
    for the hobo and the bummer"—we've been
    everywhere, seen everything.
Winning the West for the good citizens;
Driving golden spikes into the U. P.;
Harvest hands, lumbermen drifting—
    now Iowa, now Oregon—
God, how clean the sky; the lovely wine
Of coffee in a can. This land
    is our lover. How greenly beautiful
Her hair; her great pure breasts
    that are
The Rockies on a day of mist and rain.

We love this land of corn and cotton,
    Virginia and Ohio, sleeping on
With our love, with our love—
O burst of Alabama loveliness, sleeping on
In the strength of our love; O Mississippi flowing
Through our nights, a giant mother.

Pardon, and in the end
              How green is her hair,
    how pure are her breasts; the little farms
    nuzzling into her flanks
    drawing forth life, big rich life
Under the deep chant of her skies
And rivers—but we, we're driftin'
Into trouble from Kansas to the coast, clapped
    into the stink and rot of country jails
    and clubbed by dicks and cops
Because we didn't give a damn—
              remember Joe
How little we cared, how we sang
    the nights away in their filthy jails;
                and how, when

We got wind of a guy called Marx
    we sang less, just talked
And talked. "Blanket-stiffs" we were
But we could talk, they couldn't jail us
For that—but they did—
              remember Joe
Of my life be strengthened
             One Big Union:

our convention in Chi; the Red Cards,
leaflets; sleeping in the parks,
the Boul Mich; "wobblies" now, cheering
the guys that spoke our lingo, singing
down the others. "Hear that train blow,
Boys, hear that train blow."

Now confessing my crimes, I may obtain

Millions of stars, Joe—millions of miles.

          Remember Vincent St. John
In the Goldfield strike; the timid little squirt
with the funny voice, getting onto the platform
and slinging words at us that rolled
down our chins and into our hearts,
like boulders hell-bent down a mountain side.
And Orchard, angel of peace
    —with a stick of dynamite in either hand.
    Pettibone and Moyer: "The strike
Is your weapon, to hell with politics."
        Big Bill—remember him—
At Boise—great red eye rolling like a lame bull
through the furniture and men
of the courtroom—"This bastard,
His Honor."

San Diego, soap boxes,
Hundreds of them! And always
their jail shutting out the sky,
the clean rhythm of the wheels
on a fast freight; disinfectant getting
into the lung-pits, spitting blood
But singing—Christ, how we sang,
       remember the singing
Joe, One Big Union,
      One Big
         hope to be
With Thee

Hobo Convention:
(Millions of stars, Joe—millions of miles.)
"Hallelujah, I'm a bum,
Hallelujah, I'm a bum." His Honor,
the sonofabitch!
One Big Strike, Lawrence, Mass—
23,000 strong, from every neck
of every woods in America, 23,000,
Joe, remember. "We don't need
a leader. We'll fix things up
among ourselves."
"Blackie" Ford and "Double-nose" Suhr in
Wheatland—"I.W.W.'s don't destroy
property"—and they got life. "I've counted
The stars, boys, counted a million of these prison bars."

What do they matter, Joe, these rifles.
They can't reach the towns, the skies, the songs,
   that now are part of more
   than any of us—we were
The homeless, the drifters, but, our songs
   had hair and blood on them.
There are no soap boxes in the sky.
We won't eat pie, now, or ever
   when we die,
           but Joe
We had something they didn't have:
   our love for these States
   was real and deep;
          to be with Thee

In heaven. Amen.
        (How steady are
   the rifles.) We had slept
   naked on this earth on the coldest nights
   listening to the words of a guy named Marx.
Let them burn us, hang us, shoot us,

                Joe Hill

For at the last we had what it takes
   to make songs with.[20]

In *Nineteen Nineteen*, part of the trilogy *USA* published in 1937, John Dos Passos depicted the hobo as alienated from and exploited by a society increasingly mechanized and controlled by the "big money" of the trusts. Dos Passos, who had helped produce Sinclair's *Singing Jailbirds* in the 1920's, contrasted the biographies of fictional hobos Mac and Ben Compton and the real-life figures of Eugene Debs, Bill Haywood, Joe Hill, and Wesley Everest, with biographies of "big money" men such as Morgan, Mellon, Ford, and Hearst. The short, incisive portrayal of Joe Hill's life ends with a comment on his funeral: "They put him in a black suit, put a stiff collar around his neck and a bow tie, shipped him to Chicago for a bang up funeral, and photographed his handsome stony mask staring into the future. The first of May they scattered his ashes to the wind."[21]

"Rebel girl" and organizer Elizabeth Gurley Flynn recalled her acquaintance with Hill in "Joe Hill: Song Bird" which appeared in 1937.[22] In his book on the lumbering industry, *Holy Old Mackinaw*, Stewart Holbrook commented on the presence of Joe Hill's spirit in the logging camps. "Wherever there was a Wobbly . . . bunkhouse forums were sure to hear of Wobbly Joe Hill." Joe Hill's "Last Will," he maintains, was famous bunkhouse poetry.[23]

The 1940's—The *Timber Beast* (1944), a novel by Archie Binns, revived Hill's story through the ballad, "I Dreamed I Saw Joe Hill Last Night," the favorite song of the wandering Wobbly, Tag. As Tag often played his recording of the song, his non-Wobbly friends noted its appeal. The fact of Joe Hill's death ". . . was brushed aside by the singer's voice, touched with sadness, but confident and triumphant—singing of a rebel whose body died before a firing squad in a prison yard, while his spirit escaped to lead working men wherever they organized."

That Hill's guilt was accepted as fact is apparent from Binns's description—"a working stiff who took what he needed. When he ran out of money in Salt Lake City, he shot him a grocer and got caught."[24] Here is an early representation of the view that Joe Hill was indeed guilty, but nevertheless made a significant contribution to American folklore—a viewpoint which began to grow with expanding interest in Hill from outside the radical ranks.

200

In 1947 Wallace Stegner wrote an article in which he suggested that Hill was probably guilty of the Morrison murder. Concerning his introduction to Hill, Stegner has said,

> I got interested in Joe Hill not because I was interested especially in labor history, but because I had been fascinated by some songs of the Spanish Civil War, one of which, played to my five year old son, caused him to burst into tears. Well, if a child would burst into tears over a song, a man might die to it. I got interested in the songs people had died to, and one of the songs I heard a lot in those days was "I Dreamed I Saw Joe Hill Last Night." . . . The name Joe Hill was very vague to me before the song got me investigating. I probably had never heard it.[25]

Stegner's interest led to two articles and a novel based on Hill's life. Showing the song's influence, his first article was entitled "I Dreamed I Saw Joe Hill Last Night." In this and in a 1948 *New Republic* article, "Joe Hill: The Wobblies' Troubadour," he advanced the belief that, even though the state of Utah did not sufficiently prove it, Hill was probably guilty of Morrison's murder.[26]

Stegner formed his opinion after extensive research in Salt Lake City. He talked to the Morrison family, Swedish Vice Consul Oscar Carlson, the warden of the Utah State Prison, and others directly connected with the case. To their almost unanimous agreement that Hill was a "yegg," he added information from Mac McClintock, Stewart Holbrook, and James Stevens (later to write *Big Jim Turner*, a novel in which Hill appears as a character) which indicated that Hill was a "stick-up man" with a "Robin Hood nature." Stegner has said that at no time during his research did he find a trace of any conspiracy to convict Hill. Instead, he was convinced that Utah officials would have welcomed any evidence allowing them to free the condemned man.

While recognizing the pervasiveness and durability of the legend, Stegner criticized Hill's role as a martyr because of (1) his belief in Hill's guilt, (2) the lack of any evidence that Hill was actually an effective strike leader and organizer for the I.W.W., and (3) his feeling that the martyr image was tailored for Hill by the I.W.W. "A far less authentic martyr than Little, Everest, Ford, Suhr, or half a dozen others, Joe Hill was easier to blow up to martyrdom because he had the poet's knack of self-dramatization."[27] Seemingly epitomizing Stegner's ideas on Hill's martyr image, the following statement was written in answer to criticism of his 1948 *New Republic* article: "Myself, I prefer Frank Little and Wesley Everest for the martyr's role. They at least died on workers' business."[28]

To the I.W.W., even such as it was in 1948, these were fighting words. Incensed over Stegner's opinions, the organization was quick to answer. Wobblies mustered strength to picket the New York office of the *New Republic* in April 1948, saying they would continue the picketing until the magazine retracted the "slur on their hero." *Time* magazine, reporting on the picketing, said ". . . the Wobblies were on the march to keep a legend of martyrdom alive."[29] This reaction from the I.W.W. led to publication of a condensed version of the findings of a committee of Wobblies, called "Friends of Joe Hill," which reexamined the whole affair. Although they omitted some charges, such as the implication of the Mormon church in a conspiracy, the committee concluded once again that an innocent man had been framed by the authorities of Utah.[30]*

The 1950's—While the I.W.W. was busily defending Hill, Stegner was completing a novel based on his life. *The Preacher and the Slave* appeared in 1950. Although he thought Hill guilty, Stegner also found, as have many others, a man who captured his interest and stimulated his imagination. In the book, which remains the most noteworthy fictional examination of Hill, he did not try to ascertain his guilt or innocence but, rather, ". . . to make him a man, such a man as he might have been, with his legend at his feet like a lengthening shadow."[31] The Joe Hill who emerges is temperate in his habits, intelligent, sometimes gentle—but also bitter, filled with untamed passions, searching for a special identity.

Taking his cue from a letter Hill wrote to an unidentified preacher known only as Gus, Stegner created Gustave Lund, friend and confidant of Joe Hill.**

---

* Also during 1948 Ralph Chaplin's *Wobbly: The Rough-and-Tumble Story of an American Radical* (Chicago: University of Chicago Press) was published. Its portrayal of Hill lent strength to the traditional martyr image. Perhaps the controversy over Hill raised by Stegner's articles and the I.W.W.'s reply inspired an allusion to him in Alexander Saxton's novel about railroading, *The Great Midland* (New York: Appleton-Century-Crofts, Inc., 1948, pp. 3, 10, 194), in which hobos and workers on the Great Midland Railroad sang Joe Hill's "The Preacher and the Slave."

**On January 3, 1915, Hill wrote the following letter to a friend known only as Gus. It is possible that this man was another mission director or that he was somehow connected with the Sailors' Rest Mission and John Makins, but as nothing is known about him, one can only read the letter and wonder.

Dear Gus:

    Jud Ricket was telling me the other day he had had two or three contributions from you for the defense fund. You know I never was very sold on the sky pilots, but you're one preacher I'll let into heaven whenever I happen to be tending door. Ricket tells me funds keep coming in and there is going to be enough to finance the appeal clear to the supreme court. I'm still pretty sure no man is worth that much, but if I get sore and tell them to give the money to strike relief somewhere they don't pay any attention, so I have learned to keep still. Keep still and sit still. I'd make a first class toadstool.

    I was thinking the other day, when the new year rolled around, that I've been in this calaboose almost a full year, and that's a long time to live on the kind of stew they

On the last night of Hill's life, Lund, visiting to offer comfort, asks why he is willing to waste his life by dying in this way. " 'Waste?' Joe said. 'Throw myself away? You don't know what you're talking about. . . .' The grin that grew over Joe's pinched face was of an incredible impudence. 'You might call it an organizing job . . . . The union stands to gain more if they shoot me than if they turn me loose.' "[32]

It became clear to Lund that Joe Hill believed—or wanted to believe—that it was his destiny to become a martyr. As long as the I.W.W. could make people believe him innocent, Joe said, what did his true guilt or innocence really matter? He was giving the union the most for its defense money by dying a martyr. Lund left, troubled and bewildered, with an ". . . image of Joe Hillstrom, full of some ecstatic vision, living out in his last hours not his own life but his forming legend."[33]

Author and playwright Barrie Stavis combined a resumé and collection of documents explaining Hill's life with a drama in *The Man Who Never Died*, first published in 1951.[34] The play, now translated into several major languages, has been widely produced, from off-Broadway in New York City to Sweden and East Berlin.[35] It is the story of a conspiracy between a turncoat I.W.W. named Tom, who hates Joe Hill's popularity, and "Copper King Moody." The two prod the estranged husband of Joe's girlfriend into bursting in on his wife and Joe and shooting Joe, hoping to kill him. When, to their disappointment, Joe is only wounded by the shot, they frame him for the murder of a grocer named Henderson and engineer his conviction by removing the girlfriend and her husband from Salt Lake City. As Joe Hill is executed, Ed Rowan delivers the eulogy that gives the play its title.

> It all started with a man, a working man, Joe Hill, who could sing songs. Joe, you sang the things we know and feel and believe. They tried to silence you. They could not. . . . They shot you. But still they could not silence your songs. You are dead, Joe, but your voice will never be silenced. . . . As long as there are people in this land of ours who sing, Joe Hill will never die.[36]

---

serve here. The coffee is a little better than you used to make, but not enough to get excited about. Well, when we used to sit in the kitchen and drink that turpentine we never thought that pretty soon you'd be hoeing corn and I'd be where I am. I keep myself in good spirits by reminding myself that the worst is yet to come.

No chance to read anything here. Once a month or so a missionary of some kind comes around with a basket of books, but they're all full of moral uplift and angel food, and I'd rather read old letters over again than waste time on that. The missionary is a lot like you used to be. I think he prays for me.

Write me when you can. One thing this jail has made out of me is a good correspondent.

> Your friend
> Joe

(Letter in Hoover Institution on War, Revolution, and Peace, Stanford University, Stanford, California; also in Philip S. Foner, ed., *The Letters of Joe Hill* [New York: International Publishers, 1965], p. 19.)

Stavis also wrote a two-part article for the magazine *Folk Music* which told the story of Hill's life, and, with Frank Harmon, edited *Songs of Joe Hill*, a book which made both music and words to most of Hill's songs generally available for the first time.[37] *

Another interpretation was added to the Hill legend in James Stevens' *Big Jim Turner*, the story of a boy who grew up in the days when the I.W.W. was at its peak of power. Joe Hill moves in and out of the action, always on Wobbly business. Stevens had written to Wallace Stegner his opinion that Hill's songs were written by a man who had been ". . . knocking around the West for many years," and the Hill he depicts in his novel is just such a man. Half crook, half saint, with ". . . eyes that could look at you like the eyes from a picture of Jesus Christ . . . deathly in their glittering stare," Joe Hill comes to life as a sensitive man who "dreamed on Byron's songs of revolt," but one who could be tough when it came to the I.W.W.[38] The Rough Rider, unwilling to join a group of Wobblies bound for the Spokane free speech fight, discovered a deadly serious Joe Hill blocking his way.

203

> Joe Hill cat-footed over to him and said, "Where bound?"
> Rough Rider took a big spit. "No business of your'n!"
> "You could find the goin' hard," Joe Hill said, sort of chopping out each word. No saint looked from his eyes.
> "I mean, without a red card," he said. "The road has changed, comrade."
> "I'll risk it. And don't you 'comrade' me."
> "You could fink on us. You'll join for Spokane."
> "The hell I will."
> With the last word the gun was swinging. It was a big blue, mean revolver. I was looking right at the two men, but my eyes had failed to catch the motion of Joe Hill's draw. . . . The muzzle, sight down, banged the Rough Rider's left temple, then it jerked down the side of his face. The gunsight left a spreading streak of blood.[39]

In the novel *From Here to Eternity* by James Jones, published in 1951, soldier Jack Malloy, a believer in reincarnation, worshipped Joe Hill for the role he played in life. Malloy said of Hill:

> "He was a saint. He had to be one, to have been given the life he was allowed to live. . . .
> "That's the way to go out. That shows what can be done. But you have to have what it takes. And then on top of that you have to have the luck. Someday they will rank Joe Hill right up alongside old John the Baptist. He must have done something great, back a long time ago before he was ever Joe Hill to have earned a chance at a ticket like that one."[40]

---

* Hill's songs have been a continuing influence in preserving his memory. Some of the songs were recorded by Joe Glazer in 1954 (Folkways FA 2039). Recordings have also been made by Pete Seeger, John Greenway, and Joe Glazer and Bill Friedland (Labor Arts 3). Mr. Seeger said that "Pie in the Sky" is the most widely known of Hill's songs and the most firmly entrenched in American folklore. "Casey Jones" is second in popularity. The rest are currently known only among a small circle of people. Mr. Seeger stated that he frequently sang "Casey Jones" to working men—"always to roars of laughter" (quoted from a letter from Pete Seeger to the author, October 1966).

In *The Ninth Wave* by Eugene Burdick (1952),* Mike Freesmith's musician father would sit with his children in his rare moods of contentment and talk about a world where all men were brothers and there was no law.

> He told them of Joe Hill and the Wobblies who went out against the guns and bayonets of a superior enemy because they wanted to see justice done to all people. To the children it was a lovely fairy story where huge men with beards and strong knotted muscles were infinitely kind to women and children. . . .
>
> When the four children played by themselves they fought to play Joe Hill. The winner would be chased by the other three who were "Salt Lake City Special Deputies," and Joe Hill would dodge around the house throwing imaginary balls of wet phosphorus into wheat fields, binding bundles of dynamite to railroad car wheels, throwing kerosene on cribs of corn. Finally the deputies would capture Joe Hill and would stand him against the house with a bandage over his eyes. As they crouched down with their sticks leveled to fire, Joe Hill would strip the bandage from his eyes and look straight at them. Then they would make popping noises with their tongues and Joe Hill would buckle against the side of the house and finally slide in a crumpled heap to the ground. Then they would start the game over and someone else would be Joe Hill.[41]

In addition to this fictionalized treatment, several scholarly studies appeared during the 1950's. In Sweden the facts of Hill's early life were published in 1951 by Ture Nerman in his book *Arbetarsangaren, Joe Hill: Mördare Eller Martyr?*

In America, an unpublished study by James O. Morris, "The Case of Joe Hill," was completed in 1950. Concentrating on the trial, Morris gave a detailed review of the evidence and proposed that Hill could have been wounded in Morrison's store by a bullet which lodged in the ceiling and was never found. He concluded that Hill's conviction was not just and that the attempt to appeal his case was thwarted by a ". . . well settled and intense abhorrence of the I.W.W."; but he believed Hill guilty. According to Morris, Hill's silence concerning his wound was dictated by guilt rather than ". . . 'honor' or a fanatical belief in the principle of fair trial." Silence was Hill's only way of avoiding disgrace—his own and his organization's. "Reluctantly, and probably with a deeply tormented soul, he chose death."[42]

In his article "The Legend of Joe Hill" (1951), Vernon Jensen revealed the confession Hill had allegedly made to Dr. McHugh.[43] Although Jensen's article was an even harsher condemnation than Stegner's, the I.W.W. made no significant protest. Fred Thompson compiled a history of the I.W.W. in 1955 to commemorate its fiftieth anniversary which recounts the story of Joe Hill as one of the Wobbly martyrs.[44]

A 1959 program at the Old Town School of Folk Music in Chicago featured Joe Hill's songs and a short talk on the folklore of labor given by Archie

---

* Burdick was a student of Wallace Stegner during the time that Stegner was writing *The Preacher and the Slave.* His interest in and knowledge of Hill probably stem from this association.

204

Green. Fred Thompson, who attended, reported that the Joe Hill songs sung that night must have been familiar to at least some in the large audience, for they joined enthusiastically in the singing.[45]*

Archie Green, who has the John Neuhaus collection of Wobbly folklore, included some information on Hill in his 1960 article "John Neuhaus: Wobbly Folklorist."[46] Green has also commented on the fact that Hill's songs are still sung in Wobbly meetings.

> When John [Neuhaus] took me to ordinary I.W.W. branch meetings, I knew that the group singing, no instruments, was the real McCoy. Some songs were from memory and some from the little red book. Sometimes the leader would sing the first line or establish the melody and everyone would pitch in. . . . These branch meetings were regular and typical and could have taken place in any I.W.W. hall between 1905-1965.[47]

"Joe Hill," a poem by Woody Guthrie, was published in 1961, and a ballad about Hill (twenty-two verses and music) by Phil Ochs appeared in *Broadside* in November 1966.[48]

In 1964 the Canadian Broadcasting Company produced a film for television depicting Hill's life in prison. While it departed from fact in several instances, the film was basically accurate and illustrated vividly just how Hill's songs grew out of actual conditions in the workers' experience.[49] The *Industrial Worker* announced that Hill's songs had been translated into Swedish.

In 1965, fifty years after Hill's death, two books were published by Philip S. Foner. *The Letters of Joe Hill*, edited by Foner, contains most of Hill's known correspondence. *The Case of Joe Hill* is a study of the trial and the appeal and gives a brief look at Hill's life. After close examination of the evidence, Foner claims that the Mormon church, the Utah Construction Company, and the Utah Copper Company engineered Hill's apprehension, conviction, and execution with the aid of the Salt Lake City police.

> Joe Hill was arrested and convicted on suspicion. He had the misfortune of being shot on the same night that the Morrison murders were committed. This caused his arrest as a suspect and, under ordinary circumstances, the lack of any concrete evidence would have been the cause for his release. But when the police and the authorities discovered who Joe Hill was, they and all other anti-union (especially anti-I.W.W.) elements in Utah had an opportunity to "solve" a crime and get rid of a militant union agitator. There was no need to obtain real evidence to achieve this goal. Suspicion was enough to guarantee that Joe Hill would be convicted.[50]**

---

* Also in the fifties, minor mention was made of Hill in two other works of fiction. Kenneth Rexroth's work *The Dragon and the Unicorn* (Norfolk Conn.: New Directions, 1952, p. 128) mentions Joe Hill, along with Frank Little, Wesley Everest, and Sacco and Vanzetti, as a martyr of the workingmen. The science fiction novel *Not This August* by Cyril Kornbluth (Garden City, New York: Doubleday & Co., Inc., 1955, p. 152) presents the hero Billy Justin reading a comic book entitled *Joe Hill, Hero of Labor.*

**Several reviews of Foner's books have appeared. Melvyn Dubofsky, writing in *Labor History* (7, Fall 1966), criticizes Foner's views in *The Case of Joe Hill* as being "as circumstantial and as weak as the state's." Vernon Jensen, in *Dialogue: A Journal of Mormon Thought* (2, no. 1, Spring 1967), restates his story of Hill's confession to Dr. McHugh in

Joyce Kornbluh's *Rebel Voices: An I.W.W. Anthology* (1964) includes a valuable chapter, "Joe Hill: Wobbly Bard," which contains many of Hill's songs, some of his writing, letters to Sam Murray, and information on his funeral. In Patrick Renshaw's *The Wobblies* (1967), Hill is discussed in a chapter on I.W.W. martyrs. Among several Hill articles by Zapata Modesto (Barry Nichols) is "Joe Hill, Some Notes on an American Culture Hero," a compilation of references to Hill in American literature.[51]

Fiftieth Anniversary Events—In 1965 and early 1966, several gatherings were held in commemoration of the fiftieth anniversary of Hill's execution.* In Washington, D.C., Esther Peterson, a former Department of Labor official, held a "labor happening" to disprove the contention that the American labor movement does not sing any more. The festivities included the singing of Wobbly songs under the leadership of Joe Glazer.[52] At Wayne State University, the Labor History Archives devoted one program in its series of "Episodes in Labor History" to "The Legacy of Joe Hill." Held on November 19, 1965, the program included a presentation entitled "Joe Hill: Wobbly Troubadour," song and narration, with a short discussion of "The Meaning of Joe Hill Fifty Years After" presented by Fred Thompson and Carl Keller of the I.W.W.[53] At the Salt Lake City Public Library, a folk song and narrative concert-lecture, "Joe Hill and the I.W.W." was presented.[54] The modern labor movement's continuing interest in its more radical past was evidenced by an article on Hill in the United Steelworkers' paper, *Steel Labor*, in January 1966.[55]

---

taking issue with Foner's analysis of the trial. Jensen continues by attacking the popular legend, perpetuated by Foner, that Hill was an organizer for the I.W.W. and that the Mormon church was involved in a frame-up, concluding that, except for the legend which has grown up around him, Hill would have little claim to fame as a labor hero. Striking a somewhat milder note. Paul Cowan applauds Foner for making available information too commonly dropped from standard American histories. Knowledge of Hill and the I.W.W. could, if given the chance, illuminate some of the complexities and subtleties of American history, he claims ("Dying Like a Rebel," *Nation*, 203 [26 September 1966]).

Also appearing in 1965 was Philip S. Foner's book *The Industrial Workers of the World, 1905-1917*, volume four of his *History of the Labor Movement in the United States* (New York: International Publishers, 1965). Foner explained that the Hill case was to be included as a chapter in this work, but because of its length he decided to have it published as the separate book mentioned above, *The Case of Joe Hill*.

* A 1965 commemorative article on Hill appeared in the *America Swedish Historical Foundation Yearbook* (Bridgeport, Pa.: Chancellor, Inc., 1965). Also, a *New York Times* article on February 14, 1965, which was mainly concerned with a petition by the Wobblies to be removed from the Attorney General's subversive organizations list, commented that the I.W.W. lives today mostly ". . . in the dusty memories of old men and the little song book containing the Joe Hill song about 'Pie in the Sky When you Die.' " The article noted that a faded picture of Joe Hill still hangs in the old I.W.W. headquarters in Chicago.

In Sweden, *Signalen*, a magazine for railroad workers, printed an article by Carl Löfgren on the occasion of the fiftieth anniversary of Hill's death. The article contains a history of Hill's Swedish background and a statement of the martyr legend (22 January 1966, pp. 8-9).

Publications and Events in Sweden—In addition to the growing interest in America, Hill's legend has spread in Sweden in recent years, with most of the current interest dating from the publication of the articles that brought to light Hill's childhood in Gävle and the publication of Ture Nerman's book. Even before Hill gained a devoted following in Sweden, however, in a 1949 concert at Stockholm's Gardet, the traditional gathering place of Swedish workers, Paul Robeson reportedly drew intense interest from the huge audience with a poignant rendition of "I Dreamed I Saw Joe Hill Last Night."[56]

Eulogizing articles have appeared in *Ny Dag*, the Swedish Communist Party newspaper, which has claimed that Hill was ". . . murdered by the reactionary authorities in Utah,"[57] and that he died to protect the "honor" of the unnamed wife of a "prominent Salt Lake City industrialist."[58] *Arbetaren*, a Swedish labor newspaper, has protested *Ny Dag*'s interest in Joe Hill, insisting that Hill as an I.W.W. "could never have been a Bolshevik."[59] *Arbetaren* maintains that Hill was killed because he was hated by American capitalists.[60] The Joe Hill story has been reviewed and judgment has been passed in many major Swedish newspapers, including one of the largest, *Dagens Nyheter.*[61]

207

Magazine articles have appeared with some frequency, and the author has in his possession seven 1967 articles from important publications. One of these—an article in the Swedish Trade Union Council's journal— describes the efforts of a Swedish singer and composer, Matts Paulson, to popularize the translated versions of Hill's songs. With new arrangements for twelve of them, Paulson reports that the public ". . . has shown great enthusiasm for Joe Hill's songs. Joe Hill was a protest singer fifty years before his time. . . . His songs call for effective fighting for a better world."[62]

In Hill's hometown of Gävle there are plans to establish a museum for his memorabilia in the old house at 28 Nedra Bergsgatan.[63] The Gävle-Upsala theater has performed a drama on his life,[64] and the fifty-second anniversary of his execution was commemorated by a lecture in 1967.[65]

In the city of his death as well as in the town of his birth, the legend of Joe Hill endures. In 1961, Ammon Hennacy, a "humanitarian anarchist," established the Joe Hill House of Hospitality for Transients, which offered free food and beds. There was singing on Friday nights, and the house provided visitors a mimeographed songbook, "If I Were Free," containing information on Joe Hill's life and several of his songs.[66]

A group comprised of Hennacy, songwriter Bruce Phillips, and several others organized the Joe Hill Memorial Committee to preserve Hill's memory in Salt Lake City and to spearhead the erection of a monument on the site of the old prison where he was jailed and executed.[67]

Some who have become involved in the Hill controversy have been interested parties engaged in building the traditional legend, others have been attracted by the drama of the case, while still others have sought primarily to keep alive the folklore of a segment of American culture. While the various

208

Hill's influence can be seen in this picket line. The photograph is from the back cover of *Basta! La Historia de Nuestra Lucha* **(Enough! The Story of Our Struggle), issued by Farm Workers Press, Delano, California, 1966.**

interpreters have perpetuated Hill's memory, no evidence has been found to conclusively establish his guilt or innocence.

But now, more than fifty years after his execution, these questions—though they still haunt us with the possibility that an innocent man may have been put to death—tend to fade before the phenomenon of his strength in memory. A recent article reflects the change in emphasis from questions of the man's guilt or innocence to interest in the legendary figure he has become. "Joe Hill is the only American songwriter in history to get himself enshrined in such mixed company as the folklore heros Johnny Appleseed, John Henry, and Paul Bunyan, and the revolutionaries such as John Reed and Big Bill Haywood."[68] And his place in folklore is assured by the larger-than-life qualities described by Wobbly Alexander McKay: "My own impression . . . is that all militant Wobs of the period 1905-1914 were the very epitome of guts and gallantry, a handful of homeless heroes touched by the true Romance. Men and women whose spirits were stirred far above their belly-need; men and women inspired by visions of heaven on earth. . . ."[69]

There remains beneath the layers of myth the person Joe Hill, a humorous, beguiling and sentimental man, an angry, tough, and hard-bitten rebel—a man whose songs still generate energy and unity on picket lines. It is ironical in a way that might appeal to Joe Hill himself that his story still holds a fascination that prompts the asking of questions only he can answer.

ARMFA
Archives of the Royal Ministry of Foreign Affairs

ASSU
Archives of Secretary of State of Utah

DEN
Deseret Evening News

HIWRP
Hoover Institution on War, Revolution, and Peace

NA
National Archives

SLH-R
Salt Lake Herald-Republican

SLT
Salt Lake Tribune

Telegram
Salt Lake Telegram

USHSA
Utah State Historical Society Archives

WSULHA
Wayne State University Labor History Archives

Notes

CHAPTER 1

1— Fred Thompson to the author, 2 June 1967, original in author's possession.

2— Richard Brazier, "The Story of the I.W.W.'s 'Little Red Song Book,' " *Labor History*, 9 (Winter 1968): 92-95.

3— J. H. Walsh, "Developments in Spokane," *Industrial Union Bulletin*, 4 April 1908, p. 2.

4— Richard Brazier, "The Spokane Free Speech Fight, 1909," *Industrial Worker*, December 1966, p. 6.

5— Brazier, "Spokane Free Speech Fight"; Fred Thompson, *The I.W.W.: Its First Fifty Years* (1955), pp. 38-39.

6— Thompson to the author, 1 February 1967, original in author's possession.

7— Joyce L. Kornbluh, ed., *Rebel Voices: An I.W.W. Anthology* (1964), p. 65.

8— Brazier, "Spokane Free Speech Fight," p. 6.

9— Kornbluh, *Rebel Voices*, p. 95. For information on the Spokane free speech fight see n. 4 above and two articles by Richard Brazier in *Industrial Worker*, January 1967, February 1967.

10— James Wilson, "The Value of Music in I.W.W. Meetings," *Industrial Union Bulletin*, 16 May 1908, p. 1.

11— *Industrial Union Bulletin*, 24 October 1908, p. 1.

12— Brazier, "The I.W.W.'s 'Little Red Song Book,' " p. 98.

13— Brazier, "The I.W.W.'s 'Little Red Song Book,' " pp. 98-99.

14— Hill to Editor of *Solidarity*, 29 November 1914, in *Solidarity*, 19 December 1914; also in Philip S. Foner, ed., *The Letters of Joe Hill* (1965), pp. 16-17.

15— Philip S. Foner, *The Industrial Workers of the World, 1905-1917* (1965), p. 156.

16— Barrie Stavis, "Joe Hill: Poet/Organizer," *Folk Music*, June 1964, p. 43.

17— Alexander MacKay to Editor of *Industrial Worker*, 27 November 1947, Labor History Archives, Wayne State University Library, Detroit, Michigan (hereafter referred to as WSULHA).

18— *Songs of the Workers*, 29th ed. (1956), p. 9. Also see listing in Appendix A of further major references for each song.

19— Carl Sandburg, *The American Songbag* (1927), p. 222.

20— Henry F. May, *The End of American Innocence* (1959), p. 178.

21— For information on "The Preacher and the Slave" see the following: Kornbluh, *Rebel Voices*, p. 132; John Greenway, *American Folksongs of Protest* (1953), p. 184; Barrie Stavis, *The Man Who Never Died* (1954), p. 18; Sandburg, *American Songbag*, p. 222; Wallace Stegner, "I Dreamed I Saw Joe Hill Last Night," *Pacific Spectator*, 1, no. 2 (Spring 1947): 184; Barrie Stavis and Frank Harmon, eds., *Songs of Joe Hill* (1960), p. 10; Luis S. Kemnitzer, "Note on Pie in the Sky," *Western Folklore*, 18 (October 1959): 328. The song has also appeared in numerous books of folk song, among them the following: B. A. Botkin, ed., *A Treasury of American Folklore* (1944), pp. 886-87; Olin Downes and Elie Siegmeister, eds., *A Treasury of American Song* (1943), pp. 388-89; Alan Lomax, ed., *The Folk Songs of North America in the English Language* (1960), pp. 423-24; Marcus Graham, ed., *An Anthology of Revolutionary Poetry* (1929), p. 84; Richard E. Lingenfelter, Richard A. Dwyer, and David Cohen, eds., *Songs of the American West* (1968), p. 544.

22— George Milburn, *The Hobo's Hornbook* (1930), p. 83.

23— Archie Green, "John Neuhaus: Wobbly Folklorist," *Journal of American Folklore*, 73 (July-September 1960): 194.

24— Ralph Chaplin, "Joe Hill: A Biography," *Industrial Pioneer*, November 1923, p. 25; Ralph Chaplin, *Wobbly: The Rough-and-Tumble Story of an American Radical* (1948), p. 186. For further speculation on why Hill wrote "Casey Jones" see Stavis, "Joe Hill: Poet/Organizer," p. 39; William Alderson, "On the Wobbly 'Casey Jones' and Other Songs," *California Folklore Quarterly*, 1 (Winter 1942): 373-76; Greenway, *American Folksongs of Protest*, p. 186.

25— Fred Thompson, "Why Joe Hill Wrote His 'Casey Jones,' " *Industrial Worker*, February 1966, p. 5.

26— Louis B. Perry and Richard A. Perry, *A History of the Los Angeles Labor Movement, 1911-1941* (1963), p. 64.

27— Thompson, "Why Joe Hill Wrote His 'Casey Jones,' " p. 5.

28— Thompson, "Why Joe Hill Wrote His 'Casey Jones,' " p. 5.

29— Perry and Perry, *The Los Angeles Labor Movement*, pp. 63-64.

30— Thompson, "Why Joe Hill Wrote His 'Casey Jones,' " p. 5.

31— Thompson, "Why Joe Hill Wrote His 'Casey Jones,' " p. 5.

32— Carl Person, ed., *Strike Bulletin*, Clinton, Illinois, 24 March 1915, p. 2; also in *Songs of the Workers*, p. 46.

33— Greenway, *American Folksongs of Protest*, pp. 185-86. Also see Wayland D. Hand et al., "Songs of the Butte Miners," *Western Folklore*, 9 (January 1950), footnote p. 33.

34— Foner, *Workers of the World*, pp. 227-28.

35— Foner, *Workers of the World*, p. 229.

36— G. Engblem to *Solidarity*, dated 3 May 1912, printed 18 May 1912, p. 2.

37— Louis Moreau to Fred Thompson, 8 March 1967, WSULHA.

38— Moreau to Thompson, 8 March 1967, WSULHA; and Moreau to the author, 3 April 1967, original in author's possession.

39— *Industrial Worker*, 9 May 1912, p. 3.

40— *Industrial Worker*, 9 May 1912, p. 3; also in *Songs of the Workers*, p. 58.

41— Moreau to Thompson, 8 March 1967, WSULHA.

42— Foner, *Workers of the World*, p. 230.

43— Moreau to Thompson, 8 March 1967, WSULHA.

44— Foner, *Workers of the World*, p. 231. For further information on the Canadian Northern strike see Agnes C. Laut, "Revolution Yawns," *Illustrated Technical World*, 18 (May 1913): 134-44.

45— Kornbluh, *Rebel Voices*, p. 159.

46— Kornbluh, *Rebel Voices*, p. 159.

47— For a complete description of the Lawrence strike see Kornbluh, *Rebel Voices*, pp. 158-96; and Foner, *Workers of the World*, pp. 306-50.

48— U.S., Congress, Senate, "Report on Strike of Textile Workers in Lawrence, Mass.," *Senate Documents*, 62nd Cong., 2d sess., 1912, pp. 14-17.

49— *Solidarity*, 2 March 1912, p. 4.

50— *Solidarity*, 30 March 1912, p. 1.

51— "John Golden and the Lawrence Strike" can be found in Appendix A, in early editions of *Songs of the Workers*, and in Stavis and Harmon, *Songs of Joe Hill*, pp. 14-15.

52— Foner, *Workers of the World*, pp. 325-28, 340-43.

53— *Songs of the Workers*, p. 14. Oscar W. Larson told the Swedish newspaper *Ny Dag* that the song was written for Verdandi, and the newspaper published the information on 29 April 1950.

54— Hill to Sam Murray, 2 December 1914, in "The Last Letters of Joe Hill," *Industrial Pioneer*, December 1923, p. 53; also in Foner, *Letters of Joe Hill*, p. 18.

55— *Songs of the Workers*, p. 28.

56— Hill to Murray, 13 February 1915, in "The Last Letters of Joe Hill," p. 54; also in Foner, *Letters of Joe Hill*, p. 26.

57— Hill to Murray, 22 March 1915, in "The Last Letters of Joe Hill," p. 54; also in Foner, *Letters of Joe Hill*, p. 32.

58— Hill to Editor of *Solidarity*, 29 November 1914, in *Solidarity*, 19 December 1914;

also in Foner, *Letters of Joe Hill*, pp. 16-17.

59— Hill to Murray, 13 February 1915, in "The Last Letters of Joe Hill," p. 54; also in Foner, *Letters of Joe Hill*, p. 32.

60— Hill to Elizabeth Gurley Flynn, 18 November 1915, in Foner, *Letters of Joe Hill*, p. 82.

61— *Songs of the Workers*, p. 7.

62— *Songs of the Workers*, p. 39.

63— *Songs of the Workers*, p. 22.

64— *Songs of the Workers*, p. 38.

65— *Industrial Worker*, 17 April 1913, p. 2.

66— Carleton H. Parker, *The Casual Laborer and Other Essays* (1920), p. 191.

67— *Salt Lake Tribune*, 13 August 1913 (hereafter referred to as *SLT*).

68— "Nearer My Job to Thee" can be found in Appendix A and in early editions of *Songs of the Workers*.

69— "Coffee An' " can be found in Appendix A and in early editions of *Songs of the Workers*.

70— "Ta-ra-ra Boom De-ay" can be found in Appendix A, in early editions of *Songs of the Workers*, and in Stavis and Harmon, *Songs of Joe Hill*, pp. 22-23.

71— *Songs of the Workers*, p. 50.

72— *Songs of the Workers*, p. 34.

73— Hill to Murray, 9 September 1915, in "The Last Letters of Joe Hill," p. 54; also in Foner, *Letters of Joe Hill*, p. 56.

74— *Songs of the Workers*, p. 13.

75— *Songs of the Workers*, p. 54.

76— Hill to Elizabeth Gurley Flynn, 18 November 1915, in Foner, *Letters of Joe Hill*, p. 83.

77— See Appendix A.

78— *Industrial Worker*, 21 Aug. 1913, p. 2.

79— The John Neuhaus Collection of Wobbly Folklore, MS and microfilm in possession of Archie Green, microfilm copy in WSULHA; and Interview of William Chance by the author, 23 April 1967, Banning, California.

80— *Solidarity*, 27 July 1912, p. 4.

81— *SLT*, 21 June 1914.

82— *SLT*, 21 June 1914.

83— MS of "My Dreamland Girl" in Archives of the Royal Ministry for Foreign Affairs, Stockholm, Sweden (hereafter referred to as ARMFA).

84— *Los Angeles Times*, 20 November 1915.

85— Richard Brazier to Fred Thompson, n.d., original in Fred Thompson's possession.

86— *SLT*, 21 June 1914.

87— Greenway, *American Folksongs of Protest*, p. 197.

88— Stegner, "I Dreamed I Saw Joe Hill Last Night," p. 187.

89— Nels Anderson, *The Hobo: The Sociology of the Homeless Man* (1923), p. 208.

90— May, *End of American Innocence*, p. 178.

91— Sandburg, *American Songbag*, p. 222.

92— Greenway, *American Folksongs of Protest*, p. 181.

93— George Milburn, "Posey in the Jungles," *American Mercury*, 20 (May 1930): 80-86.

94— Green, "John Neuhaus: Wobbly Folklorist," p. 189.

95— Alan Calmer, "The Wobbly in American Literature," *New Masses*, 18 September 1934, p. 21.

96— *Solidarity*, 9 January 1915, p. 1.

97— *Solidarity*, 22 May 1915, p. 1.

98— Chaplin, "Joe Hill: A Biography," p. 23; Ralph Chaplin, "Joe Hill," *The Labor Defender*, 1 (November 1926): 189.

99— Bernard Kyler to Woodrow Wilson, 28 October 1915, Record Gp. 59, Records of Department of State, Decimal File, 1910-1929, File no. 311.582H55 to no. 311.582H55/35, National Archives, Washington, D.C. (hereafter referred to as State Department File, NA).

CHAPTER 2

1— Alexander MacKay to Editor of *Industrial Worker*, 27 November 1947, WSULHA.

2— Interview of William Chance by the author, 23 April 1967, Banning, California.

3— Hill to Oscar W. Larson, 30 September 1915, in *Revolt*, December 1915, p. 12; also in Philip S. Foner, ed., *Letters of Joe Hill*, p. 59.

4— Ture Nerman, *Arbetarsangaren Joe Hill: Mördare Eller Martyr?* (1951), pp. 23-24.

5— Nerman, *Mördare Eller Martyr?*, p. 24.

6— Nerman, *Mördare Eller Martyr?*, p. 29.

7— Nerman, *Mördare Eller Martyr?*, p. 25.

8— Ester Dahl to the author, 20 November 1965, original in author's possession.

9— Nerman, *Mördare Eller Martyr?*, p. 25.

10— John Takman, "Joe Hill's Sister: An Interview," *Masses and Mainstream*, March 1956, p. 28.

11— Nerman, *Mördare Eller Martyr?*, p. 27.

12— Gösta Ahlstrand, "Joe Hill From Gävle," *Gefle Dagblad*, 14 August 1967.

13— Takman, "Joe Hill's Sister," p. 25.

14— Takman, "Joe Hill's Sister," p. 25.

15— Ester Dahl to the author, 20 November 1965, and 3 July 1967.

16— Takman, "Joe Hill's Sister," p. 25.

17— Hill to Katie Phar, 4 March 1915, in Foner, *Letters of Joe Hill*, p. 29.

18— Nerman, *Mördare Eller Martyr?*, pp. 32-33.

19— Takman, "Joe Hill's Sister," p. 27; Ester Dahl to the author, 3 July 1967.

20— Ahlstrand, "Joe Hill from Gävle"; Takman, "Joe Hill's Sister," p. 27.

21— Nerman, *Mördare Eller Martyr?*, p. 27.

22— Nerman, *Mördare Eller Martyr?*, p. 29.

23— Ester Dahl to the author, 20 November 1965, and 3 July 1967. In Foner, *Letters of Joe Hill*, p. 25, Hill says he began work at the age of ten when his father died.

24— Nerman, *Mördare Eller Martyr?*, p. 33.

25— Nerman *Mördare Eller Martyr?*, p. 35.

26— Takman, "Joe Hill's Sister," p. 25.

27— Nerman, *Mördare Eller Martyr?*, p. 29.

28— Ester Dahl to the author, 15 January 1965.

29— Takman, "Joe Hill's Sister," p. 29.

30— Takman, "Joe Hill's Sister," p. 28.

31— Nerman, *Mördare Eller Martyr?*, p. 37.

32— *Salt Lake Herald-Republican*, 18 No-

vember 1915 (hereafter referred to as *SLH-R*).

33— Ralph Chaplin, "Joe Hill: A Biography," *Industrial Pioneer*, November 1923, pp. 23-26; Ralph Chaplin, *Wobbly: The Rough-and-Tumble Story of an American Radical*, p. 185.

34— Chaplin, "Joe Hill: A Biography," pp. 23-26; Chaplin, *Wobbly*, p. 185.

35— *Arbetarbladet*, 18 December 1915.

36— Nerman, *Mördare Eller Martyr?*, p. 35.

37— Nerman, *Mördare Eller Martyr?*, p. 37.

38— Ben Fletcher told Jack Sheridan of seeing Hill in Philadelphia, and Richard (Dick) Brazier said John Reed mentioned knowing Joe Hill in Philadelphia. Both incidents were reported in a letter from Fred Thompson to the author, 31 December 1966. Vaino Konga said that Frank Grad reported meeting Joe Hill in the Dakotas, probably around 1910-11. Both were presumably I.W.W.'s at the time. The incident was reported in a letter from Thompson to the author, 25 February 1967, originals of both letters in author's possession. In a letter to Fred Thompson (18 November 1947, WSULHA), Charles Anderson said he was introduced to Joe Hill in Spokane.

39— Card from Joel Hägglund to Ester Hägglund, 1905, Arbetarrörelsens Arkiv, Stockholm, Sweden, in collection of Joe Hill material.

40— Joel Hägglund to *Gefle Dagblad*, dated 24 April 1906, printed 16 May 1906; also in Nerman, *Mördare Eller Martyr?*, p. 41.

41— Mexico, "Joe Hill, A Successful Sabotage," *Brand*, 18 December 1915.

42— *SLH-R*, 18 November 1915.

43— Alexander MacKay to Editor of *Industrial Worker*, 27 November 1947, WSULHA; William Chance, interview, 23 April 1967.

44— Curt Gentry, *Frame Up* (1967), p. 63; *SLT*, 15 January 1914.

45— Chaplin, "Joe Hill: A Biography," p. 25.

46— Joe Hill, "Another Victim of the Uniformed Thugs," *Industrial Worker*, 27 August 1910, p. 3.

47— Grace Heilman Stimson, *The Rise of the Labor Movement in Los Angeles*

(1955), p. 321.

48— Ricardo Flores Magón et al. to I.W.W. members, *Industrial Worker*, 8 June 1911, p. 1.

49— Hyman Weintraub, "The I.W.W. in California: 1905-1931" (thesis, University Library, University of California at Los Angeles, 1947), p. 282.

50— William Chance, interview, 23 April 1967.

51— F. G. Peterson et al. to *Industrial Worker*, 8 June 1911, p. 1; quoted in Weintraub, "I.W.W. in California," p. 51.

52— Laura Payne Emerson, "A Visit to Mexico," *Solidarity*, no. 76 (1911): 2.

53— Chili Con Carne to *Industrial Worker*, 6 July 1911, p. 1, in Weintraub, "I.W.W. in California," p. 53.

54— *SLH-R*, 18 November 1915.

55— William Chance, interview, 23 April 1967; Alexander MacKay to Editor of *Industrial Worker*, 27 November 1947, WSULHA.

56— Sam Murray, introductory statement to "The Last Letters of Joe Hill," *Industrial Pioneer*, December 1923, p. 53.

57— Hill to Sam Murray, 13 February 1915, in "The Last Letters of Joe Hill," p. 54; also in Foner, *Letters of Joe Hill*, p. 26.

58— *Los Angeles Times*, 20 November 1915.

59— Joe Hill, "The People," in Joyce L. Kornbluh, ed., *Rebel Voices: An I.W.W. Anthology*, pp. 136-37.

60— Hill to *Industrial Worker*, 25 May 1911, p. 1.

61— Harry K. (Mac) McClintock to Wallace Stegner, 28 March 1946, Hoover Institution on War, Revolution, and Peace, Stanford University, Stanford, California (hereafter referred to as HIWRP).

62— McClintock to Editor of *Industrial Worker*, 9 July 1950, WSULHA.

63— Chaplin, "Joe Hill: A Biography," p. 24.

64— *Solidarity*, 9 January 1915, p. 1.

65— Richard Brazier told Fred Thompson in a letter dated 21 December 1966 that Fraser was not in the Spokane fight: "As to Joe Hill being in the Spokane Free Speech Fight, I feel sure that he wasn't. . . . As for Ted Fraser saying that Joe Hill was in the Spokane Free Speech Fight, Ted wasn't in that fight"; reported in a letter from Fred Thompson to the author, 31 December 1966.

66— William Chance, interview, 23 April 1967.

67— Theodore Schroeder, *Free Speech for Radicals* (1916), pp. 148-50.

68— Emma Goldman, *Living My Life*, 2 vols. (1931), 1:500-501.

69— Schroeder, *Free Speech for Radicals*, pp. 144-45; *Industrial Worker*, 18 April 1912.

70— Louis Moreau to the author, 3 April 1967, original in author's possession.

71— *San Pedro Pilot*, 24 July 1912.

72— Louis B. Perry and Richard A. Perry, *A History of the Los Angeles Labor Movement, 1911-1941*, p. 165.

73— *San Pedro Daily News*, 27 July 1912.

74— *San Pedro Daily News*, 27 July 1912.

75— *Los Angeles Times*, 20 November 1915.

76— Hill to *Salt Lake Telegram*, 15 August 1915, in *Salt Lake Telegram*, 22 August 1915 (hereafter referred to as *Telegram*); also in Foner, *Letters of Joe Hill*, p. 49.

77— Chaplin, "Joe Hill: A Biography," p. 24.

78— John Makins, *Annual Report of the Sailors' Rest Mission, San Pedro, California*, 1 February 1919, p. 2.

79— Hill to John Makins, *SLH-R*, 19 November 1915.

80— Hill to Elizabeth Gurley Flynn, 10 March 1915, in Foner, *Letters of Joe Hill*, p. 30.

81— Hill to Murray, 22 March 1915, in "The Last Letters of Joe Hill," p. 54; also in Foner, *Letters of Joe Hill*, p. 32.

82— McClintock to Stegner, 28 March 1946, HIWRP.

83— McClintock to Stegner, 28 March 1946, HIWRP.

84— McClintock to Stegner, 17 July 1947, HIWRP.

85— Stewart H. Holbrook to Stegner, 28 March 1947, HIWRP.

86— William Chance, interview, 23 April 1967.

87— H. M. Edwards in a letter to Fred Thompson, December 1966; reported in a letter from Fred Thompson to the author, January 1967.

88— Joe Hill, "The People," in Kornbluh, *Rebel Voices*, pp. 136-37.

89— Hill to Murray, 15 September 1914, in "The Last Letters of Joe Hill," p. 53; also in Foner, *Letters of Joe Hill*, p. 13.

90— Joe Hill, "How To Make Work for the Unemployed," *International Socialist Review*, 15 (December 1914): 335-36; also in Kornbluh, *Rebel Voices*, pp. 141-43.

91— Hill to E. W. Vanderleith, n.d., Frank P. Walsh Papers, Manuscript Division, New York Public Library, New York City.

CHAPTER 3

1— Ralph Chaplin, "Joe Hill: A Biography," *Industrial Pioneer*, November 1923, pp. 23-26.

2— Chaplin, "Joe Hill: A Biography," pp. 23-26.

3— There are several sources of information indicating that Hill worked in Park City: *SLH-R*, 18 November 1915; *Deseret Evening News*, 15 January 1914 (hereafter referred to as *DEN*); *Telegram*, 15 August 1915; Interview of William Chance by the author, 23 April 1967, Banning, California.

4— *DEN*, 19 January 1914. Applequist had come to Utah in 1907 and worked as a structural steel laborer. In approximately 1910 he went to the Pacific coast to work on the waterfront in San Pedro. In the late spring of 1913 he returned to Ogden, Utah, where he worked on the construction of the Eccles Building. That job finished, he moved on to the Park City mines (*SLH-R*, 15 January 1914).

5— *SLH-R*, 18 November 1915.

6— *SLT*, 15 January 1914.

7— *SLT*, 15 January 1914.

8— *SLH-R*, 24 January 1914.

9— *SLH-R*, 14 January 1914.

10— *SLH-R*, 14 January 1914.

11— Anonymous letter to O. N. Hilton from Buffalo, New York, n.d., original in ARMFA.

12— State of Utah v. Hillstrom, 46 Utah 341, 150 P. 935, 942 (1915).

13— *SLH-R*, 14 January 1914.

14— *SLH-R*, 14 January 1914.

15— *SLT*, 14 January 1914.

16— *SLH-R*, 14 January 1914.

17— Information no. 3532, supplied to Utah Board of Pardons by the Utah Third Judicial District Court concerning State of Utah v. Hillstrom, MS in Archives of Secretary of State of Utah (hereafter referred to as ASSU), p. 9.

18— Utah v. Hillstrom [Supreme Court], p. 939.

19— District Court Information no. 3532, pp. 9-10.

20— State of Utah v. Hillstrom, Case no. 3532 in the Utah Third District Court, vol. 2, Transcript of the evidence introduced on behalf of the defendant, pp. 449-50.

21— *SLH-R*, 15 January 1914.

22— Utah v. Hillstrom [Supreme Court], p. 938.

23— Utah v. Hillstrom, Case no. 3532 [District Court], p. 524.

24— District Court Information no. 3532, pp. 2-3.

25— District Court Information no. 3532, pp. 2-3.

26— *SLH-R*, 11 January 1914.

27— District Court Information no. 3532, pp. 4-5.

28— District Court Information no. 3532, pp. 6-7.

29— *SLH-R*, 11 January 1914.

30— *SLH-R*, 11 January 1914.

31— *SLT*, 11 January 1914.

32— *SLH-R*, 11 January 1914.

33— *SLH-R*, 11 January 1914.

34— Utah v. Hillstrom, Case no. 3532 [District Court], pp. 600-603.

35— *SLH-R*, 12 January 1914.

36— *SLH-R*, 12 January 1914.

37— *SLH-R*, 12 January 1914.

38— *SLH-R*, 12 January 1914.

39— *SLH-R*, 13 January 1914.

40— *SLH-R*, 13 January 1914.

41— *SLH-R*, 13 January 1914.

42— *SLH-R*, 12 January 1914.

43— *SLH-R*, 12 January 1914.

44— *SLH-R*, 3 February 1903.

45— *SLH-R*, 3 February 1903.

46— *DEN*, 3 February 1903.

47— *DEN*, 3 February 1903.

48— *SLH-R*, 3 February 1903.

49— *SLH-R*, 3 February 1903.

50— *SLH-R*, 3 February 1903.

51— *DEN*, 3 February 1903.

52— *SLH-R*, 11 January 1914.

53— *SLH-R*, 21 September 1913.

54— *SLH-R*, 11 January 1914.

55— *SLT*, 11 January 1914.

56— *SLH-R*, 11 January 1914.

57— *SLT*, 11 January 1914; *SLH-R*, 11 January 1914; *DEN*, 12 January 1914.

58— Vernon H. Jensen, "The Legend of Joe Hill," *Industrial and Labor Relations Review*, 4 (April 1951): 356-66; and Vernon H. Jensen, "The 'Legend' and the 'Case' of Joe Hill," *Dialogue: A Journal of Mormon Thought*, 2 (Spring 1967): 97-109 (this is a review of Philip S. Foner's *The Case of Joe Hill*).

59— Jensen, "The Legend of Joe Hill," p. 358.

60— Jensen, "The Legend of Joe Hill," p. 358.

61— Jensen, "The Legend of Joe Hill," pp. 358-59.

62— *SLH-R*, 14 January 1914; *DEN*, 14 January 1914.

63— Philip S. Foner, *The Case of Joe Hill* (1965), p. 21.

64— Barrie Stavis, *The Man Who Never Died*, p. 31.

65— Foner, *The Case of Joe Hill*, p. 113.

66— *SLH-R*, 23 June 1914.

67— Jensen, "The 'Legend' and the 'Case' of Joe Hill," p. 103.

68— *SLH-R*, 14 January 1914.

69— *SLH-R*, 15 January 1914.

70— *SLH-R*, 15 January 1914.

71— *SLH-R*, 14 January, 1914.

72— *DEN*, 14 January 1914; *SLT*, 14 January 1914.

73— *SLT*, 14 January 1914.

74— *DEN*, 14 January 1914.

75— *SLH-R*, 14 January 1914.

76— *SLT*, 15 January 1914.

77— *SLT*, 14 January 1914.

78— *SLH-R*, 15 January 1914.

79— *DEN*, 15 January 1914.

80— *DEN*, 19 January 1914.

81— *SLT*, 15 January 1914.

82— *DEN*, 16 January 1914.

83— *SLH-R*, 15 January 1914.

CHAPTER 4

1— *SLH-R*, 28 January 1914.

2— *SLH-R*, 28 January 1914.

3— *SLH-R*, 28 January 1914.

4— *Solidarity*, 16 October 1915, pp. 1-4; also in Philip S. Foner, ed., *The Letters of Joe Hill*, pp. 64-74.

5— Utah v. Hillstrom, 46 Utah 341, 150 P. 935, 938 (1915) [Supreme Court].

6— Information no. 3532, supplied to Utah Board of Pardons by the Utah Third Judicial District Court concerning the State of Utah v. Hillstrom, MS in ASSU.

7— *SLH-R*, 29 January 1914.

8— *SLH-R*, 29 January 1914.

9— *SLH-R*, 29 January 1914.

10— *SLH-R*, 29 January 1914.

11— *SLH-R*, 29 January 1914.

12— *SLH-R*, 29 January 1914.

13— *SLH-R*, 29 January 1914.

14— *SLH-R*, 29 January 1914.

15— *SLH-R*, 29 January 1914.

16— *Solidarity*, 16 October 1915, p. 1.

17— *SLT*, 18 June 1914.

18— *SLT*, 18 June 1914.

19— *SLT*, 18 June 1914.

20— *DEN*, 18 June 1914.

21— *SLT*, 19 June 1914.

22— *SLH-R*, 19 June 1914.

23— *SLH-R*, 19 June 1914; *DEN*, 18 June 1914.

24— *SLH-R*, 19 June 1914.

25— *SLH-R*, 20 June 1914.

26— Utah v. Hillstrom [Supreme Court], p. 943.

27— Utah v. Hillstrom [Supreme Court], p. 943.

28— Utah v. Hillstrom [Supreme Court], p. 943.

29— Utah v. Hillstrom [Supreme Court], p. 944.

30— Utah v. Hillstrom [Supreme Court], p. 944.

31— *Telegram*, 24 August 1915.

32— Utah v. Hillstrom [Supreme Court], pp. 939, 948.

33— *SLH-R*, 20 June 1914.

34— *SLH-R*, 20 June 1914.

35— *SLT*, 20 June 1914.

36— *SLH-R*, 20 June 1914.

37— Interview of William Chance by the author, 23 April 1967, Banning, California.

38— *Solidarity*, 18 April 1914.

39— *Solidarity*, 23 May 1914.

40— *SLH-R*, 21 June 1914.

41— *SLT*, 21 June 1914.

42— *Denver Post*, 16 December 1932.

43— *SLH-R*, 20 June 1914.

44— *SLT*, 21 June 1914.

45— *SLT*, 21 June 1914.

46— District Court Information no. 3532, p. 9.

47— *SLT*, 21 June 1914.

48— *SLT*, 21 June 1914.

49— District Court Information no. 3532, pp. 4-5.

50— *SLT*, 21 June 1914.

51— *SLH-R*, 23 June 1914.

52— *SLH-R*, 23 June 1914.

53— *DEN*, 22 June 1914.

54— *SLH-R*, 22 June 1914.

55— *SLH-R*, 23 June 1914.

56— *SLH-R*, 23 June 1914.

57— *SLH-R*, 21 June 1914.

58— *SLH-R*, 22 June 1914.

59— State of Utah v. Hillstrom, Case no. 3532 in the Utah Third District Court, vol. 2, Transcript of the evidence introduced on behalf of the defendant, pp. 449-50.

60— Utah v. Hillstrom, pp. 452-53.

61— Utah v. Hillstrom, p. 454.

62— Utah v. Hillstrom, pp. 466-68.

63— Utah v. Hillstrom, p. 481.

64— Utah v. Hillstrom, p. 483.

65— Utah v. Hillstrom, p. 486.

66— Utah v. Hillstrom, p. 487.

67— Utah v. Hillstrom, p. 487.

68— Utah v. Hillstrom, p. 491.

69— Utah v. Hillstrom, pp. 502-508.

70— Utah v. Hillstrom, pp. 567-69.

71— Utah v. Hillstrom, pp. 592-95.

72— Utah v. Hillstrom, p. 596.

73— Utah v. Hillstrom, p. 518.

74— Utah v. Hillstrom, p. 534.

75— Utah v. Hillstrom, p. 534.

76— Utah v. Hillstrom, pp. 540-41.

77— Utah v. Hillstrom, p. 541.

78— Utah v. Hillstrom, p. 551.

79— Utah v. Hillstrom, p. 554.

80— Utah v. Hillstrom, p. 554.

81— Utah v. Hillstrom, pp. 555-56.

82— Utah v. Hillstrom, pp. 600-603.

83— *SLH-R*, 25 June 1914.

84— *SLH-R*, 25 June 1914.

85— *Telegram*, 24 August 1915.

86— *SLH-R*, 25 June 1914.

87— *SLH-R*, 25 June 1914.

88— *SLH-R*, 25 June 1914.

89— *SLT*, 25 June 1914.

90— *SLH-R*, 26 June 1914.

91— *SLH-R*, 26 June 1914.

92— *SLH-R*, 26 June 1914.

93— *SLH-R*, 26 June 1914.

94— *SLH-R*, 27 June 1914.

95— *SLH-R*, 27 June 1914.

96— *SLH-R*, 27 June 1914.

97— *SLH-R*, 27 June 1914.

98— *SLH-R*, 27 June 1914.

99— *SLH-R*, 27 June 1914.

100— *SLH-R*, 27 June 1914.

101— *SLT*, 27 June 1914.

102— *SLH-R*, 27 June 1914.

103— *SLH-R*, 27 June 1914.

104— Utah v. Hillstrom, p. 616.

105— Utah v. Hillstrom, pp. 616-23.

106— Utah v. Hillstrom, p. 626.

107— Utah v. Hillstrom, p. 619.

108— *SLT*, 28 June 1914.

109— *SLH-R*, 28 June 1914.

110— *DEN*, 27 June 1914.

111— *DEN*, 27 June 1914.

112— Henry Campbell Black, *Black's Law Dictionary*, 4th ed. (1951), p. 107.

113— State v. City of Albuquerque, 31 N.M. 576, 249 P. 242 (1926); Burns v. State, 26 Wyo. 491, 173 P. 785 (1918).

114— Korf v. Jasper County, 132 Iowa 682, 108 N.S. 1031 (1907).

115— *Compiled Laws of Utah*, 1907, p. 1361.

116— *Compiled Laws of Utah*, 1907, p. 1422.

117— People v. Scott, 10 Utah 217, 37 P. 335 (1894).

118— State v. Hayes, 14 Utah 118, 46 P. 752 (1896).

119— State v. McKee, 17 Utah 370, 53 P. 733 (1898).

120— Griffin v. California, 380 U.S. 609 (1915).

121— People v. Tyler, 36 Cal. 522 (1869); State v. Balch, 31 Kan. 465, 2 P. 609 (1884); State v. Smokalem, 37 Wash. 91, 79 P. 603 (1905); Brown v. State, 30 Okl. Cr. 442, 106 P. 808 (1910), etc.

122— *SLT*, 9 July 1914.

123— *SLH-R*, 2 September 1914.

124— *SLH-R*, 2 September 1914.

125— *SLH-R*, 2 September 1914.

CHAPTER 5

1— Brief for Appellant, Utah v. Hillstrom, 46 Utah 341, 150 P. 935, 942 (1915) [Supreme Court]. Copy in Utah State Historical Society Archives (hereafter referred to as USHSA).

2— Brief for Appellant, Utah v. Hillstrom, pp. 3-8.

3— Brief for Appellant, Utah v. Hillstrom, pp. 7-10.

4— Brief for Appellant, Utah v. Hillstrom, p. 11.

5— Brief for Appellant, Utah v. Hillstrom, p. 16.

6— Brief for Appellant, Utah v. Hillstrom, p. 16.

7— Brief for Appellant, Utah v. Hillstrom, p. 15.

8— Brief for Appellant, Utah v. Hillstrom, p. 18.

9— Brief for Appellant, Utah v. Hillstrom, p. 21.

10— Brief for Appellant, Utah v. Hillstrom, p. 24.

11— Brief for Appellant, Utah v. Hillstrom, p. 25.

12— Brief for Appellant, Utah v. Hillstrom, p. 28.

13— Brief for Appellant, Utah v. Hillstrom, p. 38.

14— Brief for Appellant, Utah v. Hillstrom, p. 44.

15— Brief for Appellant, Utah v. Hillstrom, p. 49.

16— Brief for Appellant, Utah v. Hillstrom, p. 53.

17— Brief for Appellant, Utah v. Hillstrom, p. 54.

18— Brief for Appellant, Utah v. Hillstrom, p. 33.

19— Brief for Respondent, Utah v. Hillstrom, 46 Utah 341, 150 P. 935, 942 (1915) [Supreme Court]. Copy in USHSA.

20— Brief for Respondent, Utah v. Hillstrom, p. 24.

21— Brief for Respondent, Utah v. Hillstrom, p. 12.

22— Brief for Respondent, Utah v. Hillstrom, p. 13.

23— Brief for Respondent, Utah v. Hillstrom, p. 24.

24— Brief for Respondent, Utah v. Hillstrom, pp. 26-27.

25— Brief for Respondent, Utah v. Hill-strom, pp. 10-11.

26— Hill to Sam Murray, 6 June 1915, in "The Last Letters of Joe Hill," *Industrial Pioneer*, December 1923, p. 54; also in Philip S. Foner, ed., *The Letters of Joe Hill*, p. 34.

27— Hill to Murray, 12 August 1915, in "The Last Letters of Joe Hill," p. 54; also in Foner, *Letters of Joe Hill*, p. 47.

28— Utah v. Hillstrom [Supreme Court], pp. 935, 942.

29— Utah v. Hillstrom [Supreme Court], pp. 942-43.

30— Utah v. Hillstrom [Supreme Court], p. 943.

31— Utah v. Hillstrom [Supreme Court], p. 941.

32— Utah v. Hillstrom [Supreme Court], p. 941.

33— Utah v. Hillstrom [Supreme Court], p. 941.

34— Utah v. Hillstrom [Supreme Court], p. 942.

35— Utah v. Hillstrom [Supreme Court], p. 942.

36— Utah v. Hillstrom [Supreme Court], p. 943.

37— Utah v. Hillstrom [Supreme Court], pp. 944-45.

38— Utah v. Hillstrom [Supreme Court], p. 946.

39— Utah v. Hillstrom [Supreme Court], pp. 946-47.

40— Utah v. Hillstrom [Supreme Court], p. 947.

41— Utah v. Hillstrom [Supreme Court], p. 947.

42— Utah v. Hillstrom [Supreme Court], pp. 948-49.

43— Hill to Elizabeth Gurley Flynn, 7 July 1915, in Foner, *Letters of Joe Hill*, p. 35.

CHAPTER 6

1— Max Eastman, "The Great American Scapegoat," *New Review*, 2, no. 8 (August 1914): 466.

2— Helen Zeese Papanikolas, "Life and Labor among the Immigrants of Bingham Canyon," *Utah Historical Quarterly*, 33, no. 4 (Fall 1965): 292-96.

3— Papanikolas, "Immigrants of Bingham Canyon," pp. 296-301.

4— Papanikolas, "Immigrants of Bingham Canyon," pp. 301-303.

5— Papanikolas, "Immigrants of Bingham Canyon," pp. 304-306.

6— Papanikolas, "Immigrants of Bingham Canyon," p. 294.

7— A. S. Embree, "Bingham Strike," *Solidarity*, 9 November 1912, p. 3.

8— Alfred Hayes and Earl Robinson, "I Dreamed I Saw Joe Hill Last Night," *Fireside Book of Folk Songs*, Margaret Bradford Boni and Norman Lloyd, eds. (1947), pp. 48-49.

9— Lee Pratt, "Conditions in Utah," *Solidarity*, 19 August 1911, p. 1.

10— *Solidarity*, 5 July 1913, p. 1.

11— *SLT*, 13 June 1913.

12— *SLT*, 13 June 1913.

13— *DEN*, 10 June 1913.

14— *DEN*, 11 June 1913.

15— *SLT*, 14 June 1913.

16— *SLT*, 14 June 1913.

17— *Industrial Worker*, 19 June 1913, p. 1.

18— *Industrial Worker*, 3 July 1913, p. 1.

19— *Solidarity*, 5 July 1913, p. 1.

20— *Solidarity*, 5 July 1913, p. 1.

21— *SLT*, 13 August 1913.

22— *SLT*, 13 August 1913.

23— *SLH-R*, 21 September 1913.

24— *SLT*, 13 August 1913.

25— *SLT*, 14 August 1913.

26— *DEN*, 13 August 1913.

27— *SLT*, 14 August 1913.

28— *Solidarity*, 30 August 1913, p. 1.

29— *Solidarity*, 3 January 1914, p. 1.

30— *SLH-R*, 23 January 1914.

31— *Telegram*, 15 August 1915.

32— *Solidarity*, 23 May 1914, p. 1.

33— *Solidarity*, 18 April 1914, p. 2.

34— Ralph Chaplin, *Wobbly: The Rough-and-Tumble Story of an American Radical*, pp. 160-61.

35— *Solidarity*, 23 May 1914, p. 1.

36— *Solidarity*, 11 July 1914, p. 1.

37— William D. Haywood, "On Friday Morning September 4, 1914, Joe Hill Is To Be Judicially Murdered," *Solidarity*, 25 July 1914, p. 1.

38— Ralph Chaplin, "Joe Hill," *Solidarity*, 12 September 1914, p. 3.

39— *Solidarity*, 26 September 1914, pp. 1-4.

40— *SLT*, 30 August 1914.

41— *Solidarity*, 23 November 1914, p. 1.

42— *Solidarity*, 9 January 1915, p. 1.

43— *Solidarity*, 23 November 1914, p. 1.

44— *Solidarity*, 27 February 1915, p. 1.

45— *Solidarity*, 22 May 1915, pp. 1-4.

46— *Solidarity*, 17 July 1915, p. 1.

47— *Appeal to Reason*, 11 September 1915, p. 4.

48— *Solidarity*, 6 June 1915, p. 4.

49— *Solidarity*, 14 August 1915, p. 1.

50— *SLH-R*, 6 November 1915.

51— *SLH-R*, 2 November 1915.

52— *SLH-R*, 9 November 1915.

53— *SLH-R*, 20 November 1915.

54— *DEN*, 16 February 1916.

55— *SLH-R*, 8 November 1915.

56— *DEN*, 19 June 1914.

57— Theodora Pollok to W. A. F. Ekengren, 2 October 1915, ARMFA.

58— Vernon H. Jensen, "The Legend of Joe Hill," *Industrial and Labor Relations Review*, 4 (April 1951): 365.

59— *Industrial Worker*, 13 November 1948, pp. 1-4.

60— Ralph Chaplin to Wallace Stegner, 10 April 1946, HIWRP.

61— Mrs. A. C. Pollok, Theodora Pollok, and Charlotte Anita Whitney to Frank P. Walsh, 11 August 1915, Frank P. Walsh Papers, Manuscript Division, New York Public Library, New York City.

62— Hill to E. W. Vanderleith, 4 September 1914, Frank P. Walsh Papers, New York Public Library.

63— Hill to Elizabeth Gurley Flynn, 18 January 1915, in Foner, *Letters of Joe Hill*, p. 21.

64— Hill to Elizabeth Gurley Flynn, 6 August 1915, in Foner, *Letters of Joe Hill*, p. 45.

65— Hill to E. W. Vanderleith, n.d., Frank P. Walsh Papers, New York Public Library.

CHAPTER 7

1— Hill to Elizabeth Gurley Flynn, 18 August 1915, in Philip S. Foner, ed., *The Letters of Joe Hill*, p. 53.

2— Sample petition to be sent to the Utah Board of Pardons, *Solidarity*, 21 August 1915, p. 2.

3— *Solidarity*, 21 August 1915, p. 4.

4— *SLT*, 15 September 1915.

5— Frank Caurll, Clara K. Schade, and John F. C. Holler to William Spry and the Utah Board of Pardons, n.d., ASSU.

6— Emil S. Lund to William Spry and the Utah Board of Pardons, 14 September 1915, ASSU.

7— Letters in Joe Hill File, USHSA.

8— Letters in Joe Hill File, USHSA.

9— Otto J. Guosa to Utah Board of Pardons, 10 August 1915, ASSU.

10— Paul Jones to Utah Board of Pardons, n.d., Joe Hill File, USHSA.

11— Eugene V. Debs to Utah Board of Pardons, n.d., Joe Hill File, USHSA.

12— Utah Board of Pardons, statement of denial of Joe Hill's application for a pardon or a commutation of sentence, MS in ASSU, p. 7.

13— *SLH-R*, 21 September 1915.

14— Utah Board of Pardons, statement of denial of Joe Hill's application for pardon, p. 7.

15— Utah Board of Pardons, statement of denial of Joe Hill's application for pardon, pp. 7-8.

16— Utah Board of Pardons, statement of denial of Joe Hill's application for pardon, p. 8.

17— Utah Board of Pardons, statement of denial of Joe Hill's application for pardon, p. 8.

18— Utah Board of Pardons, statement of

denial of Joe Hill's application for pardon, p. 9.

19— Utah Board of Pardons, statement of denial of Joe Hill's application for pardon, p. 9.

20— Utah Board of Pardons, statement of denial of Joe Hill's application for pardon, p. 10.

21— Utah Board of Pardons, statement of denial of Joe Hill's application for pardon, p. 1.

22— *Solidarity*, 25 September 1915, p. 1.

23— Utah Board of Pardons, statement of denial of Joe Hill's application for pardon, p. 9.

24— *SLH-R*, 24 September 1915.

25— Utah Board of Pardons, statement of denial of Joe Hill's application for pardon, p. 9.

26— Utah Board of Pardons, statement of denial of Joe Hill's application for pardon, p. 12.

27— Utah Board of Pardons, statement of denial of Joe Hill's application for pardon, p. 12.

28— Utah Board of Pardons, statement of denial of Joe Hill's application for pardon, p. 12.

29— Utah Board of Pardons, statement of denial of Joe Hill's application for pardon, p. 12.

30— Utah Board of Pardons, statement of denial of Joe Hill's application for pardon, p. 13.

31— Utah Board of Pardons, statement of denial of Joe Hill's application for pardon, pp. 14-15.

32— Utah Board of Pardons, statement of denial of Joe Hill's application for pardon, p. 14.

33— *SLH-R*, 21 September 1915.

34— *Telegram*, 21 September 1915.

35— *SLH-R*, 21 September 1915.

36— *SLT*, 20 September 1915.

37— *SLH-R*, 22 September 1915.

38— *International Socialist Review*, 16 (October 1915): 22.

39— *Solidarity*, 25 September 1915, p. 1.

40— *Solidarity*, 25 September 1915, p. 4.

41— Emma B. Little, editorial in *Solidarity*, 25 September 1915, p. 2.

42— Telegram, William D. Haywood to W. A. F. Ekengren, 20 September 1915, ARMFA.

43— Telegram, Ekengren to Oscar W. Carlson, 22 September 1915, ARMFA.

44— Telegram, Carlson to Ekengren, 24 September 1915, ARMFA.

45— Telegram, Tom Mooney to Ekengren, n.d., ARMFA.

46— *SLH-R*, 28 September 1915.

47— Jane Addams to Ekengren, 29 September 1915, ARMFA.

48— Letters collected in ARMFA.

49— Telegram, Ragnar Johanson and others to Ekengren, 26 September 1915, ARMFA.

50— Swedish workers at Model Steam Laundry, Thief River Falls, Minnesota, to Ekengren, 24 September 1915, ARMFA.

51— Telegram, F. B. Scott to Ekengren, 24 September 1915, ARMFA.

52— *SLH-R*, 26 September 1915.

53— *SLH-R*, 21 September 1915.

54— *SLH-R*, 29 September 1915.

55— *SLH-R*, 24 September 1915.

56— *SLH-R*, 22 September 1915.

57— *Los Angeles Times*, 19 November 1915.

58— *SLH-R*, 29 September 1915.

59— *SLH-R*, 29 September 1915.

60— *SLH-R*, 28 September 1915.

61— Curt Gentry, *Frame Up*, p. 74.

62— *Solidarity*, 25 December 1915, p. 3.

63— *DEN*, 6 December 1915.

64— *SLH-R*, 2 October 1915.

65— *SLH-R*, 26 September 1915.

66— *SLH-R*, 26 September 1915.

67— Telegram, Ekengren to Frank L. Polk; Telegram, Polk to William Spry, 25 September 1915, State Department File, NA.

68— *SLH-R*, 26 September 1915.

69— Telegram, Spry to Polk, 26 September 1915, State Department File, NA.

70— Spry to Ekengren, 27 September 1915, ARMFA.

71— *SLH-R*, 26 September 1915.

72— Telegram, Ekengren to Polk, 28 September 1915, ARMFA.

73— Telegram, Ekengren to Spry, 28 September 1915, ARMFA.

74— *SLH-R*, 29 September 1915.

75— *SLH-R*, 29 September 1915.

76— *SLH-R*, 29 September 1915.

77— Joe Hill, "A Few Reasons Why I Demand a New Trial," *Solidarity*, 16 October 1915, p. 4; also in Foner, *Letters of Joe Hill*, pp. 64-74, and Appendix B of this book.

78— *SLH-R*, 30 September 1915.

79— *SLH-R*, 30 September 1915.

80— *SLH-R*, 30 September 1915.

81— Telegram, Spry to Ekengren, 29 September 1915, ARMFA.

82— Telegram, Spry to Ekengren, 29 September 1915, ARMFA.

83— Elizabeth Gurley Flynn, *I Speak My Own Piece* (1955), p. 181.

84— Telegram, O. N. Hilton to Joseph Tumulty, 29 September 1915, State Department File, NA.

85— Telegram, Frank B. Scott to Tumulty, 29 September 1915, State Department File, NA; also in *SLH-R*, 30 September 1915.

86— Telegram, Mrs. J. Sargent Cram to Ekengren, 29 September 1915, ARMFA.

87— Telegram, Ekengren to Woodrow Wilson, 29 September 1915, ARMFA.

88— Telegram, Ekengren to Hill, 30 September 1915, ARMFA.

89— Telegram, Ekengren to Spry, 30 September 1915, ARMFA.

90— *SLT*, 30 September 1915.

91— Hill to Sam Murray, 30 September 1915, "The Last Letters of Joe Hill," *Industrial Pioneer*, December 1923, p. 56; also in Foner, *Letters of Joe Hill*, p. 57.

92— Hill to Oscar W. Larson, 30 September 1915, in *Revolt*, December 1915; also in Foner, *Letters of Joe Hill*, p. 59.

93— Hill to Ben Williams, in *Solidarity*, 9 October 1915, p. 2; also in Foner, *Letters of Joe Hill*, p. 60.

94— Hill to Elizabeth Gurley Flynn, 30 September 1915, in Foner, *Letters of Joe Hill*, p. 62.

95— Telegram, Woodrow Wilson to William Spry, 30 September 1915, Woodrow Wilson Papers, Library of Congress.

96— *SLH-R*, 1 October 1915.

97— *SLH-R*, 1 October 1915.

98— *SLH-R*, 1 October 1915.

99— William Spry, "Order of Respite," *SLH-R*, 1 October 1915.

100— Joe Hill, "The People," in Joyce L. Kornbluh, ed., *Rebel Voices: An I.W.W. Anthology*, p. 136.

101— Telegram, Wilson to Spry, 1 October 1915, Woodrow Wilson Papers, Library of Congress.

102— Telegram, Frank L. Polk to Ekengren, 1 October 1915, ARMFA.

103— Telegram, Hill to Ekengren, 1 October 1915, ARMFA; also in Foner, *Letters of Joe Hill*, p. 63.

104— *SLH-R*, 30 September 1915.

105— *SLH-R*, 1 October 1915.

106— *DEN*, 1 October 1915.

107— *SLT*, 1 October 1915.

108— *SLH-R*, 1 October 1915.

109— Charles Ashleigh, "Reflections on Joe Hill's Reprieve," *Solidarity*, 9 October 1915, p. 2.

110— *Solidarity*, 9 October 1915, p. 2.

CHAPTER 8

1— Telegram, Ekengren to *Salt Lake Tribune*, 2 October 1915, ARMFA.

2— Telegram, Ekengren to Isaac B. Reinhardt, 8 October 1915, ARMFA.

3— Telegram, Ekengren to Henry G. Gray, 8 October 1915, ARMFA.

4— Telegram, Henry G. Gray to Ekengren, 9 October 1915, ARMFA.

5— Telegram, Ekengren to Mrs. J. Sargent Cram, 14 October 1915, ARMFA.

6— O. N. Hilton to Ekengren, 10 October 1915, ARMFA.

7— Reed Smoot, unpublished diaries, book 20, copy of MS currently in possession of University of Utah Press.

8— Hilton to Ekengren, 11 October 1915, ARMFA.

9— Telegram, Hill to Ekengren, 11 October 1915, ARMFA.

10— Ekengren to Jerome Sabath, 11 October 1915, ARMFA.

11— Telegram, William D. Haywood to Ekengren, 13 October 1915, ARMFA.

12— Telegram, Hilton to Ekengren, 13 October 1915, ARMFA.

13— Ekengren to Wilson, 13 October 1915, ARMFA.

14— Office Memorandum to President Wilson, 15 October 1915, Woodrow Wilson Papers, Library of Congress.

15— Telegram, Wilson to Ekengren, 15 October 1915, Woodrow Wilson Papers, Library of Congress.

16— Telegram, Ekengren to Hill, 15 October 1915, ARMFA.

17— Ekengren to Timothy Walsh, 18 October 1915, ARMFA.

18— Telegram, Ekengren to Hilton, 15 October 1915, ARMFA.

19— Telegram, Ekengren to Spry, 15 October 1915, ARMFA.

20— Ekengren to Hilton, 21 October 1915, ARMFA.

21— Ekengren to Timothy Walsh, 18 October 1915, ARMFA.

22— Hilton to Ekengren, 22 October 1915, ARMFA.

23— *SLH-R*, 17 October 1915.

24— *SLH-R*, 17 October 1915.

25— *SLH-R*, 17 October 1915.

26— Transcript, meeting of Utah Board of Pardons, 16 October 1915, MS in ASSU.

27— *SLH-R*, 17 October 1915.

28— Telegram, Jerome Sabath to Ekengren, 11 October 1915, ARMFA.

29— O. N. Hilton, "Open Letter to the Board of Pardons of Utah," 17 October 1915, in *Solidarity*, 30 October 1915, p. 4.

30— Telegram, Hilton to Ekengren, 19 October 1915, ARMFA.

31— *SLH-R*, 19 October 1915.

32— Hill to Hilton, 27 October 1915, ARMFA; also in Philip S. Foner, ed., *The Letters of Joe Hill*, p. 78. The records of the Joe Hill case were deposited in the I.W.W. headquarters as Hill requested, but were subsequently destroyed by a fire which consumed many of that organization's official records. Those records that survived the fire were confiscated and destroyed by federal officials during the Palmer raids on I.W.W. headquarters.

33— Isaac B. Reinhardt to Ekengren, 30 October 1915, ARMFA.

34— Hilton to Ekengren, 17 October 1915, ARMFA.

35— Enclosure in letter from Reinhardt to Ekengren, 30 October 1915, ARMFA.

36— Hilton to Hill, 30 October 1915, ARMFA.

37— Hilton to Ekengren, 21 October 1915, ARMFA.

38— Telegram, Hill to Ekengren, 28 October 1915, ARMFA.

39— Telegram, Hill to Ekengren, 12 November 1915, ARMFA; also in Foner, *Letters of Joe Hill*, p. 81.

40— Telegram, Waldemar VanCott to Ekengren, 25 October 1915, ARMFA.

41— E. B. Critchlow to Ekengren, 6 November 1915, ARMFA.

42— Critchlow to Ekengren, 6 November 1915, ARMFA.

43— Critchlow to Ekengren, 10 November 1915, ARMFA.

44— Critchlow to Ekengren, 12 November 1915, ARMFA.

45— Telegram, Ekengren to Critchlow (no. 1), 17 November 1915, ARMFA.

46— Telegram, Ekengren to Critchlow (no. 2), 17 November 1915, ARMFA.

47— Telegram, Critchlow to Ekengren, 17 November 1915, ARMFA.

48— *Solidarity*, 13 November 1915, p. 3.

49— *Solidarity*, 5 November 1915, p. 1.

50— *Solidarity*, 5 November 1915, p. 3.

51— *Solidarity*, 20 November 1915, p. 1.

52— *Solidarity*, 20 November 1915, p. 1.

53— *Solidarity*, 20 November 1915, p. 1.

54— *Solidarity*, 13 November 1915, p. 1.

55— Elizabeth Gurley Flynn, *I Speak My Own Piece*, pp. 181-82.

56— *SLH-R*, 17 November 1915.

57— Telegram, Samuel Gompers to Wilson,

16 November 1915, Woodrow Wilson Papers, Library of Congress.

58— Telegram, Helen Keller to Wilson, 16 November 1915, Woodrow Wilson Papers, Library of Congress.

59— Telegram, Wilson to Helen Keller, 17 November 1915, Woodrow Wilson Papers, Library of Congress.

60— Telegram, J. P. Tumulty to Samuel Gompers, 17 November 1915, Woodrow Wilson Papers, Library of Congress.

61— Telegram, Wilson to Spry, 17 November 1915, Woodrow Wilson Papers, Library of Congress.

62— Telegram, Spry to Wilson, 18 November 1915, Woodrow Wilson Papers, Library of Congress.

63— *SLH-R*, 19 November 1915.

64— *DEN*, 18 November 1915.

65— *SLT*, 19 November 1915.

66— *SLH-R*, 19 November 1915.

67— *Ogden Standard-Examiner*, 19 November 1915.

68— *Ogden Standard-Examiner*, 18 November 1915.

69— *SLH-R*, 14 November 1915.

70— *SLH-R*, 20 November 1915.

71— *SLT*, 19 November 1915.

72— *SLT*, 14 November 1915.

73— *New York Tribune*, 19 November 1915.

74— *SLH-R*, 18 November 1915.

75— *SLH-R*, 19 November 1915.

76— *SLH-R*, 19 November 1915.

77— *SLH-R*, 19 November 1915.

78— *Los Angeles Times*, 19 November 1915.

79— *SLH-R*, 19 November 1915.

80— *SLH-R*, 16 November 1915.

81— *SLH-R*, 12 November 1915.

82— *SLH-R*, 19 October 1915.

83— *SLH-R*, 19 November 1915.

84— *SLH-R*, 19 November 1915.

85— *SLH-R*, 19 November 1915.

86— *SLH-R*, 19 November 1915.

87— *SLH-R*, 19 November 1915.

88— *SLH-R*, 19 November 1915.

89— *SLH-R*, 19 November 1915.

90— Telegram, Hill to William D. Haywood, 18 November 1915, in *SLH-R*, 19 November 1915; also in Foner, *Letters of Joe Hill*, p. 84.

91— Telegram, Haywood to Hill, 18 November 1915, in Ralph Chaplin, *Wobbly: The Rough-and-Tumble Story of an American Radical*, p. 189; also in Foner, *Letters of Joe Hill*, p. 84.

92— Telegram, Hill to Haywood, 18 November 1915, in *SLH-R*, 19 November 1915.

93— Telegram, Hill to Elizabeth Gurley Flynn, 18 November 1915, in *SLH-R*, 19 November 1915; also in Foner, *Letters of Joe Hill*, p. 83.

94— Hill to James Rohn, 18 November 1915, in *SLH-R*, 19 November 1915; also in Foner, *Letters of Joe Hill*, p. 85.

95— *SLH-R*, 19 November 1915.

96— Hill to San Francisco Local of the I.W.W., 18 November 1915, in *SLH-R*, 19 November 1915; also in Foner, *Letters of Joe Hill*, p. 86.

97— Hill to Elizabeth Gurley Flynn, 18 November 1915, in Flynn, *I Speak My Own Piece*, pp. 160-61; also in Foner, *Letters of Joe Hill*, p. 82.

98— Hill to John Makins, 18 November 1915, in *SLH-R*, 19 November 1915.

99— *SLH-R*, 20 November 1915.

100— Joe Hill, "My Last Will," *Songs of the Workers*, p. 5.

101— *SLH-R*, 20 November 1915.

102— *Seattle Post Intelligencer*, 21 November 1915.

103— *Seattle Post Intelligencer*, 21 November 1915.

104— *SLH-R*, 20 November 1915.

105— *SLH-R*, 19 November 1915.

106— *SLH-R*, 20 November 1915.

107— *SLH-R*, 20 November 1915.

108— *Seattle Post Intelligencer*, 20 November 1915.

109— *SLH-R*, 20 November 1915.

110— *SLH-R*, 20 November 1915.

111— *SLH-R*, 20 November 1915.

112– *SLH-R*, 20 November 1915.

113– *SLH-R*, 20 November 1915.

114– *New York Tribune*, 20 November 1915.

115– *SLH-R*, 20 November 1915.

CHAPTER 9

1– *Park Record* (Park City, Utah), 19 November 1915; quotation from *Goldfield Tribune* (Goldfield, Nevada) reprinted in *Ogden Standard-Examiner*, 26 November 1915, among others.

2– *New York Tribune*, 19 November 1915; *Chicago Daily Tribune*, 20 November 1915; *San Francisco Chronicle*, 20 November 1915; *Los Angeles Times*, 30 November 1915.

3– *DEN*, 19 November 1915.

4– *New York Times*, 20 November 1915.

5– *Ogden Standard-Examiner*, 30 November 1915.

6– *SLH-R*, 30 November 1915.

7– *SLH-R*, 21 November 1915.

8– *Ogden Standard-Examiner*, 2 December 1915.

9– Mrs. C. W. Jenkins to the author, 5 July 1967, original in author's possession. Mrs. Jenkins and Mrs. Nellie McIntosh, acquaintances of Virginia Snow Stephen Filigno in Willow Creek, California, say that she taught school in Willow Creek for several years after moving there. She remained interested in education all her life and often, in the summer, traveled to Los Angeles to study in libraries. Mrs. Filigno reportedly had an extensive library in her isolated home in Willow Creek and died there in the early 1950's.

10– *Park Record*, 10 December 1915.

11– Hilton to Ekengren, 13 December 1915, ARMFA.

12– *In re Hilton*, 158 P. 691 (1916). Hilton was later readmitted to the Utah Bar on 14 September 1923. By then only Justice Frick remained of the court that heard Joe Hill's case and disbarred Hilton.

13– Joseph F. Merrill to Wilson, 13 October 1916, Woodrow Wilson Papers, Library of Congress.

14– *SLH-R*, 21 November 1915.

15– S. P. Wise to Ralph Chaplin, 12 February 1948, WSULHA.

16– *SLH-R*, 21 November 1915.

17– *SLH-R*, 22 November 1915.

18– *SLH-R*, 22 November 1915.

19– *SLH-R*, 22 November 1915.

20– *Sun* (Price, Utah), 26 November 1915.

21– Ralph Chaplin, "Joe Hill's Funeral in Chicago," *Solidarity*, 4 December 1915, p. 1.

22– Announcement of Joe Hill's funeral, in collection of Joe Hill material, Arbetarrörelsens Arkiv, Stockholm, Sweden.

23– Funeral program for Joe Hill's Chicago funeral, Arbetarrörelsens Arkiv.

24– *Chicago Daily Tribune*, 25 November 1915.

25– Chaplin, "Joe Hill's Funeral in Chicago," p. 1.

26– *Chicago Daily Tribune*, 26 November 1915.

27– Chaplin, "Joe Hill's Funeral in Chicago," p. 1; also in *Chicago Daily Tribune*, 26 November 1915.

28– Ralph Chaplin, *Wobbly: The Rough-and-Tumble Story of an American Radical*, p. 160.

29– *New York Tribune*, 26 November 1915.

30– Chaplin, "Joe Hill's Funeral in Chicago," p. 4.

31– Funeral oration delivered by O. N. Hilton at Joe Hill's Chicago funeral, p. 4, USHSA.

32– Hilton's funeral oration, pp. 22-23.

33– Hilton's funeral oration, p. 24.

34– Hilton's funeral oration, p. 28.

35– Hilton's funeral oration, p. 29.

36– Chaplin, "Joe Hill's Funeral in Chicago," p. 4.

37– Chaplin, *Wobbly*, p. 191.

38– Ralph Chaplin, "Joe Hill's Funeral," *International Socialist Review*, 16 (January 1916): 401.

39– Chaplin, "Joe Hill's Funeral in Chicago," p. 4.

40– Mary Gallagher, "An Interview with Mary Gallagher," typed transcript of a tape-recorded interview conducted by Willa Baum, University of California General Library Regional Cultural History Project (Berkeley, 1955), p. 19.

41— Chaplin, *Wobbly*, p. 192.

42— Funeral program for Joe Hill's Chicago funeral, Arbetarrörelsens Arkiv.

43— Chaplin, "Joe Hill's Funeral," p. 404.

44— Chaplin, "Joe Hill's Funeral," p. 404.

45— Chaplin, *Wobbly*, p. 193.

46— *New York Times*, 26 November 1915.

47— *Los Angeles Times*, 27 November 1915.

48— *Ogden Standard-Examiner*, 27 November 1915.

49— *SLH-R*, 27 November 1915.

50— W. S. Van Valkenburgh, "The Murder of Joseph Hillstrom," *Mother Earth*, 10 (December 1915): 326.

CHAPTER 10

1— Fred Thompson to the author, 21 January 1967, original in author's possession.

2— Vernon Jensen, "The Legend of Joe Hill," *Industrial and Labor Relations Review*, 4 (April 1951): 366.

3— Robert Franklin Hoxie, *Trade Unionism in the United States* (1923), p. 150.

4— Ralph Chaplin, "Joe Hill," *Songs of the Workers*, 29th ed., p. 6.

5— John E. Nordquist, "November Nineteenth," *Songs of the Workers*, 29th ed., p. 26; *Solidarity*, 27 November 1915, p. 3.

6— Ralph Chaplin, "Joe Hill: A Biography," *Industrial Pioneer*, November 1923, pp. 23-26.

7— [Joe Hill], "The Last Letters of Joe Hill," *Industrial Pioneer*, December 1923, pp. 53-56.

8— For information on "I Dreamed I Saw Joe Hill Last Night" see Richard A. Reuss, "The Ballad of 'Joe Hill' Revisited," *Western Folklore*, 26 (July 1967): 187.

9— Patrick Renshaw to the author, 28 March 1967, original in author's possession, in which Renshaw tells of his father's reaction to Robeson.

10— Alfred Hayes and Earl Robinson, "I Dreamed I Saw Joe Hill Last Night," *Fireside Book of Folk Songs*, Margaret Brad-ford Boni and Norman Lloyd, eds., pp. 48-49. Other folk song books that have included "I Dreamed I Saw Joe Hill Last Night" are the following: Edith Fowke and Joe Glazer, eds., *Songs of Work and Freedom* (1960), pp. 20-21; Irwin Silber, ed., *Lift Every Voice* (1953), p. 39; Olive Woolley Burt, *American Murder Ballads* (1958), pp. 95-96.

11— Michael Loring: Theme Records T-100; Paul Robeson: Columbia Records M 534.

12— Upton Sinclair, *Singing Jailbirds* (1924); Upton Sinclair, *The Autobiography of Upton Sinclair* (1962), p. 233.

13— Ralph Chaplin, "Joe Hill," *The Labor Defender*, 1 (November 1926): 187-90; Ralph Chaplin, "Casey Jones," *New Masses*, 4 (January 1929): 14.

14— Carl Sandburg, *The American Songbag*, p. 222.

15— Carl Sandburg, *The People, Yes* (1936), p. 42.

16— Wallace Stegner to the author, 8 October 1966, original in author's possession.

17— Archie Green, "John Neuhaus: Wobbly Folklorist," *Journal of American Folklore*, 73 (July-September 1960): 210.

18— Pete Seeger to the author, October 1966, original in author's possession. It has not been conclusively determined whether Hill originated the phrase "pie in the sky" or just popularized it.

19— Archie Green to the author, 16 October 1966, original in author's possession.

20— Kenneth Patchen, "Joe Hill Listens to the Praying," *Proletarian Literature in the United States: An Anthology*, Granville Hicks et al., eds. (1935), pp. 179-82.

21— John Dos Passos, *Nineteen Nineteen* (1937), p. 423. For an analysis of the hobo in the works of Dos Passos, Jack London, and Jack Kerouac, see Frederick Feied, *No Pie in the Sky* (1964).

22— Elizabeth Gurley Flynn, "Joe Hill: Song Bird," *Sunday Worker*, 14 November 1937.

23— Stewart Holbrook, *Holy Old Mackinaw* (1938), p. 240.

24— Archie Binns, *The Timber Beast* (1944), p. 143.

25— Stegner to the author, 8 October 1966.

26— Wallace Stegner, "I Dreamed I Saw Joe Hill Last Night," *Pacific Spectator*, 1 (Spring 1947): 184-87; Wallace Stegner, "Joe Hill: The Wobblies' Troubadour," *New Republic*, 5 January 1948, pp. 20-24.

27— Stegner, "Joe Hill: The Wobblies' Troubadour," p. 24.

28— Wallace Stegner, letter in *New Republic*, 9 February 1948, p. 39.

29— "The Wobblies March Again," *Time*, 19 April 1948, p. 26.

30— Friends of Joe Hill Committee, "Joe Hill: I.W.W. Martyr," *New Republic*, 15 November 1948, pp. 18-20.

31— Wallace Stegner, *The Preacher and the Slave* (1950), p. x (Foreword).

32— Stegner, *Preacher and the Slave*, p. 379.

33— Stegner, *Preacher and the Slave*, pp. 381, 386.

34— Barrie Stavis, *The Man Who Never Died*.

35— Sweden: Evert Anderson, "Joe Hill, I.W.W. Rebel, Is Honored in Sweden," *Industrial Worker*, 20 May 1964, p. 1; East Berlin: *Dagens Nyheter* (Sweden), 27 February 1956.

36— Stavis, *The Man Who Never Died*, p. 204.

37— Barrie Stavis, "Joe Hill: Poet/Organizer," *Folk Music*, June 1964, pp. 3-4, 38-50; August 1964, pp. 27-29, 38-50; Barrie Stavis and Frank Harmon, eds., *Songs of Joe Hill*.

38— James Stevens, *Big Jim Turner* (1948), pp. 87-88.

39— Stevens, *Big Jim Turner*, pp. 167-68.

40— James Jones, *From Here to Eternity* (1951), pp. 647-48.

41— Eugene Burdick, *The Ninth Wave* (1956), pp. 22-23.

42— James O. Morris, "The Case of Joe Hill" (thesis, Labadie Collection, University Library, University of Michigan, 1950), p. 133.

43— Vernon Jensen, "The Legend of Joe Hill," pp. 356-66.

44— Fred Thompson, *The I.W.W.: Its First Fifty Years.*

45— Correspondence between Archie Green and Gertrude Soltker (of the Old Town School of Folk Music) October 1959, copies in author's possession.

46— Green, "John Neuhaus: Wobbly Folklorist," pp. 189-217.

47— Archie Green to the author, 16 October 1966.

48— Woody Guthrie, "Joe Hill," *American Folksong*, Moses Asch, ed. (1961), p. 22; Phil Ochs, "Joe Hill," *Broadside*, no. 76 (November 1966): 5.

49— From the Canadian Broadcasting Company film *The Man Who Never Died*, loaned to the author by Ammon Hennacy.

50— Philip S. Foner, ed., *The Letters of Joe Hill*; Philip S. Foner, *The Case of Joe Hill*, p. 108.

51— Joyce L. Kornbluh, ed., *Rebel Voices: An I.W.W. Anthology*, pp. 127-57; Patrick Renshaw, *The Wobblies* (1967); Zapata Modesto [Barry Nichols], "Joe Hill, Some Notes on an American Culture Hero," *Wobbly No. 3* (a publication of the Berkeley, California, branch of the General Recruiting Union, Industrial Workers of the World), October 1963, pp. 2-11, mimeographed; Zapata Modesto, "The Death of Joe Hill," *Mainstream*, September 1962, pp. 3-16.

52— Mimeographed invitation issued by the Petersons announcing the party, copy in author's possession.

53— Brochure printed by Wayne State University announcing the program, copy in author's possession.

54— *SLT*, 15 November 1965; account reprinted in *Western Folklore*, 25, no. 2 (April 1966): 129.

55— "Joe Hill ... The Man Who Never Died," *Steel Labor* (Western Edition, Indianapolis, Indiana), 31, no. 1 (January 1966): 9.

56— *Ny Dag*, 19 August 1952; 29 April 1950.

57— *Ny Dag*, 19 November 1955.

58— *Ny Dag*, 29 April 1950.

59— *Arbetaren*, 20 August 1952.

60— *Arbetaren*, 14 January 1949.

61— *Dagens Nyheter*, 27 February 1956.

62— "Young Swede Gives New Life to Joe

Hill's Songs," *Fackföreningsrörelsen* (journal of the Swedish Trade Union Council), 1967, copy in author's possession.

63— Gösta Ahlstrand, "Joe Hill—from Gävle," *Gefle Dagblad*, 14 August 1967.

64— *Ny Dag*, 16 December 1963.

65— Kjell Persson to the author, August and December 1967.

66— Ammon Hennacy et al., eds., "If I Were Free" (mimeographed; Salt Lake City, Utah: Utah Wobbly Press, 1967).

67— Certificate of Incorporation of The Joe Hill Memorial Committee, copy in author's possession.

68— David Anderson, "Wobblies Still Strive for 'Labor Revolution,' " *Los Angeles Times*, 17 March 1967.

69— Alexander MacKay to Editor of *Industrial Worker*, 22 November 1947, WSULHA.

Appendix

A

PART I: The "Little Red Song Books"

My list of books is intended for collectors and students, as well as a "time setting" for Joe Hill's songs. Twenty-seven songs or poems are listed below in chronological order of appearance in the little red songbooks and by pages within the books. Early books are coded **A** to **O**, rather than by editions. They are dated by announcements in *The Industrial Worker* and are identified by short references to lines printed on the red cover or title page. The songbooks generally indicated the tunes to which I.W.W. songs were composed; these tunes are further identified below by additional titles, original composers, and an occasional comment on variation.

In compiling this Checklist I have drawn heavily on material left to me by the late John Neuhaus (see "John Neuhaus: Wobbly Folklorist," *Journal of American Folklore*, 73 [July 1960]). My notes are intended to supplement the following two basic references, in which detailed comments can be found:

Barrie Stavis and Frank Harmon, eds. *Songs of Joe Hill*. New York: People's Artists, 1955. Reprint. New York: Oak Publications, 1960.

Joyce L. Kornbluh, ed. *Rebel Voices: An I.W.W. Anthology*. Ann Arbor: University of Michigan Press, 1964.

A

Industrial Worker

19 August 1909, first ad for first ed.

Front Cover

Rear 412-420 Front Avenue
Spokane, Wash.

B (I have never seen this edition.)

Industrial Worker

21 May 1910, new ad probably indicates a second edition

C

Industrial Worker

20 August 1910, a third, very much improved edition

Front Cover

Box 616 Front Avenue
Spokane, Wash.

D

Industrial Worker

6 July 1911, new songbook includes "Long Haired Preachers" (note early use of popular title)

Front Cover

Published by Spokane Local, I.W.W.
Spokane, Washington

A Joe Hill song checklist compiled by Archie Green

232

Above, early "Little Red Song Book" cover (D)
and right, spread from same edition. Below,
cover of Ninth Edition (K). Actual size.

THE PREACHER AND THE SLAVE.

Tune: "Sweet Bye and Bye."

(By F. B. Brechler.)

Long-haired preachers come out every night,
Try to tell you what's wrong and what's right;
But when asked how 'bout something to eat
They will answer with voices so sweet:

Chorus.

You will eat, bye and bye,
In that glorious land above the sky;
Work and pray, live on hay,
You'll get pie in the sky when you die.

The starvation army they play,
They sing and they clap and they pray
'Till they get all your coin on the drum,
Then they'll tell you when you're on the bum:

Chorus.

Holy Rollers and jumpers come out,
They holler, they jump and they shout.
Give your money to Jesus they say,
He will cure all diseases today.

Chorus.

If you fight hard for children and wife—
Try to get something good in this life—
You're a sinner and bad man, they tell,
When you die you will sure go to hell.

Chorus.

Workingmen of all countries, unite,
Side by side we for freedom will fight;
When the world and its wealth we have gained
To the grafters we'll sing this refrain:

Chorus.

You will eat, bye and bye,
When you've learned how to cook and to fry.
Chop some wood, 'twill do you good,
And you'll eat in the sweet bye and bye.

26

MEET ME IN THE JUNGLES LOUIE.

(Written by Richard Brazier.)

Louie was out of a job,
Louie was dead on the hog;
He looked all around,
But no job could be found,
So he had to go home and sit down.
A note on the table he spied,
He read it just once, and he cried.
It read: "Louie, dear, get to hell out of here,
Your board bill is now overdue."

Chorus.

Meet me in the jungles, Louie,
Meet me over there.
Don't tell me the slaves are eating,
Anywhere else but there;
We will each one be a booster,
To catch a big, fat rooster;
So meet me in the jungles, Louie,
Meet me over there.

Louie went out of his shack,
He swore he would never come back;
He said, "I will wait, and take the first freight,
My friends in the jungles to see;
For me there is waiting out there,
Of a mulligan stew a big share.
So away I will go and be a hobo,
For the song in the jungles I hear."

Chorus.

Meet me in the jungles, Louie,
Meet me over there.
Don't tell me the slaves are eating,
Anywhere else but there;
We will each one be a booster,
To catch the scissor Bill's rooster;
So meet me in the jungles, Louie,
Meet me over there.

27

233

Page 26

THE PREACHER AND THE SLAVE

"Sweet Bye and Bye," gospel song
Lyrics, S. Fillmore Bennett;
music, J. P. Webster

This song was originally credited to
F. B. Brechler, not to Hill. It was also
assigned to Brechler in Book **E**, but was
finally credited to J. Hill in Book **F**. See
note on page 21 for hypotheses which
have been advanced in explanation.

Stavis and Harmon, p. 10;
Kornbluh, p. 132.

E

Industrial Worker

11 July 1912, new book to include
"Casey Jones"

Front Cover

Published by The Industrial Worker
PO Box 2129
Spokane, Washington

Page 1

CASEY JONES—THE UNION SCAB

(no tune given) popular song
Lyrics, Tallifero Lawrence Sibert; music,
Eddie Walter Newton; copyright 1909

This song was credited to J. Hill and
assigned first place in the book. Songs
through "The Tramp" (below), with
the exception of "Coffee An'," were
similarly credited to J. Hill when they
appeared.

Stavis and Harmon, p. 8;
Kornbluh, p. 133

Page 33

EVERYBODY'S JOINING IT

"Everybody's Doin' It," popular song
Lyrics and music, Irving Berlin;
copyright 1911; correct name: "Everybody's Doin' It Now"

Stavis and Harmon, p. 16

Page 39

WHERE THE FRAZER RIVER FLOWS

"Where the River Shannon Flows,"
popular song
Lyrics and music, James I. Russell;
copyright 1905

In later editions "Frazer" is corrected
to "Fraser."

Stavis and Harmon, p. 12;
Kornbluh, p. 134

Page 42

COFFEE AN'

"Count Your Blessings," gospel song
Lyrics, Johnson Ottman;
music, E. O. Excell

This song first appeared without any
composer credit. However, in Book **H** it
was credited to J. H. of the I.W.W. In the
seventeenth edition (ca. 1922) it was
retitled "Count Your Workers—Count
Them!"

Kornbluh, p. 134

Page 43

JOHN GOLDEN AND THE LAWRENCE STRIKE

"A Little Talk with Jesus"

This song gave John Neuhaus an opportunity to mark variation in song style. He
identified Hill's tune as a " Christian
religious song very popular in Sunday
Schools and [skid road] Rescue Missions
around 1900." The text derived from a
Negro spiritual, but the gospel tune
differed from the spiritual's tune.
Neuhaus specifically noted that the Stavis
and Harmon melody was not the tune
used by I.W.W. members. To further
distinguish the spiritual's melody
from the gospel song, he cited the
"correct" I.W.W. tune in *Sunshine
Choruses*, p. 64 (Kansas City, Mo.:
Lillenas Publishing Company).

Stavis and Harmon, p. 14;
Kornbluh, p. 180

F

Industrial Worker

6 March 1913, new edition adds
eleven new songs

Front Cover

FIFTH EDITION

Page 5

SHOULD I EVER BE A SOLDIER

"Colleen Bawn," popular song
Lyrics, Ed Madden; music,
J. Fred Helf; copyright 1906

John Neuhaus noted that this tune was
not to be confused with the folk song
"Colleen Bawn" or the aria
"Colleen Bawn" from the opera *The
Lily of Killarney* by Jules Benedict.

Stavis and Harmon, p. 18

Page 9

WHAT WE WANT

"Rainbow," popular song
Lyrics, Alfred Bryan;
music, Percy Wenrich; copyright 1908

Stavis and Harmon, p. 26;
Kornbluh, p. 138

Page 17

SCISSOR BILL

"Steamboat Bill," popular song
Lyrics, Ren Shields;
music, Leighton Brothers;
copyright 1910

Stavis and Harmon, p. 29;
Kornbluh, p. 136

Pages 18-19

MR. BLOCK

"It Looks to Me Like a Big Time
Tonight," popular song
Lyrics, Harry Williams; music, Egbert
Van Alstyne; correct name: "It Looks
Like a Big Night Tonight,"
copyright 1908

Stavis and Harmon, p. 19;
Kornbluh, p. 135

Page 23

STUNG RIGHT

"Sunlight, Sunlight," gospel song
Lyrics, J. W. DeVenter;
music, W. S. Weeden

Stavis and Harmon, p. 32;
Kornbluh, p. 140

Page 27

THERE IS POWER IN A UNION

"There Is Power in the Blood,"
gospel song
Lyrics and music, L. E. Jones

Stavis and Harmon, p. 37;
Kornbluh, p. 140

Page 32

THE WHITE SLAVE

"Meet Me Tonight in Dreamland,"
popular song
Lyrics, Beth Slater Whitson; music,
Leo Friedman; copyright 1909

Stavis and Harmon, p. 30

Page 35

WE WILL SING ONE SONG

"My Old Kentucky Home"
Lyrics and music, Stephen Collins Foster

Kornbluh, p. 137

Page 42

THE TRAMP

"Tramp, Tramp, Tramp, the Boys Are
Marching," Civil War song
Lyrics and music, George Frederick Root

Stavis and Harmon, p. 27;
Kornbluh, p. 138

G

Industrial Worker

21 August 1913, another press run
of books

Front Cover

SIXTH EDITION

H

Front Cover

Published By
The Seattle Locals, I.W.W.
Seattle, Washington

Page 1

NEARER MY JOB TO THEE

(no tune given) hymn
Lyrics, Sarah F. Adams;
music, Lowell Mason

In Book **H** all Hill's songs taken from
previous editions were credited to J. Hill,
but his "new" songs (pages 1, 18, 28-

235

29, 35) were credited to J. H. of the I.W.W. Is it possible that this book's editorial committee didn't know that both sets of songs were composed by the same person?

Kornbluh, p. 141

Page 18

DOWN IN THE OLD DARK MILL

"Down by the Old Mill Stream," popular song
Lyrics and music, Tell Taylor

Pages 28-29

THE OLD TOILER'S MESSAGE

"Silver Threads among the Gold," popular song
Lyrics, Eben E. Rexford; music, Hart Pease Danks; composed 1872

Page 35

THE GIRL QUESTION

"Tell Mother I'll Be There," gospel song
Lyrics and music, Charles M. Fillmore; copyright 1898

I _____

Title Page

Seventh Edition
Cleveland
June, 1914

J _____

Title Page

Joe Hill Edition
Eighth
December, 1914

Page 52

THE REBEL'S TOAST

This eight-line untitled poem appeared in Book J headed by a drawing of a wooden shoe. The poem appeared under the song "Liberty Forever," but I do not believe the two pieces are related. There is no evidence that Hill intended the poem to be sung.

K _____

Front Cover

Joe Hill Memorial Edition
Ninth Edition
Cleveland

Title Page

March 1916

Pages 1-2

WORKERS OF THE WORLD, AWAKEN!

(no tune given)
The music was composed by Hill but not so stated in the book. The I.W.W. published sheet music for this piece as well as for "Don't Take My Papa Away from Me" and "The Rebel Girl."

This lead song was the very first to be credited to Joe Hill rather than to J. Hill or J. H. of the I.W.W.

Stavis and Harmon, p. 42; Kornbluh, p. 143

Pages 17-18

TA-RA-RA BOOM DE-AY

(no tune given) popular song
Authorship disputed but attributed to Henry J. Sayers, 1891 composition

Stavis and Harmon, p. 22; Kornbluh, p. 143

Page 28

DON'T TAKE MY PAPA AWAY FROM ME

Book states words and music are by Joe Hill; sheet music published by I.W.W.

Stavis and Harmon, p. 44; Kornbluh, p. 139

Page 35

THE REBEL GIRL

Book states words and music are by Joe Hill; sheet music published by I.W.W.

Stavis and Harmon, p. 39; Kornbluh, p. 145

Page 56

JOE HILL'S LAST WILL

(no tune given)
It is unlikely that Hill intended this last poem to be sung. However, it

was subsequently set to music. John Neuhaus sang it to the tune "Abide with Me," a gospel song with words by Henry F. Lyte and music by William H. Monk. Other melodies for this piece can be heard on LP recordings by Joe Glazer and by Pete Seeger.

Stavis and Harmon, p. 46; Kornbluh, p. 146

Page 56 (also fourteenth edition, p. 56)

JOE HILL'S FAREWELL MESSAGE

(no tune given)
Hill's farewell message "Don't waste any time mourning—organize!" appeared in the form of an aphorism under his "Will" for several editions. However, for the fourteenth edition (April 1918) the message was set to music and, hence, turned into a "song."

L _____

Front Cover

Joe Hill Memorial Edition

Title Page

Tenth Edition
February, 1917
Chicago

M, N _____

(I have never seen editions eleven and twelve. Presumably, they were issued during the half-year between February and September of 1917.)

O _____

Front Cover

Joe Hill Memorial Edition

Title Page

Thirteenth Edition
September 1917
Chicago

From the fourteenth edition (April 1918) to the present, all books are clearly marked on the front cover or on the title page.

Page 28 (twenty-fifth edition, 1933)

IT'S A LONG WAY DOWN TO THE SOUPLINE

"Tipperary," English popular song Lyrics, Jack Judge; music, Harry Williams; correct name: "It's a Long, Long Way to Tipperary," written 1912, published 1914

Songs from "The Preacher and the Slave" to "The Rebel's Toast" appeared while Hill was still alive. Songs from "Workers of the World, Awaken!" to "Joe Hill's Farewell Message" appeared shortly after his death. Curiously, this song, composed in 1915 and printed on cards, was not "revived" for songbook publication until the Great Depression. It was the last new Hill song to appear in a "Little Red Song Book."

Stavis and Harmon, p. 34; Kornbluh, p. 145

PART II: Other songs and poems

Labor songs

LET BILL DO IT

A poem first printed in *The Industrial Worker*, 10 October 1912, p. 2; there is no evidence that Hill intended it to be sung. It is reprinted as a poem by Stavis and Harmon, p. 25.

BRONCO BUSTER FLYNN

While Hill was in jail he sent this poem to Elizabeth Gurley Flynn for her son. It was set to "Yankee Doodle" and printed in Stavis and Harmon, pp. 38-40.

There are probably other labor poems by Hill which remain to be found. In addition to the published songs, Joe Hill composed songs which were preserved only in the memories of his fellow workers. John Neuhaus knew of such numbers, but felt these pieces to be of lesser importance than Hill's "official" material in the songbooks. To my knowledge, Neuhaus never transcribed such "oral" songs, nor do I know of anyone who did. At least three titles were retained by Louis Moreau from British Columbia railroad construction days, and the available verses of these songs appear in this book.

WE WON'T BUILD NO MORE RAILROADS FOR OVERALLS AND SNUFF, p. 26

238

Above, cover of Twenty-ninth Edition, issued July 1956, and right, spread from same book. Below, cover of Thirty-first Edition, issued May 1964.

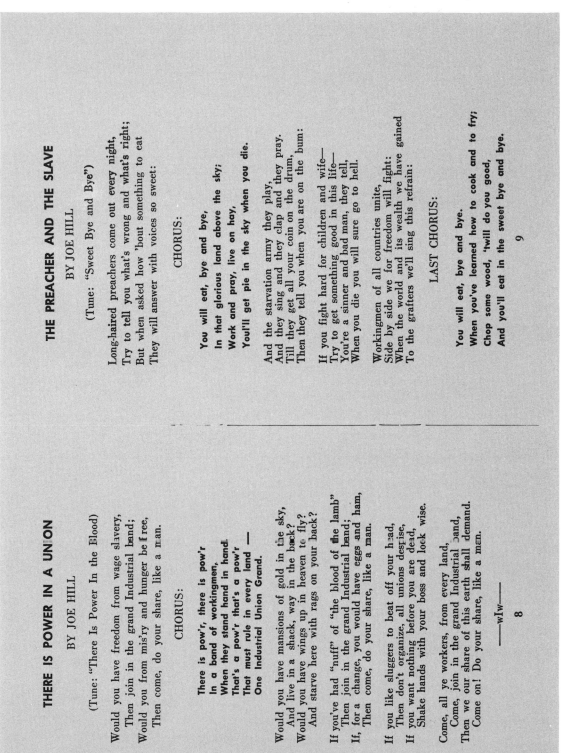

THE PREACHER AND THE SLAVE

BY JOE HILL

(Tune: "Sweet Bye and Bye")

Long-haired preachers come out every night,
Try to tell you what's wrong and what's right;
But when asked how 'bout something to eat
They will answer with voices so sweet:

CHORUS:

You will eat, bye and bye,
In that glorious land above the sky;
Work and pray, live on hay,
You'll get pie in the sky when you die.

And the starvation army they play,
And they sing and they clap and they pray.
Till they get all your coin on the drum,
Then they tell you when you are on the bum:

If you fight hard for children and wife—
Try to get something good in this life—
You're a sinner and bad man, they tell,
When you die you will sure go to hell.

Workingmen of all countries unite,
Side by side we for freedom will fight:
When the world and its wealth we have gained
To the grafters we'll sing this refrain:

LAST CHORUS:

You will eat, bye and bye.
When you've learned how to cook and to fry;
Chop some wood, 'twill do you good,
And you'll eat in the sweet bye and bye.

9

THERE IS POWER IN A UNION

BY JOE HILL

(Tune: "There Is Power In the Blood)

Would you have freedom from wage slavery,
Then join in the grand Industrial band;
Would you from mis'ry and hunger be free,
Then come, do your share, like a man.

CHORUS:

There is pow'r, there is pow'r
In a band of workingmen,
When they stand hand in hand
That's a pow'r that's a pow'r
That must rule in every land —
One Industrial Union Grand.

Would you have mansions of gold in the sky,
And live in a shack, way in the back?
Would you have wings up in heaven to fly?
And starve here with rags on your back?

If you've had "nuff" of "the blood of the lamb"
Then join in the grand Industrial band;
If, for a change, you would have eggs and ham,
Then come, do your share, like a man.

If you like sluggers to beat off your head,
Then don't organize, all unions despise,
If you want nothing before you are dead,
Shake hands with your boss and look wise.

Come, all ye workers, from every land,
Come, join in the grand Industrial band,
Then we our share of this earth shall demand.
Come on! Do your share, like a man.

——wIw——

8

APPENDIX A

240

PART III: Joe Hill's labor songs

Following are the complete texts of Joe Hill's labor songs as they
have appeared in the many editions of the "Little Red Song Book."

THE PREACHER AND THE SLAVE
Words, Joe Hill
Music, "Sweet Bye and Bye"

Long-haired preachers come out every night,
Try to tell you what's wrong and what's right;
But when asked how 'bout something to eat
They will answer with voices so sweet:

> Chorus
> You will eat, bye and bye,
> In that glorious land above the sky;
> Work and pray, live on hay,
> You'll get pie in the sky when you die.

The starvation army they play,
They sing and they clap and they pray
'Till they get all your coin on the drum,
Then they'll tell you when you're on the bum:

> Repeat chorus

Holy Rollers and jumpers come out,
They holler, they jump and they shout.
Give your money to Jesus they say,
He will cure all diseases today.

> Repeat chorus

If you fight hard for children and wife—
Try to get something good in this life—
You're a sinner and bad man, they tell,
When you die you will sure go to hell.

> Repeat chorus

Workingmen of all countries, unite,
Side by side we for freedom will fight;
When the world and its wealth we have gained
To the grafters we'll sing this refrain:

APPENDIX A

Chorus
You will eat, bye and bye,
When you've learned how to cook and to fry.
Chop some wood, 'twill do you good,
And you'll eat in the sweet bye and bye.

CASEY JONES–THE UNION SCAB
Words, Joe Hill
Music, "Casey Jones"

The Workers on the S. P. line to strike sent out a call;
But Casey Jones, the engineer, he wouldn't strike at all;
His boiler it was leaking, and its drivers on the bum,
And his engine and its bearings, they were all out of plumb.

    Chorus
    Casey Jones kept his junk pile running;
    Casey Jones was working double time;
    Casey Jones got a wooden medal,
    For being good and faithful on the S. P. line.

The Workers said to Casey: "Won't you help us win this strike?"
But Casey said: "Let me alone, you'd better take a hike."
Then some one put a bunch of railroad ties across the track,
And Casey hit the river bottom with an awful crack.

    Chorus
    Casey Jones hit the river bottom;
    Casey Jones broke his blessed spine;
    Casey Jones was an Angelino,
    He took a trip to heaven on the S. P. line.

When Casey Jones got up to heaven, to the Pearly Gate,
He said: "I'm Casey Jones, the guy that pulled the S. P. freight."
"You're just the man," said Peter; "our musicians went on strike;
You can get a job a'scabbing any time you like."

    Chorus
    Casey Jones got up to heaven;
    Casey Jones was doing mighty fine;
    Casey Jones went scabbing on the angels,
    Just like he did to workers of the S. P. line.

The angels got together, and they said it wasn't fair,
For Casey Jones to go around a'scabbing everywhere.
The Angels' Union No. 23, they sure were there,
And they promptly fired Casey down the Golden Stairs.

    Chorus
    Casey Jones went to Hell a'flying.
    "Casey Jones," the Devil said, "Oh fine:
    Casey Jones get busy shovelling sulphur;
    That's what you get for scabbing on the S. P. line."

EVERYBODY'S JOINING IT

Words, Joe Hill
Music, "Everybody's Doin' It Now"

Fellow workers, can't you hear,
There is something in the air.
Everywhere you walk everybody talks
'Bout the I.W.W.
They have got a way to strike
That the master doesn't like—
Everybody sticks, That's the only trick,
All are joining now.

Chorus

Everybody's joining it, joining what? joining it!
Everybody's joining it, joining what? joining it!
One Big Union, that's the workers' choice,
One Big Union, that's the only noise,
One Big Union, shout with all your voice;
Make a noise, make a noise, make a noise, boys,
Everybody's joining it, joining what? joining it!
Everybody's joining it, joining what? joining it!
Joining in this union grand,
Boys and girls in every land;
All the workers hand in hand—
Everybody's joining it now.

Th' Boss is feeling mighty blue,
He don't know just what to do.
We have got his goat, got him by the throat,
Soon he'll work or go starving.
Join I.W.W.,
Don't let bosses trouble you,
Come and join with us—everybody does—
You've got nothing to lose.

Repeat chorus

Will the One Big Union grow?
Mister Bonehead wants to know.
Well! what do you think, of that funny gink,
Asking such foolish questions?
Will it grow? Well! Look a here,
Brand new locals everywhere,
Better take a hunch, join the fighting bunch,
Fight for Freedom and Right.

Repeat chorus

WHERE THE FRASER RIVER FLOWS

Words, Joe Hill
Music, "Where the River Shannon Flows"

Fellow workers pay attention to what I'm going to mention,
For it is the fixed intention of the Workers of the World.
And I hope you'll all be ready, true-hearted, brave and steady,
To gather 'round our standard when the Red Flag is unfurled.

APPENDIX A

Chorus
Where the Fraser river flows, each fellow worker knows,
They have bullied and oppressed us, but still our Union grows.
And we're going to find a way, boys, for shorter hours and better pay, boys;
And we're going to win the day, boys; where the river Fraser flows.

For these gunny-sack contractors have all been dirty actors,
And they're not our benefactors, each fellow worker knows.
So we've got to stick together in fine or dirty weather,
And we will show no white feather, where the Fraser river flows.

Repeat chorus

Now the boss the law is stretching, bulls and pimps he's fetching,
And they are a fine collection, as Jesus only knows.
But why their mothers reared them, and why the devil spared them,
Are questions we can't answer, where the Fraser river flows.

Repeat chorus

243

"COFFEE AN' "
Words, Joe Hill
Music, "Count Your Blessings"

An employment shark the other day I went to see,
And he said come in and buy a job from me,
Just a couple of dollars, for the office fee,
The job is steady and the fare is free.

Chorus
Count your pennies, count them, count them one by one,
Then you plainly see how you are done,
Count your pennies; take them in your hand,
Sneak into a Jap's and get your coffee an'.

I shipped out and worked and slept in lousy bunks,
And the grub it stunk as bad as forty-'leven skunks,
When I slaved a week the boss he said one day,
You're too tired, you are fired, go and get your pay.

Repeat chorus

When the clerk commenced to count, Oh holy gee!
Road, school and poll tax and hospital fee.
Then I fainted, and I nearly lost my sense
When the clerk he said: "You owe me fifty cents."

Repeat chorus

When I got back to town with blisters on my feet,
There I heard a fellow speaking on the street.
And he said: "It is the workers' own mistake.
If they stick together they get all they make."

Repeat chorus

And he said: "Come in and join our union grand.
Who will be a member of this fighting band?"
"Write me out a card," says I, "By Gee!
The Industrial Workers is the dope for me."

Chorus

Count your workers, count them; count them one by one,
Join our union and we'll show you how it's done.
Stand together, workers, hand in hand,
Then you will never have to live on coffee an'.

JOHN GOLDEN AND THE LAWRENCE STRIKE
Words, Joe Hill
Music, "A Little Talk with Jesus"

In Lawrence, when the starving masses struck for more to eat
And wooden-headed Wood tried the strikers to defeat,
To Sammy Gompers wrote and asked him what he thought,
And this is just the answer that the mailman brought:

Chorus
A little talk—
A little talk with Golden
Makes it right, all right;
He'll settle any strike,
If there's coin enough in sight;
Just take him up to dine
And everything is fine—
A little talk with Golden
Makes it right, all right.

The preachers, cops and money-kings were working hand in hand,
The boys in blue, with stars and strikes were sent by Uncle Sam;
Still things were looking blue 'cause every striker knew
That weaving cloth with bayonets is hard to do.

Repeat chorus

John Golden had with Mr. Wood a private interview,
He told him how to bust up the "I double double U."
He came out in a while and wore the Golden smile.
He said: "I've got all labor leaders skinned a mile."

Repeat chorus

John Golden pulled a bogus strike with all his "pinks and stools."
He thought the rest would follow like a bunch of crazy fools.
But to his great surprise the "foreigners" were wise,
In one big solid union they were organized.

Chorus
That's one time Golden did not
Make it right all right;
In spite of all his schemes
The strikers won the fight.
When all the workers stand
United hand in hand,
The world with all its wealth
Shall be at their command.

SHOULD I EVER BE A SOLDIER

Words, Joe Hill
Music, "Colleen Bawn"

We're spending billions every year
    For guns and ammunition,
"Our Army" and "our Navy" dear,
    To keep in good condition;
While millions live in misery
    And millions died before us,
Don't sing "My Country 'tis of thee,"
    But sing this little chorus.

  Chorus
    Should I ever be a soldier,
       'Neath the Red Flag I would fight;
    Should the gun I ever shoulder,
       It's to crush the tyrant's might.
    Join the army of the toilers,
       Men and women fall in line,
    Wage slaves of the world! Arouse!
       Do your duty for the cause,
    For Land and Liberty.

And many a maiden, pure and fair,
    Her love and pride must offer
On Mammon's altar in despair,
    To fill the master's coffer.
The gold that pays the mighty fleet,
    From tender youth he squeezes,
While brawny men must walk the street
    And face the wintry breezes.

  Repeat chorus

Why do they mount their gatling gun
    A thousand miles from ocean,
Where hostile fleet could never run—
    Ain't that a funny notion?
If you don't know the reason why,
    Just strike for better wages,
And then, my friends—if you don't die—
    You'll sing this song for ages.

  Repeat chorus

WHAT WE WANT

Words, Joe Hill
Music, "Rainbow"

We want all the workers in the world to organize
Into a great big union grand
And when we all united stand
The world for workers we'll demand

If the working class could only see and realize
What mighty power labor has
Then the exploiting master class
It would soon fade away.

> Chorus
> Come all ye toilers that work for wages,
>> Come from every land,
>> Join the fighting band,
>> In one union grand,
> Then for the workers we'll make upon this earth a paradise
> When the slaves get wise and organize.

We want the sailor and the tailor and the lumberjacks,
And all the cooks and laundry girls,
We want the guy that dives for pearls,
The pretty maid that's making curls,
And the baker and staker and the chimneysweep,
We want the man that's slinging hash,
The child that works for little cash
In one union grand.

> Repeat chorus

We want the tinner and the skinner and the chamber-maid,
We want the man that spikes on soles,
We want the man that's digging holes,
We want the man that's climbing poles,
And the trucker and the mucker and the hired man,
And all the factory girls and clerks,
Yes, we want every one that works,
In one union grand.

> Repeat chorus

SCISSOR BILL

Words, Joe Hill
Music, "Steamboat Bill"

You may ramble 'round the country anywhere you will,
You'll always run across that same old Scissor Bill.
He's found upon the desert, he is on the hill,
He's found in every mining camp and lumber mill.
He looks just like a human, he can eat and walk,
But you will find he isn't, when he starts to talk.
He'll say, "This is my country," with an honest face,
While all the cops they chase him out of every place.

> Chorus
> Scissor Bill, he is a little dippy,
> Scissor Bill, he has a funny face.
> Scissor Bill, should drown in Mississippi,
> He is the missing link that Darwin tried to trace.

And Scissor Bill he couldn't live without the booze,
He sits around all day and spits tobacco juice.
He takes a deck of cards and tries to beat the Chink!
Yes, Bill would be a smart guy if he only could think.
And Scissor Bill he says: "This country must be freed
From Niggers, Japs and Dutchmen and the gol durn Swede.
He says that every cop would be a native son
If it wasn't for the Irishman, the sonna fur gun.

    Chorus
    Scissor Bill, the "foreigners" is cussin',
    Scissor Bill, he says: "I hate a Coon";
    Scissor Bill, is down on everybody,
    The Hottentots, the bushmen and the man in the moon.

Don't try to talk your union dope to Scissor Bill,
He says he never organized and never will.
He always will be satisfied until he's dead,
With coffee and a doughnut and a lousy old bed.
And Bill, he says he gets rewarded thousand fold,
When he gets up to Heaven on the streets of gold.
But I don't care who knows it, and right here I'll tell,
If Scissor Bill is goin' to Heaven, I'll go to Hell.

    Chorus
    Scissor Bill, he wouldn't join the union,
    Scissor Bill, he says, "Not me, by Heck!"
    Scissor Bill, gets his reward in Heaven,
    Oh! sure. He'll get it, but he'll get it in the neck.

MR. BLOCK
Words, Joe Hill
Music, "It Looks Like a Big Night Tonight"

Please give me your attention, I'll introduce to you
A man that is a credit to "Our Red, White and Blue";
His head is made of lumber, and solid as a rock;
He is a common worker and his name is Mr. Block.
And Block he thinks he may
Be President some day.

    Chorus
    Oh Mr. Block, you were born by mistake,
      You take the cake,
      You make me ache.
    Tie a rock on your block and then jump in the lake,
    Kindly do that for Liberty's sake.

Yes, Mr. Block is lucky; he found a job, by gee!
The sharks got seven dollars, for job and fare and fee.
They shipped him to a desert and dumped him with his truck,
But when he tried to find his job, he sure was out of luck,
He shouted, "That's too raw,
I'll fix them with the law."

    Repeat chorus

247

Block hiked back to the city, but wasn't doing well.
He said, "I'll join the union—the great A.F. of L."
He got a job next morning, got fired in the night,
He said, "I'll see Sam Gompers and he'll fix that foreman right."
Sam Gompers said, "You see,
You've got our sympathy."

    Repeat chorus

Election day he shouted, "A Socialist for Mayor!"
The "comrade" got elected, he happy was for fair,
But after the election he got an awful shock,
A great big socialistic Bull did rap him on the block.
And Comrade Block did sob,
"I helped him to his job."

    Repeat chorus

The money kings in Cuba blew up the gunboat Maine,
But Block got awful angry and blamed it all on Spain.
He went right in the battle and there he lost his leg,
And now he's peddling shoestrings and is walking on a peg.
He shouts, "Remember Maine,
Hurrah! To hell with Spain!"

    Repeat chorus

Poor Block he died one evening, I'm very glad to state,
He climbed the golden ladder up to the pearly gate.
He said, "Oh Mr. Peter, one word I'd like to tell,
I'd like to meet the Astorbilts and John D. Rockefell."
Old Pete said, "Is that so?
You'll meet them down below."

    Repeat chorus

STUNG RIGHT
Words, Joe Hill
Music, "Sunlight, Sunlight"

When I was hiking 'round the town to find a job one day,
I saw a sign that thousand men were wanted right away,
To take a trip around the world in Uncle Sammy's fleet,
I signed my name a dozen times upon a great big sheet.

    Chorus
    Stung right, stung right, S-T-U-N-G
    Stung right, strung right, E. Z. Mark, that's me;
    When my term is over, and again I'm free,
    There'll be no more trips around the world for me.

The man he said, "The U.S. fleet, that is no place for slaves,
The only thing you have to do is stand and watch the waves."
But in the morning, five o'clock, they woke me from my snooze,
To scrub the deck and polish brass and shine the captain's shoes.

    Repeat chorus

248

One day a dude in uniform to me commenced to shout,
I simply plugged him in the jaw and knocked him down and out;
They slammed me right in irons then and said, "You are a case."
On bread and water then I lived for twenty-seven days.

    Repeat chorus

One day the captain said, "Today I'll show you something nice,
All hands line up, we'll go ashore and have some exercise."
He made us run for seven miles as fast as we could run,
And with a packing on our back that weighed a half a ton.

    Repeat chorus

Some time ago when Uncle Sam he had a war with Spain,
And many of the boys in blue were in the battle slain,
Not all were killed by bullets, though; no, not by any means,
The biggest part that died were killed by Armour's Pork and Beans.

    Repeat chorus

249

THERE IS POWER IN A UNION

Words, Joe Hill
Music, "There Is Power in the Blood"

Would you have freedom from wage slavery,
    Then join in the grand Industrial band;
Would you from mis'ry and hunger be free,
    Then come! Do your share, like a man.

    Chorus
    There is pow'r, there is pow'r
    In a band of workingmen,
    When they stand hand in hand,
    That's a pow'r, that's a pow'r
    That must rule in every land—
    One Industrial Union Grand.

Would you have mansions of gold in the sky,
    And live in a shack, way in the back?
Would you have wings up in heaven to fly,
    And starve here with rags on your back?

    Repeat chorus

If you've had "nuff" of "the blood of the lamb,"
    Then join in the grand, Industrial band;
If, for a change, you would have eggs and ham.
    Then come, do your share, like a man.

    Repeat chorus

If you like sluggers to beat off your head,
    Then don't organize, all unions despise,
If you want nothing before you are dead,
    Shake hands with your boss and look wise.

    Repeat chorus

Come, all ye workers, from every land,
    Come join in the grand Industrial band,
Then we our share of this earth shall demand.
    Come on! Do your share, like a man.

    Repeat chorus

THE WHITE SLAVE

Words, Joe Hill
Music, "Meet Me Tonight in Dreamland"

One little girl, fair as a pearl,
Worked every day in a laundry;
All that she made for food she paid,
So she slept on a park bench so soundly;
An old procuress spied her there,
She came and whispered in her ear:

    Chorus

    Come with me now my girly,
    Don't sleep out in the cold;
    Your face and tresses curly
    Will bring you fame and gold,
    Automobiles to ride in, diamonds and silk to wear,
    You'll be a star bright, down in the red light,
    You'll make your fortune there.

Same little girl, no more a pearl,
Walks all alone 'long the river,
Five years have flown, her health is gone,
She would look at the water and shiver,
Whene'er she'd stop to rest and sleep,
She'd hear a voice call from the deep:

    Repeat chorus

Girls in this way, fall every day,
And have been falling for ages,
Who is to blame? you know his name,
It's the boss that pays starvation wages.
A homeless girl can always hear
Temptations calling everywhere.

    Repeat chorus

WE WILL SING ONE SONG

Words, Joe Hill
Music, "My Old Kentucky Home"

We will sing one song of the meek and humble slave,
    The horn-handed son of the soil,
He's toiling hard from the cradle to the grave,
    But his master reaps the profits from his toil.

Then we'll sing one song of the greedy master class,
    They're vagrants in broadcloth, indeed,
They live by robbing the ever-toiling mass,
    Human blood they spill to satisfy their greed.

Chorus

Organize! Oh, toilers, come organize your might;
    Then we'll sing one song of the workers' commonwealth,
    Full of beauty, full of love and health.

We will sing one song of the politician sly,
    He's talking of changing the laws;
Election day all the drinks and smokes he'll buy,
    While he's living from the sweat of your brow.
Then we'll sing one song of the girl below the line,
    She's scorned and despised everywhere,
While in their mansions the "keepers" wine and dine
    From the profit that immoral traffic bear.

Repeat chorus

We will sing one song of the preacher, fat and sleek,
    He tells you of homes in the sky.
He says, "Be generous, be lowly, and be meek,
    If you don't you'll sure get roasted when you die."
Then we'll sing one song of the poor and ragged tramp,
    He carries his home on his back;
Too old to work, he's not wanted 'round the camp,
    So he wanders without aim along the track.

Repeat chorus

We will sing one song of the children in the mills,
    They're taken from playgrounds and schools,
In tender years made to go the pace that kills,
    In the sweatshops, 'mong the looms and the spools.
Then we'll sing one song of the One Big Union Grand,
    The hope of the toiler and slave,
It's coming fast; it is sweeping sea and land,
    To the terror of the grafter and the knave.

Repeat chorus

THE TRAMP

Words, Joe Hill
Music, "Tramp, Tramp, Tramp, the Boys Are Marching"

If you all will shut your trap,
I will tell you 'bout a chap,
That was broke and up against it, too, for fair;
He was not the kind that shirk,
He was looking hard for work,
But he heard the same old story everywhere.

251

Chorus

Tramp, tramp, tramp keep on a-tramping,
Nothing doing here for you;
If I catch you 'round again,
You will wear the ball and chain,
Keep on tramping, that's the best thing you can do.

He walked up and down the street,
'Till the shoes fell off his feet,
In a house he spied a lady cooking stew,
And he said, "How do you do,
May I chop some wood for you?"
What the lady told him made him feel so blue.

252

Repeat chorus

'Cross the street a sign he read,
"Work for Jesus," so it said,
And he said, "Here is my chance, I'll surely try,"
And he kneeled upon the floor,
'Till his knees got rather sore,
But at eating-time he heard the preacher cry—

Repeat chorus

Down the street he met a cop,
And the Copper made him stop,
And he asked him, "When did you blow in to town?
Come with me up to the judge."
But the judge he said, "Oh fudge,
Bums that have no money needn't come around."

Repeat chorus

Finally came that happy day
When his life did pass away,
He was sure he'd go to heaven when he died,
When he reached the pearly gate,
Santa Peter, mean old skate,
Slammed the gate right in his face and loudly cried:

Repeat chorus

In despair he went to Hell,
With the Devil for to dwell,
For the reason he'd no other place to go.
And he said, "I'm full of sin,
So for Christ's sake, let me in!"
But the Devil said, "Oh, beat it, you're a 'bo."

Repeat chorus

NEARER MY JOB TO THEE

Words, Joe Hill
Music, "Nearer My God to Thee"

Nearer my job to thee,
Nearer with glee,
Three plunks for the office fee,
But my fare is free.
My train is running fast,
I've got a job at last,
Nearer my job to thee
Nearer to thee.

Arrived where my job should be,
Nothing in sight I see,
Nothing but sand, by gee,
Job went up a tree.
No place to eat or sleep,
Snakes in the sage brush creep.
Nero a saint would be,
Shark, compared to thee.

Nearer to town! each day
(Hiked all the way),
Nearer that agency,
Where I paid my fee,
And when that shark I see
You'll bet your boots that he
Nearer his god shall be.
Leave that to me.

DOWN IN THE OLD DARK MILL

Words, Joe Hill
Music, "Down by the Old Mill Stream"

How well I do remember
   That mill along the way,
Where she and I were working
   For fifty cents a day.
She was my little sweetheart;
   I met her in the mill—
It's a long time since I saw her,
   But I love her still.

   Chorus
   Down in the Old Black Mill,
      That's where first we met.
   Oh! that loving thrill
      I shall ne'er forget;
   And those dreamy eyes,
      Blue like summer skies.
   She was fifteen—
      My pretty queen—
   In the Old Black Mill.

We had agreed to marry
    When she'd be sweet sixteen.
But then—one day I crushed it—
    My arm in the machine.
I lost my job forever—
    I am a tramp disgraced.
My sweetheart still is slaving
    In the same old place.

    Repeat chorus

THE OLD TOILER'S MESSAGE

Words, Joe Hill
Music, "Silver Threads among the Gold"

"Darling I am growing old"—
    So the toiler told his wife—
"Father Time the days have tolled
    Of my usefulness in life.
Just tonight my master told me
    He can't use me any more.
Oh, my darling, do not scold me,
    When the wolf comes to our door."

    Chorus
    To the scrap heap we are going
        When we're overworked and old—
    When our weary heads are showing
        Silver threads among the gold.

"Darling, I am growing old—"
    He once more his wife did tell—
"All my labor pow'r I've sold,
    I have nothing more to sell.
Though I'm dying from starvation
    I shall shout with all my might
To the coming generation.
    I shall shout with all my might—

    Repeat chorus

THE GIRL QUESTION

Words, Joe Hill
Music, "Tell Mother I'll Be There"

A little girl was working in a big department store,
Her little wage for food was spent; her dress was old and tore.
She asked the foreman for a raise, so humbly and so shy,
And this is what the foreman did reply:

Chorus
Why don't you get a beau?
Some nice old man, you know!
He'll give you money if you treat him right.
If he has lots of gold,
Don't mind if he is old.
Go! Get some nice old gentleman tonight.

The little girl then went to see the owner of the store,
She told the story that he'd heard so many times before.
The owner cried: "You are discharged! Oh, my, that big disgrace,
A ragged thing like you around my place!"

Repeat chorus

The little girl she said: "I know a man that can't be wrong,
I'll go and see the preacher in the church where I belong."
She told him she was down and out and had no place to stay.
And this is what the holy man did say:

Repeat chorus

Next day while walking round she saw a sign inside a hall,
It read: THE ONE BIG UNION WILL GIVE LIBERTY TO ALL.
She said: I'll join that union, and I'll surely do my best,
And now she's gaily singing with the rest:

Chorus
Oh, Workers do unite!
To crush the tyrant's might.
The ONE BIG UNION BANNER IS UNFURLED—
Come slaves from every land,
Come join this fighting band,
It's named INDUSTRIAL WORKERS OF THE WORLD.

REBEL'S TOAST
Poem, Joe Hill

If Freedom's road seems rough and hard,
    And strewn with rocks and thorns,
Then put your wooden shoes on, pard,
    And you won't hurt your corns.
To organize and teach, no doubt,
    Is very good—that's true,
But still we can't succeed without
    The Good Old Wooden Shoe.

WORKERS OF THE WORLD, AWAKEN!

Words and music, Joe Hill

Workers of the world, awaken!
    Break your chains, demand your rights.
All the wealth you make is taken
    By exploiting parasites.
Shall you kneel in deep submission
    From your cradles to your graves?
Is the height of your ambition
    To be good and willing slaves?

    Chorus
    Arise, ye prisoners of starvation!
    Fight for your own emancipation;
    Arise, ye slaves of every nation.
        In One Union grand.
    Our little ones for bread are crying,
    And millions are from hunger dying;
    The end the means is justifying,
        'Tis the final stand.

If the workers take a notion,
    They can stop all speeding trains;
Every ship upon the ocean
    They can tie with mighty chains.
Every wheel in the creation,
    Every mine and every mill,
Fleets and armies of the nation,
    Will at their command stand still.

    Repeat chorus

Join the union, fellow workers,
    Men and women, side by side;
We will crush the greedy shirkers
    Like a sweeping, surging tide;
For united we are standing,
    But divided we will fall;
Let this be our understanding—
    "All for one and one for all."

    Repeat chorus

Workers of the world, awaken!
    Rise in all your splendid might;
Take the wealth that you are making,
    It belongs to you by right.
No one will for bread be crying,
    We'll have freedom, love and health.
When the grand red flag is flying
    In the Workers' Commonwealth.

    Repeat chorus

APPENDIX A

TA-RA-RA BOOM DE-AY
Words, Joe Hill
Music, "Ta-Ra-Ra Boom De-Ay"

I had a job once threshing wheat, worked sixteen hours
    with hands and feet.
And when the moon was shining bright, they kept me
    working all the night.
One moonlight night, I hate to tell, I "accidentally"
    slipped and fell.
My pitchfork went right in between some cog wheels of
    that thresh-machine.

    Chorus
    Ta-ra-ra-boom-de-ay!
    It made a noise that way,
    And wheels and bolts and hay,
    Went flying every way.
    That stingy rube said, "Well!
    A thousand gone to hell."
    But I did sleep that night,
    I needed it all right.

Next day that stingy rube did say, "I'll bring my eggs to
    town today;
You grease my wagon up, you mutt, and don't forget to
    screw the nut."
I greased his wagon all right, but I plumb forgot to
    screw the nut,
And when he started on that trip, the wheel slipped off
    and broke his hip.

    Chorus
    Ta-ra-ra-boom-de-ay!
    It made a noise that way,
    That rube was sure a sight,
    And mad enough to fight;
    His whiskers and his legs
    Were full of scrambled eggs:
    I told him, "That's too bad—
    I'm feeling very sad."

And then that farmer said, "You turk! I bet you are
    an I-Won't Work."
He paid me off right there, By Gum! So I went home
    and told my chum.
Next day when threshing did commence, my chum was
    Johnny on the fence;
And 'pon my word, that awkward kid, he dropped his
    pitchfork, like I did.

Chorus

Ta-ra-ra-boom-de-ay!
It made a noise that way,
And part of that machine
Hit Reuben on the bean.
He cried, "Oh me, oh my;
I nearly lost my eye."
My partner said, "You're right—
It's bedtime now, good night."

But still that rube was pretty wise, these things did open
    up his eyes.
He said, "There must be something wrong; I think I work
    my men too long."
He cut the hours and raised the pay, gave ham and eggs
    for every day,
Now gets his men from union hall, and has no "accidents"
    at all.

Chorus

Ta-ra-ra-boom-de-ay!
That rube is feeling gay;
He learned his lesson quick,
Just through a simple trick.
For fixing rotten jobs
And fixing greedy slobs,
This is the only way,
Ta-ra-ra-boom-de-ay!

DON'T TAKE MY PAPA AWAY FROM ME

Words and music, Joe Hill

A little girl with her father stayed, in a cabin
    across the sea,
Her mother dear in the cold grave lay; with her father
    she'd always be—
But then one day the great war broke out and the
    father was told to go;
The little girl pleaded—her father she needed.
    She begged, cried and pleaded so:

Chorus

Don't take my papa away from me, don't leave me there all alone.
He has cared for me so tenderly, ever since mother was gone.
Nobody ever like him can be, no one can so with me play.
Don't take my papa away from me; please don't take papa away.

Her tender pleadings were all in vain, and her father
    went to the war.
He'll never kiss her good night again, for he fell 'mid the
    cannon's roar.
Greater a soldier was never born, but his brave heart was pierced
    one day;
And as he was dying, he heard some one crying,
    A girl's voice from far away:

Repeat chorus

APPENDIX A

THE REBEL GIRL

Words and music, Joe Hill
(*Copyrighted 1916*)

There are women of many descriptions
    In this queer world, as everyone knows.
Some are living in beautiful mansions,
    And are wearing the finest of clothes.
There are blue blooded queens and princesses,
    Who have charms made of diamonds and pearl;
But the only and thoroughbred lady
    Is the Rebel Girl.

    Chorus

    That's the Rebel Girl, that's the Rebel Girl!
    To the working class she's a precious pearl.
    She brings courage, pride and joy
    To the fighting Rebel Boy.
    We've had girls before, but we need some more
    In the Industrial Workers of the World.
    For it's great to fight for freedom
    With a Rebel Girl.

Yes, her hands may be hardened from labor,
    And her dress may not be very fine;
But a heart in her bosom is beating
    That is true to her class and her kind.
And the grafters in terror are trembling
    When her spite and defiance she'll hurl;
For the only and thoroughbred lady
    Is the Rebel Girl.

    Repeat chorus

JOE HILL'S LAST WILL

(*Written in his cell, November 18, 1915,
on the eve of his execution*)

My will is easy to decide,
For there is nothing to divide.
My kin don't need to fuss and moan—
"Moss does not cling to a rolling stone."

My body? Ah, If I could choose,
I would to ashes it reduce,
And let the merry breezes blow
My dust to where some flowers grow.

Perhaps some fading flower then
Would come to life and bloom again.
This is my last and final will.
Good luck to all of you,

              Joe Hill

IT'S A LONG WAY DOWN TO THE SOUPLINE
Words, Joe Hill
Music, "It's a Long, Long Way to Tipperary"

Bill Brown was just a working man like others of his kind.
　He lost his job and tramped the streets when work was hard to find.
The landlord put him on the stem, the bankers kept his dough,
　And Bill heard everybody sing, no matter where he'd go:

　Chorus
　It's a long way down to the soupline,
　　It's a long way to go.
　It's a long way down to the soupline
　　And the soup is thin I know.
　Good bye, good old pork chops,
　　Farewell, beefsteak rare;
　It's a long, long way down to the soupline,
　　But my soup is there.

So Bill and sixteen million men responded to the call
　To force the hours of labor down and thus make jobs for all.
They picketed the industries and won the four-hour day
　And organized a General Strike so men don't have to say:

　Repeat chorus

The workers own the factories now, where jobs were once destroyed
　By big machines that filled the world with hungry unemployed.
They all own homes, they're living well, they're happy, free and strong,
　But millionaires wear overalls and sing this little song:

　Repeat chorus

Appendix

B

The original spelling and punctuation have been preserved in documents (2), (3), and (4).

1— Article based on a letter from a woman in Salt Lake City, Utah, which appeared in the Swedish newspaper *Arbetarbladet* on 18 December 1915. The author was presumably Athana Saccoss.

THE SWEDE WHO WAS EXECUTED IN AMERICA

Strange information by one of the witnesses at the court proceedings. The man came from Gävle and his name was Hägglund.

Arbetarbladet [The Workers' Daily] has described in detail the sensational court proceedings against the Swede Joseph Hillstrom. Hillstrom was accused of and sentenced for the murder of a grocer named Morrison and his son in Salt Lake City, and, according to the latest information in this case, was executed toward the end of the month of November. We have also mentioned the storm of opinion his sentence caused, especially among the organized workers in America, and the powers which worked to try to change the sentence. The executed man seems to have had a high reputation within the socialistic worker world in Salt Lake City, and, it is therefore easy to believe that he was the victim of a powerful plot within the capitalistic circles there. Such is not unusual in America. Also, it seems to have been the decided opinion of the organized workers that he was innocent.

However, a Swedish lady who lived in Salt Lake City at the time of the murder and who, because of her personal acquaintance with the murderer, testified at his trial, has given us an account of the case which indicates that the man really committed the murder.

First, this Swedish-American woman informs us that the sentenced man, whom the papers have always called Joseph Hillstrom, was really named Joel Hägglund, and that he came from Gävle. He emigrated from here about thirteen years ago together with a few other people from Gävle. During his stay in America he used several different names: first Hägglund, Hill, Nilsson, and now Hillstrom.

The woman who sent us this information is also from Gävle. She knew Hägglund very well before his emigration, she says, and when she met him by surprise in a cafe in Salt Lake City they talked quite a while about the conditions here. She hadn't been in America very long. She invited him and his companion, who was also a Swede, to her home. This was only a few days before the murder. Hägglund was an accomplished pianist and, therefore, she asked him to come on an evening when she had invited many people to her home, to play for her guests. Her party was planned for the same evening that the murder was committed. Hägglund's companion Applequist was also invited. However, they seemed to have difficulty giving a final answer. Finally they explained that they probably would come, a promise which they didn't keep.

Concerning the murder, the lady tells us that the grocer Morrison and his two sons were in the store and were just ready to close it when two men who had masked themselves by tying handkerchiefs over their faces forced their way in. With a cry, one said, "Finally I got hold of you!" raised his pistol, and shot the killing bullet at Morrison. The older of Morrison's sons ran over to a box and took from it a pistol with which he shot toward the murderer. The bullet hit the man's chest, but the man had strength enough to fire three more shots which all hit Morrison's older son. He also fell dead to the floor. The youngest son was in a storeroom nearby and from there he witnessed the happening, but he didn't dare to show himself. The shots of course aroused the attention of the neighbors, and therefore both the murderer and his companion fled.

The most telling testimony against Hägglund was given by the doctor whom he visited on the night of the murder to get some help for a wound which he had received from a bullet in the chest. The bullet had pierced the lung, but the wound was not deadly. Hägglund explained before the court the story he had also given the doctor that he had been shot during an argument concerning a love affair. He said he could not give the name of the other person in that drama as he then would involve a lady whose honor he would protect even if it cost him his life.

However, other incriminating circumstances were also brought to light. The handkerchief that the murderer had held over his face at the time of the murder was found outside the Morrison's store, and when the police went through Hägglund's possessions, they found there an exact copy of that handkerchief. Also, a woman testified that about half an hour before the murder she observed Hägglund outside the store. The young Morrison who was saved explained definitely, even though he could not be a witness, that the murderer and Hägglund were the same person. Hägglund's companion Applequist disappeared from the place when the suspicion fell on Hägglund, and he has not been found despite many searches and a reward for catching him. It was also established that the pistol which H. had been shot with was of the same caliber as the weapon which the murdered Morrison had used for self-defense. Other telling evidence was also brought forth against H. during the proceedings.

As to the motive for this terrible deed—our informer explains that H. seldom had any orderly work and that he seems to have gained his livelihood in a way that could not stand police investigation. About ten years ago Morrison was police commissioner and he is supposed to have run across Hägglund's criminal plans, whereby H. started a deadly hate against M.

Then why have the socialistic organizations so energetically taken the side of the man if he was a simple murderer and a criminal before the crime? He was endowed in his way, the lady explained, and had written several workers' songs which had been hits. It was possible that he stayed with the socialistic organization only to hide his criminal activities. The workers thus should have been informed concerning his character.

These are in short the information and presumptions of our informer. They must, of course, be her own; however, the history seems strange. On one side, the testimony against H. seems to be completely incriminating. On the other side, it is clearly unbelievable that all the labor organizations in America, without exception, stood up in defense of the executed if he really was a criminal by profession as the Swedish-American lady seems to think. One of the foremost female socialistic agitators in America has traveled far and wide and held meetings where she has represented the sentenced man as innocent. On these occasions she has collected large sums which have been used to gain testimony on behalf of the sentenced man. The opinion against the sentence has also, as mentioned before, been tremendous in the labor circles. What can we believe?

2— Letter from Joe Hill to the editor of the *Salt Lake Telegram* on 15 August 1915, in which Hill explains why he discharged his attorneys, maintains his innocence, and discusses the extent of his "criminal record." The *Salt Lake Telegram* printed the letter on 22 August 1915.

State Prison
Aug. 15, 1915.

Editor, Salt Lake Telegram,
Salt Lake City, Utah

Sir—

I have noticed that there have been some articles in your paper wherein the reason why I discharged my attorneys E. B. Scott and E. D. McDougall, was discussed pro and con. If you will kindly allow me a little space, I think I might be able to throw a little light on the question.

There were several reasons why I discharged, or tried to discharge these attorneys. The main reason, however, was because they never attempted to cross-examine the witnesses for the state, and failed utterly to deliver the points of the defense.

When I asked them why they did not use the records of the preliminary hearing and pin the witnesses down to their former statements, they blandly informed me that the preliminary hearing had nothing to do with the district court hearing and that under the law they had no right to use said records.

I picked up a record myself and tried to look at it, but Mr. Scott took it away from me, stating that "it would have a bad effect on the jury." I then came to the conclusion that Scott and McDougall were not there for the purpose of defending me, and I did just what any other men would have done—I stood up and showed them the door. But, to my great surprise, I discovered that the presiding judge had the power to compel me to have these attorneys, in spite of all my protests.

The main and only fact worth considering, however, is this: I never killed Morrison and do not know a thing about it.

He was, as the records plainly show, killed by some enemy for the sake of revenge, and I have not been in this city long enough to make an enemy. Shortly before my arrest, I came down from Park City, where I was working in the mines. Owing to the prominence of Mr. Morrison, there had to be a "goat," and the undersigned being, as they thought, a friendless tramp, a Swede, and worst of all, an I.W.W., had no right to live anyway, and was therefore selected to be "the goat."

There were men sitting on my jury, the foreman being one of them, who were never subpoenaed for the case. There are errors and perjury that are screaming to high heaven for mercy, and I know that I, according to the laws of the land, am entitled to a new trial, and the fact that the supreme court does not grant it to me only proves that the beautiful term, "equality before the law," is merely an empty phrase in Salt Lake City.

Here is what Judge Hilton of Denver, one of the greatest authorities on law, has to say about it:

"The decision of the supreme court surprised me greatly, but the reason why the verdict was affirmed is, I think, on account of the rotten records made by the lower court."

This statement shows plainly why the motion for a new trial was denied and there is no explanation necessary. In conclusion I wish to state that my records are not quite as black as they have been painted.

In spite of all the hideous pictures and all the bad things said and printed about me, I had only been arrested once before in my life, and that was in San Pedro, Cal. At that time of the stevedores' and dock workers' strike I was secretary of the strike committee, and I suppose I was a little too active to suit the chief of the burg, so he arrested me and gave me thirty days in the city jail for "vagrancy"—and there you have the full extent of my "criminal record."

I have worked hard for a living and paid for everything I got, and my spare time I spend by painting pictures, writing songs and composing music.

Now, if the people of the State of Utah, want to shoot me without giving me half a chance to state my side of the case, then bring on your firing squads—I am ready for you.

I have lived like an artist and I shall die like an artist. Respectfully yours,

Joseph Hillstrom

3— Joe Hill's reply to the Utah Board of Pardons after his appeal for a new trial had been denied. "A Few Reasons Why I Demand A New Trial" gives Hill's point of view on his arrest, preliminary hearing, and trial.

TO THE UTAH BOARD OF PARDONS

October 3, 1915

A Few Reasons Why I Demand A New Trial

When I was up before the highest authorities of the state of Utah I stated that I wanted a new trial and nothing but a new trial, and I will now try to state some reasons why I am entitled to that privilege. Being aware of the fact that my past record has nothing to do with the facts of this case, I will not dwell upon that subject beyond saying that I have worked all my life as a mechanic and at times as a musician. The mere fact that the prosecution never attempted to assail my reputation proves that it is clean. I will therefore commence at the time of my arrest.

On the night of January 14, 1914, I was lying in a bed at the Eselius house in Murray, a town located seven miles from Salt Lake City, suffering from a bullet wound in my chest. Where or why I got that wound is nobody's business but my own. I know that I was not shot in the Morrison store and all the so-called evidence that is supposed to show that I was is fabrications pure and simple. As I was lying there half asleep, I was aroused by a knock on the door, somebody opened the door and in came four men with revolvers in their hands. A shot rang out and a bullet passed right over my chest, grazing my shoulder and penetrating my right hand through the knuckles, crippling me for life. There was absolutely no need of shooting me at that time because I was helpless as a baby and had no weapons of any kind. The only thing that saved my life at that time was the officer's inefficiency with fire-arms.

I was then brought up to the county jail where I was given a bunk and went to sleep immediately. The next morning I was pretty sore on account of being shot in three places. I asked to be taken to a hospital but was instead taken upstairs to a solitary cell, and told that I was charged with murder and had better confess right away. I did not know anything about any murder and told them so. They still insisted on that I confess, and told me they would take me to a hospital and "treat me white" if I did. I told them I knew nothing of any murder. They called me a "liar," and after that I refused to answer all questions. I grew weaker and weaker, and for three or four days I was hovering between life and death, and I remember an officer coming up and telling me that according to the doctor's statement I had only one hour to live. I could, of course name all these officers if I wanted to, but I want it distinctly understood that I am not trying to knock any officers, because I realize that they were only doing their duty, and in my opinion the officers who were in charge of the county jail then, were as good officers as can be found anywhere. Well! I finally pulled through because I made up my mind not to die.

When the time came for my preliminary hearing, I decided to be my own attorney, knowing that it could be nothing against me. I thought I'd let them have it all their own way, and did not ask any questions. When the court went into session, I was asked if I objected to having the witnesses remain in the courtroom during the trial, and I replied that it was immaterial to me who remained in the courtroom. All the witnesses then remained inside, and I noted that there was a steady stream of "messengers" going back and forth between the witnesses and the county attorney during the whole trial, delivering their messages in a whisper. When the trial commenced, there were first some witnesses of little importance, but then a man came up that made me sit up and take notice. He put up his hand and swore that he positively recognized me and that he had seen me in the Morrison store in the afternoon of the same day that Morrison was shot. I did not say anything, but I thought something. This man was a tall lean man with a thin pale face, black hair and eyes, and a very conspicuous black shiny mustache. I don't know his name and have never been able to find out. (Keep this man in mind, please.) The little boy, Merlin Morrison, was the next witness that attracted my attention. He was the first one to come up and look at me in the morning of the day after my arrest. Being only a little boy, he spoke his mind right out in my presence, and this is what he said: "No, that is not the man at all. The ones I saw were shorter and heavier set."

When he testified at the preliminary hearing, I asked him if he did not make that statement, but he then denied it.

I accidentally found a description of the bandit in a newspaper, however, and the description says that the bandit was 5 feet 9 inches tall and weighed about 155 pounds. That description seems to tally pretty well with Merlin Morrison's statement, "The ones I saw were shorter and heavier set." My own height is six feet and I am of a slender built.

The next witness of importance was Mrs. Phoebe Seeley. She said she was coming home from the Empress Theater with her husband and she met two men in a back street in the vicinity of Morrison's store. One of them had "small features and light bushy hair." This description did not suit the county attorney, so he helped her along a little by saying, "You mean medium colored hair like Mr. Hillstrom's, don't you?" After leading her along that way for a while, he asked her this question: "Is the general appearance of Mr. Hillstrom anything like the man you saw?" She answered, "No, I won't, I can't say that."

This is the very same woman who at the district court proved to be the star witness for the prosecution. She did not only describe me into the smallest details, but she also told the jury that the man she saw had scars on both sides of his face, on his nose, and on his neck. I have such scars on my face, and that was practically the testimony that convicted me. Just think of it, a woman not knowing a thing about the murder passing a man in a back street in the dead of a winter night, and six months later she described that man to the smallest details, hat and the cut and color of clothes, height and built, color of eyes and hair, and a number of scars, and when asked, "Is the appearance of Mr. Hillstrom anything like the man you saw?" she answered, "No, I won't, I can't say that." Her husband who was with her was not even there to testify. It is true that the prosecuting attorney put his questions in such a way that all she had to say was "yes, sir" and "all the same, sir," but she said that just the same. With a hostile judge and attorneys, who merely acted as assistant prosecuting attorney, the prosecuting attorney had what in the parlance of the street would be called "easy sailing."

The next witness was Mr. Zeese, detective. When I was sick in bed at the Eselius house in Murray, the lady gave me a red bandana handkerchief to blow my nose on. At the trial she told that she had several dozen bandana handkerchiefs that were used by her boys and brothers when they worked in the smelter. After my arrest Mr. Zeese went to the Eselius house looking for clues. He found this handkerchief, and with his keen, eagle eyes he soon discovered some "creases at the corners." With the intelligence of a super-man, he then easily drew the conclusion that this handkerchief had been used for a mask by some "bandit." Then he capped the climax by going on the stand and telling his marvellous discovery to the judge. Mr. Zeese is well known in Salt Lake City, and comments are unnecessary.

The next witness at the preliminary hearing, Mrs. Vera Hanson, said she saw two or three men outside of the Morrison store shortly after the shooting. She heard one of the men exclaim "Bob," or "Oh Bob," and she thought that my voice sounded the same as the voice she heard on the street. I then asked Mrs. Hanson this question: "Do you mean to tell me that you, through that single word Bob, were able to recognize my voice?" Now I am coming to the point.

After the preliminary hearing I got a record of the hearings and took it to my cell in the county jail. I immediately discovered that it had been tempered with, that everything I had said had been misconstrued in a malicious way. It was a little hard to prove it at first but on page 47, I found the questions that I had put to Mrs. Vera Hanson, and there the tampering was so clumsly that a little child could see it. In the records the question reads like this, "Do you mean to tell me that you through the single word (mark, 'single word') 'Oh, Bob, I'm shot,'" four or five words. Here anyone can see that the official court records were altered for the express purpose of "proving" that someone was shot in the Morrison store. I then started to look for testimony of a man with a black shiny mustache but to my great surprise I could not find it anywhere in the records in spite of the fact that this man had positively recognized me at the preliminary hearing. No wonder that this very dignified stenographer, Mr. Rollo, who is also stenographer for the United States supreme court, was shaking life a leaf when he put up his hand and swore that the records were "correct" in every detail. The strange part of it is that the supreme court in a statement prepared by them for the press are, so my attorney told me (I am not allowed to see any papers), making the very same mistake. They say that Mrs. Vera Hanson said in her testimony, "O, Bob, I'm shot," which is not correct.

At the time when I was shot I was unarmed. I threw my hands up in the air just before the bullet struck me. That accounts for the fact that the bullet hole in my coat is four inches and a half below the bullet hole in my body. The prosecuting attorney endeavors to explain that fact by saying "that the bandit would throw one hand up in surprise when Arlin Morrison got hold of his father's pistol." He also states that the bandit might have been leaning over the counter when he was shot. Very well. If the bandit "threw up his hands in surprise," as he said, that would of course raise the coat some, but it would not raise it four inches and one-half. "Leaning over the counter" would not raise the coat at all. Justice McCarthy agrees with the prosecuting attorney and says that throwing his hands up would be just the very thing that the bandit would do if the boy Arlin made an attempt to shoot him. Let me ask Mr. McCarthy a question. Suppose that you would some night discover that there was a burglar crawling around in your home, then suppose that you would get your gun and surprise that burglar right in the act. If the burglar should then reach for his gun, would you throw up your hands and let the burglar take a shot at you and then shoot the burglar afterward? Or would you shoot the burglar before he had a chance to reach for his gun? Think it over. It is not a question of law but one of human nature. I also wish Mr. McCarthy would try to find it possible to raise a coat on a person four and a half inches in the manner described by the prosecuting attorney.

We will now go back to the bullet. After the bullet had penetrated the bandit, the prosecuting attorney says that it "dropped to the floor" and then disappeared. It left no mark anywhere that an ordinary bullet would. It just disappeared, that's all. Now gentlemen, I don't know a thing about this bullet, but I will say this, that if I should sit down and write a novel, I certainly would have to think up something more realistic than that, otherwise I would never be able to sell it. The story of a bullet that first makes an upshoot of four inches and a half at an angle of 90 degrees, then cuts around another corner and penetrates a bandit and finally makes a drop like a spit ball and disappears forever, would not be very well received in the twentieth century. And just think of it that the greatest brains in Utah can sit and listen to such rot as that and then say that "Hillstrom" got a fair and impartial trial.

I have heard this case rehashed many times and I wish to state that I have formed my own opinion about this shooting. My opinion is this: Two or three bandits entered the Morrison store for the express purpose of killing Mr. Morrison. As they entered, both of them shouted "We've got you now!" and started to blaze away with automatic Colt pistols caliber "38," and having the advantage of a surprise, it does not seem reasonable that they would allow a boy to shoot them. The story about that remarkable disappearing bullet; the fact that the official records were changed for the purpose of proving that someone was shot in that store; all that goes to show that there is a decided lack of evidence that anybody was shot in that store outside of the two victims. Nobody saw the Morrison gun fired. Merlin Morrison ran in deadly fright into some back room and hid himself. In spite of the fact that he was almost scared to death he "counted seven shots" and that is supposed to be some more proof that the Morrison gun was discharged. Six shots were fired by the bandits and all the bullets found. But there had to be seven shots fired, otherwise there would be no case against me. The boy "counted seven shots" and that "evidence" is introduced by the state as "proof" that the Morrison gun was discharged. Any sensible person can readily see what chance a frightened boy, or anybody else for that matter, would have to count the shots when two bandits are blazing away with automatic pistols. There were some officers there who claimed that they smelled the end of the gun and that thereby they could tell that the gun had been recently discharged, but the gun expert from the Western Arms Co. exploded that argument. He stated that it was a physical impossibility to determine with any degree of certainty at what time a gun had been discharged, in a case where smokeless powder is used, on account of the fact that the odor of powder is always there. Then there was that empty chamber in the Morrison gun. An officer testified that it was customary among police officers to keep an empty chamber under the hammer of their guns. Morrison used to be a sergeant of police, I was told.

Then there was a "pool of blood" found two or three blocks away from the Morrison store and the prosecution made a whole ocean out of it in spite of the fact that the Utah state chemist would not say that it was human blood. He said that the blood was of "Mammalian origin."

Then there is Miss Mahan, who is supposed to have heard somebody say "I'm shot." At the preliminary hearing she was very uncertain about it. She said she thought she heard somebody say those words but she was not by any means sure about it.

Now, that's all there is, to my knowledge, and I am positively sure that all this so-called evidence which is supposed to prove that the Morrison gun was discharged on the night of Jan. 10, 1914, would not stand the acid test of a capable attorney, such as I am not in a position to get. At the time of my arrest I did not have money enough to employ an attorney. Thinking that there was nothing to my case, and always being willing to try anything once, I decided to "go it" alone and be my own attorney which I did at the preliminary hearing.

A few days after that hearing an attorney by the name of McDougall came to see me at the county jail. He said he was a stranger in town and had heard about my case and would be willing to take the case for nothing. Seeing that that proposition was in perfect harmony with my bankroll, I accepted his offer. I will say for McDougall, though, that he was honest and sincere about it and would no doubt have carried the case to a successful finish if he had not got mixed up with that miserable shyster Mr. Scott. Before my trial, I pointed out the fact that the preliminary hearing records had been altered, but they said that the said record did not amount to anything anyway, and that it would do no good to make a holler about it.

Then the trial commenced. The first day went by with the usual questioning of jurors. The second day, however, something happened that did not look right to me. There was a jury of eight men entered the courtroom. They had been serving on some other case and came in to deliver their verdict, which was one of "Guilty." Then the court discharged all the jurors and they all started to go home, but then for some reason Judge Ritchie changed his mind and told three of them to come back and go up in the jury box and be examined for my case. I noted that these men were very surprised and that they did not expect to be retained for jury service. I have therefore good reason to believe that they were never subpoenaed for the case, but just simply appointed by the court. One of these men, a very old man by the name of Kimball, was later on made "foreman" of the jury. During the course of the trial I was surprised to see that some of the witnesses were telling entirely different stories from the ones told by them at the preliminary hearing and I then asked my attorney why they did not use the records of the preliminary hearing and pin the witnesses down to their former statements. They then told me that the preliminary hearing had nothing to do with the district court hearing and that they did not amount to anything. They did, however, use said record a little, but only for a bluff. After I had watched this ridiculous grand stand play for a while I came to the conclusion that I had to get rid of these attorneys and either conduct the case myself or else get some other attorney. I therefore stood up the first thing in the morning one day and showed them the door. Being the defendant in the case, I naturally thought I should have the right to say who I wanted to represent me, but to my surprise I discovered that the presiding judge had the power to compel me to have these attorneys in spite of all my protests. He ruled that they remain as "friends of the court" and that settled it. Mr. Scott went after one of the state witnesses in a way that convinced me that he really could do good work when he wanted to. After he got through with this witness (Mrs. Seeley) he came up to me and said, "Now then, how did you like that?" I said, "That's good, but why didn't you do some of that before?" "Well—er" he hesitated. "This was the first witness we had marked for cross-examination." If that is not a "dead give-away," then I don't know anything. It will be noted that Mrs. Seeley is one of the best witnesses for the state.

I will now say something about the pistol which I had in my possession when I called at

Dr. McHugh's office to have my wound dressed. The pistol was a "Luger" caliber 30, a pistol of German make. I laid my pistol on the table while the doctor dressed my wound and I thought that he would be able to tell it from other pistols on account of its peculiar construction. He said he did not know, however, what kind of pistol mine was. That was an even break, and whenever I get an even break I am not complaining. He did not, like most of the state witnesses, commit perjury, and is therefore in my opinion a gentleman. There was another doctor, however, by the name of Bird, who dropped in while Dr. McHugh was dressing my wound. He only saw the pistol as I put it in my pocket, he said so at the preliminary hearing, but at the district court hearing he came up and deliberately swore that my pistol was exactly the same kind of pistol as the one that Morrison and his son were killed with.

As I said before, my pistol was a "Luger" 30. It was bought less than a month before my arrest in a second hand store on West South Temple street, near the depot. I was brought down there in an automobile by three officers and the record of the sale was found on the books: price, date of sale, and everything just as I had stated. The books did not show what kind of gun it was, however, and as the clerk who had sold it was in Chicago at the time a telegram was sent to him to which he sent this answer: "Remember selling Luger gun at that time. What's the trouble?" I bought the pistol on Dec. 15, 1913, for $16.50. Anybody may go to the store and see the books.

Now, anyone can readily understand that I am not in a position where I could afford to make any false statements. I have stated the facts as I know them in my own simple way. I think I shall be able to convince every fair-minded man and woman who reads these lines that I did not have a fair and impartial trial in spite of what the learned jurists may say to the contrary. Now if you don't like to see perjurors and dignified crooks go unpunished, if you don't like to see human life being sold like a commodity on the market, then give me a hand. I am going to stick to my principles no matter what may come. I am going to have a new trial or die trying.

Yours for Fair Play,

Joseph Hillstrom.

4— The Board of Pardons' statement of its reasons for denying Joe Hill a commutation of sentence (prepared by Justice Straup).

BEFORE THE BOARD OF PARDONS,
Consisting of the
Governor of the State, the
Three Justices of the Supreme
Court and the Attorney General.

In the Matter of the
Application of
JOSEPH HILLSTROM for
Commutation of Sentence.

The applicant, Joseph Hillstrom, in the District Court of Salt Lake County, by an impartial jury of twelve men, against whom no complaint of prejudice, bias or unfairness has been made, was on the 27th day of June, 1914, convicted of murder in the first degree. Under the statutes of this State, when one is found guilty of such an offense, the jury, by their verdict, may recommend that he be imprisoned for life. In the absence of such a recommendation the court is required to impose the death sentence. The jury refused to make the recommendation and hence the court imposed that penalty. The statute further provides that the accused so found guilty may choose whether death shall be inflicted by hanging or by shooting. The applicant chose the latter. The court thereupon sentenced him to death by shooting. From that judgment the applicant prosecuted an appeal to the Supreme Court of the State.

One of the principal contentions made on the appeal was, that the evidence was insufficient to connect the applicant with the commission of the murder. The court, upon a complete transcript of all the evidence adduced before the trial court, and upon a complete record of the cause, reviewed that question and in its written opinion filed July 3, 1915, and published in 150 Pac. 935, ____Utah____, set forth at considerable length the evidence which, in its judgment, justified the verdict of the jury. For a better understanding of the facts of the case a copy of the opinion is hereto attached. It is not necessary to here make a detailed statement of them. Let it suffice by noting some of them.

As appears by the opinion, and as shown by the record, two men with red bandana handkerchiefs over their faces as masks, and with guns in hand, at about 10 o'clock at night, on the 10th of January, 1914, entered the store of the deceased, J. G. Morrison, in Salt Lake City and there shot and killed him and his son. The undoubted purpose of the assailants entering the store was either murder, or roberry, or both. The deceased was shot twice; his son three times. In the attack one of the assailants was himself shot by the son. The gun with which the son did the shooting was found near the outstretched hand of his dead body with one chamber discharged. One of the assailants, as he ran from the store, was heard to exclaim, as if in great pain, "Oh Bob," and "I am shot." Considerable blood was found on the sidewalk and in an alley near the store, and where the assailants, after the shooting, were seen and heard to mutter to themselves. There was one living eye witness to the shooting,—a younger son of the deceased. Because of the handkerchiefs over their faces portions of the facial features of the assailants were hidden from him; but he testified that the general features of one of the assailants were about the same as those of the applicant, and that he had the same shaped head, was about the same size, and wore the same clothes as was shown the applicant wore that night. There also was testimony of two other witnesses, whose attention was attracted by the shooting, that the size and appearance of one of the perpetrators of the crime, and whom they saw running from the store after the shooting in a stooping posture, were similar to the size, appearance and build of the applicant, and that his voice as he spoke "Oh Bob" and "I am shot" was similar to the voice of the applicant. One of the witnesses testified that they were exactly the same. Another witness testified that she saw the assailants near the store just a few minutes before they entered it. They then had red bandana handkerchief tied around their necks. She had particular reason to observe one of them because of their crowding her off the sidewalk as she and her husband met and passed them. There was some snow on the ground, the night a bright moonlight night, and the surroundings well lighted by electric arc lights. As some of the witnesses expressed it, it was about as light as day. She testified that one of the assailants, just as they had passed, turned and looked at her and that she looked at him and that close by she had a direct view of his face. She described that man as being rather tall and slim, with light hair and of light complexion; that he had a peculiarly sharp nose, sharp fac, and large nostrils, and a scar on the side of his face and neck, and that these were very lik' the sharp nose and face, and large nostrils of the applicant and the scar on the side of his face and neck; and that the build, size and appearance of that man and the applicant were alike. She gave such a particular and minute description that with it the applicant, among many, could well be identified. Many men have light hair and are tall and slim. That is a description not uncommon of others; but the peculiarly sharp nose and sharp face, and large nostrils of the applicant and the scar on his face and neck gave him most pronounced and unusual marks of identification, and features which may not readily be mistaken for another. In addition to that the applicant, about two hours after the commission of the murder, and about two and one-half miles from the place of the homicide, was found seeking aid at a doctor's office for a fresh gunshot wound through his lungs and chest. He then was in a condition about to collapse because of loss of blood. He volunteered to the doctors who attended him that he "had had a quarrel with someone over a woman and that in the quarrel he was shot, and that he was as much to blame as the other fellow and wanted it kept quiet, kept private." He then had a gun in his possession, which, when he was dressing after the wound had been attended, dropped from his clothes to the floor. The physicians testified that in their opinion, the applicant's wound was produced by a bullet shot from a .38 calibre gun. It was also shown that the gun which lay near the out-

269

stretched hand of the deceased's son, with one chamber freshly discharged, and with which he had shot one of the assailants, was a .38 calibre gun. One of the doctors, in his automobile, took the applicant to Murray, a town about five miles south of the place of the homicide, and there left him with his friends. On the way there the applicant threw his gun away. As they approached the house to which he was being taken, he requested the doctor to turn down the lights of the automobile, and as they drew nearer he gave two shrill, penetrating whistles. He was arrested two or three days thereafter. The officer then told him that if he would disclose the place where and the circumstances under which he received his wound, and if the facts were as stated by him to the physician, he would be given his liberty. He declined to give the officer any information whatever.

There thus, as disclosed by the opinion of the court and by the record, is good evidence to connect the applicant with the commission of the murder.

The applicant was not a witness in the case. And, other than what he stated to the physicians, gave no explanation whatever to show where or the circumstances under which he received the gunshot wound. He made no offer or attempt to prove anything of that kind at the trial, nor did he offer any evidence whatever to show his movements, whereabouts, or doings, on the night of the homicide. All these at all times have been withheld by him.

It also was contended before the Supreme Court that the applicant had not had a fair trial in the particular, as claimed in one breath, that he was not represented by counsel, in the next that he was not permitted to conduct his defense alone and in person without counsel. These matters are also fully and in detail referred to and set forth in the opinion. They show that the applicant was represented by two counsel of his own selection and hire. When the state was about half through its case the defendant, without any warning or notice to his counsel, arose before the court and jury and in a most unseemly manner, and wholly without cause, demanded that his counsel be summarily discharged and that he be permitted to conduct his defense in person and without counsel. The court advised him that he had the right to discharge his counsel and himself to examine witnesses and to conduct his defense. But the court further stated that he would request his counsel to remain and safeguard and protect his rights and interests. Colloquies were had between the court, the defendant and his counsel, when the trial was suspended to enable counsel to consult with the defendant and his friends. That was just shortly before adjournment for the noon hour. As a result of such consultation the defendant and his counsel returned into court when his counsel announced that "we will proceed to act in behalf of the defendant on the court's appointment unless the court chooses to appoint someone else in our place. If the defendant wishes some other attorney appointed we will cheerfully withdraw." The applicant did not then ask that his counsel withdraw or that other counsel be appointed for him, but assented to his counsel proceeding in his behalf with the understanding, however, that he be given the right to examine witnesses himself. The court granted him that right and the trial thereupon was resumed. Shortly thereafter the noon hour adjournment was taken. When the court convened in the afternoon additional counsel appeared for the defendant and asked that his name, at the request of the defendant and of his friends, be entered as counsel for the defendant. That was done and from thence on for four days taking testimony in the case all three counsel, with the defendant's consent, represented him and took part in all of the proceedings to the end of the trial without any objection from any one. It was not claimed before the Supreme Court that the applicant's counsel had been unfaithful or disloyal to him, or that they had not done all in protecting and safeguarding the rights and interest of the applicant that was proper for anyone to do.

Other alleged errors also were considered by the Supreme Court, but the contentions made with respect to them also were held unfounded. The court, upon a review of the whole record, stated that "we are satisfied that there is sufficient evidence to support the verdict; that the record is free from error; and that the defendant had a fair and impartial trial in which he was granted every right and privilege vouchsafed by the law." The judgment thus, on the 3d day of July, 1915, was affirmed.

The applicant, within twenty days thereafter, had the right to file a petition for rehearing. The court also, upon application therefor, had the right to extend that time. No petition was filed and no attempt whatever made to do so.

Upon remittitur, the applicant was, by the district court, again sentenced to death by shooting on the 1st day of October, 1915. He thereupon applied to this board for a commutation of sentence. The application was heard on the 18th of September, 1915. Upon that hearing the applicant was represented by O. N. Hilton of Denver and Soren X. Christensen of Salt Lake City, attorneys, and who also prosecuted the appeal for him to the Supreme Court. One of them also represented him at the trial in the district court. The applicant also was present at the hearing before the board from beginning to end. So also were representatives or a committee of the Industrial Workers of the World. The grounds stated for a commutation were, that the evidence was insufficient; that the applicant had not had a fair trial, his counsel stating that he had had "a legal trial but not a fair trial"; that the case rested on circumstancial evidence and that the life of one should not be taken on that kind of evidence; and that the infliction of the death penalty was barbarous and ought not to be imposed in any case. Here let it be observed that the applicant before verdict and judgment was entitled to every presumption of innocence; but after a verdict finding him guilty and after judgment and its affirmance the presumption of innocence no longer prevails. The presumption then to be indulged is that the judgment is right and that the applicant is guilty. He, after that, had the burden to show, or bring forward, or point out, something to justify a commutation of sentence, or clemency in his favor. But neither he nor his counsel before the board attempted to point out anything wherein, or in what particular, they claimed the evidence was insufficient to justify the verdict. Nor did they offer or attempt to show anything respecting the applicant's life, habits, morals, or previous character, or what trade, profession or occupation had been followed by him, or who he was, or what he had done, or where he was from, or what kind of life had been lived by him. Nor did they offer or attempt to show anything new or additional respecting the case, or anything in favor of the applicant, or anything to justify commutation or clemency. What was urged in support of the application is this: Cases were referred to wherein we were told convictions rested alone on circumstantial evidence and where later it was disclosed that the persons convicted were innocent. It, however, was not claimed, nor was there any attempt made to show, that the facts in those cases and in this case were similar or even analogous. Frequent assertions were made by counsel that the conviction here rested alone on circumstantial evidence and that the applicant's life ought not to be taken on that kind of evidence. But, as stated by the Supreme Court in its decision, and as shown by the record, the conviction here does not rest on circumstantial evidence alone. There is direct evidence, testimony of eye witnesses, to identify the applicant as one of the perpetrators of the crime. No reference whatever was made to that testimony by counsel, nor did they in any manner offer or attempt to review the evidence, or to inform the board wherein or for what reason the evidence did not support the conviction, or that the conviction rested alone upon circumstantial evidence. Indeed, counsel, before the board, for some reason avoided all references to the real facts of the case and as disclosed by the record, and in such respect contented themselves with fervid exhortations on the horros of an execution on circumstantial evidence and with unwarranted assaults on the good names of the States of Utah and Colorado.

It further was contended before the board that the applicant was denied representation by counsel. As to that, we may here say, as was said by the Supreme Court upon a review of the whole matter, that "under all the circumstances the argument in one breath that the defendant was denied his constitutional right to appear and defend in person and in the next was proceeded against without counsel is as groundless as was senseless the defendant's action discharging his counsel in the forenoon and reemploying or reengaging them in the afternoon."

Counsel also, before the board in criticism of the Supreme Court, contended that it in its opinion had held that the failure of the applicant to be a witness on the trial of the case before the district court was a circumstance to be considered against him and as an inference of guilt. Notwithstanding counsel were told that they had misconceived the opinion and did not properly reflect it, they, nevertheless, impatiently persisted in their misconception and misconstruction of the opinion, and argued, as though this board were clothed with power to review and correct what counsel chose to assert were errors of law of the Supreme Court. They were asked that, if they were in good faith in their contention, why it was they had not filed a petition in the Supreme Court for a rehearing. No answer was made to this and no reason given for their failure to do that, except that one counsel was in Denver and that he had left the matter in hands of counsel in Salt Lake City. From the fact that no petition was filed, when counsel had every opportunity to do so, it may well be presumed that they thought there was no just or meritorious ground on which to ask a rehearing.

Reference also was made to the applicant's alleged attitude in protecting the honor of a woman. This, because of the testimony of the doctor that the applicant had told him that he had received the gunshot wound in a quarrel over a woman in which he "was to blame as much as the other fellow." Here it may be well to note that there was good evidence adduced by the state to show that the applicant received his gunshot wound in the store at the time of the homicide. Neither at the trial nor before this board was there any evidence whatever adduced to show the contrary; nor was there anything offered on behalf of the applicant to show where, or in what manner, or under what circumstances he received the wound. There was, of course, the testimony of the doctor that the applicant had stated to him that he had received the wound in a quarrel over a woman. But that was not evidence of the fact. It was but evidence of his claim, of his declaration. Suppose he had said to the doctor that he accidentally had shot himself. That would be but evidence of such claim, of such contention. But such an extrajudicial, selfserving, and unsworn declaration would be no evidence of the fact that the wound was caused in such manner. So here. If the applicant claimed that the wound was produced in a quarrel over a woman, then it was his duty, and he was afforded full opportunity, to bring forward something to support it. He cannot ask anyone to believe his claim with no evidence whatever to support it and with no effort or attempt even to produce or furnish any. Hence it is time enough to consider the applicant's alleged attitude in protecting the honor of some woman when there is some evidence to show that he received his wound at some place other than at the place of the homicide. His mere general, extrajudicial, selfserving and unsworn statement to the doctor that he received the wound at some undisclosed place, in a quarrel with some unnamed and undescribed man over some unnamed and undescribed woman, is so vague and lax as even not to present an issue; much less can it be accepted as evidence of the fact. Further, his declaration to the doctor does not even imply that the honor of a woman was involved. He but said that "he had had a quarrel with someone over a woman and that in the quarrel he was shot." A quarrel between two men over a woman may or may not involve her honor. It depends upon what the quarrel is about. Yet upon this weird, vague and selfserving statement, wholly unsupported by any evidence, the board was in effect asked to make a finding that the applicant was shot in a quarrel over some unknown woman at some unknown place and by some unknown man, and to ignore all the evidence adduced at the trial and in the record that he was shot in the store at the time of the homicide.

When counsel concluded their argument, without any attempt even to point out in what particular they claimed the evidence was insufficient to connect the applicant with the commission of the offense; without giving or offering anything as to the character, morals, habits or past life of the applicant, or as to who or what he is or was, or where he lived, or what he had done; without attempting to offer anything new or additional in the case, or any new information, or anything in his favor, or where he was or what he did on the night of the homicide, the chairman of the board asked the applicant if he desired to make any statement or to say anything in his own behalf. His reply was that he would not give the board any information, nor make any statement, until he was first granted a new trial; and that then he, on such new trial, would prove his innocence and send several perjurers to the penetentiary where, as he said, they belonged. What or whom he meant by the statement he did not disclose. Nor did he disclose or attempt or offer to disclose what, if anything, were he granted a new trial, he would or could produce or prove, nor did he in any manner even indicate or intimate the nature or character of such proof. He was informed that the board was not clothed with power to grant him a new trial; that all by way of favorable action that it could do was to grant a pardon or to commute the sentence. He stated that he did not want either a pardon or a commutation of sentence; that what he wanted was a new trial and an acquittal by a jury. He was asked why he did not make his defense and put in his evidence on the trial. His reply was that he thought the law presumed him innocent and that he would not be convicted on the evidence which was adduced against him. He again was told that the board was powerless to grant him a new trial and that a pardon would be equivalent to an acquittal; and that at this hearing was his opportunity to say or show whatever he desired to say or show. His counsel were asked if they desired to ask him any questions, or if there was anything that they desired to show by him. They replied in the negative. The applicant then was asked if he would be willing that any member of the board ask him questions which he might answer or decline to answer as he saw fit. He replied that unless the board first granted him a new trial he was unwilling that any questions be asked him or to make answer to any. His counsel were asked if they had informed and advised him that the board could not grant him a new trial and that if he desired to say or show anything in his behalf that he was required to say or show it at this hearing. They replied that they had so adviced him, and had requested him to make a statement and to tell the board whatever he claimed to be the truth about the case, but that he had declined to give any information, or to make any statement, or to answer any question, except on a new trial of the case before a jury, which, they had advised him, this board was powerless to grant. Some members of the board almost pleaded with him that if he was innocent he ought to give the board some information, or something, which at least might raise a reasonable doubt in the minds of the members of the board and thus give them some ground upon which to commute the sentence. One of the representatives of the Industrial Workers of the World was asked if he desired to be heard in behalf of the applicant and if he would not consult with him in view of furnishing whatever information the applicant had in his favor. The representative but replied that the applicant knew his own mind and was quite capable of determining for himself his own desires in the premises, and that he did not care to advise him either one way or the other. Some members of the board even went so far as to say to the applicant that if he would give his attorneys and the warden the name of the man whom he claimed to the doctor had shot him, the name of the woman and the place and the circumstances of the shooting, so that the matter could be investigated, and if on such investigation it should be found that he was shot in such manner he would be given an unconditional pardon; and that the names of the parties to the affair, if any such had occurred, would be kept secret and made known to no one except to the warden, his attorneys and those investigating the matter. But after a conference with his attorneys he declined the proposition, his attorneys stating to the board, that he declined to give any further information, and that "he wanted to die a martyr."

There were also before the board a number of letters which were received by the chairman of the board from many different states. A few of them were from those seeking information as to the real facts of the case. Some of them were threatening demands to release and discharge the applicant regardless of whether he be guilty or innocent. Others were from those who, though in remote parts of the country, nevertheless claimed to know what the facts in the case are, and stated that there was no evidence to show the applicant's guilt, that he is innocent, and that he had not had a fair trial, and for these reasons asked that he be discharged. But in every such instance it is apparent from statements made by them that they have been misinformed as to the real facts and that they have been misguided and misdirected. If those who seek clemency on these grounds could but read the record in its entirety, as we have, and not some mere garbled reports and pamphlets prepared and sent out by partisans, they would reach a different conclusion. For, it is almost inconceivable how any impartial and unbiased mind reading the record in its entirety can reach any reasonable conclusion other than that of the applicant's guilt. Other letters and communications were from those who, wholly unfamiliar with and uninformed of the real facts of the case, labored under the impression that the applicant was arrested and prosecuted because of his membership of and connection with an organization known as the Industrial Workers of the World and that the trial involved something that the applicant had done as a member of, or in pursuance of that organization, or in furtherance of its principles, and that hence, the real contest involved the rights and general welfare of members of that organization, and of laborers and workers of the world. And while they protested against the applicant's execution and threatened and demanded his immediate discharge, yet indicated, in the event their protests and demands should be unavailing, that they exalted the applicant as a martyr dying in and for a most righteous cause. It is indeed, difficult to perceive how anyone, unless grossly misinformed of the facts of the case, could entertain any such views. It is natural and proper enough for the organization of which it is claimed the applicant is a member to aid him in his defense and to see that his trial was had in accordance with the laws of the state and of our country. But this controversy in no way involved any rights, doctrines or principles of any organization. There is nothing in the record whatever, nor in the history of the case, to support any such claim. Confessedly a most revolting double murder, without any extenuating or mitigating circumstances whatever, was committed by the two assailants who entered the store with faces masked and guns in hand. Certainly no one can exalt a perpetrator of such a crime a martyr. The only question, then, is, was the applicant one of the perpetrators who committed the crime? If he was, then ought he to suffer the consequences of his wilful and criminal acts, not because he is or is not a member of any organization, but because of the awful offense committed by him. If he was not, then is he entitled to a discharge, again not because he is or is not a member of any organization, but because of his innocence of the charged offense. As heretofore observed the state, at the trial, produced good and sufficient evidence to connect the applicant with the commission of the offense. Against that evidence the applicant produced nothing and at all times withheld everything.

When thus nothing whatever was made to appear before the board to justify clemency or a commutation of sentence, and when the applicant, after a conference and consultation with his counsel asserted that he did not wish a commutation of sentence, but demanded a new trial, which we, as he was advised, were powerless to grant him, and when, too, no showing whatever was made to justify the granting of a new trial though we had the power to grant it, there was but one course open to the board, and that was to deny the application, which was done.

To have reached any other conclusion requires a holding that capital punishment should not be inflicted in any case of first degree murder no matter how revolting the commission of it may have been, and to disregard the constitution and the statute of this state on the subject. This opinion and report is concurred in by all the members of the board. Let it be recorded and filed with the records of the cause before the board and made a part thereof. Such is the order.

(signed)   A. R. Barnes
        Secretary of the Board

                                (signed)   William F. Spry
                                        Chairman of the Board

274

Bibliography

Books listed in the Joe Hill bibliography are either primarily about Hill as indicated by their titles, have a chapter or other notable mention of Hill (indicated by C), or allude briefly to Hill (indicated by † with page numbers supplied when available).

Books

Aaron, Daniel. *Writers on the Left.* New York: Harcourt, Brace & World, 1961. († p. 270)

Anderson, Nels. *The Hobo: The Sociology of the Homeless Man.* Chicago: University of Chicago Press, 1923. Reprint. Chicago: University of Chicago Press, Phoenix Books, 1961. († pp. 208-10)

Binns, Archie. *The Timber Beast.* New York: Charles Scribner's Sons, 1944. (Novel † pp. 130, 140-41, 279, 281)

Blaisdell, Lowell L. *Desert Revolution.* Madison, Wis.: University of Wisconsin Press, 1962. (†)

Botkin, B. A., ed. *A Treasury of American Folklore.* New York: Crown Publishers, 1944. († pp. 886-87)

———, ed. *A Treasury of Western Folklore.* New York: Crown Publishers, 1951. (C pp. 627-30, 730)

Burdick, Eugene. *The Ninth Wave.* Boston: Houghton Mifflin Co., 1956. (Novel † pp. 22-23)

Burt, Olive Woolley. *American Murder Ballads.* New York: Oxford University Press, 1958. Reprint. New York: Citadel Press, 1964. († pp. 95-96)

Chaplin, Ralph. *Wobbly: The Rough-and-Tumble Story of an American Radical.* Chicago: University of Chicago Press, 1948. (C)

Dos Passos, John. *Nineteen Nineteen.* New York: Random House, 1937. (Novel † pp. 456-57)

Downes, Olin, and Elie Siegmeister, eds. *A Treasury of American Song.* New York: Alfred A. Knopf, 1943. († pp. 388-89)

Dunson, Josh. *Freedom in the Air.* New York: International Publishers Co., 1965. († pp. 14-16)

Egbert, Donald Drew, and Stow Parsons, eds. *Socialism and American Life.* Vol. 2. Princeton Studies in American Civilization, no. 4. Princeton: Princeton University Press, 1952. († p. 494)

Feied, Frederick. *No Pie in the Sky.* New York: Citadel Press, 1964. († pp. 42, 53)

Filler, Louis. *A Dictionary of American Social Reform.* New York: Philosophical Library, 1963. († p. 351)

Flynn, Elizabeth Gurley. *I Speak My Own Piece.* New York: Masses and Mainstream, 1955. (C)

Foner, Philip S. *The Case of Joe Hill.* New York: International Publishers Co., 1965.

———. *The Industrial Workers of the World, 1905-1917. History of the Labor Move-*

276

ment in the United States, vol. 4. New York: International Publishers Co., 1965. (†)

———, ed. *The Letters of Joe Hill.* New York: Oak Publications, 1965.

Fowke, Edith Fulton, and Joe Glazer, eds. *Songs of Work and Freedom.* Garden City, N.Y.: Doubleday & Co., 1960. Reprint. New York: Dolphin Books, 1961. († pp. 20-21)

Gentry, Curt. *Frame Up.* New York: W. W. Norton & Co., 1967. (†)

Graham, Marcus, ed. *An Anthology of Revolutionary Poetry.* New York: The Active Press, 1929. († p. 84)

Greenway, John. *American Folksongs of Protest.* Philadelphia: University of Pennsylvania Press, 1953. Reprint. New York: A. S. Barnes & Co., 1960. (C "Migratory Workers," pp. 173-208)

Guthrie, Woody. "Joe Hill." In *American Folksong,* edited by Moses Asch. New York: Oak Publications, 1961. (†)

Hall, Covington [Covami]. "A Fair Trial." In *Battle Hymns of Toil* (collected poems of Covington Hall). Oklahoma City: General Welfare Reporter, n.d. (Poem † p. 30)

Hayes, Alfred, and Earl Robinson. "I Dreamed I Saw Joe Hill Last Night." In *Fireside Book of Folk Songs,* edited by Margaret Bradford Boni and Norman Lloyd. New York: Simon & Schuster, 1947. (Song †)

Haywood, William D. *The Autobiography of Big Bill Haywood.* New York: International Publishers Co., 1927. Reprint. New York: International Publishers Co., 1967. (†)

Hennacy, Ammon, et al., eds. "If I Were Free." Mimeographed. Salt Lake City: Utah Wobbly Press, 1967. (C)

Hille, Waldemar. "Joe Hill." In *Reprints from the People's Songs Bulletin, 1946-1949,* edited by Irwin Silber. New York: Oak Publications, 1961. († p. 59)

Holbrook, Stewart H. *Holy Old Mackinaw.* New York: Macmillan Co., 1938. († p. 240)

Jones, James. *From Here to Eternity.* New York: Charles Scribner's Sons, 1951. (Novel † pp. 640-42, 647-48)

Kornbluh, Joyce L., ed. *Rebel Voices: An I.W.W. Anthology.* Ann Arbor, Mich.: University of Michigan Press, 1964. (C "Joe Hill: Wobbly Bard," pp. 127-57)

Kornbluth, Cyril N. *Not This August.* Garden City, N.Y.: Doubleday & Co., 1955. (Novel † pp. 152, 161)

Lingenfelter, Richard E.; Richard A. Dwyer; and David Cohen, eds. *Songs of the American West.* Berkeley and Los Angeles: Univ. of California Press, 1968. (†)

Lomax, Alan, ed. *The Folk Songs of North America in the English Language.* Garden City, N.Y.: Doubleday & Co., 1960. († pp. 423-24)

Makins, John. *Annual Report of the Sailors' Rest Mission, San Pedro, California.* 1 February 1919. (Pamphlet †)

May, Henry F. *The End of American Innocence.* New York: Alfred A. Knopf, 1959. Reprint. Chicago: Quadrangle Books, 1964. (†)

Milburn, George. *The Hobo's Hornbook.* New York: Ives Washburn, 1930. († pp. 83-84)

Nerman, Ture. *Arbetarsangaren, Joe Hill: Mördare Eller Martyr?* Stockholm: Federativs Förlag, 1951.

O'Conner, Harvey. *Revolution in Seattle.* New York: Monthly Review Press, 1964. († pp. 54, 66, 233)

Patchen, Kenneth. "Joe Hill Listens to the Praying." In *Proletarian Literature in the United States: An Anthology,* edited by Granville Hicks et al. New York: International Publishers Co., 1935. (Poem †)

Renshaw, Patrick. *The Wobblies.* Garden City, N.Y.: Doubleday & Co., 1967. (C)

Rexroth, Kenneth. *The Dragon and the Unicorn.* Norfolk, Conn.: New Directions, 1952. (Poem † p. 128)

Sandburg, Carl. *The American Songbag.* New York: Harcourt, Brace & Co., 1927. (†)

———. *The People, Yes.* New York: Harcourt, Brace & Co., 1936. (Poem † p. 42)

Saxton, Alexander. *The Great Midland.* New York: Appleton-Century-Crofts, 1948. (Novel † pp. 3, 10, 194)

Silber, Irwin. *Lift Every Voice.* New York: Oak Publications, 1953. († p. 37)

———, and Earl Robinson. *Songs of the Great American West*. New York: Macmillan Co., 1967. († pp. 298-301)

Sima, Jonas. "Joe Hill: The Man Who Never Died." In *America Swedish Historical Foundation Yearbook*. Bridgeport, Penn.: Chancellor, Inc., 1965. (C pp. 59-64)

Sinclair, Upton. *Singing Jailbirds*. Long Beach, Calif.: By the author, 1924. (Play † pp. 6, 10, 14-15, 31, 38, 40, 70-71, 75-76, 78)

Songs of the Workers. 29th ed. Chicago: Industrial Workers of the World, 1956. ("Little Red Song Book")

Stavis, Barrie. *The Man Who Never Died*. New York: Haven Press, 1954 (copyright 1951 under the title *Joe Hill*). Reprint. New York: Dramatists Play Service, 1959. (Play)

———, and Frank Harmon, eds. *Songs of Joe Hill*. New York: People's Artists, 1955. Reprint. New York: Oak Publications, 1960. (Songbook)

Stegner, Wallace. *The Preacher and the Slave*. Boston: Houghton Mifflin Co., 1950. (Novel)

Stevens, James. *Big Jim Turner*. Garden City, N.Y.: Doubleday & Co., 1948. (Novel C pp. 85-89, 92-95, 158-73, 211-12, 275)

Thompson, Fred. *The I.W.W.: Its First Fifty Years*. Chicago: Industrial Workers of the World, 1955. (C)

Warrum, Noble, ed. *Utah Since Statehood*. Chicago and Salt Lake City: S. J. Clarke, 1919. (C "The Hillstrom Case," pp. 686-90)

Articles

Alderson, William. "On the Wobbly 'Casey Jones' and Other Songs." *California Folklore Quarterly* 1 (Winter 1942): 373-76.

Bearse, Ray; Ragnar Johanson; Oscar W. Larson. "Dramat Joe Hill." *Folket i Bild* (Sweden), 18 November 1949 (three short articles combined under a general title).

Calmer, Alan. "The Wobbly in American Literature." *New Masses*, 18 September 1934, pp. 21-22.

Chaplin, Ralph. "Casey Jones." *New Masses*, January 1929, p. 14.

———. "Joe Hill." *The Labor Defender* 1 (November 1926): 187-90.

———. "Joe Hill: A Biography." *Industrial Pioneer*, November 1923, pp. 23-26.

———. "Joe Hill's Funeral." *International Socialist Review* 16 (January 1916): 400-405.

"Correspondence: Joe Hill" (letters by Fred Thompson, Meyer Friedkin, Wallace Stegner). *New Republic*, 9 February 1948, pp. 38-39.

Cowan, Paul. "Dying Like a True Rebel." *Nation* 203 (26 September 1966): 201-202.

Dubofsky, Melvyn. Review of *The Case of Joe Hill* and *The Letters of Joe Hill* by Philip S. Foner. *Labor History* 7 (Fall 1966): 354-58.

Emrich, Duncan. "Songs of the Western Miners." *California Folklore Quarterly* 1, no. 3 (July 1942): 216-20.

"The Execution of the I.W.W. Poet." *Survey*, 27 November 1915, p. 200.

Friends of Joe Hill Committee. "Joe Hill: I.W.W. Martyr." *New Republic*, 15 November 1948, pp. 18-20.

Green, Archie. "American Labor Lore: Its Meanings and Uses." *Industrial Relations: A Journal of Economy and Society* 4 (February 1965): 51-68.

———. "John Neuhaus: Wobbly Folklorist." *Journal of American Folklore* 73 (July-September 1960): 189-217.

Hand, Wayland D., et al. "Songs of the Butte Miners." *Western Folklore* 9 (January 1950): 1-49.

Haywood, William D. "Sentenced To Be Shot—Act Quick!" *International Socialist Review* 16 (August 1915): 110.

Hill, Joe. "How To Make Work for the Unemployed." *International Socialist Review* 15 (December 1914): 335-36.

———. "The Last Letters of Joe Hill." *Industrial Pioneer*, December 1923, pp. 53-56.

———. "A Letter in Swedish from Joseph Hillstrom" (contributed by Oscar W. Larson). *Revolt*, December 1915, p. 12.

Hilton, Orrin N. "A Challenge." *International Socialist Review* 16 (December 1915): 328.

——. "The Joe Hill Case." *International Socialist Review* 16 (September 1915): 25-31.

"The I.W.W. Scare in Salt Lake City." *Sunset Magazine* 35 (November 1915): 854-55.

Jensen, Vernon H. "The 'Legend' and the 'Case' of Joe Hill." Review of *The Case of Joe Hill* by Philip S. Foner. *Dialogue: A Journal of Mormon Thought* 2 (Spring 1967): 97-109.

——. "The Legend of Joe Hill." *Industrial and Labor Relations Review* 4 (April 1951): 356-66.

"Joe Hill." *International Socialist Review* 16 (December 1915): 325-30.

"Joe Hill's Will." *Sing Out*, Summer 1961, p. 29.

Kemnitzer, Luis S. "Note on Pie in the Sky." *Western Folklore* 18 (October 1959): 328.

Larkin, Jim. "Murder Most Foul." *International Socialist Review* 16 (December 1915): 330-31.

Löfgren, Carl. "Joe Hill, The Man Who Never Died." *Signalen* (Sweden), 22 January 1966, pp. 8-9.

Mattson, Edward. "Joe Hill." *Signalen* (Sweden), 1941.

Mexico. "Memory of Joe Hill. Sabotage that Succeeded." *Brand* (Sweden), 18 December 1915.

Milburn, George. "Posey in the Jungles." *American Mercury* 20 (May 1930): 80-86.

Modesto, Zapata [Barry Nichols]. "The Death of Joe Hill." *Masses and Mainstream*, September 1962, pp. 3-16.

——. "In Salt Lake City a Living Memorial to Joe Hill." *Sing Out* 12 (October-November 1962): 14-16.

——. "Joe Hill." *Wobbly No. 3* (a publication of the Berkeley, Calif., branch of the General Recruiting Union, Industrial Workers of the World), October 1963, pp. 2-11. Mimeographed.

Ochs, Phil. "Joe Hill" *Broadside*, no. 76 (November 1966): 5. (Song)

"Petition To Be Sent to Governor Spry of Utah." *International Socialist Review* 16 (October 1915): 222.

Reuss, Richard A. "The Ballad of 'Joe Hill' Revisited." *Western Folklore* 26 (July 1967): 187.

Stavis, Barrie. "Joe Hill: Poet/Organizer." *Folk Music*, (Part 1) June 1964, pp. 3-4, 38-50; (Part 2) August 1964, pp. 27-29, 38-50.

Stegner, Wallace. "I Dreamed I Saw Joe Hill Last Night." *Pacific Spectator* 1 (Spring 1947): 184-87.

——. "Joe Hill: The Wobblies' Troubadour." *New Republic*, 5 January 1948.

Sturges, Philip C. "Utah Mining Folklore." *Western Folklore* 18 (April 1959): 137-39.

Takman, John. "Joe Hill's Sister: An Interview." *Masses and Mainstream*, March 1956, pp. 24-30.

VanValkenburgh, W. S. "The Murder of Joseph Hillstrom." *Mother Earth* 10 (December 1915): 326-28.

Waring, John. "Questioned the Executioners." *International Socialist Review* 16 (January 1916): 405. (Poem)

Weisberger, Bernard A. "Here Come the Wobblies!" *American Heritage* 18, no. 4 (June 1967): 30-35, 87-93.

"The Wobblies March Again." *Time*, 19 April 1948, p. 26.

"Young Swede Gives New Life to Joe Hill's Songs." *Fackföreningsrörelsen* (journal of the Swedish Trade Union Council), 1967.

Newspapers *Articles with an author and title are given alphabetically under the name of the newspaper.*

Appeal to Reason (Girard, Kansas), 11 September 1915.

Arbetar-Tidningen (Stockholm, Sweden), 5 July 1961.

Arbetarbladet (Sweden), 18 December 1915.

Arbetaren (Stockholm, Sweden), 14 January 1949; 20 August 1952.

Box Elder Journal (Brigham City, Utah), 25 November 1915.

Catholic Worker (New York, N.Y.).

Hennacy, Ammon. "Joe Hill House," December 1965, p. 3; December 1966, p. 3; April 1967, p. 3.

Chicago Daily Tribune, 20, 25-26 November 1915.

Chicago Sun-Times.

Anderson, David. "Pie in the Sky: It's Still There for the Wobblies," 12 December 1966.

Dagens Nyheter (Sweden), 27 December 1955; 27 February 1956.

Dala Demokraten (Stockholm, Sweden), 18 November 1955.

Deseret Evening News (Salt Lake City, Utah), February 1903; 10 June, 13 August, September 1913; January 1914-December 1915.

Deseret News (Salt Lake City, Utah), "Joe Hill's Ghost," 13 January 1954; "Joe Hill—Is He Really Dead?" 25 November 1965.

Gefle Dagblad (Gävle, Sweden).

Ahlstrand, Gösta. "Joe Hill—from Gävle," 14 August 1967.

Hill, Joe. "Catastrophe in San Francisco" (letter written by Hill, 24 April 1906), 16 May 1906.

Industrial Worker (Chicago), 13 November 1948.

Anderson, Evert. "Joe Hill, I.W.W. Rebel, Is Honored in Sweden," 20 May 1964, p. 1.

Thompson, Fred. "Why Joe Hill Wrote His 'Casey Jones,' " Feb. 1966, p. 5.

Industrial Worker (Spokane), 1912-1913.

Hill, Joe. "Another Victim of the Uniformed Thugs," 27 August 1910, p. 3.

Los Angeles Times, 19-20, 27, 29 November 1915.

Anderson, David. "Wobblies Still Strive for 'Labor Revolution,' " 17 March 1967, p. 4-1A.

Morgen Tidningen (Sweden), 19 November 1955.

New York Times, 20, 26 November 1915; 14 February 1965.

New York Tribune, 19-20, 26 November 1915.

Ny Dag (Stockholm, Sweden), 29 April 1950; 19 August 1952; 30 April, 19 November 1955; 12 September 1958; 16 December 1963.

Ogden Standard-Examiner, 19-20, 26-27 November, 2 December 1915.

Park Record (Park City, Utah), 19 November, 10 December 1915.

Salt Lake Herald-Republican, 3 February 1903; 21 September 1913; January 1914-December 1915.

Salt Lake Telegram, 1915.

Hill, Joe. "Letter to the Editor," 15 August 1915.

Salt Lake Tribune, 3 February 1903; 13-14 June, 13-14 August 1913; January 1914-December 1915; 30-31 January 1919; 6 September 1964; 15 November 1965.

Long, Theodore. "Joe Hill Myth Finds a Home in Russia," 6 March 1966, p. 16A.

San Francisco Chronicle, 20 November 1915.

San Pedro Daily News, July-August 1912.

San Pedro Pilot, July-August 1912.

Seattle Post Intelligencer, 20-21 November 1915.

Solidarity (Cleveland), 19 August 1911; 1912-1916.

Ashleigh, Charles. "Reflections on Joe Hill's Reprieve," 9 October 1915, p. 2.

Brazier, Richard. "Joe Hill—A Tribute," 14 August 1915. (Poem)

Chaplin, Ralph. "Joe Hill," 12 September 1914, p. 3.

——. "Joe Hill's Funeral in Chicago," 4 December 1915.

Debs, Eugene V. "Murder of Joe Hill," 8 January 1916, p. 2.

Haywood, Wm. D. "On Friday Morning September 4, 1914, Joe Hill Is To Be Judicially Murdered," 11 July 1914, p. 1.

Hill, Joe. "A Cheerful Note from Joe Hill," 19 December 1914.

——. "A Few Reasons Why I Demand a New Trial," 16 October 1915, p. 4.

Hilton, Orrin N. "Open Letter to the Board of Pardons of Utah" (written 17 October 1915), 30 October 1915, p. 4.

279

Lewis, W. H. "Our Martyr," 11 December 1915.

Little, Emma B. Editorial, 25 September 1915, p. 2.

Nordquist, John E. "November Nineteenth," 27 November 1915, p. 3. (Song)

O'Carrol, Joseph. "To the Governor of the Sovereign State of Utah," 13 November 1915. (Poem)

Steel Labor (Indianapolis, Indiana).

"Joe Hill . . . The Man Who Never Died." Western ed., 31, no. 1 (January 1966).

Sun (Price, Utah), 26 November 1915.

Sunday Worker.

Flynn, Elizabeth Gurley. "Joe Hill: Song Bird," 14 November 1937.

Utah Chronicle (University of Utah, Salt Lake City, Utah). "Bomb Thrower Is Brought to Trial," 13 December 1915.

Washington Post (Washington, D.C.).

Lalley, J. M. "Martyr Minstrel of the Wobblies," 8 February 1960.

Other Media

Film. *The Man Who Never Died.* Produced by the Canadian Broadcasting Company and shown on Canadian television.

Recordings.

Glazer, Joe. "The Songs of Joe Hill." Folkways FA 2039.

Glazer, Joe and William Friedland. "Songs of the Wobblies." Labor Arts 3.

Legal Sources

State of Utah v. Hillstrom, 46 Utah 341, 150 P. 935 (1915).

State of Utah v. Hillstrom. Case No. 3532 in the Utah Third District Court, vol. 2, Transcript of evidence introduced on behalf of the defendant (vol. 1 lost).

Miscellaneous Unpublished Material

Archives

Ann Arbor. Labadie Collection, University Library, University of Michigan; Joe Hill file box contains much primary material relating to the I.W.W.

Detroit. Wayne State University Labor History Archives, Wayne State University; official repository for the papers and files of the I.W.W.

New York City. New York Public Library, Manuscript Division. Frank P. Walsh Papers.

Salt Lake City. Archives of the Secretary of State of Utah, State Capitol Building.

Salt Lake City. Utah State Historical Society Archives, Historical Society Building; houses Governor Spry's papers and, in the Joe Hill file, many letters and petitions relating to the Hill case.

Stanford. Hoover Institution on War, Revolution, and Peace, Stanford University; contains Wallace Stegner's collection of material on Hill.

Stockholm. Arbetarörelsens Arkiv; contains copies of Swedish writings on Hill.

Stockholm. Archives of the Royal Ministry for Foreign Affairs; houses official papers of Swedish government concerning the Hill case, which include correspondence of Swedish Minister Ekengren with various American officials and petitions sent to Ekengren asking him to aid Hill.

Washington, D.C. Library of Congress. Woodrow Wilson Papers.

Washington, D.C. National Archives. Record Group 59, "Records of the Department of State," Decimal File 1910-1929, File no. 311.582H55 to 311.582H55/35.

Interviews

Gallagher, Mary. "An Interview with Mary Gallagher," typed transcript of a tape-recorded interview conducted by Willa Baum, University of California General Library Regional Cultural History Project, Berkeley, California, 1955, p. 19.

Interview of William Chance by the author, Banning, California, 23 April 1967.

Manuscripts

Morris, James O. "The Joe Hill Case." Thesis, Labadie Collection, University Library, University of Michigan, 1950.

Smoot, Reed. Diaries, book 20. MS copy

currently in possession of University of Utah Press.

Weintraub, Hyman. "The I.W.W. in California: 1905-1931." Thesis, University Library, University of California at Los Angeles, 1947.

GENERAL BIBLIOGRAPHY
used in preparation of this book

Books

Adamic, Louis. *Dynamite*. New York: Viking Press, 1931.

Black, Henry Campbell. *Black's Law Dictionary*. 4th ed. St. Paul: West Publishing Co., 1951.

Brissenden, Paul Frederick. *The I.W.W.: A Study of American Syndicalism*. Studies in History, Economics and Public Law. New York: Columbia University Press, 1919. Reprint. New York: Russell & Russell Publishers, 1957.

———. "The Industrial Workers of the World." In *Encyclopedia of the Social Sciences*, edited by Edward Seligman, vol. 8, 1935.

Brooks, John Graham. *American Syndicalism: The I.W.W.* New York: Macmillan Co., 1913.

Cannon, James P. *The I.W.W.: The Great Anticipation*. New York: Pioneer Publishers, 1956.

Compiled Laws of Utah, 1907.

Coombs, Whitney. *The Wages of Unskilled Labor in Manufacturing Industries in the United States, 1890-1924*. New York: Columbia University Press, 1926.

Douglas, Paul H. *Real Wages in the United States*. Boston: Houghton Mifflin Co., 1930.

Dowell, Eldridge Foster. *A History of Criminal Syndicalism Legislation in the United States*. The Johns Hopkins University Studies of Historical and Political Science, vol. 57, no. 1. Baltimore: Johns Hopkins University Press, 1939.

The General Strike. Chicago: Industrial Workers of the World, 1946. (Pamphlet)

Goldman, Emma. *Living My Life*, vol. 1. New York: Alfred A. Knopf, 1931.

Hennacy, Ammon. *The Book of Ammon*.

Salt Lake City: By the author, 1965.

Hoxie, Robert Franklin. *Trade Unionism in the United States*. New York: C. D. Appleton & Co., 1923.

The I.W.W. in Theory and Practice. 5th ed. Chicago: Industrial Workers of the World, n.d. (Pamphlet)

Jensen, Vernon H. *Heritage of Conflict*. Ithaca, N.Y.: Cornell University Press, 1950.

Lawless, Ray M. *Folksingers and Folksongs in America*. New York: Duell, Sloan & Pearce, 1960.

London Jack. Introduction to first edition of *The Cry for Justice* by Upton Sinclair. New York: By the author, 1915. Reprint. New York: Lyle Stuart, 1963.

Murray, Robert K. *Red Scare*. Minneapolis: University of Minnesota Press, 1955.

Parker, Carleton H. *The Casual Laborer and Other Essays*. New York: Harcourt, Brace & Co., 1920.

Perlman, Selig, and Phillip Taft. *Labor Movements. History of Labor in the United States, 1896-1932*, edited by John R. Commons, vol. 4. New York: Macmillan Co., 1935.

Perry, Louis B., and Richard A. Perry. *A History of the Los Angeles Labor Movement, 1911-1941*. Berkeley and Los Angeles: University of California Press, 1963.

Preston, William, Jr. *Aliens and Dissenters*. Publications for the Study of the History of Liberty in America. Cambridge: Harvard University Press, 1963. Reprint. New York: Harper & Row, 1966.

Russell, Bertrand. *Roads to Freedom: Socialism, Anarchism, and Syndicalism*. London: George Allen & Unwin, Ltd., 1918.

Saposs, David J. *Left Wing Unionism: A Study of Radical Policies and Tactics*. New York: International Publishers Co., 1926.

Schroeder, Theodore. *Free Speech for Radicals*. Riverside, Conn.: Free Speech League, 1916.

Stimson, Grace Heilman. *The Rise of the Labor Movement in Los Angeles*. Berkeley and Los Angeles: University of California Press, 1955.

Twenty-five Years of Industrial Unionism. Chicago: Industrial Workers of the World, n.d. Commemorative pamphlet containing the following articles:

Baldwin, Roger N. "Free Speech Fights of the I.W.W."

Chaplin, Ralph. "How the I.W.W. Defends Labor."

Thompson, James P. "Revolutionary Class Union."

Tyler, Robert L. *Rebels of the Woods: The I.W.W. in the Pacific Northwest.* Eugene Ore.: University of Oregon, 1967.

U.S., Congress, Senate, "Report on Strike of Textile Workers in Lawrence, Mass." *Senate Documents*, vol. 31, 62nd Cong., 2d Sess., 1912.

Articles

Balch, Elizabeth, "Songs of Labor." *Survey*, 3 January 1914, pp. 409-26.

Brazier, Richard. "The Story of the I.W.W.'s 'Little Red Song Book.' " *Labor History* 9 (Winter 1968): 91-105.

Davies J. Kenneth. "The Accommodation of Mormonism and Politico-Economic Reality." *Dialogue: A Journal of Mormon Thought* 3, no. 1 (Spring 1968): 51-52.

Eastman, Max. "The Great American Scapegoat." *New Review* 2 (August 1914): 466-68.

Holbrook, Stewart H. "Wobbly Talk." *American Mercury* 7 (January 1926): 62-65.

Laut, Agnes C. "Revolution Yawns." *Illustrated Technical World* 18 (May 1913): 134-44.

Papanikolas, Helen Zeese. "Life and Labor among the Immigrants of Bingham Canyon." *Utah Historical Quarterly* 33, no. 4 (Fall 1965): 289-315.

Putnam, Samuel. "Red Days in Chicago." *American Mercury* 30 (September 1933): 64-71.

Talbott, E. Guy. "The Armies of the Unemployed in California." *Survey*, 22 August 1914, pp. 523-24.

Newspapers

Denver Post, 16 December 1932.

Industrial Union Bulletin, 25 July 1908.

Walsh, J. H. "Developments in Spokane," 4 April 1908, p. 2.

Wilson, James. "The Value of Music in I.W.W. Meetings," 16 May 1908, p. 1.

Industrial Worker (Chicago).

Brazier, Richard. "The Spokane Free Speech Fight, 1909" (three pts.), December 1966; January, February 1967.

Solidarity (Cleveland).

Embree, A. S. "Bingham Strike," 9 November 1912, p. 3.

Pratt, Lee. "Conditions in Utah," 19 August 1911, p. 1.

Strike Bulletin (Clinton, Ill.). Carl Person, ed., 1913-1915.